OCEAN
MOUNTAINS
San Antonio de los Cobres
JUJUY
Jujuy
Salta
SALTA
Tucumán
TUCUMÁN
CATAMARCA
Catamarca
SANTIAGO DEL ESTERO
Santiago del Estero
La Rioja
LA RIOJA
SAN JUAN
San Juan
MT. ACONCAGUA
Mendoza
MENDOZA
Santiago
San Luis
SAN LUIS
Río Salado
Córdoba
CÓRDOBA
Santa Rosa
LA PAMPA
Río
PARAGUAY
Pilcomayo
Asunción
FORMOSA
Bermejo
Formosa
CHACO
Resistencia
Corrientes
CORRIENTES
Posadas
MISIONES
R. Iguazú
Río Paraguay
Paraná
Salado
SANTA FE
Santa Fe
ENTRE RÍOS
Paraná
Monte Caseros
Uruguay
Rosario
San Nicolás
Tigre
Buenos Aires
La Plata
BUENOS AIRES
Azul
URUGUAY
Montevideo
Río de la Plata
BRAZIL
OCEAN

The Argentine Republic

BY

YSABEL F. RENNIE

NEW YORK
THE MACMILLAN COMPANY
1945

First printing.

PRINTED IN THE UNITED STATES OF AMERICA

The author wishes it understood that although she is at present employed by the United States government, this work was completed before she entered government employ, and represents no opinions but her own, and no information but that available from public printed sources.

The author wishes it understood that although she is at present employed by the United States government, this work was completed before she entered government employ, and represents no opinions but her own and no information but that available from public printed sources.

AN EXPLANATION AND AN APOLOGY

As a history of Argentina this book has deficiencies which must be at once apparent to the critical reader. Why, for instance, no colonial history? What of the story of Argentine foreign relations, of Argentina and the other American Republics? And what of constitutional history?

I can only plead guilty to all these omissions. A book has to begin somewhere, and the colonial period is a volume by itself. More important, Argentine colonial history has been raked over with a fine-tooth comb, and there are numberless volumes on the Wars of Independence. This is the story of the Argentine Republic, which was founded in 1853; I have carried the story back to Rosas because there is no understanding the Republic without knowing the system it was rebelling against. Above all, there is no understanding the nationalist revolution without knowing how deep and native its roots are.

A book has physical limitations. I early decided to hew to the line where Argentina's development was concerned. I have tried to tell, not everything there is to know, not even all that is interesting and worth while, but what is essential. The book was written backwards. I spent more than a year hunting the issues, looking for the questions to ask, before I even began my research. They were all on the surface, like open boils: it was a wonderful, if tragic, moment.

Those problems, as the most unlettered Argentine could tell you, were the disastrous economic unbalance of the country, between Buenos Aires and the interior, between agriculture and nascent industry; they were the slow economic decline of the landed oligarchy, and the death struggle by which the landed class was trying to exclude other classes from effective participation in national life; they were the anger and frustration of the immigrant millions in the face of fraud and political exclusion; they were the dying hold of those foreign enterprises that had first brought wealth to the young Republic, and whose hegemony that Republic had outgrown.

Like most foreigners, I saw Buenos Aires first. Then I visited the far south, the deserts and mountains of Patagonia to the Straits of Magellan. What I saw gave me an exaggerated idea of Argentine wealth and prosperity. It was when I saw the north, the rachitic and tuberculous people of the sugar plantations and *yerbatales* and quebracho forests, that I first realized the unbridgeable division between Buenos Aires and the interior. I heard Santafecinos and Santiagueños speak only with bitterness of their proud capital city. Useless to try to tell my porteño friends about it when I got back: they wouldn't listen, as they had not been listening for a hundred and thirty years.

There are two Argentinas, and the whole history of the nation is the story of their struggle. I have tried to show it in all its aspects: what the civil wars were about, what economic liberalism really meant, who benefited from Argentina's colonial economy, and why that economy had to come to an end. The dichotomy in the country is that of creole and European, protectionist and free trader, the provinces and Buenos Aires, or, as Sarmiento liked to put it, the poncho and the *frac*.

1943 is the gauchesque reaction. It is the poncho and chiripá, the intensely indigenous—even, if you like, the barbarian. In its extreme form it is something at once terrible and pitiable. But the other extreme was an extreme, too, and on it was based nearly a century of exploitation. Until the two Argentinas are brought together, that nation will have no peace. Neither a blind provincialism on the one hand, nor an aping of Europe on the other, can create a whole and healthy culture.

I realize that in telling this story I have ignored too much that was not germane to the theme. It is very probable that I have made errors of judgment and fact. But I plead, in my own excuse, that I have told the story for the first time anywhere, in any language, and with precious little material to go on. This book is only spadework, and far from resenting criticisms of it, I shall be only too glad if they stimulate others to do better.

THE ARGENTINE REPUBLIC

THE MACMILLAN COMPANY
NEW YORK · BOSTON · CHICAGO · DALLAS
ATLANTA · SAN FRANCISCO
MACMILLAN AND CO., Limited
LONDON · BOMBAY · CALCUTTA · MADRAS
MELBOURNE
THE MACMILLAN COMPANY
OF CANADA, Limited
TORONTO

CONTENTS

ILLUSTRATIONS

A GLOSSARY OF ARGENTINE TERMS USED IN THIS BOOK

aduana—customhouse.
aftosa—hoof-and-mouth disease.
almacén—grocery store.
almacenero—groceryman.
al portador—"To the bearer" (way of writing a check which requires no endorsement).
angelito ("little angel")—a child who has died.
ánimas en pena ("souls in pain")—earthbound spirits.
asado—roast. *asado al asador*—roast cooked on a stake driven into the ground.
bastos—hard leather cylinders that are part of the Argentine *recado*, or saddle.
bienes raíces—real property.
bigotes federales—Federal whiskers, worn as a sign of loyalty to Rosas.
bodega—wine cellar; winery.
boite (from the French)—night club of a respectable variety.
bolas, boleadoras—instrument of leather-covered stones tied together with thongs, used by Indians and gauchos to capture or kill animals.
boleada—a hunt with bolas.
bombachas—baggy trousers worn by modern peon and estanciero.
bombilla—silver tube through which mate is sucked.
bota de potro—boot made of the hide of a colt's hind leg.
cabaña—stud farm.
cacique—Indian chief.
campo—field, country. *campesino*—countryman.
caña—liquor distilled from sugar.
capataz—overseer.
capiango—according to legend, a man who can turn himself into a tiger.
caudillo—military chieftain; political boss.
chambergo—soft felt hat. (From Chamberga, a Spanish regiment serving as guard to Charles II.)
che!—Hey! or Say! Argentine interjection of indefinite meaning indicating confidence with the person addressed.
colectivo—microbus.

colegio—high school.
comisario—chief of a district police station.
comparsa—group, gang; especially, band of carnival celebrators all dressed alike.
conchabador—agent who furnishes peons to plantations for a percentage of their wages.
confitería—confectionery; in Argentina, a combination tearoom, pastry shop, and bar.
consorcio—consortium, partnership, financial group.
correntino—native of Corrientes province.
criador—man who raises calves to sell at less than one year.
criollo—creole, son of a Spaniard born in America. In Argentina it is used loosely as a synonym for Argentine, or especially to differentiate the Indo-Hispanic colonial stock from the descendants of recent immigrants.
cuadra—a block 150 yards square.
cuña—"pull." Literally, a wedge.
divisa punzó—the red Federal ribbon worn by Rosistas.
ejido—common public land around a town.
empanada—meat pie.
entrerriano—native of Entre Ríos.
estancia—cattle ranch, sheep farm.
estanciero—owner of an estancia.
facón—double-edged dagger.
Federal—member of nineteenth century party which favored a federal form of government; a follower of Rosas or the caudillos.
fonda—country inn, eating house.
frac—frock coat.
frigorífico—packing house.
gallego—Gallician. In Argentina, any Spaniard.
galleta—hardtack.
ganadero—livestock raiser.
gaucho—seminomadic horseman of the pampa of the eighteenth and nineteenth centuries. *gaucho malo*, outlaw.
hacendado—owner of livestock, ganadero, estanciero.
hacienda—livestock; wealth in general. *Ministro de Hacienda*—Minister of Finance.
hectare—2.471 acres.
hombre de campo—man who devotes himself to the land.
ingenio—sugar refinery, plantation.
invernador (literally, "winterer")—estanciero who fattens animals for market.
jefe de frontera—frontier chief or commanding officer.

jerga—a kind of loosely woven saddle blanket.
Juarista—follower of President Juárez Celman.
Junta de Mayo—committee of the May, 1810, revolution.
kilo—kilogram (2.2 pounds).
league—five kilometers, or about three miles. A square league is 2,500 hectares, or 6,176 acres.
libreta de enrolamiento—military service enrollment book which entitles a man to vote.
littoral—that part of Argentina bordering on the lower Paraná: the provinces of Buenos Aires, Santa Fe, Entre Ríos, and Corrientes.
matadero—slaughterhouse.
mataperros—dog-killer. Applied contemptuously to the colonial militia that was sent to kill wild dogs on the pampa.
mate—an infusion of *yerba mate*, or Paraguay tea (*Ilex paraguayensis*). Also the gourd from which it is drunk.
Mazorca—Rosas's secret police.
mazorquero—member of the Mazorca; thug, assassin, terrorist.
mendocino—native of Mendoza.
montonera—guerrilla or bandit group.
negrero—literally, slave-trader; applied to conchabadores of the North.
niño bien—aristocratic youth, dandy, playboy.
Noventa—literally, ninety. The year 1890, and the Revolution of 1890.
paisano—countryman, peasant; fellow countryman.
palabra de inglés—word of an Englishman, promise on which you can rely.
pampa—the grassy plains of southwestern Argentina, including most of Buenos Aires, and parts of Santa Fe, Córdoba, San Luis, and La Pampa.
partido—a section of land twenty kilometers square.
pasto fuerte—coarse pampa grass.
pasto tierno—clover and other tender grasses.
Pato, El—"the duck." A game played on horseback using as guerdon a duck sewed in a leather hide.
patria—fatherland, *patrie*.
payada de contrapunto—a verse contest in which the competing minstrels improvise questions and answers in rhyme.
payador—a gaucho minstrel.
peon—common laborer.
peso—Argentine money, in 1944 worth about 25 U. S. cents.
pialar—to lasso by the feet. *El Pialar*—a gaucho game in which a horseman runs the gantlet of players who try to lasso and throw his mount.

poncho—a wool cape with a slit in the middle so that it will fit over the head.

pordiosero—beggar.

porteño—native of the city of Buenos Aires.

puchero—dish of boiled meat and vegetables.

puerto habilitado—legal port; during the colonial period, Buenos Aires.

puestero—man who has a section of an estancia to take care of. He is above a peon in that he has a small house and is better paid.

pulpero—keeper of a pulpería.

pulpería—country store and bar.

quebracho—a tree (*Quebrachia lorentzii*) of very hard wood whose bark is a rich source of tannin. (From *quiebra-hacha*, break-ax.)

Quichua (or *Quechua*)—a South American Indian group, and the language spoken by its members.

quintal—100 kilograms, 220 lbs.

rancho—poor country hut.

recado—Argentine saddle of *bastos* and sheepskins.

Restaurador, El—The Restorer (of the Laws). Title given to Rosas by the Buenos Aires legislature.

riojano—native of La Rioja.

Rosista—follower or modern admirer of the dictator Rosas.

Sala de Representantes—House of Representatives.

saladero—meat-salting plant.

salteño—a native of Salta.

sanjuanino—a native of San Juan.

santafecino—a native of Santa Fe.

santiagueño—a native of Santiago del Estero.

Siglo de Oro—"Golden Century," the Spanish sixteenth century. (Sometimes includes the seventeenth.)

soldado federal—Federal soldier, soldier of Rosas or his allies.

suerte de estancia—one and a half square leagues, minimum tolerable holding of a colonial estanciero.

taba—foot bone of a cow; gambling game played with the taba.

tambo—dairy; negro colony.

tierra adentro—inland, in the interior; in Indian country.

tropilla—troop of horses trained to stay together.

tú—thou.

tulpo—corn prepared with mutton grease.

unicato ("unicate")—one-man government, especially of President Juárez Celman.

Unitario—member of party in nineteenth century which favored centralized government.

velorio—wake, vigil.

verdadero—real, true.
vicuña—a wild humped animal (*Lama vicunna*) related to the llama and alpaca; the soft, warm wool of the vicuña.
yerba mate—Paraguay tea (*Ilex paraguayensis*).
yerbal (*yerbatal*)—yerba plantation.
Yrigoyenista—follower of Hipólito Yrigoyen.

THE ARGENTINE REPUBLIC

Argentines, of whatever class they may be, educated or ignorant, have a high concept of their value as a nation; all the other American nations hold this vanity against them, and are offended by their presumption and arrogance. I believe that the charge is not unfounded, and I am not sorry for it. Too bad for the people that does not have faith in itself!

—DOMINGO F. SARMIENTO, *Facundo* (1845).

THE SETTING

THE PAMPA

Now, I wonder what impression there must leave in the Argentine the simple act of fixing his eyes on the horizon and seeing . . . and not seeing anything? —SARMIENTO, *Facundo.*

"Argentina's tragedy is its vastness," wrote Domingo F. Sarmiento a hundred years ago; "the desert hems it in on all sides and works into the heart of it; the solitude, the desolation without a single human dwelling, divide province from province. There, immensity on all sides: immense the plains, immense the forests, immense the rivers, the horizon always uncertain, always confounding itself with the earth between clouds and tenuous mists . . . where earth ends and sky begins." [1]

It was a country rich in potentialities when its greatest writer wrote these lines from his exile in Chile. But none knew better than he how poor was the present. In a million square miles there was not a single highway, not a single railroad. The country was watered by navigable rivers: there was not a single boat, not a single bridge. From Salta in the north to Buenos Aires in the south goods and men came by bullock cart, taking three months for the trip, and—ironically—following the Paraná River for most of their slow and painful journey. The soil was as fantastic then as it is now, three to eleven feet of alluvial black mold, so rich that fertilizers were unknown in the Argentine Republic. Yet the estanciero imported flour from the United States. Men whose cattle could be counted in the thousands had neither milk nor butter.[2]

It was a country of sudden death. A man might die from crossing the southern frontier into Indian country. He might die in a drunken fight with knives at close quarters in some country tavern. He might die in civil war. Every province had its gaucho army: some had two. Life was not sacred, nor was it comfortable.

In Buenos Aires the cruel Juan Manuel de Rosas set the style for caudillos, and one might be stabbed in the street or in his own house, or shot by firing squad. Argentina's great—the men who believed in democracy, as Alberdi and Sarmiento did, or who believed in the nation's greatness, as San Martín did, or who just did not like Juan Manuel de Rosas (most fell into this category)—were in exile in France, in Chile, and in Uruguay. In 1845 Argentina's independence was thirty-five years old, and the country was wretched, underpopulated, and in complete anarchy. "Society has completely disappeared," said Sarmiento; "there remains only the feudal family, isolated, self-contained." [3]

The pampa was beautiful. There was the tall, coarse pampa grass, high enough to hide the wild deer and partridges that covered the open country. There were rich green clover, thistles with green and white foliage, rye grass, wild flowers: the scarlet vervain, the purple and white verbena, and the purple *flor morada*. The thistle grew to three yards. In spring it flowered in rose-purple, and in midsummer it turned to seed that fed herds of cattle and sheep. In the marshes were wild birds: ducks, plovers, cranes, spoonbills, flamingoes, geese, swans, and turkeys.[4] The land was rich in soil and clays, white for making porcelain, red and yellow for coloring, and strong for tiles and earthenware. There were chalk and sand in the earth, a sparkling black sand for writing desks, a fine white sand for hourglasses.[5] Where there were houses, men planted trees for shade and fruit: willows and Lombard poplars, *paraísos* and acacias, pears, nectarines, apricots, and peaches. These groves stood out like islands on the flat, monotonous pampa, and signalled the lonely ranch or estancia house.

Best of all was the ombú. The ombú is part of the legend that is Argentina, the native tree of the pampa that botanists aver is only a giant herb. Its gnarled roots stand out from the soil, and give it the look of oak sturdiness that it has. To the solitary traveller it was shade and company, and when the criollo built his hut on the plain, it was beside a friendly ombú, or a copse of them. The estancia of W. H. Hudson, who, writing in English, was yet the most authentic of all Argentine novelists, was called

Los Veinticinco Ombúes—The Twenty-five Ombúes. It is said that one rarely or never sees a nest in the ombú, for at night its leaves are noxious. That is why it never would occur to the *hombre de campo* to sleep beneath it.[6]

When Hudson was a boy he used to lie in a hammock under the trees and watch the birds. He came to know them by heart, and years later, as an old man in London, he wrote feelingly of the wild life he had known so intimately, of the red-breasted military starling, of the kinglet with yellow breast and brown wings. In the autumn the storks came, and the owls. He hated the owls and tried to kill them; but there were always more, and finally he tired of the useless slaughter. After the rains one saw flocks of black-necked swans, because the air was so clear. But, of all the birds, he liked the hummingbird best, "this formless cloud on which the glittering body hangs suspended . . . like the silvery lace woven by the Epeïra." [7] There were the crested screamer, with its pale, slaty-blue body and eyes rimmed in red, the chocolate tyrant with breast of washed orange, the peacock with its "crest and starry train." [8] And finally there was the rhea, the American ostrich, the great bird that runs like a man with his hands in his pockets. The gauchos used to hunt ostriches with bolas, and finally they disappeared from the pampa. You can still see them in the deserts of Patagonia, where they will run sideways at the approach of a car or a man on horseback. They are fast, and seem desperately anxious to take off and fly.

Beside nature's prodigality, man's habitation was poor indeed. If he was a peon, he lived in a thatched hut plastered with mud, or perhaps in just a cave covered with skins and corrugated iron.[9] The floor was beaten earth, the furniture an ox skull to sit on. The married peon might have a few utensils: a copper pot to boil water, an iron pot for meat, a bull's horn to drink from, a few wooden spits to roast meat.[10] There were fleas everywhere. "In the gaucho's *rancho,* in the lady's drawing room, or in the open country, they are equally present, and equally energetic and insatiate in their attacks; they are generally rather larger than those met with in England, and seem to have keener appetites." [11]

The master did not live much better than his peon. The estancia might be of mud, too, although as the century progressed mud gave way to brick and adobe, with tiled roof. The Englishman, Beaumont, travelling through Buenos Aires in 1827, described the estancia house as "shed-like buildings with mud walls and thatched roof." [12] Each room was a building by itself, and they might total three or four: sitting room, bedroom, guest room, and a storeroom for jerked beef, hides, and tallow. The kitchen was off by itself. Sometimes the nakedness of country life was softened by man-planted trees—mulberries, ombúes, poplars, willows, or acacias. There were two classes of estancieros: those who lived relatively Europeanized lives (they were in the minority), and those who lived like their peons. McCann, who rode two thousand miles on horseback through the Argentine provinces in the middle of the century, and who therefore might be presumed to know what he was talking about, told how a rich estanciero lived. "His costume was that of a gaucho," he said. "The bedroom had not been cleaned for perhaps half a year; under my bed a favorite gamecock was tied by the leg, that he might be at hand to amuse his master; spurs, stirrups and other equestrian equipments, of silver, hung round the walls; our food consisted of beef, and beef only, without either salt, bread, biscuit or vegetable of any sort; water was our drink, and the floor was our table." [13]

THE GAUCHO

> *The vast plains of Buenos Ayres are inhabited only by Christian savages known as Guachos* (sic) *whose furniture is chiefly composed of horses' skulls, whose food is raw beef and water, and whose favorite pastime is running horses to death.*
>
> —Sir Walter Scott, *Life of Napoleon Bonaparte.*

This, then, was the background of the man whose figure has become legendary, the gaucho of the Río de la Plata. In those days he had no prestige. Even the word "gaucho" was a term of offense: he preferred to be called a peon.[14] The first man to use "gaucho" in any but a contemptuous sense was Martín Güemes, whose ragged gaucho army beat the Spaniards in Salta and wrote an heroic chapter in the history of Argentine independence. To him, they were his "beloved gauchos." To Sarmiento the gaucho represented all that was worst, that was most savage in the Argentine character, and he called his remarkable study of the gaucho mentality *Facundo; or Civilization and Barbarism.* Well, the gaucho has gone the way of the American Bad Man, or Ouida's Algerian Tirailleurs, and the controversy is dead. Being extinct, he is, like the dodo or the buffalo, merely picturesque. Now the Argentines are proud of him, and he is a part of their Heroic Legend.

The authentic gaucho of Rosas' time must have looked very much like a desert nomad. His lean brown body was hung with loose-fitting robes, and his face was black, his hair long and matted. Sarmiento, who had seen the Arabs of the Sahara, was amazed at how much they and his countrymen had in common, from horse trappings to physiognomy. The rein, the whip, and the bit showed their Moorish-Andalusian descent. "Not to speak of faces: I have known Arabs I would have sworn I had seen in my country."[15] This nomad horseman was a cross between Spanish father and Indian mother, and he had the Spaniard's dignity and the Indian's savage skills. He owned what he could wear or ride—his horses, his weapons and his clothes. Dismounted, he waddled like a good American cowboy. Hence the phrase "to walk without feet," * in other words, to be off your horse. Hudson tells of asking an idle peon why he was not working, and getting the reply: "Because I am too poor." Not an illogical answer at all. The man was so poor he had no horse. That is why he was not working.

It was a country of centaurs. Mail and newspapers were delivered on horseback, even in the big towns. Even beggars rode on horseback.[16] Milk was churned by tying it in a hide to the saddle girth and galloping over the plain. Sometimes the gauchos cured

* *Andar sin pies.*

meat by putting it between the saddle and the horse's back, and after a good gallop it was "turned out very tender, well soaked in gravy, and enough done."[17] This was perhaps not the most hygienic possible treatment, but some of the gauchos' other customs were not particularly hygienic, either—for instance, that of masticating their meat over a common pot so as not to lose any of its drippings. The squeamish visitor was apt to be revolted the first time, although hunger usually broadened his mind if he had to spend many days in the country.

Sarmiento was not mistaken in noting the likeness of gaucho and Arab. The gaucho's clothes were burnooselike in their looseness. He wore a shirt and long white cotton drawers with a fringe at the bottom; and over his drawers went a kind of long diaper, the chiripá, girdled at the waist with a sash or a leather-and-silver belt. The chiripá left eighteen inches of fringed drawer showing on either side. This strange garment, probably of Indian origin (from the Quichua *chilipá* or *chiripá?*), was not known as late as 1831 in the central and Andean regions, according to Sarmiento; but it is described by all travellers in the province of Buenos Aires. It finally gave way to the baggy cossack trousers called bombachas which are in general use today. Bombachas were an invention of European exporters to the Argentine, or rather an adaptation of foreign dress to their horseman customers.

The gaucho wore a short bolero jacket and, thrown over his shoulders, his poncho of sheep- or vicuña-wool. His hat was a felt chambergo—a shapeless kind of headpiece with high crown and narrow brim; and under his hat he usually tied his long hair in a colored handkerchief. The general effect of these haphazard garments was that of trailing and ill-fitting apparel. They were, as a matter of fact, quite comfortable and utilitarian. The poncho did double duty as raincoat-overcoat by day, and blanket by night.

The most curious article of all was the *bota de potro*, or horsehide boot, made from the hide of a colt's hind leg. The skin was cut in the middle of the thigh, and again about nine inches above the fetlock, and it was stripped off. The upper part formed the boot's leg, the hock fitted over the heel, and the remainder covered the foot, leaving the big toe showing. This boot was fitted to a man's leg while it was still moist, and it dried to the foot's shape. With his free toe the horseman grasped the stirrup, which might be the usual kind, though smaller, but was frequently a button or a bone dangling on a leather thong that the rider gripped between his two toes for support. The result of this extraordinary exercise was, as might be imagined, deformed toes.

The gaucho carried his weapons and utensils. His knife was single-edged, and was used to strip hide from cows or cut ribs from roasting meat. He thrust the meat into his mouth with his left hand, and sawed off the excess with his right, taking care not to slice his nose in the process. "The use of the fork is avoided," said McCann, "because it would occasion trouble, and necessitate the adoption of other domestic habits which are also considered troublesome: a knife and fork require a plate, which needs to be placed on a table; for to sit on the floor, with a plate, knife and fork, would be too ludicrous and inconvenient even for this paradoxical people, however amusing it may be in pic-nic party; therefore a table must be had. This want creates another: a table involves the necessity of a chair; and thus the consequences resulting from the use of forks involve a complete revolution in the household." [18]

For fighting the gaucho had a long double-edged dagger, the facón. After a few drinks at a country pulpería he might challenge all comers to a duel "at first sight." So at least goes the legend. He let the edge of his poncho touch the ground, and drew it trailing after him as he made the rounds of those present: "Nobody dares step on my poncho!" If anyone did, the two men went to it with daggers, their ponchos rolled over their left arms to shield their bodies. [19]

The criollo horse gear is unique. Sarmiento thought it Arabic in the rein of woven leather, the whip, and the bit. The saddle, however, differed sharply both from the Arab and from the Andalusian, which took a line of evolution that has ended in the Mexican and American Western saddles. The criollo recado consists of layer upon layer of blanket and sheepskin topped by two hard leather bastos, horizontal cylinders that lie on either side. Over the bastos goes another sheepskin, then a square of leather, and the whole is tied round the middle with a leather cinch. The resulting saddle is bulky in the extreme, and forces the rider to bend his knees as if he were sitting in a chair. A hundred years ago the effect was even more pronounced: contemporary drawings show horsemen with their knees at ninety-degree angles. The lasso is coiled and fastened behind the recado and lies over the rump of the horse.

A hundred years ago the boleadoras were in general use, and the boleada was a favorite country sport. The boleadoras have two or three leather-covered stones which are tied together by thongs. The bolas are whirled rapidly over the head and shot at the feet of an animal, to throw it, or at the head, to kill it. This instrument, an Indian invention, also had its war uses. One of the most important campaigns of the civil wars came to an abrupt termination when General José M. Paz was captured by a lucky throw of the bolas. As a sport, the boleada was an animal and ostrich hunt by a great group of riders who formed a circle and closed in, killing all they trapped. In theory the boleada was limited to game, but in the enthusiasm of the chase other people's cattle and horses were frequently included in the slaughter. At night the hunters gathered at the campfire to drink mate and play the guitar. Boleando was also a profession. Boleadores made a living selling skins.[20]

Thus, the travelling gaucho carried his knife and his bolas at his belt, and with his lasso he was prepared for what might come. Firearms were not in general use: the gaucho feared guns, and was a wretched shot, and indeed, McCann relates the amazement and childlike joy of the gauchos when he killed an animal with a bullet instead of stabbing it to death.[21] The Argentine was prodigal in his waste of animal life. The *gaucho malo,* the outlaw, might kill a cow to eat its tongue. Flesh was less than worthless. A hungry man killed his animal and saved the hide. It was the hide that had value in those days when neither the chilling of meat, nor the export of beef on the hoof, was yet known. In the Buenos

Aires market in the middle of the century beef sold for nine English pence per twenty-five pounds. One paid the same price for a turkey as for fifty-five pounds of beef. As for mutton, there was a time when even the meanest slave wouldn't eat it. In 1827 one could buy a whole sheep for a peso, then worth twenty English pence.[22] This prodigality with meat is by no means confined to the past, for the people of Argentina are the world's greatest meat-eaters, consuming more than twice as much as either England or the United States per capita.[23] In Patagonia one can still buy a lamb for a dollar and a half, at the butcher shop, dressed. Meat has always been the staple diet of the Argentine. In the nineteenth century he literally ate nothing else. The only variant to a straight-beef diet was yerba mate, the green Paraguay tea which is drunk from a gourd through a silver tube. The gaucho used to carry yerba mate tied in a handkerchief to his saddle. It was his breakfast, and his only refreshment on long rides.

Dinner in the campo was easily arranged. He lassoed a calf or steer, stabbed it, skinned it, and cut off a piece of the ribs. If he had an iron stake, he impaled the side of beef on it; if he did not, a green stick of wood served just as well. He built a fire of brush, or bones, or dung, and drove the stake into the ground beside it, roasting the meat slowly on one side, then the other. Then he filled his mate—the gourd—with yerba, and poured boiling water over it, sucking in the drink bitter. If he had tobacco, a luxury, he might roll a cigarette. When the asado was done he carved himself a choice chunk with his knife and ate until he was gorged. Probably four-fifths of the animal was thrown away or left to rot. He wiped his hands and knife on the ground. Washing was a luxury not in general acceptance.

This nomad horseman's pastimes were as rough as he was. He might go to a pulpería and drink caña (a fiery sweet rum) or pale yellow Holland gin. Gambling was with cards, dice, or the taba—the knee bone of a cow, which is thrown for heads and tails. The taba is still a common game in provincial taverns, and I have seen it myself. A skilled player can make the bone come up as he likes, and it is a test of dexterity, like horseshoes, or bowls. The pulpería was the social center of the campo. The peon went there to drink, or for occasional dances; there he swapped information on cattle brands, the price of hides (the pulpero was often the buyer of all hides and wool in his district), or the news, as it came from Buenos Aires; and there he bought boots, liquor, reins, cloth, yerba, flour, sugar, and salt—everything, indeed, that one could buy in the campo.

The gaucho's games, as might be expected, were equestrian. The most famous was *el pato,* prohibited by Rosas because it often led to pitched battles. A cooked duck was sewed in a hide with a leather point at each end for the hand to grasp, and all the horsemen tried to get away with it. No less dangerous—possibly worse—was *el pialar* (from *pialar,* to lasso by the feet). A horseman had to gallop through a double line of riders as each tried to lasso his mount's feet and throw him. If the horse was snagged, the rider was supposed to land on his feet.[24]

Most of these men could play the guitar after a fashion. Among them were those who with their improvisations in song and verse were a kind of gaucho minstrel and wandered from pulpería to pulpería, playing at fiestas. These were the payadores, who have been immortalized in the Argentine ballad of *Martín Fierro.* Tradition says that when two or more of these minstrels were together they composed a kind of extemporaneous dialogue in verse, the *payada de contrapunto.* One payador invented a question in verse, and his rival answered it. These poetic jousts went on for hours, sometimes, until one or the other admitted defeat. Criollo tradition has puffed the payador into a brilliant minstrel, although contemporaries were not unanimous in their approval. "Set a Gaucho to dance," wrote one unimpressed Englishman, "and he moves as if he were on a procession to his execution; ask him to sing, and he gives utterance to sounds resembling an Irish keen, accompanied with nasal drones suggestive of croup; put him to play the guitar, and you feel your flesh beginning to creep, for the tinkling elicited is as if a number of sick crickets were cracking their legs over the fingers of the player." [25] Argentine music is not now, and never has been remarkable; but it has a kind of monotonous charm and sadness in keeping with its background. And modern Argentina has given the world at least one original dance form, which is the tango.

The gaucho mentality was as primitive as the environment that formed it. These men were illiterate. This, in itself, broke down the language, for a man who has never seen words written has no standard against which to judge his speech. Argentine Spanish is probably the most deformed of all the Hispanic-American dialects, in spite of the almost total lack of Indian traces in the speech. The pronunciation shows a decided Andalusian influence, with a dropping of *d*'s and a slurring of *s*'s, and the mispronunciation of the *ll*. The most marked changes, however, have been brought about by Italian and French immigration. Italian is enough like Spanish to make a bastardization easy, and the long cultural tutelage of France has introduced Gallicisms into the language. This has come about since 1860. Before, the speech was simply that of unlettered country people living in isolation from one another and from Spain. The language of the gaucho was soft, dignified, and simple; and much that was picturesque in daily life found its way into the language.

The gaucho had much of the child in him. Sarmiento tells the suggestive story of Facundo Quiroga and a soldier thief. A piece of gear was missing, and no one knew the culprit. Quiroga called his soldiers to him, and after asking the guilty man to give himself up, and getting no reply, he cut identical wands and gave one to each man. "Now," he said sternly, "tomorrow I shall know the thief, because his wand will grow longer tonight." The next morning he lined up his gauchos again, and found his man: the poor culprit, in guilty terror, had whittled off his stick in the night. This is a most curious tale, and needs no underlining. It shows at once the primitive mentality of the age, and how well Quiroga understood it. He was a gaucho among gauchos.

Rosas understood this mentality, and his understanding was the source of the great power he had over the country people and the Indians of his generation. He and Quiroga were both caudillos in the purest sense of the word. They inspired both devotion and terror. Rosas could out-gaucho any gaucho in Buenos Aires, and everyone knew it. He was ferocious but just. The most terrible tales are told of this dictator: how he sewed up his enemies in the bloody hides of animals, for instance. But there were other stories that told of his fairness. On his estancia he had forbidden the carrying of arms under penalty of flogging. One day he appeared with a knife in his belt, and a peon made some malicious remark about it. "You are quite right," said Rosas, and he ordered himself to be flogged before his astonished peons.* After that example, they never questioned his justice.

The provincial caudillos of the civil wars—Rosas in Buenos Aires, Quiroga in La Rioja, Estanislao López in Santa Fe, and all the others—were men that appealed to superstition and to the admiration of physical skill and bravery. Quiroga, for example, enjoyed the reputation of having *capiangos* in his army. When Paz, before a battle, asked the commandant of certain deserting troops of his what capiangos were supposed to be, he replied that they were men who had the ability to turn themselves into tigers. "And so you see," added the commandant, "four hundred wild beasts turned loose against a camp at night will finish it beyond remedy." [26] And with this, he took his men and deserted.

Country people believed then, as they still do, whole-heartedly in ghosts and all that went with them. *Animas en pena* (souls in pain) were popularly supposed to wander about suffering and frightening the living, because they had been treacherously murdered or had not been buried in holy ground. Some of the beliefs about the dead led to gruesome customs. For instance, it was popularly held that a small child, dying, was a "little angel," an *angelito*, called by God, and on the occasion of infant funerals there was held the so-called *velorio del angelito*, or "wake of the little angel." Alfredo Ebelot, a Frenchman, has given a graphic description of the first wake he ever saw. It was at a country pulpería in the province of Buenos Aires. The main room of the fonda was lighted by candles, and there was an odor of grease,

* For a slightly different version, see Darwin's *Voyage of H.M.S.* Beagle *Round the World* (New York, 1846), I, 93.

cigar smoke, and gin. In the center of the room was the corpse of a little boy in his best clothes, seated in a chair on boxes of gin, arranged on top of a table like a pedestal. The child's eyes were fixed, and his arms hung lifelessly at his side. This was the second night the angelito was on exhibit. Beside it sat a white-haired gaucho with guitar on his knees, and drunken couples were dancing about the corpse, and making love. In the corners the older people were smoking, and discussing horses and politics. Across the table from the guitarrist, the child's mother sat with hands crossed, staring fixedly ahead. "El angelito está en el cielo" (The little angel is in heaven), people would say to her; and she would reply, "Yes, in heaven." The point of this strange scene is that wakes were occasions for festivity, perhaps the best occasions that turned up during the year, and when the family was through with the corpse neighbors frequently borrowed it for themselves. It was kept as long as possible: by day it was put in a cold room to keep it from flies. Pulperos were especially enthusiastic about wakes, since they brought good business.[27]

As in all primitive peoples, there was a thin border line between fact and fancy, between hard reality and the dim world of spirits and *ánimas en pena*. Lucio V. Mansilla, who has left a remarkable record of an expedition against the Indians, tells the story of a Correntino corporal named Gómez, who was given to occasional hallucinations. He had once murdered the woman he lived with out of jealousy, as he explained to Colonel Mansilla. At night, when they were sleeping, he dreamt another man was making love to her, and he became so exasperated with this dream that one night he stabbed her as she lay beside him.[28]

It is not surprising that such men had to be ruled by force. All that the gaucho had of the democratic spirit was a sense of personal liberty that was anarchic. The border line between gaucho and gaucho malo was tenuous. Both had probably done their share of violent killing; but one, from bad luck perhaps, had gone beyond the pale of the law. "Law" was at best a relative term. It stood for the right of provincial militia to stop the traveller and demand a passport, or perhaps throw him in jail on a technicality and keep him there until he had raised money for a whacking fine or to bribe his way out. In Buenos Aires law was what Rosas said it was. Each caudillo was his own law, with as much order thrown in as he could enforce. Distances were too great, communication too poor, and the population too thinned out to make real organization possible.

THE CITY

> *It alone, in all the vast extension of Argentina, is in contact with the European nations; it alone enjoys the advantages of foreign trade; it alone has power and income.* —SARMIENTO, *Facundo.*

Buenos Aires always has been, and perhaps always will be, the tail that wags Argentina. In the first census it had 10 per cent of the population of the entire Republic. Now it has 20 per cent. It has historically controlled the wealth, the national income, the political power. It has been a force for centralization and for anarchy, for great good and for greater evil. It made the Revolution, and it wrecked the Confederation.

In the early years of the nineteenth century the Queen of the Plata had little of the regal in her appearance. A dull, flat-roofed, colorless little town, squatting on the mud banks of a muddy river, it had not even a port to offer the ships that brought it Europe's woollens and silks, cutlery and ironware, cheese and olive oils and wines. The boats anchored in the river at high tide, and stayed in the mud as the water receded, and passengers and merchandise were unloaded in giant-wheeled bullock carts. The town, like all Spanish colonial towns, was cut into square blocks, with streets intersecting each other, as prescribed by the Laws of the Indies, every 160 yards. Some streets were paved, but well into the middle of the century the unwary who ventured too close to the edge of town saw their animals mired down, and sometimes left to die and rot. The Spanish viceroys had argued against paving the streets. With impeccable logic the Marquis of Loreto, for instance, had shown that carts rolling over pavement would rattle so hard the houses would shake down. Furthermore, said the Marquis, the cost of shoeing horses for paved streets was greater than the value of the animals themselves. (In this he was quite correct.) In spite of these and other logical subtleties, however, paving began in 1795, and by Rivadavia's time, in the 1820's, was virtually completed.[29]

The buildings were one story high, of whitewashed brick or adobe, and looked at each other across streets that were—again, as prescribed by the Laws of the Indies—just ten yards wide. The furniture was generally of "the most tawdry North American manufacture," and the walls might be decorated with French prints.[30] Heating was primitive, and both Beaumont and Woodbine Parish, who visited Buenos Aires in the 1820's, concur in the total lack of fireplaces. Heating was by braziers filled with wood ashes from the kitchen fire, and they had the double disadvantage of giving off choking fumes and being inadequate to a climate that was extremely damp and chill in winter.

Public hygiene was unknown. There were neither sewers nor drainpipes nor waterworks until almost the end of the century. The better families drained water from their roofs into patio cisterns, but the poor had to buy from the water carts that were pulled by oxen from door to door. Even in 1850, says Parish, well water was brackish and bad. Milk was peddled on horseback in large cans that hung from the sides of the saddles (as it still is in Jujuy). It is not surprising then that typhoid was endemic, and that there were terrible outbreaks of yellow fever even as late as the 1870's. Meat was delivered in carts hung with horribly bleeding carcasses. The rest of the provisions—vegetables, fruit, and eggs—were brought in by gauchos on horseback, whose service was haphazard and irregular. Food, except for meat, was high; and out of season it was scarce.[31]

In the opening years of the last century, the porteño was colorful. European modes had not sifted to the poorer classes, and the town was thronged with men in bright ponchos and bright caps, with merchants and soldiers and friars. There were all races: Indians and mestizos, negroes and mulattos, and pure whites. Ladies of society dressed more demurely for mass, in black silk, with black or white mantillas, and white silk shoes and stockings. But on their shoulders they usually wore a colored shawl, and they carried brilliant rugs over their arms to kneel on in church. The young men of society dressed after the European fashion.[32] But pure whites were not common. As Samuel Haigh said, "the rank and file are such a mixture of white, Indian and Negro, that it is difficult to tell their origin." [33]

In Buenos Aires, as in the Pampa, people lived on horseback. In this city, beggars rode. They were called *pordioseros*, because they were always begging things "por el amor de Dios"—for the love of God. J. P. Robertson, who lived in Buenos Aires at various times between 1807 and 1830, claimed that the pordiosero did very well in his profession. He went from door to door with knapsack and saddlebags, collecting beef and lamb, bacon, vegetables, fish, fruit, and perhaps even a brace or two of partridges. Having finished his rounds, he would return home, turn his nag to graze, and cook dinner. He did not work after lunch. It was the hour of the siesta.[34]

Even fishing was done on horseback. At low tide enormous nets were spread on the mud banks, and the rising water brought in fish by the thousands. When the tide was up, three or four horses and riders swam out to the nets and began hauling them in. As they got closer to shore and the nets grew heavier with the weight of their wriggling load, the horsemen stood up in their saddles like circus riders and pulled. When they got to shore they spilled their captives on the banks. Since the catch was indiscriminate, including flounders, *pacúes*, *pejerreyes* and all the fishes, large and small, of the Río de la Plata, the fishermen would choose the best and leave the rest to rot.[35]

In spite of its quaintness, this was the most important city in South America, and the economic heart of the Argentine provinces. Buenos Aires lived from its hides and salted beef. The outskirts stank with slaughterhouses and *saladeros* (meat-salting plants). In return for leather and tallow, the capital imported all that it used from Europe. England and Scotland furnished woollens from Halifax and Leeds, cottons from Glasgow, Paisley, and Manchester, cutlery from Sheffield and Birmingham, pottery from Worcester and Staffordshire.[36] England was the first to tap this market, and has never lost her lead. But as the century progressed, merchandise from the whole world found its way to the Plata. There were silks from Lyons, cashmeres from Louviers, Sedan and Elbeuf, cambrics from Paris, wines from Bordeaux, Provence, and Languedoc. Germany and Flanders sent linens, woollens, Rhenish cottons, ironmongery and hardware, cutlery, glass, muskets and sabers, laces and veils, cotton stockings, furniture. From Holland came cheeses, butter, and gin in pipes and case bottles. There were Westphalian hams, Spanish and Sicilian wines, Spanish olive oils in casks and jars, macaroni and vermicelli from Genoa, Spanish olives and dried fruits, and condiments and sausages from Italy. From the Baltic came iron, cordage, canvas, pitch, tar, and deals; from the United States, tobacco, soap, sperm candles, and unbleached cloth; and from Brazil, sugar, coffee, rice, tobacco, and cacao.[37] Local industries were of the simplest kinds, being restricted to the making of felt hats and clothes; and there were silversmiths and blacksmiths, carpenters, shoemakers, and tailors.[38]

In a very true sense Buenos Aires occupied a colonial position with relation to Europe. It was a provider of raw materials and a consumer of manufactured goods. Why should the porteño buy his ponchos in Santiago del Estero, paying the price plus 100 per cent for transportation by oxcart, when he could buy an English-made poncho for less? Why should he buy his wines in San Juan and Mendoza when he could get French wines? Why should he bring rice and sugar from Tucumán, with painful slowness, and at exorbitant cost, when they could be brought by ship from Brazil? This was the nub of the problem. This was the issue that made the Revolution, and the civil war between the capital city and the starving provinces. Spain had protected local industry by prohibiting all commerce of the colony with other countries. Smuggling, as might be imagined, thrived, and the prohibition was honored far more in the breach than in the observance. The best proof of the handicap Buenos Aires had suffered under the viceroys was that when the port was opened in 1809 to free commerce with the English, as a result of Dillon and Company's pressure on the Viceroy Cisneros, customs receipts jumped, prices of English goods dropped and a million and a half hides that had been a drug on the market were exported to England.[39]

The secret of this curious situation—that the interests of Buenos Aires should be directly opposed to the interests of all the rest of the Republic—was transportation. The capital had access to the sea. It was the *only* city with access to the sea. Its privileged position was sanctioned by law, even under Spanish rule, when it was the *puerto habilitado*, the only legal port of the viceroyalty of the Río de la Plata. But in contrast with its easy and cheap access to Europe by sea, was its isolation from the interior by land. Trains of oxcarts could make just one round trip between Buenos Aires and Salta per year, and one cart could carry one and a half to two tons. A man who wanted to travel on main routes might get fresh horses at post houses which were some ten to twenty-five miles apart; but the chances were that where he wanted to go he had to take his own *tropilla* of four horses with a belled mare to keep them together. If his tropilla strayed or was stolen, bad luck. A tropilla took months to train, and was worth money. And the traveller had to go armed against violence, and sleep on the ground. It was not a tempting trip. When ladies travelled they had to take heavy coaches with six to eight horses, each ridden by a postillion, and they carried their own kitchens and beds.[40] In comparison, the trip to England or France by ship was luxurious.

So the Queen City turned her back on the provinces and her face to London and Paris. Buenos Aires learned what to wear, and how to heat her houses, from the English. She took her poetry and literature from the French. Where the provincial ate his beef without salt, without bread, without vegetables, and drank Correntine caña and wine from Mendoza, the porteño ate bread and fruit and vegetables as well as the finest beef, and drank the best that

Spain and France had to offer. In the city the poor might dress like the gauchos, but the estanciero and merchant class wore satins and silks. The campesino drank from a gourd mate, and the porteño from a mate of wrought silver. The gaucho wore *botas de potro,* the porteño silver-buckled shoes. And so was born the porteño mentality, which may be roughly summed up as the inner conviction that Argentina exists for Buenos Aires, and that all outside the limits of Buenos Aires is outside the limits of civilization.

THE PROVINCES

> *Several of the provinces are now in a worse condition than when under the government of the Spaniards; and the vicinity of Buenos Ayres alone appears to have materially benefited by the changes which have taken place.* —J. A. B. BEAUMONT, *Travels in Buenos Ayres.*

It is the Pampa that has given Argentina its fame as a breeder of livestock, a grower of wheat and corn; and perhaps it was but right to introduce first this region of incomparable richness and fertility. Yet to do so was to point up again the injustice that has always been done to the northern provinces, an injustice of historical perspective as well as of economic distribution. For the Pampa is only one of the four great geographical regions of the country. It embraces the largest and richest province, Buenos Aires, and segments of Santa Fe, Córdoba, San Luis, and La Pampa. This treeless plain has the best of Argentina's land, and three-quarters of all its manufacturing. In the nineteenth century, in addition, it had the only outlet to foreign markets. Its heart was the city of Buenos Aires, and it claimed to speak for the Republic.

In comparison, the misery and isolation of all the rest of the nation would be difficult to paint. The railroads have saved some of the provinces, but when the Revolution of 1810 opened the European market to Buenos Aires, the effect was the most sudden and complete disaster. The interior had lived by its handicrafts: weaving, leatherwork, and metalwork. When the Junta de Mayo threw open the doors for all that Europe could send, English ponchos sold at three pesos where Argentine cost seven, and English cotton cloth cost one real and a quarter, against domestic cloth's two to three. Small, autarchic economic units of the interior that had supported servants, serfs, and slaves, now found themselves with no buyers for what they produced, and the provinces sank into unemployment and economic stagnation.[41]

There are three great regions in addition to the Pampa. South of the Río Negro lies Patagonia, a cold, windy desert plain that stretches down to Tierra del Fuego between the Cordillera of the Andes and the Atlantic Ocean. In this period it was Terra Incognita. Magellan had wintered at San Julián in his epochal voyage of discovery, and in the eighteenth century Antonio de Viedma had founded San Julián and Puerto Deseado. In the nineteenth, Darwin, on the *Beagle*, stopped on this desolate coast to seek specimens of plant and animal life. But settlements hugged the coast, and it was not until the third quarter of the century that General Julio A. Roca, with his Expedition to the Desert, was to open these bleak stretches of land to the sheepmen that came from Scotland and the Basque regions of Spain.

The old Spanish settlements were in the north and west, in the dry, rolling hills of Córdoba, in the rocky Andean region of Cuyo, in green, subtropical Tucumán, in hot Santiago del Estero, and in the Argentine littoral that lies along the Paraná River. The north is a warm, swampy, subtropical plain that includes the Territories of Chaco, Formosa, and Misiones, where Argentina, Brazil, and Paraguay meet; and the provinces of Salta, Tucumán, Santiago del Estero, Corrientes, and a part of Santa Fe. Here the rainfall is the heaviest in the Republic: in the Chaco it averages 63 inches.[42] Here are the quebracho forests, and the *yerbales*, the plantations of yerba mate, that were first cultivated by the Jesuit missionaries of Paraguay in the eighteenth century as a monopoly. Here are the sugar and the rice and the tobacco. But in the nineteenth century the north was poor, for there were no railroads and no one had thought to navigate the Paraná. All that the north produced came by oxcarts that had to be unloaded at every stream and river and floated across on inflated hide rafts. The carts were made in Tucumán of the toughest timber, but fell apart in two years under the pounding the trails gave them.[43]

Something of what this journey meant is told by Parish. Trains of fourteen carts used to leave Salta in April or May, when the rivers were falling, to avoid being caught on the road in the dry months from July to October when water and pasturage were scarce. The carts were built with an eye to the swamps and streams they would have to cross. The wheels were higher than a man, and the oxen were harnessed with one pair close to the wagon, and another far ahead, to help traction should the cart bog down. They took eighty to ninety days to reach Buenos Aires, rarely making more than fifteen miles a day. It took three relays of oxen for the journey: the first to Tucumán, the second to the edge of Buenos Aires, and the third across the province to the capital city. Twenty to twenty-five drivers were employed by a train of oxcarts, and the hire of the fourteen vehicles was 2,800 pesos from Salta to Buenos Aires, and 2,200 pesos from Buenos Aires back to Salta.[44]

It was these freight costs that killed the provinces. Even Santa Fe, which shared the fertile Pampa with its southern neighbor, Buenos Aires, could not beat the handicap. Until the railroad and the river port of Rosario finally gave it an outlet to Europe, it was as poor as the rest. The interior suffered not only as an exporter, but as an importer. A Frenchman who was in Argentina in the fifties said that a hide that sold for five francs in Buenos Aires cost 1.8 francs to transport to Córdoba, 2.5 francs to San Luis, and four to five francs to Tucumán.[45]

The last great geographical division of Argentina is the west, the region of the Andes, and it includes Mendoza, San Juan, La Rioja, and Catamarca. This is the highest and the driest part of the Republic: rainfall averages three to eleven inches, and in Mendoza the Cordillera reaches the highest point in the Americas with Mount Aconcagua at nearly 23,000 feet. San Juan and Mendoza are, and always have been, the great wine producers of Argentina; and when a man is well gone in his cups, the Argentines say he is "between San Juan and Mendoza." Mendoza is so rich that the federal government has to forbid further planting of grapes, and it has a practical monopoly on table beverages in the country. But in the nineteenth century it suffered like all the interior: it could not get its wines to market. Buenos Aires preferred French Burgundies and Spanish sherries.

The provincial economy was primitive, like all pre-industrial economies. Corrientes made cinches and *jergas* (coarsely woven saddle blankets). Córdoba wove cloaks and ponchos and blankets, and raised cattle and mules. Santa Fe, very poor, lived from its mules, and both Córdoba and Santa Fe sold their animals in the annual fair in Salta, destined for Alto Perú (Bolivia) and Bajo Perú, during colonial times. La Rioja, San Juan, and Mendoza made wines and liquors. Salta lived by providing winter pasture for the mules of Córdoba. Santiago made stirrups and ponchos. Tucumán grew rice, and Jujuy cultivated sugar cane.[46] This was the economy of the interior, sufficient for the feudal society of the age so long as there was trade with Buenos Aires, but too close to starvation to leave any margin when the industrial revolution, in the person of England, came to compete in the market.

Sarmiento, in his *Recuerdos de Provincia,* tells what life was like in his native province of San Juan when his mother was a girl. Her father had been "owner of half the Zonda valley, and of troops of mules and carts"; but the family fell on evil times, and the girl, then twenty-three, took a Negro slave and a servant and set herself up as a weaver of serges for the religious orders of the province. "The manual industries of my mother are so many and so various," writes Sarmiento, "that to enumerate them would tire the memory with names that no longer have any meaning. She made suspenders of silk, kerchiefs of vicuña to send as samples to the curious in Spain, and ties and ponchos of the same soft wool." She made altar cloths, albs, laces, nets, "and a multitude of thread work employed in the adornment of women's clothes." And with the money she saved by her work, Paula Albarracín built the little house where she was to live after her marriage, and where Domingo Sarmiento was born.[47]

All this handiwork, especially after the Revolution, added up to poverty. Joseph Andrews made a trip through Santiago, Tucumán, and Salta in 1825, and wrote of the misery he saw everywhere. Santiago, he said, was "inconceivably backward," and the people were not only poor but lazy. The government made its chief income from transit duties on goods passing through the province on their way to Upper Perú. (All the provincial governments relied on tariffs for revenue. They had nothing else.) Tucumán, the Garden of the Republic, as Argentines call it, he found luxuriant in vegetation, but poor in human resources. The rich soil yielded fruits, vegetables, and pasturage for livestock, but the inhabitants lived miserably on meat and corn. "It is really sad," wrote Andrews, "to contemplate these people, in the very garden of the universe, wasting their time so painfully. Their lazy habits were undoubtedly inherited from their former masters." There seemed to be little incentive to labor, however, for Andrews adds that peons were paid three to five pesos a month, and *capataces* (overseers) only eight to ten.

The buildings of Tucumán were in a deplorable state. As for the cultural level of the province, it may be judged by the fact that, when Andrews wanted to get a contract with the government printed, there was not enough type in the whole town. Tucumán was depopulated: probably ten out of forty thousand inhabitants had died in the Wars of Independence, or emigrated to Buenos Aires. Salta was in the same condition, and its mines were abandoned.[48]

Twenty years later the condition of the interior was, if anything, worse. In his *Facundo,* Sarmiento paints a dismal picture of his native San Juan. In a city of forty thousand there was not one lawyer, and there was only one doctor. There was not a single public school. The one girls' *colegio,* or high school, closed in 1840. Three boys' high schools successively opened and closed between 1840 and 1843. There were three young people being educated outside the province. There was only one person in the whole city who had ever studied mathematics. And there were not ten people who knew more than how to read and write.[49] As for La Rioja, after a quarter-century in the hands of caudillos like Facundo Quiroga, it had fallen to a level at which culture could no longer be said to exist. Sarmiento reports this dialogue with Dr. Manuel Ignacio Castro Barros six months after the latter had fled La Rioja for Chile:

Question. Approximately what is the population of La Rioja?
Answer. Scarcely fifteen hundred souls. It is said that there are only five hundred men and boys in the city.
Q. How many outstanding citizens live there?
A. In the city, six or seven.
Q. How many lawyers have opened offices?
A. None.
Q. How many doctors are there for the sick?
A. None.
Q. How many judges are there?
A. None.
Q. How many men wear European dress?
A. None.
Q. How many young Riojanos are studying in Córdoba or Buenos Aires?
A. I know of only one.
Q. How many schools are there, and how many pupils?
A. None.
Q. Are there any public charitable institutions?
A. No, nor primary schools. The only Franciscan friar in the monastery has a few pupils.
Q. How many ruined churches?
A. Five. Only La Matriz can be used.
Q. Are new houses being built?
A. None, nor are fallen ones repaired. . . .
Q. Are there fortunes of fifty thousand pesos? How many of twenty thousand?
A. None. Everybody is very poor.
Q. Has the population increased or decreased?
A. It has decreased by one-half.
Q. Is there any feeling of terror among the people?
A. The greatest terror. Even the innocent are afraid to speak.[50]

This, then, from the jungles of Misiones to the rocky Cordillera, from the Bolivian border to the Straits of Magellan, was the Argentine Republic that had turned from a brave war for national independence to a half-century of bloody and ruinous civil war.

BLOODY ROSAS

UNITARIO OR FEDERAL?

> *The Argentine revolution has been double: first, the war of the cities, initiated into European culture, against the Spaniards, to the end of giving that culture wider extension; second, the war of the caudillos against the cities, to try to free themselves of all civil subjection and to give free rein to their hatred of civilization. The cities triumph over the Spaniards, and the country over the cities.*
>
> —SARMIENTO, *Facundo.*

In 1826, Bernardino Rivadavia was President of the precariously United Provinces of the Río de la Plata. "Don Bernardino Rivadavia seems to be between forty and fifty years of age," wrote Beaumont, who had known him in London, and did not like him; "about five feet in height and much about the same measure in circumference; his countenance is dark, but not unpleasing, it denotes acuteness, and, with his features, appears to belong to the ancient race which formerly sojourned at Jerusalem; his coat is green, buttoned *à la Napoleon;* his small clothes, if such they can be called, are fastened at the knee with silver buckles, and the short remainder of his person is clad in silk hose, dress shoes, and silver buckles; his whole appearance is not very unlike the caricature portraits of Napoleon: indeed, it is said he is very fond of imitating that once great personage in such things as are within his reach, such as the cut or colour of a coat, or the inflation of an address." [1]

Rivadavia's days as Napoleon were fated to be short. It was one of those moments in history when a momentary balance of forces gives a short stability. Argentina was on the eve of her civil wars.

The Revolution had been a premature birth. When the battle with Spain was over it became appallingly clear that there were several—and strong—class interests that had not been served by Independence, and that were to be the element of disunion. The cattlemen had been for independence only to break the Spanish monopoly: they were an inherently conservative class. The merchants who had benefited from the Spanish monopoly hated the Revolution and all its works, and they were to form the backbone of Rosas' reaction. And as for the provinces, their market gone, their income stopped at the source, they gave themselves over to war against the capital city. The more one surveyed the situation, the more it seemed that the only class that had evidently benefited from Independence, and that continued revolutionary, was the importers of English merchandise. This was not enough to hold a nation together. Buenos Aires wanted to unite the provinces, but on her own terms, and under her hegemony; and from this movement grew one of the two great parties of the civil wars, the Unitario party.* The provinces were in the hands of their caudillos now, and were fiercely for their provincial rights. "It is not possible to satisfy local demands, in the present stage of development, except in a federal system," said Quiroga. "The provinces will be torn to pieces, perhaps, but never dominated." [2] So the interior united against the capital city, and thus was born the opposition party, the Federales.

The Unitarian constitution of 1819 had failed to unite the nation. Congress met, but the provinces were in anarchy. In Mendoza, José de San Martín, who had liberated the southern half of the continent, waited impatiently for Congress's permission to cross the Andes again. He was thinking in terms of the freedom and union of all South America; but provincial self-interest was too strong, and Congress relieved him of his command. San Martín lost his army, and Congress lost its sovereignty, almost at the same moment. Congress dissolved itself, because there was nothing else to do, and Argentina's greatest patriot crossed the mountains into exile. Buenos Aires, losing the hope of organizing the nation, created its own provincial legislature, the Junta de Representantes, and left the provinces to fend for themselves. In Tucumán, Bernabé Araoz declared himself "President of the Free and Independent Republic of Tucumán." In Santa Fe, government was in

* So called because it wanted a United Argentina, rather than a Federation.

the hands of caudillo Estanislao López, who had taken up arms for the Federal cause. In La Rioja, Juan Facundo Quiroga had also taken up arms: "I and my men have sworn never to give up our arms until the nation is constituted by the expression and free vote of the Republic," he wrote to General Paz.[3]

For five years there was no national government. Then the Constituent Congress met and elected Rivadavia president. It was at this juncture that there seemed to be a momentary, but only a fleeting, hope of counteracting the drift to anarchy. In reality, Rivadavia had no hopes from the first, because he held office illegally: Congress was authorized to make a constitution, not elect a chief executive, and the reaction from the provinces took only as long as it took the news to travel. But, in that brief interlude before the whole false structure fell down, the President worked ambitiously to encourage immigration and capital investment in Argentina. It was probably not his fault that his ambitious schemes began backfiring almost at once. A law was passed to encourage immigrants to come to Argentina, promising to provide work for them, to maintain them their first fifteen days at government expense, and to furnish their passage money up to 100 pesos.* Ignacio Núñez, secretary of the Argentine legation in London, published a book in English to encourage immigration. "The provinces of the Río de la Plata do not present a very flattering prospect for those who enjoy the world, nor of such persons do they now stand in need. There, the things which interest the most are capital; and that class of people which, in other parts, is considered the least provided for, and consequently the most needy of society. The artisan, the labourer, the mechanic, the man who works with his hands, are the most valuable acquisitions that can be made by that country."[4]

If this sounded promising to the men who "worked with their hands," the reality proved disillusioning. Several hundred families did immigrate, having been promised farms in Entre Ríos; and when they got to Buenos Aires, the government tried to send them

* The peso and dollar signs are identical. In this book, $ will refer to United States dollars; when pesos are meant, that word will appear.

to man a fort in Patagonia. They were robbed of their agricultural implements. And in spite of the wide advertising, in Spanish, French, English, and German, of Argentina's promise to pay their passage money, the government made them work it off at the rate of one-fifth their monthly wages until it was paid. As for the unfortunate English agent who had been employed by Rivadavia to collect the six hundred fifty immigrants, he lost between twenty and thirty thousand pounds on the deal, if we are to believe his son's account. His wrath could not have been soothed much when, after presenting his complaints to the President, he was given Rivadavia's answer: "It is of no consequence. I will employ some-one else." [5]

Rivadavia's efforts to encourage capital investment seemed to have come to no better end. In 1823 he had authorized the formation of the Río de la Plata Mining Association, and Núñez, with more of a flair for advertising than for truth, signed a certified description of the properties to be exploited. "We can affirm," he wrote, "without hyperbole, that the two first curacies, Rinconada and Santa Catalina, contain the greatest riches in the universe. I am going to prove it by a single assertion, which is attested by thousands of witnesses. In its fields the gold springs up with the rain, as in the others, weeds. The great mass of this soil is composed of earth, stone, water, and larger and smaller grains of gold; these last appear in sight when the rain washes away the dust which covers the surface. After a very heavy rain, a woman stepping forth from her hut, a few yards from her door, found a piece of gold weighing twenty ounces; another, wnen gathering wood, on pulling up some grass, discovered among the roots a grain of from three to four ounces." Stockholders in the Río de la Plata Mining Association, of which Rivadavia had graciously accepted the presidency, lost between sixty and seventy thousand pounds.[6]

Rivadavia's most spectacularly big undertaking came to the most spectacularly bad end of all. It was the famous loan of 1824 from the English firm of Baring Brothers, which had been first negotiated by Buenos Aires when it was under its provincial government. A provincial law of 1822 authorized the negotiation of a loan of three or four million pesos to build a port and waterworks. Since the province had nothing but its land to put up as security, the sale of public lands was forbidden, and they were put under the orders of the Minister of Finance to be given out in emphyteusis, a kind of life lease that involved no ownership. In July, 1824, the London bankers, Baring Brothers, accepted the terms of the loan, and advanced the money, which was to be for £1,000,000. It was the beginning of Baring Brothers' excursion into Argentine finances, which were finally to reach the heady total of £81,000,000 by 1894, and bring this firm to bankruptcy along with the republic it had helped to create.[7]

The history of Baring Brothers' relations with Argentina is an expensive lesson in loose financial practices. The first loan was the worst. It was not used for the purposes specified, and it took half a century to liquidate. Furthermore, it has been used both by those Argentines who detest foreign capital as an object lesson in the dangers of borrowing money, and by foreign capitalists with a grudge against Latin America as an object lesson in the dangers of lending money. The Argentines claim that a loan which was supposed to net them three to four million pesos, and actually netted them less, cost them twenty-three millions to liquidate. This is true. The loan was for £1,000,000, but Baring Brothers deducted the amortization and interest up to January 12, 1827, so that only £570,000 was advanced to the Argentine government. The outbreak of war with Brazil in 1825, followed by the outbreak of the civil wars and the French and English blockades of Buenos Aires, sent the peso spiralling from a value of 45 English pence in January, 1823, to 20 in 1827, 7½ in 1837, and 2⅝ in 1847.[8] And as the peso dropped, naturally the servicing of the loan became heavier and heavier. During the tyranny of Rosas it stopped altogether. Before the Republic finally cleared it, it had become a nightmare to both creditor and debtor.

But the evil effects of the loan of 1824 did not end with the loan itself. A greater ill was the indirect, but determining, effect it was to have on the distribution and ownership of land in Argentina. To furnish collateral for this English loan, Congress in 1826 passed the law of emphyteusis to provide for the distribution of public lands without their outright sale. By this law, men who took up the land had a life lease on it, their rent to be fixed every ten years. The error of this law, which was sponsored by Rivadavia, was that it did not fix the amount of land any one man might own. Thus it was grabbed up immediately by speculators and sublet, and before the decade was over two of Argentina's perennial evils were born: the concentration of seigniorial tracts of land in the hands of a few families, and the subletting of the land down through several hands to the poor man who actually worked it.

Anyone who had ever studied the history of emphyteusis in the late Roman Empire and early Middle Ages could have prophesied what would happen, even though the Argentine system differed in important respects. It has been axiomatic that possession, when it is old enough, becomes ownership. The idea of emphyteusis broke down early in Argentina, and was finally abandoned. To read the roll call of the men who profited by the government's distribution of land between 1822 and 1830 is to read the roll call of the landed aristocracy of the twentieth century: Aguirre, Anchorena, Alzaga, Alvear, Lynch, Pereyra, Quiroga, Rozas, Sáenz, Viamonte. Five hundred thirty-eight men obtained 3,206 leagues—in English equivalents, approximately 20,000,000 acres, an average of some 37,000 acres each.* Some of these land speculators took fabulous amounts. Tomás M. de Anchorena took up 119 leagues (some 735,000 acres) in six different parts of the province. Eustaquio Díaz Vélez took 143 leagues (some 880,000 acres).[9] Nor did they ask for this land with any eye to working it themselves. They sublet it. When Rosas later allowed them to take title to it, there began that pyramiding of wealth that was accomplished by the automatic rise in land values. These families did not have to earn their wealth. They neither worked the land, nor risked their fortunes in speculative ventures. All that they had

* An Argentine metric league is 2,500 hectares (6,176 acres). One hectare equals 2.471 acres. These early nineteenth century leagues were not metric, and were so inexactly measured as to be difficult to translate, so I have calculated them at the metric equivalent for the sake of simplicity, even though slight error results.

to do to become multimillionaires was to wait, and their fortunes piled up by themselves. This is the origin of the Argentine landed aristocracy. But the land is a chapter by itself. Rivadavia's emphyteusis was at least a well intentioned venture. It was Rosas who was to be the real villain.

In spite of Rivadavia's vanity, in spite of his lending himself to financial schemes of a doubtful character, in spite of the bad consequences of his land policy—in spite, in short, of the fact that his presidency was a failure in less than a year, and that it precipitated the civil wars—Rivadavia must be counted as one of Argentina's greatest statesmen. He had the best vision of what his country ought to be of any man of his time. Events were out of his hands, and his failure was really the failure of Argentina's political maturity.

He was right in encouraging immigration and foreign investment in Argentina. An Argentina without ports, without roads, without great cities, without a population worthy of the name—one inhabitant to every two square miles—had neither a present nor a future. England needed a market and needed to export capital, and the English loans, public and private, had logic in them. Where both Rivadavia and the English investors erred was in their optimism. Argentina was not yet ready to be a nation. Economics was on the side of foreign investors, but politics was not. Probably the President had no real notion of how close the Argentine nation was to dissolution. His administration foundered on the question of Unitarianism *vs.* Federalism. It was the province of Buenos Aires that broke the federal government. On February 9, 1826, the day after he took office, Rivadavia sent Congress a bill to make Buenos Aires the national capital, and to dissolve its provincial government. The province had the only port, and therefore had all the national income which came from import duties. The customs—the *aduana*, as it is called in Spanish—was the young nation's only source of income, and since the Revolution Buenos Aires had simply appropriated the funds in their totality for its own provincial treasury. This meant that every other province was paying a toll to the capital. This is the explanation of the interprovincial tariffs which were so hard on trade. The interior provinces had literally *no money at all*. Bad as internal tariffs are, and truly as they contributed to the economic poverty of the already desperate north, there was no alternative for the provincial governments to raise money for their expenses. Rivadavia proposed to nationalize the aduana, and divide the customs receipts among all the provinces.

The question was debated in Congress on the false issue of Unitarianism *vs.* Federalism. The debates, which took place in February and March, and were often brilliant (perhaps there have never been more interesting debates in the history of the Argentine Congress), revolved around a number of irrelevant questions. Rivadavia and his party were called Unitarios, and the party representing the private interests of Buenos Aires were called Federales; but the names were misnomers. You have only to read the speech of Manuel Moreno,* the chief Federal, to see what the real issue was. Buenos Aires had everything to lose by the nationalization of the port and its revenues, and the dissolution of its government. Moreno tried to put the debate on constitutional grounds by saying that Congress had no right to dissolve the provincial government before the constitution was sanctioned (this was true, just as it was true that Congress had had no right to elect Rivadavia President). But that was not what was worrying Moreno or the Buenos Aires party. This law would strike where it hurt most: at the pocketbook. Buenos Aires had all the wealth, all the richest land, all the national revenues, and the only city worthy of the name. If this had to be divided with the other provinces, they would be the gainers, and she the loser.

Rivadavia's government was doomed the day this law was presented. The province of Buenos Aires was stronger than the Argentine nation, and was to prove it. No matter whether the Unitario or the Federal plan of government were to triumph, Buenos Aires would be the natural leader of the Republic. But Rivadavia wanted the province to organize the nation, at its expense, and the provincial party which called themselves Federales wanted to let the

* Not to be confused with his more important brother, Mariano Moreno.

rest of the nation go hang. Buenos Aires was richer and stronger by itself than acting as a crutch for the misery and poverty of the rest of the country. For the next fifty years there were really two parties within the province: the Buenos Aires Unitarios, who wanted to organize the nation and run it themselves; and the Buenos Aires Federales, who did not want to organize the nation, and who wanted to monopolize the national revenues. There was a third party, which is not usually recognized as such, and hence the confusion of names and issues in the titles "Unitario" and "Federal." The third party was the provincial Federales, the Federales of the interior, whose evolution in political sophistication was finally to result in national union. The Federales of La Rioja and Córdoba and Santa Fe were at first only caudillos who wanted provincial autonomy. These were the men who contributed to the anarchy of the civil wars, the barbarians of Sarmiento's "Civilization and Barbarism." Provincial federalism was nothing but the rule of the gaucho mentality when the civil wars broke out. But in thirty years it matured enough to make the union of the nation. It matured faster than the narrow interests of the province of Buenos Aires, which still fought the Republic when every despised caudillo of the north had given his support to the national constitution.

The Buenos Aires Federales broke Rivadavia's government over the issue of dissolving the provincial government. No sooner was the project presented than Colonel Juan Manuel de Rosas went about the province getting signatures for a petition against it. In Chascomús he was jailed for his agitation, but Rivadavia ordered him released. The Buenos Aires Sala de Representantes was in the greatest agitation, uncertain whether to acquiesce in its own dissolution should this be ordered. In Congress the majority was for the project, a fact which again points up the difference between the Federales of the province of Buenos Aires, and the Federales of the North. On March 3, the law passed 25 to 14. The interior voted with the Unitarios because they wanted a share in the national revenues, and they were delighted to see the power of Buenos Aires broken. On March 7 Rivadavia asked the governor of

Buenos Aires to close his office, and he did, going into voluntary exile. The legislature had a tumultuous meeting, and disbanded.

This law was the undoing of the Constituent Congress. Many of the interior provinces disowned their own representatives for voting with the Unitarios. The men in Congress were men of exceptional caliber, and understood better than the caudillos the real interests of the interior. They voted with Rivadavia because they wanted to share the national government with Buenos Aires. But there were many provincial governors who still put autonomy above the national interests, and who did not see that a Unitarian constitution would have meant the economic salvation of the north. When Buenos Aires rebelled against the nation, they joined her, against their own best interests. Federalism for Buenos Aires meant economic prosperity and a monopoly of wealth. For the interior it could only mean an aggravation of misery. But the interior was to learn the hard way. Catamarca and Tucumán declared for the Unitarios. Estanislao López in Santa Fe and Juan Facundo Quiroga in La Rioja declared for the Federales. Facundo raised a black banner with the motto "Religion or Death," and he invaded Catamarca and Tucumán and deposed the governors. In Buenos Aires, Congress and President were left isolated and unheeded. Finally Rivadavia saw that his situation was hopeless, and in July, 1827, a year after taking office, he resigned. Congress simply fell apart. The civil wars had begun.

THE CAUDILLOS

> *The spirit of the Argentine Revolution existed only in the small Europeanized nuclei of the cities, while the Indo-Hispanic spirit was preserved intact in the rest of the population.*
>
> —José Ingenieros, *La Evolución de las Ideas Argentinas.*

The caudillo was the political counterpart of the gaucho. He was the kind of leader that would naturally spring from an isolated and feudal society without political experience. If he was brutal, so were the men he ruled. If they were ignorant, so usually was he. It is axiomatic in politics that people have the kind of government they deserve and want, and the caudillo belonged supremely to the brutal and primitive society that was then Argentina.

The caudillos of all provinces had several features in common. Most of them were rich in the kind of wealth that then counted, which was land. In this respect they were like the feudal lords of Europe before capitalism made money the basis of wealth. (And like the medieval baron, who ceded political power to the merchant class when he ceded it economic power, the caudillos' decline paralleled the rise of merchant wealth in Argentina.) Among the landowners benefiting from Rivadavia's emphyteusis were both Quiroga and Rosas. General Justo José de Urquiza, the caudillo who finally broke Rosas, was one of the greatest estancieros of Entre Ríos. Juan Manuel de Rosas was not only a landowner, he had a monopoly on the *saladeros* of Buenos Aires, and so great was his control of the meat market that the government had once had to close his saladeros for causing a meat shortage.[10]

The caudillos had a kind of picturesque cruelty in common. Facundo Quiroga, for instance, publicly boasted he had burned down his father's house while his father and mother were taking a nap, because his father had refused him money.[11] Rosas was the kind of man who exhibited his enemies' heads on pikes. It was a savage age, and as in any period when the normal tenor of life is violent, punishments tended towards the barbarous. Among Rosas' prisoners once was a twelve-year-old boy, and when the colonel wrote to Rosas to ask if the boy should be shot with the other prisoners, the caudillo replied that his throat was to be slit.[12] As for what the less-than-capital punishment was like, it can be seen in the provincial museum at Luján, where a gaucho of the period hangs in effigy: he is strung up by his armpits in a dungeon, preparatory to being flogged. But even in an age of barbarism, punishments knew class distinction. General José M. Paz was once a prisoner in the same building, but upstairs, in a bedroom.

One of the most ferocious of the caudillos was the Mendocino Felix Aldao, one of the few to have distinguished themselves in the Wars of Independence. Aldao was a priest, and began his career in 1817 as an army chaplain. In the battle of Guardia Vieja he fought with so much cruelty that General Las Heras reprimanded him. He finally quit the church for a military career, and he became drunken and ferocious. When he was captured by Paz's men at the battle of Oncativo, during the civil wars, he screamed, "Don't touch me!" and took out the sacred Host and consecrated it, saying, "I am a priest and I have in my hands the body of Our Lord Jesus Christ." He kept the Host while he was in prison, and used it to intimidate his ignorant jailers, who thought it made him sacred. Aldao finally died of delirium tremens, suffering the most horrible hallucinations of being tormented by his victims.

The caudillos had an excess of the qualities that made the gaucho what he was: physical courage, cruelty, independence, and the vices of gambling and women. Facundo, for instance, was the kind of man who would stake his last cent on a card. (He usually did not lose, because it was fatal to win from him.) In his youth, when he was only a peon, he once left the house where he had worked for a year with his whole year's wages, seventy pesos. His first stop was a pulpería, and his first act was to put his year's wages on a card, and lose. He afterwards said that this was the highest wager he ever made: not in money, because later he used to play for ounces of gold, but in what that money stood for. It had taken him less than a minute to lose what it cost him twelve months to earn. The sequel to the story is typical. He left the pulpería and rode off aimlessly, not knowing where to go. At this point he was stopped by a local official, who demanded to see his papers. Quiroga drew near on his horse, pretending to fumble for them, and he left the man lying in the road, stabbed to death.[13]

The caudillo thrived on a reputation for daredeviltry. Paz tells of a conversation with a *paisano* about Facundo. "*Señor*, you may think what you like," said the man; "but experience teaches us that Sr. Quiroga is invincible in war, in gambling"—lowering his voice—"and in love. Thus there isn't an example of a battle which he has not won; a game which he has lost"—lowering his voice again—"or a woman he has asked for that he has not conquered." [14]

To the simple country people the caudillos represented their interests against the city and the merchants. Güemes, said Paz, "was adored by the gauchos, who saw in their idol the representative of the lowest class, the protector and father to the poor." [15] Aldao shot the merchants of Mendoza, and sacked their shops. In La Rioja, Quiroga had property owners shot, and their property distributed among his soldiers. When he took Córdoba, the negroes and mulattoes of the city assaulted the stores, and the houses of the Unitarios.[16] Paz, who was never a caudillo, and wanted to make himself one, could not understand why taking the city of Córdoba with his army was not sufficient to win the kind of support Quiroga or Rosas had. "The opposition against me, principally towards the last of my government," he wrote years later, "was, rather than personal, directed against the class they considered an enemy, and which they believed supported me. . . . The gauchos, the people without property, were our enemies." [17]

It is ironic that a man like Rosas, a rich estanciero, a man with a monopoly on the meat of Buenos Aires, should have come to be considered by the country people as a representative of their interests. The only interests he represented were those of the cattlemen of Buenos Aires, an essentially reactionary class. He certainly did not represent the interior, and it is difficult to understand why a man like Facundo Quiroga, who, for all his faults, was possibly the one caudillo who wanted a united Argentina, should have given his support to this Governor-Dictator of Buenos Aires. If Quiroga did not see that Rosas was his enemy, Rosas was not so blind. Quiroga was finally murdered, if not at the instigation of Juan Manuel de Rosas, at least with his blessing.

Rosas was the most aristocratic of the caudillos. He came from a family of Spanish hidalgos, his great-granduncle having been governor and captain-general of the province. His father was Don León Ortiz de Rozas, and his mother, Doña Agustina López de

Osornio, and Juan Manuel was born with the aristocratic family name of Juan Manuel José Domingo Ortiz de Rozas. The surname was as much of a political handicap as Vanderbilt would be in the United States, and Juan Manuel dropped the Ortiz and changed Rozas to Rosas. Both the Ortiz de Rozas and the López de Osornios were rich landowners, and Doña Agustina's father was one of the richest *hacendados* of Buenos Aires. Juan Manuel grew up on his mother's estancia near Salados, and in his adolescence acted as majordomo for his parents. He had little schooling. When he was thirteen, school closed because of the English invasion of 1806, and Rosas, who was still only a child, led a group of boys to fight against the invader. In 1808 his father sent him to manage an estancia.

At the age of twenty he married and left his parents' estancia to work for himself. "I wished to receive no capital from my parents," he said afterwards; "nor did I wish to have my own brand or livestock or land or money while their estancias were in my care. When they tried to force me to accept land and cattle for my services, I asked them only to let me have the pleasure of serving them, and the proud satisfaction of being able always to say that what I have I owe entirely to my own work and my own honor. I went out to work without any other capital than my credit and my industry." [18] It is said that Rosas wrung a reluctant parental consent to his marriage with the young Encarnación Ezcurra y Asguirel by spreading the rumor she was going to have a baby. At any rate, it was a good match. Doña Encarnación had a head no less hard than her husband's, and she was the kind of woman who could be depended on to watch out for his interests when he was away from Buenos Aires. Three women were important in his life: his mother, Doña Agustina; his wife, Doña Encarnación; and his daughter, Manuela. All three were women of considerable force of character.

It remains to be explained how this young estanciero came to be the caudillo of Buenos Aires. He had been born with a silver spoon in his mouth, but he turned out to be tough and competent. Above all, he turned out to be a born leader of men. When Rosas left his parents' estancia he went to work for the Anchorenas, who were relatives of his. (It was Tomás M. de Anchorena who staked claim to the record 735,000 acres of public land, and founded one of the greatest fortunes in Argentina.) This gives an idea of young Juan Manuel's connections. There never was a more respected estanciero than Rosas, and his famous instructions on how to manage an estancia can still be bought in any Buenos Aires bookstore. He inspired awe and respect in the men under him. He could break horses, lasso, throw the boleadoras, brand calves, or play the dangerous *juego del pato* with the best: better than the best. The gauchos worshipped him. His justice was proverbial. I have already told the story of the peon who criticized him for carrying a knife in his belt when he himself had forbidden the wearing of arms; and how Rosas had ordered himself flogged for disobeying orders. He also knew when to be merciful if it would make friends. One time he caught three Indians in the act of cutting up one of his mares. Cut off without escape, they pleaded that they had robbed because they were hungry. Rosas spoke to them gently. "Don't steal, amigos. Whenever you need anything, tell me, and I will give it to you." And he made them a gift of two dozen animals.[19] As might be well imagined, they were deeply impressed, and in the future they left his horses alone.

Rosas made friends both with the Indians of the south, and with the negroes in Buenos Aires. He is the only Argentine executive who ever made peace with the Indians without exterminating them. In 1833, when he was sent by the legislature of Buenos Aires to campaign against them, he made a treaty that lasted twenty years. In this he was unique. After the revolution the Argentines had decreed a war of extermination. As Rivadavia once said to an English acquaintance, "They are bad people—they must be got rid of." Rivadavia's imaginative friend Núñez, who had been so persuasive in luring English capital to Argentina, put the matter very well: since the Indians insisted on being paid for their lands, "no choice is now left to the government of the United Provinces but to resort to violence." [20] But Rosas thought it would be cheaper to buy off the Indian tribes, and he made a pact with them, which both sides rigidly observed. A southern boundary was drawn, and the Indians were not to cross it without a military pass. They had to give military service when asked. And in return each cacique (chief) was given mares and colts for his tribe to eat, as well as yerba mate, tobacco, and salt. The cost to the government ranged from six to fifteen depreciated paper pesos per Indian per month.[21] Rosas' policy worked, because in his administration the frontier was farther south than it was ever to be again until the Conquest of the Desert of 1874–1883.

He made friends with the negroes, too, and the laundresses and servants of Buenos Aires formed a vast volunteer spy system in the homes of his enemies. The question, What happened to the negroes? is one of the more intriguing riddles of Argentine history. They certainly formed a considerable segment of the population during the Wars of Independence. In 1825, one-fourth of the population of the province of Buenos Aires was black. Fifty years before, the negroes were one-third of the population.[22] But there seems to have been an unacknowledged but tacit policy on the part of the government to get as many into dangerous military service as they could. Rosas, who assiduously cultivated the negroes of Buenos Aires, and made uniformed visits to their colonies on the outskirts of the city, put as many as possible into the army, where they got killed off fighting Indians (another race the Argentines were interested in exterminating). In Rosas' time some ten to fifteen thousand negroes lived on the fringes of the city in colonies called *tambos*, and they had their own kings. On Sundays, Rosas, with Doña Encarnación on his arm, paid regular visits to the tambos, and ostentatiously seated himself beside their "kings." His attentions were well repaid: all the porters, carters, carriers, and drivers, not to mention the washerwomen, of Buenos Aires formed a vast and enthusiastic network of spies for Juan Manuel.[23]

It is rare to see a negro in Argentina today. That is why one is always surprised at the important role the blacks once played. Five thousand of them fought in the Wars of Independence, and an uncounted number in the civil wars. In the colonial period they were slaves but were kindly treated, and employed only in household tasks. The revolution freed them. Wars and disease took their toll; and finally came the flood of white immigration. Quite the contrary to what happened in the southern United States, the blacks multiplied more slowly than the whites, and were swallowed up. Parish reported that in the middle 1820's the births among negroes barely exceeded deaths. His figures for the province of Buenos Aires show a remarkable decline just in the years 1822–1825. In 1822, there were 1,246 negro baptisms and 1,117 negro deaths, or an excess of 129 baptisms; and in 1825 there were 1,192 negro baptisms and 1,292 negro deaths, or an excess of 100 deaths. The colored population, said Parish, was on the wane, and "ere long must be entirely lost in the rapid increase of the white population and the continual immigration of fresh settlers from Europe." [24]

Rosas used the negroes, just as he used the poor classes of the country and city: and he was as much the "friend" of one as the other. One is continually struck, when one reads about these caudillos, by the way they appealed to a primitive mentality. Paz's comment on his own failure in Córdoba is eloquent: "The gauchos, the people without property, were our enemies." Rosas was no friend of the masses, however you consider him. He was a friend of the landed aristocracy, and he even betrayed them eventually. Yet the masses loved Rosas. The Mazorca, Rosas' private army of terrorists and thugs, was largely recruited from the peons of his saladeros and mataderos.[25]

His rise to wealth and position was rapid. With the aid of Luis Dorrego and Juan N. Terrero, Rosas founded the first saladero in the province of Buenos Aires, near the town of Quilmes. He doubled his capital in two years, and he had his own ships exporting directly to Rio de Janeiro and Havana. His control of the meat supplies of Buenos Aires was so tight that the butchers' union finally appealed to the government to close his saladeros because they were causing a shortage. He and his partners invested in land, too. They bought vast tracts on the Indian frontier. With this land, with what the legislature of Buenos Aires later gave him, and with what he seized from his enemies, Rosas became one of the greatest landowners of the century.

He got into political power on the wave of discontent that washed Rivadavia from office. When the great Unitario's attempt to subordinate the province of Buenos Aires to the good of the nation failed, Rosas was already distinguishing himself in the opposition. Juan Manuel proclaimed himself a Federal, and he became the hero of the province. He stood for all the egocentrism of Buenos Aires, for the doctrine that the wealth of the nation belonged to the province, and that Buenos Aires spoke for Argentina. In the period of confusion that followed the breakdown of the national government, the province returned to its own local government, and Manuel Dorrego was chosen governor. But in 1828 Dorrego, a Federal, was murdered on orders of the Unitario General Juan Lavalle. Lavalle had acted on the best Unitario advice. His friend Salvador María del Carril advised him to murder Dorrego in a letter that shows well the atmosphere of the times: "Revolution is a game of chance in which one wins even the lives of the losers, if it is believed necessary to dispose of them." [26] Lavalle killed Dorrego and dissolved the provincial legislature, trying to do what even the greater Rivadavia had been unable to do: break the provincial government. It was this last Unitario maneuver that threw Buenos Aires into the arms of the strong Juan Manuel de Rosas. In 1829 Rosas was elected governor and captain-general of the province of Buenos Aires by the Sala de Representantes. No one dreamed what kind of man he was. He was handsome, popular, and universally beloved. In relief at the passing of the Unitario nightmare, the province granted him dictatorial powers, and the legislature bestowed on him the rank of brigadier general and the title *Restaurador de las Leyes*, Restorer of the Laws.

EL RESTAURADOR

> *The provinces have asked in vain that Buenos Aires share with them a little of its culture, its industry, its European population; a stupid and colonial policy has made it deaf to these clamors. But the provinces revenged themselves, sending it in Rosas much, and too much, of their excess barbarism.* —SARMIENTO, *Facundo.*

When the Sala first proposed his new title, Rosas made a prophetic reply. "The conversion of this success in a permanent title of honor," he told them, "though it proves the generosity of the Representatives, is a step dangerous to the people's liberty . . . *for it is not the first time in history that a prodigality of honors has lifted public men to the seats of tyrants.*"[27] No one had yet had time to try the temper of this new master, and the handsome young governor had the worship of the masses, and the support of some of the most famous patriots in the country.

In 1829, the year that the Federales came to power in Buenos Aires, the Unitario General José M. Paz marched on Córdoba to overthrow the government and carve out a nation of his own in the interior. Paz took Córdoba, and he beat the army that Facundo Quiroga sent against him. He beat Quiroga twice. The history of this whole adventure of Paz in the interior is a curious one, because there is no doubt he had no political support whatever, as he himself admits in his memoirs. But the fact is that Paz was far and away the ablest general of the civil wars, which were not notable for able generals. Within a year after marching out of Buenos Aires with a thousand men, Paz had the whole of the interior: Córdoba, Mendoza, San Luis, Salta, Tucumán, La Rioja, and Santiago del Estero. Thus by 1830 Argentina was divided between Unitarios and Federales. The littoral (the states bordering on the Río de la Plata and the Río Paraná—Santa Fe, Entre Ríos, Corrientes, and Buenos Aires) was Federal, and the interior was nominally, at least, Unitario. In that year the littoral provinces sent representatives to a meeting in Santa Fe to consider their position, and to make a pact of union and commerce.

The story of that meeting, and the debates that took place there, illustrate beautifully the division of economic interests that made the civil wars inevitable. It developed that all was not harmony even among the littoral provinces, for General Pedro Ferré of Corrientes turned out to favor the Unitario point of view. He proposed to protect the provinces of the interior against the free-trade theories of the May Revolution by forbidding the entry of all products that competed with local industry; and he demanded the distribution among all the provinces of the customs duties which Buenos Aires was appropriating for itself. The opposition of Buenos Aires made it impossible to realize his proposals, and Ferré retired from the conference, leaving only Santa Fe and Entre Ríos with Buenos Aires.

The arguments of Dr. José María Rojas y Patrón, representing Buenos Aires, are as good an exposition of the grazing interests as anyone can find. "The almost exclusive industry of Buenos Aires, Santa Fe, and Entre Ríos is cattle-raising," he said; "and even in Corrientes it is the basis of the rest. It is the most worth while because all the capital it needs is human labor, and it employs even the least useful. Furthermore, our lands are for the most part unpopulated, for that reason being cheap; and since the foreign demand for leather and other cattle products is constantly growing, the men and capital employed make an exorbitant profit. It is a certified fact that a cattle generation duplicates itself every three years, and this fact, and its utility, will explain everything. If it still needs confirmation, look at the way men of all professions are abandoning their livings to dedicate themselves to this business which produces more than any other, and needs no further protection than that of heaven. Why should these men and their families be obliged to buy at high cost, and scarce, what they can have cheaply and abundantly, and to waste money they could save? You will reply that it is to contribute to the well-being of others that are not in such an advantageous position. Before everything, one should investigate whether it is the majority or the minority that spend more in this transaction. Buenos Aires, Santa Fe, and Entre Ríos have nothing to provide the consumers of Corrientes. . . . San Juan and Mendoza only export in return for foreign goods. . . . The return is metallic, with few exceptions. And so, even if you put into the balance the leather soles of Tucumán, the textiles of Córdoba, and some other things, there will still be an immense difference of value in favor of the livestock raisers. I will add to this that Corrientes, San Juan, and Mendoza will not for many years be able to provide the country with sugar and liquors, either in sufficient quantity or at a reasonable enough price, lacking as they do both labor and money." [28]

On January 4, 1831, the three remaining littoral provinces signed the famous Pacto Federal. The pact provided for mutual defense against the interior, for the abolition of provincial tariffs between the three provinces, and for the calling of a congress to draw up a federal constitution. (Events were to prove that the last was not sincere—at least, not so far as Rosas was concerned. Of the triumvirate of caudillos, Rosas-Quiroga-López, only Facundo Quiroga was really interested in constituting the nation. Could his situation as a Riojano have had anything to do with this?) The Federales raised an army to invade the provinces held by Paz, and the short-lived Unitario government of Córdoba came to a surprising end when the Unitario general was caught by a lucky throw of the boleadoras, and there began his eight years of internment as the prisoner of Rosas and López. For the moment the Unitarios were completely crushed.

Now for the first time the Buenos Aires dictator began to show his hand. The first indication that the province was to have of his cruelty came when he ordered López to shoot his prisoners and to cut the throat of a twelve-year-old child who had been captured with them. That servile adulation of the dictator which was finally to reach unimagined depths of ignominy began, too, to make itself felt. The custom for which Rosas' dictatorship became famous, that of wearing the *divisa punzó*, the red Federal ribbon, began at this time. Red—a deep scarlet, the color of blood—was Rosas' color, and it became symbolic of his cruel rule. At a solemn

Te Deum celebrated in the Buenos Aires cathedral on January 27, 1832, a number of people went with red ribbons over their hearts, and the idea caught on. By the next week Rosas ordered everyone to wear the ribbon as a badge of loyalty. For the next twenty years fashions in ribbons were to come and go. One day they would be long, the next short, and the next wide. The printed motto they bore changed, too, but the theme was always the same: "Viva la Federación! Mueran los salvajes Unitarios!" ("Long live the Federation! Death to the Unitario savages!") As the dictatorship wore on, the term *salvajes Unitarios* developed in the direction of worse and worse insult, and by the 1840's it had been standardized to that prize Argentine insult "*salvajes inmundos asquerosos Unitarios*," which may be translated "the loathsome, filthy Unitario savages." Even the finest ladies did not dare be seen on the street without their red ribbon. Legislators, justices of the supreme court, priests—no one was safe in public unless he wore his loyalty clearly blazoned in red across his breast. Scarlet became the symbol of this terrible dictatorship. Doña Encarnación wore evening dresses of red satin. Estancieros wore scarlet ponchos. And Rosas finally dressed his soldiers in the same gruesome color: the *soldado federal*, in cap, poncho, and shirt, looked as though he had emerged from a blood bath.

The provincial legislature began to look with certain alarm on some of Rosas' activities, and an opposition party took shape. The interior, too, saw that Rosas was no friend, and that he represented only the most selfish interests of the estancieros of Buenos Aires. Quiroga wanted a constituent congress to draw up a federal constitution, and he and López issued invitations to various of the provinces to send representatives to a *Comisión Representativa* in Córdoba. The provinces realized that now was the time to strike, or it would be too late. "You know perfectly well that if we do not now make the arrangements proposed in Article 5, our country will always be in chaos," wrote Dr. Manuel Leiva, delegate from Corrientes, to the governor of Catamarca. "Buenos Aires is the only one which will resist the formation of a congress, because in the proposed organization and accords it will lose the management of our wealth, with which it has made war against us." Dr. Juan Bautista Marín of Córdoba wrote in much the same terms: "Let us not fool ourselves: in place of happiness, Buenos Aires will never give us anything but the bars and chains of poverty. We are seeing that it is quite content with our misery." [29] These letters fell into the hands of Quiroga, and he foolishly made them public. Rosas used them as an excuse for postponing the congress indefinitely.

In the middle of 1832 Rosas' high-handed ways had so alarmed his own provincial legislature that the opposition found itself in the majority, and withdrew the dictatorial powers he had been granted. Rosas then resigned his governorship, and said that his health was so delicate he thought he might die at any moment. Experience had shown him, he said, that he lacked the knowledge and talent to govern "in accordance with the desires of the Sala." But he accepted in return the command of the army to make a campaign against the Indians.

For three years Buenos Aires had been suffering from a drought so severe that entire regions of the province had been left without vegetation. In one estancia near Chascomús, 11,000 head of cattle had died of thirst. Everywhere there could be seen rotting carcasses and bleaching bones.[30] It became imperative to open new lands to the south, and for this reason it was necessary to dislodge the Indians. Rosas, as one of the greatest estancieros of Buenos Aires, had everything to gain and nothing to lose from this campaign. First, his resignation of the governorship made him a martyr to the common people. Second, he left behind him a powerful and intriguing faction, headed by Doña Encarnación, to look out for his interests in Buenos Aires. And finally, he had a chance to stake out for himself and his friends vast new tracts of land on the southern frontier. The campaign was a success on all these scores. Two governors in rapid succession tried to hold the power in Buenos Aires and failed, and Rosas returned from the south more of a hero than ever. The legislature, which had learned by bloody street fighting how strong the Restaurador was, even when he was absent, received him with the greatest honors. It voted him the island of Choele Choel in Patagonia, a sword decorated with gold and precious stones, and a commemorative medal. The hero patriotically refused the island, which needed a garrison to keep it out of the hands of the Indians, and settled for seventy leagues, some 430,000 acres, of good grazing land in less dangerous parts of the province.[31]

Buenos Aires was really in his hands now, economically and politically. He owned hundreds of thousands of acres of the best land. He owned slaughterhouses and salting plants. He owned his own ships, exporting directly to Brazil and Cuba. And he was politically so strong that no government in Buenos Aires could exist without his support. In two years, six men were chosen governor by the Sala: two refused, and the other four had to resign. The Mazorca, Rosas' dread secret police, began functioning in the streets of Buenos Aires, shouting vivas for the Restorer of the Laws, and shooting at the houses of his enemies. The government was in a state of paralysis. And finally Facundo Quiroga, the last caudillo whom Rosas had any reason to fear, was obligingly ambushed and murdered in Córdoba under circumstances that would indicate that, if Rosas was not the direct instigator of the crime, he did nothing to prevent it. Juan Manuel made a great show of indignation, and the trial of the assassins lasted two years and ended in shooting. But the murder was highly convenient for the Buenos Aires caudillo: it freed him of his rival, and also of the only man who persistently embarrassed him by insisting that the nation must be organized.

There was nothing now for the legislature to do but give Rosas the power *de jure* that he already possessed *de facto*. In 1835 he was elected governor by the Sala with dictatorial powers for five years. Only seven legislators—and they must have been brave men—dared vote against him. After the fashion of dictators, who like to have a show of popular sanction, he called a plebiscite. In each parish the people were summoned from their houses one by one and asked to declare their political ideas, and whether they were for or against the Restaurador. Out of 9,320 voters, only eight felt that they disliked the Restaurador enough to say so.[32]

Now lukewarm adherence was not to be enough. Rosas declared a war to the death against his enemies. There were two organizations to enforce public enthusiasm. One was the Sociedad Popular Restauradora, whose backbone was that class of Spanish monopolistic merchants which had been ruined by the revolution.[33] And the other was the Mazorca, made up of the lower classes, and always ready for a political assassination on orders from above. Rosas' enemies began emigrating in great numbers to Montevideo, which finally became so packed with Argentine refugees and foreign—especially Italian and French—volunteers that the Uruguayans lost control of it completely. In Buenos Aires there reigned the greatest terror. The Federal clergy were strongly with the new dictator, and they put his portrait on all church altars and celebrated continual masses in his honor. People fell over backward to exteriorize their loyalty. If the fashion in Federal ribbons changed—if they became longer, or wider, or the motto grew more insulting to the Unitarian savages—everyone hastened to copy the style. The most fantastic fashions were imposed. It occurred to Rosas, for instance, to decree *bigotes federales*, Federal whiskers, and all the men who did not have mustaches (which included the majority, for the style was then to go clean-shaven) pasted on false ones, or drew them in with burnt cork. There were processions of carts down the streets of Buenos Aires, carrying pictures of the dictator. The Federal hymn was composed in his honor by José Rivera Indarte, comparing Rosas to the condor "cleaving his way through the clouds of the ethereal regions," destroying "odious tyrants," and giving "life to the laws and the union." [34]

Intellectual reaction went hand in hand with terror. Rosas on the one hand appropriated funds to restore religious houses and churches, and on the other closed down schools throughout the province for lack of money to keep them open. By 1842 there were only 2,200 pupils in a population of 180,000.[35] If primary education suffered, the university was almost finished. Rosas issued a decree that candidates for the doctorate might study in one faculty and transfer to another: a harmless-looking edict designed to make it possible for students of the monastery of San Francisco to be granted a degree from the University of Buenos Aires. It was also ordered that theses, heretofore presented in Spanish, should in the future be presented in Latin. This barred degrees to all but theologians. Political interference with the university was quite direct. One student whose thesis displeased the dictator was expelled by the Rector on Rosas' order and made to serve three months without pay on a barge in the harbor of Buenos Aires.[36]

Rosas made the church a cornerstone of his dictatorship. Jesuits expelled from Spain by Queen María Cristina were welcomed in Buenos Aires by Rosas and his cousin Tomás de Anchorena. The first group of six arrived in 1836, and were given a college * and church, and a pension of 450 pesos a month. It was expected that gratitude would make the fathers of the Society loyal supporters of the régime, and when circumstances proved otherwise (the head of the order conspired with the Unitarios) the college and church were closed down, and the superior left Buenos Aires. Perhaps Rosas would never have discovered the treason if General Juan Lavalle had not invaded the province in 1840. When it looked as though the Salvaje Unitario would make a clean sweep of Buenos Aires the Jesuits rather openly showed their sympathies for the invader; and when the danger was over, Rosas took his revenge. In 1843 the Jesuits were formally expelled.

THE OPPOSITION

> *I bring only one party: the Nation. I bring only one cause: Liberty. I bring only one ambition: to break the last link of my country's slavery and to lay my sword at the feet of the Argentine people. I recognize but one enemy: the enemy of the people: the tyrant Rosas.*
>
> —Proclamation of Lavalle, 1839.

Rosas had three great sources of opposition. In descending order of importance they were: the French and English, who did

* *Colegio,* in Argentina, is a secondary school.

not like his trading policies, and who laid a blockade around the port of Buenos Aires; the old Rivadavian Unitarios, who conspired against him from their safe citadel in Montevideo; and the young Utopian socialists, who under the influence of European liberalism and of the ideas of the Count of Saint-Simon, formed the anti-Rosista *Asociación de Mayo* to combat Rosas' intellectual reaction.

The intervention of European powers stemmed directly from the porteño tariff policy, which was aimed at keeping trade from Montevideo and from the north. Buenos Aires imposed a straight 20 per cent extra duty on all imports from boats that had touched at Montevideo or any Argentine port before reaching the capital. And there was a 20 per cent export duty on goods shipped from the provinces abroad. This was a measure to give Buenos Aires a monopoly on all sea-borne trade. Because of provisions of the Treaty of Friendship, Commerce, and Navigation of 1825, the English were exempted from this duty; but other nations had to pay it, and the French government tried in vain to negotiate a similar pact with Rosas. A year of bickering came to nothing, and when the French vice-consul, Aimé Roger, exasperated at Rosas' obstinacy, and at mistreatment and imprisonment of French subjects by the Buenos Aires dictator, threatened naval intervention, the stubborn Juan Manuel replied by an amended tariff law: henceforth, transshipped goods would pay 25 per cent duty on top of what they already paid. Thus, relations with France were broken in 1836. Two years later a French fleet under Admiral Leblanc began the blockade of Buenos Aires.

The blockade was disastrous to the estancieros of Buenos Aires, with the notable exception of Juan Manuel de Rosas. Rosas had his own cattle, his own saladeros, and—what was supremely important—his own fleet of ships to carry his meat abroad. To encourage ships to run the French blockade, he issued a new tariff decree that during the continuation of the blockade all goods entering Buenos Aires would pay one-third less duty than the law specified. But trade was strangled, and work stopped on the estancias of the province. Between the second half of 1837 and the second half of 1838, imports dropped from 19,000,000 paper pesos to 4,000,000;

exports, from 19,000,000 to 900,000.[37] It was apparent now that the Restorer of the Laws no longer represented any interests but his own. The estancieros, faced with ruin, revolted against the dictator and were bloodily subdued at the battle of Chascomús. Rosas decapitated the leaders and exhibited their heads on pikes in the town of Dolores. The soldiers who had participated in the slaughter were rewarded in land: generals were given six leagues; colonels, five; lieutenant-colonels, four; sergeant majors, two; captains, one; and lesser ranks from three-quarters of a league down to one-quarter. In acres this ranged from 1,500 to 37,000 acres per person.[38]

Indirectly, though, the three blockades of Buenos Aires by foreign powers (the Brazilian, 1826, lasting 1,004 days; the French, 1836, lasting 949; and the joint English and French, 1845, lasting 1,000) had a good effect on the cattle industry of Buenos Aires. By stopping the slaughter of animals for export, it led to great increases in the herds. Eight years of blockade tripled the herds. Where there were an estimated three to four million cattle in 1837, by 1850 there were ten to twelve millions.[39] The point was that the estancieros were not in a position to appreciate the long view in the matter. Their income was stopped. When Rosas killed them ruthlessly and exposed their heads as a public reminder to others who might be considering disloyalty, he broke with the class that had put him in power.

In Buenos Aires the terror grew. The president of the Sala, who had supported Rosas from the first, was murdered by the Mazorca. People were afraid to show their faces in the streets after dark, and Paz, who after eight years as Rosas' prisoner, was allowed to return to Buenos Aires, tells in his *Memoirs* how he never let his servant open the front door of his house without first spying on the visitor from an upstairs window. One night Paz went to the home of Rosas. "It is impossible to describe the silence and the darkness of that street," he said; "few people ever walked in it, and I have known many who made long detours to avoid it, when some necessity forced them into its neighborhood. And what can I say of the house? There was no guard, or show of arms; an entrance lighted by a single lantern, and a man who acted as porter; a somber and deserted patio in which there reigned the most profound silence, were all I saw." [40]

The only organized opposition to Rosas was literary. The Unitarios had been forced to emigrate to Montevideo, where they were holding forth under the Comisión Argentina, and squabbling among themselves. Montevideo, at this time a city of 31,000 had only 11,000 Uruguayans in its population: the rest were Spanish, French, Argentine, and Italian adventurers, holding the fort against the hated Rosas across the river.[41] In Buenos Aires the opposition had gone so far underground it was invisible. The only group that managed any protest at all was one that both Federales and Unitarios looked on with misgiving—the salon of young poets and (so they imagined) socialists headed by Esteban Echeverría, that was later to be known as the Asociación de Mayo.

Echeverría was a young romantic with a French education who had picked up a kind of foggy socialism from reading the doctrines of Saint-Simon, and who had returned from four years in Paris to face the ugly realities of Rosas' reaction. Echeverría was welcomed at the Salón Literario which used to meet at the home of Marcos Sastre, who had the best private library in the city. Among the men who met at Sastre's house were Juan María Gutiérrez and Juan Bautista Alberdi, the man whose ideas were to father the Argentine Constitution; and from this small nucleus were to come some of the nation's greatest leaders. The Salón seems to have been metamorphosed into a secret society after the Jesuit fathers, who had not yet fallen into Rosas' bad graces, persuaded the government to close up Sastre's library on the ground that it contained books of a dangerous and liberal nature—which it did. Taking Young Italy as their model, Echeverría and their friends formed a society called Joven Argentina (Young Argentina); and they held their first meeting on the night of June 23, 1837, when more than thirty-five young people gathered to hear Echeverría speak. These were the words he was later to edit as his *Dogma Socialista.* "The tyrants have sown dissension and erected their iniquitous thrones on the debris of anarchy," he began. "For us there is neither law, nor rights, nor country, nor freedom. . . . Our heritage is obscurity, humiliation, servitude." [42] (Echeverría was a young man who wrote Romantic poetry.)

The platform of Young Argentina was somewhat vague, but full of good intentions:

"We wanted then, as we want now, Democracy as a *tradition*, as a *principle*, and as an *institution*.

"Democracy as a tradition is *May*,* *continuous progress*.

"Democracy as a principle—*fraternity, equality, liberty*.

"Democracy as an institution conservative of the principle—is *suffrage* and *representation* in city, department, province, and nation.

"We wanted furthermore as institutions to come out of this, Democracy in education and, through education, in the family; Democracy in industry and in property; in the distribution and retribution of work; in the registering and distribution of taxes; in the organization of the national militia; in the hierarchy of capacities; in short, in all the intellectual, moral, and material movement of Argentine society." [43]

Luckily for these young socialists, Rosas did not take them very seriously. "Even the exiled Unitarios abroad looked with pity on these young people," wrote Gutiérrez, who was the spark plug of the group, "—mistrusted them, looked down on them . . . because they considered them Federalists and frivolous. They did not hide from Rosas that the intelligence and future of his time were not with him, and he tried to humiliate these youths who represented the aspiration for the good and just, and who were the agents of destruction for his power and policy." [44] Young Argentina, whose name Echeverría later changed to the Asociación de Mayo, limited its activities in Buenos Aires to publishing *La Moda*, a weekly which was dedicated to "music, poetry, literature, and manners," [45] according to its own caption, but which came out with some powerful political satire. Alberdi was its editor, and he found it expedient to emigrate. Echeverría and Gutiérrez finally followed.

In Montevideo these young men did not find the atmosphere

* A reference to the May revolution of 1810.

congenial. They were disliked by the Unitarios. Echeverría came to consider himself a misunderstood genius, and devoted himself to his poetry. He called the Unitarios a "beaten minority, with good tendencies, but without local bases for a socialist platform, and somewhat disagreeable because of their proud fits of exclusivism and supremacy." [46] The Unitarios were a motley crew of conspirators who devoted more energy to bickering among themselves than to overthrowing Rosas. Lavalle was their military leader, and later Paz joined them. Paz was the only general worthy of the name in the whole group, but he was hated and mistrusted by the Unitarios. Lavalle, who in 1840 invaded the province of Buenos Aires and botched the campaign, was the same man who had killed Dorrego and set off Rosas' reaction. His character may be judged by the following letter to a friend on the subject of what to do with the Buenos Aires Sala de Representantes should he take the province. "What to do with the legislature? The opinion of my friends is that if it is believed they cannot count on its members they must have nothing whatever to do with it; but without saying they will dissolve it. But if they can count on a certain majority, take hold of it immediately; convoke it with pomp and urgency; tell it the facts and our motives and give the government over to it, putting all the forces at its disposition, certain that the man they want will be elected. In this way an air of dignity and legality will be given to the matter, and everyone will be pledged." [47]

Lavalle was a bad general, and his campaigns were quite typical of the haphazard fighting of the civil wars. The army was weighted down with camp followers, to whom Lavalle distributed handkerchiefs and silk stockings, just as he distributed ponchos and shirts to the men. There was no organization of any kind. There were neither maneuvers nor roll calls, and the men were absent whenever they felt like it. When Lavalle wanted to get them together he had to resort to ruses, like announcing that he was going to hand out money, or that they were about to do battle. Clothing was distributed so haphazardly that the soldiers worked simple frauds like standing in line three or four times and getting three or four handouts.[48] Under the circumstances it is not surprising that when Lavalle invaded Entre Ríos in 1840 with 4,000 men, he was easily beaten by an opposing army of 1,000. He managed to embark the remainder of his army in French vessels and get to Buenos Aires, where he gave Rosas a bad scare, but he retired with the city within his grasp.

In the years 1840–1841, Lavalle was beaten not once but several times, thus demonstrating that he was probably as bad a general as Paz always said he was. He fled to Salta, then to Jujuy, the northernmost province of Argentina. There, ironically enough, he died for another man. A squad of soldiers fired on the house he was lodged in, intending to kill the owner, and Lavalle was killed in his place. It is a small colonial house on a quiet side street of the city, and today's tourist can know it by the metal plate that commemorates the event. Lavalle's friends carried the corpse to Potosí. Only his bones were buried. His flesh had rotted, and had to be cut away.

This left the Unitarios with only one good general, Paz, who had escaped to Uruguay by boat. The Comisión Argentina in Montevideo received him with a notable lack of enthusiasm. "There goes General Paz," said Lavalle's brother, José. "He thinks he will be chief of staff, but up there they don't need that job." [49] The envy and malice of the Unitarios did more to defeat Paz than Rosas ever did. The Comisión hampered him in every way they could devise. They sent him subordinate officers who were directly answerable to the Comisión, not to Paz. When Paz invaded Buenos Aires province with a Correntine army, and with excellent prospects of winning, the Governor of Corrientes came and took his army home. He did not want them fighting on "foreign" soil. Provincialism, jealousy, small-mindedness, and lack of imagination made Paz's task all but hopeless. The only time he got co-operation from the Unitarios was when they were scared, and their first bad scare came when a Federal army laid siege to Montevideo. Paz was named defender of the city, and there began one of the most tiresome sieges in history. The Federal army under Manuel Oribe sat down outside the city, and the Unitarios sat down inside the city, and nothing happened. In spite of all attempts to paint the siege of Montevideo as heroic—it had all the elements of heroism, including Giuseppe Garibaldi and a group of Italian volunteers—it was not heroic, and not even comprehensible. Oribe made no real attempt to get into the city, which he could probably have taken easily. The English refused to recognize the blockade, and not only supplied Montevideo with all kinds of contraband, but even disembarked marines to help in its defense. As for Garibaldi, the action for which he is best remembered is piracy. When both England and France broke with Rosas in 1845 the English seized the Argentine fleet and turned it over to him. Garibaldi took the fleet and sacked towns up and down the river, a purely private enterprise.

Neither France nor England came out of their adventure in Argentine intervention with either profit or honor. They got a bad press in the Americas, especially in the United States, which viewed the intervention as a violation of the Monroe Doctrine. San Martín, who was then in exile in France, wrote a sympathetic letter to the Buenos Aires dictator, offering Rosas his sword for his defense of Argentine sovereignty. The British and French mediators who had been sent by their governments to negotiate a peace, instead had turned their hands to speculation and were getting rich supplying contraband to Montevideo and exploiting its customs receipts. Finally, in 1849, sick of the whole adventure, the British signed a peace that gave all the honors of war to Rosas. They abandoned the island of Martín García, in the middle of the Plata, which they had occupied. They recognized the Paraná as an interior, and thus purely Argentine river (one of the bones of contention with Rosas having been the internationalizing of the Paraná). And, to crown the capitulation, they saluted the Argentine flag with twenty-one guns. Thus the decade of the forties ended in a complete triumph for Juan Manuel de Rosas.

Rosas never looked stronger than he did in 1851. His enemies abroad were divided and impotent. His enemies at home were terrorized and without hope. In Buenos Aires silence and fear bespoke a tacit consent to things as they were. People had forgotten what it was like to be against Rosas, or to be without him. In that year, as was his immemorial custom, Rosas sent his resignation to the Sala de Representantes so that they might have the chance to renew their protestations of loyalty and tell him that he was indispensable to the government of the province. He had been doing this for so long it had gotten to be a habit with him. His resignation was also sent to the governors of the provinces as their representative in foreign relations, and all the governors wrote back immediately protesting that he was, of course, indispensable, and that they would not think of having anyone else in his place. Then, on May 1, General Justo José de Urquiza, caudillo of Entre Ríos, who had been one of Rosas' most faithful henchmen, and had led the Federal army against Paz, did the unthinkable: he published a decree accepting the resignation of Brigadier General Juan Manuel de Rosas, and announced that Entre Ríos resumed its sovereign right to make war and peace and manage its own foreign relations. He also published another decree that was perhaps even more ominous. Henceforth, he said, government documents in Entre Ríos would not carry the motto, "Long Live the Argentine Confederation! Death to the Unitarian savages!" but "Long live the Argentine Confederation! Death to the enemies of national organization!"

The structure that had looked unassailable cracked from within. Not the British and French, with their fleets and marines, not the Unitarios with their hatred, not the romantic socialists with their doctrines of democracy, but the Federal caudillos, the men who had worn the red ribbons and cried, "Death to the filthy, loathsome, Unitarian savages!" were the men who broke the tyranny of Rosas. Urquiza was a caudillo, like any other. Probably Sarmiento was right when he told him, "You are the man who, after Artigas, Quiroga, and Rosas, has murdered the most prisoners." [50] Urquiza was a Federal, not an Unitario. Every caudillo in Argentina except the governor of Corrientes joined him against Rosas. On February 3, 1852, he beat Rosas at the battle of Caseros, and the beaten and deserted dictator took refuge in the British legation. A British warship carried him to exile in England. The unshakable tyranny had fallen almost without a push. "Rosas survived his fall like a worm-eaten tree," said Sarmiento, "because there came no light wind to make him fall of his own weight." [51] But the nightmare was over, and from Uruguay, from Chile, from France, the men who had lived almost a generation in exile came flocking back to their native land. As for Rosas, he left behind him the Black Legend of Argentine history. In our own times the native fascists of Argentina have proclaimed themselves Rosistas and tried to rehabilitate the hated Juan Manuel. But Argentina, that has named streets and plazas after Paz, Lavalle, and Urquiza, that has even erected statues to Estanislao López, has not a single park or boulevard to commemorate the man who ruled it longest. His house is gone from Palermo, the Buenos Aires park that was once his estate. When he died in England in 1877, an old man of eighty-four, and his relatives tried to organize a funeral mass for him in Buenos Aires, the government forbade it. A mass was held, but not for Rosas: the Unitarios, headed by Bartolomé Mitre, held a public funeral for his victims.

There remains, perhaps, but one comment on this long and terrible dictatorship. It died from within. The *caudillos killed it.* Twenty years of anarchy had taught them a lot. It taught them that Rosas' was a pseudo-Federalism. It taught them that he was serving, not the interests of Argentina, but the interests of Buenos Aires, and finally only the interests of himself. And it taught them finally, and most important, that their interests lay not in provincial isolationism but in national union. When their political education reached this point, the one-man dictatorship of the governor of Buenos Aires fell of its own weight. One might well ask, Who, at the end, did Rosas represent? Not the provinces. They were starving. Not the estancieros. The blockade had ruined them. He represented nobody, not a class, not a province, and certainly not the nation. Urquiza, the victor of Caseros, marched into Buenos Aires wearing the red Federal ribbon, but this time it stood for Confederation, not for Juan Manuel de Rosas. The returning Unitarios were not to forgive Urquiza the wearing of the red, or the fact that it was he, and not they, who had unseated the tyrant. But that is another chapter.

Perhaps there might be a postscript to the story of Juan Manuel. He was not entirely forgotten, not entirely unloved. There were two social groups—the lowest, the poorest—that remembered and loved him: the Indians, with whom he had kept the peace, and to whom he had kept his word of honor; and the negroes, who did not forget that in the days of Juan Manuel they had had their place in society. Mansilla, who visited the Ranqueles of the southern frontier a quarter of a century later, found that among the Indians, and among the Christian exiles that had taken refuge with them, the memory of Rosas was still green. The chief of the Ranqueles, Mariano Rosas, had once been taken prisoner and served for several years as a peon on Rosas estancia El Pino. Rosas had been his godfather in baptism, and the cacique had taken Juan Manuel's name as his own. "Mariano Rosas retains the greatest feeling of veneration towards his godfather," wrote Colonel Mansilla; "he speaks of him with the deepest respect, and says that all he knows he owes to him; that after God he has not had a better father; that because of him he knows how to hitch a team; how to care for cattle and horses and sheep, so that they will fatten quickly and be good to eat at all seasons; that it is he who taught him to lasso (*pialar*) and to throw the bolas like a gaucho." [52]

In the Indian camp was a drunken old negro who played the accordeon. "I am a Federal," he told Mansilla. "When our father Rosas, who freed the negroes, fell, I was left without anything. . . . I shall not leave here until the Restaurador comes back again, which will be soon." And here the old negro interrupted his story to sing Mansilla a song:

"Long live the nation
Free of its chains,
And long live the great Rosas
To defend it." [53]

THE LAND—I

MATADERO, SALADERO

In the nineteenth century, land in Argentina was only a dimension of space. There was so much land that nobody knew what to do with it. The land divided town from town, and region from region. It was unfenced and unsettled. Whatever lived in it seemed savage, from the stringy long-horned cattle and the wild dogs that harried them, to the Indian and the half-Christian gaucho. It was the land, unpopulated, unmeasured, and unconquered, that swallowed up the provinces and made them nations unto themselves, and that created the mentality of division. To Corrientes, Buenos Aires was a foreign country, and so the governor called back his troops and left Paz without an army when he might have beaten Rosas and won the nation. The land was not wealth, but distance.

In the opening years of the century there were few to believe that this treeless plain that was Buenos Aires was richer than gold mines. It was pasture for animals, and the animals were worth less than nothing. You could buy a sheep for six centavos,[1] and what you did with it after you bought it was up to you. Even a slave would sniff at mutton. Cows were small, and gave little meat and less milk.[2] The beef was so tough it made your teeth and gums sore, partly because the cattle were a bastard lot, and partly because the gaucho roasted his meat as soon as it was killed, and then elected to eat the toughest part.[3] Both cows and sheep had run wild in the country since the sixteenth century, when they were brought down from Peru by Juan Torres de Vera y Aragón. They were hunted by packs of wild dogs, and the dogs, in colonial times, were hunted by militiamen whom the Argentines laughingly called *mataperros* (dog killers—the soldiers hated both the name and the task).

Animals were poor, and worth no more than the coarse wool or hides or tallow they produced, but agriculture was poorer. The estancia, from colonial times to the end of Rosas, smothered the farm. The farmer had neither social standing nor economic security. Usually his little holding was sandwiched between estancias, and since there were no fences—holdings were divided by geographical accidents, or by streams—cattle got into his crops and ate them, and sometimes his bigger and stronger neighbors simply took his farm away.[4] The estanciero himself despised whatever grew out of the ground, and something of his attitude was reflected in his peons: they would brand and lasso and skin, but they would not dig. No self-respecting peon would dig a hole at any price. Irishmen coming into the country drew down fantastic wages making ditches and fences. Perhaps the attitude of the criollo stemmed from a Spanish scorn for manual labor, but it was a social fact. As a result, the criollo went on eating meat and drinking mate, and the corn and potatoes and green vegetables that might have varied his diet and decorated his table remained potential in the soil.

In terms of wealth, the land produced little. Even in colonial times holdings were large—but never as large as they were to get under the land policies of the Republic. You had to have a lot of land to make anything, with meat worthless and hides cheap. The minimum respectable holding in colonial Argentina was the *suerte de estancia*, one and a half square leagues, or 10,000 acres.[5] In the eighteenth century it cost less to buy land than to register it: the price was three to twenty pesos a league, but notary fees came to four hundred pesos, and government red tape made transfer of title so slow that it might take anywhere up to eight years.

Until Rosas and his partners opened the first saladero in Buenos Aires, beef, on which Argentina's subsequent wealth was to be built, was entirely worthless. Even in colonial times the estancieros felt uneasily that something should be done about the meat. But what? There was not even the necessary transportation to get it into the capital without its rotting first, let alone to get it by sailing vessel to European markets. The shipment of cattle on the hoof was unknown, and meat salting as a preservative had never been tried. In the closing years of the eighteenth century the slaughter of wild cattle for their hides, by the Indians of Chile and the inhabitants of Corrientes, Mendoza, and Santa Fe, so reduced the herds that the hacendados of Buenos Aires sent a memorial to the minister Don Diego Gardoqui. Six hundred thousand cattle a year were killed and left to rot, complained the memorial, asking for some "means of providing for the utilization and exportation of the cow's meat." [6]

It was Rosas who, with Luis Dorrego and Juan N. Terrero, founded the first saladero in the province of Buenos Aires, near Quilmes. This was probably the first, and certainly a most important, forward step in the history of the Argentine livestock industry, for now meat, which had been economically without value, could be salted for export to the Americas and Europe. Slaughterhouses and saladeros grew up around the outskirts of Buenos Aires, and an unsavory but profitable business was born. T. J. Hutchinson has left a stomach-turning description of both institutions. Barracas and Saladeros, where the animals were slaughtered, were surrounded by screaming birds of prey, and gave off a sickening stench. The matadero, or abattoir, was a long shed and three corrals. Animals were dragged from the corrals by peons on horseback, who lassoed them by the horns; and at the gate a butcher hamstrung them by gashing their haunches. The hamstrung animals were dragged farther, and at a convenient place the butcher drove his knife into their throats and left them to bleed.

The saladero was scarcely more pleasant. Here, reports Hutchinson, cows were knifed in the spine. The meat was hung up to cool, then cut into slices and heaped on the floor between layers of salt. It was salted several times, then put on palings to dry. The saladero employed Cadiz salt because it was less soluble than other varieties.[7] Salted meat, although it seemed to find a market abroad, was never particularly satisfactory. Salt is a powerful solvent and forms a brine which extracts the nutritive value of meat: its phosphoric acid, its potash, and its albuminous content.[8] Meat salting was a forward step, but it was not yet the solution to the problem of getting Argentine beef to the English and European markets.

CHEAP MEAT, CHEAP LAND: THE FOUNDING OF AN ARISTOCRACY

If there was a king of France who could say, "I am the State," in Argentina there is a small group of citizens who can say, "We are the State." —ROBERTO KURTZ, *La Argentina ante Estados Unidos.*

In a society where land is wealth and land is cheap, the earth means more than pasture for cattle or soil for grain. In nineteenth century Argentina it was a political weapon of reward and punishment, buying support for a caudillo or financing a war to overthrow one; it was as fluid as money in the bank, but safer; it was a speculative venture; it was wealth and social prestige; and it set a pattern for the society of the age. To be rich, a man had to own thousands of acres, and those who were farsighted and lucky got the land into their hands in any way they could. Tomás M. de Anchonera was both farsighted and lucky, staking out his claims under Rivadavia's emphyteusis, buying the land into outright ownership when Rosas decreed its public sale, and getting great tracts along the southern frontier when the generosity of his caudillo kinsman led him to give away public lands to favored families. Anchorena was not the only man with vision, nor was he the only one favored by the Buenos Aires dictator. When Rosas in 1832 began giving away land along the new frontier line of the Arroyo Azul, among the settlers who claimed title were names that, added to the list from Rivadavia's time, went to make up the landed aristocracy of Argentina: Anchorena, Alzaga, Unzué, Harilaos, Pereyra, Iraola, Videla, Dorna, Olmos, Duggan, Ballester, Saavedra, Elizalde, Lynch. Some had been scarcely more than cattle rustlers. Others were poor Irish immigrants. But all realized that land meant wealth. How much wealth, even they probably did not dream.

The breakdown of Rivadavian emphyteusis is a study in what happens when a piece of legislation is outside a period's frame of ideas. Land tenure without ownership would not have been foreign to the comprehension of medieval Europe, but it was foreign to the nineteenth century. By 1832, the landlords, secure in possession, were letting their rent lapse, and were coming to consider themselves as owners. It was not part and parcel of that society to understand that land might belong to the government and be theirs only to use. But also the government had changed, and instead of Rivadavia, with his ample vision, it had Juan Manuel de Rosas, the apotheosis of the colonial estanciero mentality. Argentina had many evils to rue in Rosas, but none left a more lasting mark than his land policy. In 1836 he decreed the first great public sale of land, fifteen hundred square leagues, including estancias held in emphyteusis; and, to make purchase easy, he allowed installment payments in kind, and without interest. Some cases were notorious: Francisco Rozas paid for part of ten leagues of land (costing 45,000 pesos) with 578 steers at 45 pesos apiece, and nine cows at 40 pesos apiece. Segundo and Juan F. Girado paid for their land in cows. Paper pesos had dropped to 13 centavos gold, which is just about 13 American gold cents; and, paying in devalued paper, this is what some of the larger buyers took, and what it cost them.[9]

Name	Area		Price
	Leagues	= Acres	(Paper pesos)
Anchorena, Tomás M.	30⅓	187,000	119,130
Alzaga, Felix D.	43¾	270,000	91,330
Alzaga y Chueco	20	124,000	84,840
Díaz Vélez, Eustaquio	27	167,000	82,801
Fernández, Mariano	22⅘	141,000	75,657
Fernández, Juan W.	29	179,000	91,000
Miguens, Felipe S.	34¼	212,000	90,000
Peña, Juan B.	20	124,000	62,060
Selva, Juan M.	24	148,000	96,000
Vela, Pedro J.	64½	398,000	236,900

Rosas' policy was to get public land into private hands as quickly as possible. He gave land to the soldiers that helped him put down the insurrection of Buenos Aires estancieros during the blockade. He gave land to himself. In 1838 he doubled the rent on land held in emphyteusis in order to force the holders to buy outright, and disposed in this way of another 1,936 leagues.[10] A caudillo paid his supporters by the league as he might write a check, and the weapon was used against Rosas, as well as by him. In 1841 Corrientes raised money for its war against the porteño dictator by selling public lands to the value of 50,000 pesos, and using the rest as guarantee for a paper issue of 100,000 pesos.[11]

There were only two kinds of wealth. One was land, the other livestock. Rosas gave away animals as he gave away land, with both hands; but animals multiply, and land does not. To the victorious armies of Sauce Grande and Quebrachito (1840), and of San Carlos (1841), Rosas distributed cattle and sheep stolen from the Unitarios. To give an idea of the numbers given away, here is a list for those participating in the defeat of Lavalle at Sauce Grande, Entre Ríos, as decreed by the Buenos Aires legislature:[12]

Rank	*Cattle*	*Sheep*
Commanding general	3,000	3,000
Second general	2,500	2,500
Colonels	1,500	1,500
Majors	500	600
Captains	400	500
Lieutenants	300	400
Second lieutenants	200	300
Sergeants	100	200
Corporals	80	180
Soldiers	50	150

In the fight with the other provinces, Buenos Aires always had the advantage that it could afford to pay and equip its armies best. It had the best livestock, the best land, and all the customs revenue. Indeed, from an economic point of view, it is hard to see how the provinces could make war so long when they were so poor. The civil wars could go on because the armies ate the animals that came to hand, and varied their flesh diet only with mate. A wool poncho was uniform and bedding. If the criollo soldier had not been able to subsist at this level, it would never have been possible to challenge Buenos Aires at all.

With the fall of Rosas, the alienation of public land went on the same as ever. In 1857 the Buenos Aires legislature leased vast new tracts of land (rent-free to those who would settle outside the Indian frontier). Some of the landholders from the time of Rosas turn up again on the list, but there are new additions in this period, and the aristocracy is enlarged: Alvear, Bullrich, Bunge, Elizalde, Gowland, Guerrero, Herrera, Irigoyen, Lynch, Pereyra, Santamarina, Saavedra, Unzué. Ten years later the leases terminated, and the holders were permitted to buy outright at from 4,800 to 16,000 gold pesos per league. Land was beginning to rise perceptibly. This same land had been worth 650 gold pesos in 1836.[13]

The rise in land values was to be spectacular. Jacinto Oddone calculates that land that sold for 44–55 centavos per hectare in 1836, sold for 4.40–5.60 pesos in 1857, 4.00–13.50 pesos in 1867, and an average of 1,840 pesos per hectare in 1927.[14] Merely to *hold* land was to make a fortune—a sure and easy way if one got it when it was cheap enough. There were many factors at work that made this the safest and easiest speculation. Population growth in itself was one. The building of the railroads was another, because it brought the outlying estancias within range of the Buenos Aires market. Land alongside the railroads, or in new railroad towns, multiplied in value fantastically. Thomas J. Hutchinson, who was British consul in Rosario, tells how a certain Sr. Alcorta bought two and a half leagues near what was to be Moreno Station, paying 600 paper pesos per cuadra (a block 150 yards square). After the station was built, he divided the land into lots and sold it for as high as 35,000 to 40,000 pesos per cuadra. At Morón a miller, M. de la Roche, in 1855 bought thirty cuadras of land for 15,000 pesos. Then he treated with the railroad to bring the line through his property, offering them three cuadras for a station, and room for their rails. When the line was built he auctioned off his lots for as much as 100,000 pesos *per cuadra*.[15]

Improved methods of preserving and marketing meat were certainly to be a factor in the rise in land values, but in the middle nineteenth century salt was still the only preservative known, and it did not tap the better-paying markets of Europe. Bringing in better blood lines to get more meat and a finer grade of wool boosted livestock prices, and helped make the land more valuable, although this is a history in itself. Francis Clark Ford, secretary of the British legation in Buenos Aires, made a report to Parliament on the profits to be had in sheep raising, and even in the sixties they were considerable. An investment of 78,000 gold pesos, he estimated, would sell in eight years for 119,500—a 53 per cent profit—besides yielding an additional 9 per cent per year return. Total profit, eight years, 125 per cent.[16]

Truth is, the estanciero had nature on his side. A livestock generation doubles in three years. The early sheep- and cattle-breeders took no interest in blooded stock, in improving of strains, or in running an estancia like a business. They were content to see that their herds multiplied in number, without caring whether they improved in quality. The cattle herds trebled between 1837 and 1850, and this was money in pocket to the estancieros. Hide exports trebled, wool quadrupled, and tallow shipments went up in value nearly 700 per cent.[17] In the same period land was rising fast, and the men who had land were getting rich without trying. As they ignored scientific breeding, so did they ignore the potential agricultural wealth of the Argentine soil. In the first sixty-two years after the revolution, planting increased only half a million hectares, probably less than the total holdings of Anchorena or Eustaquio Díaz Vélez.[18]

TARQUIN: A STUDY IN TRANSFORMATION

It would have taken a subtle eye to see much change in the nation's face between the rise and the fall of Rosas. The estancia was almost as primitive in the middle of the century as it had been at the beginning. Land was unfenced. Cattle were long-horned and lean. The most luxurious estancia house was adobe, but by far the majority were of twigs or straw. The plains were open, and the scattered houses were signalled by ombúes and paraísos. The first railroad was yet to be built. People lived simply, even the estancieros. On the cattle estancias the classic gaucho led a nomadic existence, content with his daily portion of meat and yerba mate. On the sheep farm the *puestero* watched his section of land, eating his allotment of three-year-old wethers, but providing his own yerba, sugar, biscuit, and salt. Skin, grease, tallow went to the master. This was the rigid rule. Sheep outnumbered cattle by more than four to one, and McCann described all the country within a ninety-mile radius of Buenos Aires as "one vast sheep-walk." [19]

But if the province of Buenos Aires seemed to present no different aspect to the casual eye than it had presented a quarter of a century earlier, appearances were deceiving, for there had been innovations that were to change the livestock industry of the country. The first fence had been built on the pampa. The first blooded bull had been introduced. And sheep farmers were already experimenting with new breeds. The innovations went hand in hand, for, until blood-lines were improved, Argentine meat and wool would remain second-class, and until the pampa was fenced, scientific breeding was impossible.

The importance of the fence to the Argentine livestock industry cannot be exaggerated. Before land was divided and enclosed, the only cattle that could exist on the pampa were the tough and resistant longhorns. The herds were wild, and the fatter and finer Durhams, or shorthorns, could not live under conditions that forced herds to migrate at random, and sometimes over great distances, to find water and pasture. Nor was it possible to control breeding. Rams ran with the flocks, and bulls with the herds, from one end of the year to the other. When an estancia is fenced, it is possible to put onto one parcel of land only as many animals as there is feed for them, and after the pasture has been eaten they can be moved to another place. In Argentina, where landholdings are so seigniorial, where herds number into the tens of thousands of animals, fencing is the only control left to the estanciero. Baled hay as feed in winter months, or times of drought, has never been used. When herds cannot be moved at will, they are at the mercy of sun and rain, and only the tough survive.

The first man to fence an estancia was an Englishman, Richard Newton, who in the year 1844 put up iron posts and a wire fence on his estancia Los Jagüeles.[20] In this period landholdings were still divided from each other by ditches, which were expensive—because criollos did not like to dig—and ineffectual. After Newton set the example, a few of the richest estancieros followed it. Wire cost too much to make fencing general. The first fences had posts of ñandubay from the coasts of the Paraná, where the wood was plentiful and cheap; and they were set in the ground every three yards. Three strands of brittle iron wire ran from post to post, and instead of being run through holes, were nailed on. A ditch ran alongside the fence to supplement it, because the wire broke easily, and sheep would crawl under it and escape. But later wire went down in price, and as the Paraná was stripped clean of ñandubay, posts went up. Wood of lapacho, quebracho, and caldén had to be sent from Santiago del Estero and the Chaco for posts, which were now set twenty yards apart. Iron wire gave place to steel, and the strands were drawn taut with tourniquets. Fencing became general, not only to divide estancia from estancia, but to divide field from field. The last stage was the introduction of barbed wire, which is still in use.[21] Leather men disagree on whether it is an improvement: the fine barbs can catch and scar a hide, and spoil a good piece of leather.

Tentative experiments with breeding had begun in Rivadavia's time with an attempt to improve the quality of wool of the criollo sheep. Merinos from Spain and southdowns from England were both introduced by Rivadavia, whose vision extended even to his country's livestock industry. The first hundred merinos were imported in 1825, and by the middle of the century Argentine sheep were a cross between criollos and merinos. Wool resulting from the cross was poor: too short, too brittle, too fine. Southdowns were originally considered to have better wool, but as they came to be bred more and more for meat, the wool degenerated. Nevertheless, wool exports soared. In 1829, the year that Rosas was elected governor and captain-general of Buenos Aires, wool exports were 384,000 kilograms.* In 1850, they were 7,681,000. In 1870 they were 65,704,000.[22]

But this tentative experiment in sheep breeding was halfhearted at best. Most estancieros lacked the money to improve their breeds, or the incentive. With cattle the case was even more serious, for fine bulls are far more costly than blooded rams, and, however rich the estanciero may have been in land and animals, he was not rich in cash. It was in the midst of general indifference, therefore, that there took place what, in retrospect, was the most important single event in the early history of the Argentine livestock industry. In 1848 John Miller, an Englishman, imported the first Durham bull from England for an English estanciero named White. The bull's name was Tarquin, and he added a new word to the Argentine vocabulary: Tarquin's descendants, half criollo, half English shorthorn, were known as *tarquinos*, and the gauchos corrupted the word to *talquino*, a term still current among country people.

Tarquin, in his day, was almost an isolated phenomenon. In 1856–1857 a few Durhams were introduced by progressive estancieros, but the experiment was disheartening. "The value and importance of this movement can hardly be overestimated," wrote Wilfrid Latham. "Nevertheless it has not found general favor, as few have hitherto derived that direct pecuniary benefit which is needful to give it wide-spread acceptation." [23] The trouble was simple. The chief value of cattle was still hide, tallow, and grease, not the tough salted meat. So long as this was so, so long as cattle had small value and Argentina was no more than a purveyor of cheap hides to a low-paying world market, the high capital investment that a fine bull represented was, from the estanciero's point of view, ruinous. Owning a cabaña, or stud farm, has always been the riskiest end of the livestock business. It means a high investment and a dangerous gamble against epidemics and the rapid fluctuations of the market. In the middle of the last century there

* One kilogram = 2.2 lbs.

was no market for pedigreed bulls. The Sociedad Rural had not been founded. There were no annual auctions. The first brave souls to import English shorthorns found that they had imported white elephants, and wrote them off as a bad investment. It was evident that the livestock industry had reached an impasse, and that if it were to make any further advances, it must wait for imagination and technics to solve the riddle: how could *meat*, without losing both substance and value, be somehow, miraculously, carried from the pampa to the market of Europe? The railroad could get it to Buenos Aires. But from Buenos Aires to Bordeaux and Liverpool was a three months' ocean voyage. If meat were not salted, it rotted. And who would eat salted meat if he could get fresh meat?

URQUIZA AND THE LIBERALS

THE WEARING OF THE RED

This trivial act is in large part responsible for all the succeeding evils. The people are like that: they work by reactions. The ribbon of Rosas was despotism, the Mazorca, barbarism, humiliation, everything. To impose it was to chill the spirits, revive discontents, bring doubts, division, alarm for the future.

—SARMIENTO, Letter to Urquiza, October 13, 1852.

The tyrant Rosas was gone. From Montevideo, from Chile, from Europe, a generation that had lived their lives in exile came flocking back to Buenos Aires, bringing old grudges and new hopes. There was Salvador María del Carril, an old Rivadavian Unitario, he who had so many years before advised Lavalle to murder Dorrego with the words: "Revolution is a game of chance in which one wins even the lives of the losers, if it is believed necessary to dispose of them." Carril had been Lavalle's man all through the years of that general's fruitless campaigns against Rosas, and he had spent his exile in Montevideo. Now, almost alone among the returning Unitarios, he joined the Federal Urquiza in his attempt to reorganize the nation.

There was Valentín Alsina, who had been in Montevideo since 1835. Alsina was a porteño Unitario to the bone, and he was to head the movement that took Buenos Aires out of the Confederation. Another porteño was Dalmacio Vélez Sarsfield, whose position during the dictatorship had been equivocal. He had spent some time in Montevideo, but he had been on good terms with Rosas. Vélez Sarsfield was an eminent jurisconsult and authority on church-state relations. Rosas had once consulted him in a quarrel with the papal nuncio. He too joined the porteño Unitarios that were to defy Urquiza.

And there was young Bartolomé Mitre. Mitre had just turned

thirty, and no one yet dreamed that he was to be the greatest Unitario of them all. Mitre had followed his father into exile to Montevideo. He had already made himself a brilliant military career, first in Bolivia, then in the defense of Montevideo, and finally in the battle of Caseros, where he had reached the rank of colonel. He had lived in Chile, editing papers both in Valparaíso and Santiago. Mitre, too, was a porteño, and he was to break early with Urquiza. In Buenos Aires he founded *Los Debates* to combat the caudillo from Entre Ríos.

There was Juan Bautista Alberdi. He had been an exile in Montevideo, but not an Unitario. He had belonged to Echevería's Asociación de Mayo, that group of young utopian socialists that had found the Unitarios quarrelsome, petty, and tiresome. Alberdi had no more use now than he had ever had for this faction. A lawyer and theorist, his ideas were to be the basis of the Argentine constitution. With Carril, he was willing to put the national organization above partisan politics, and he joined Urquiza in his fight to bring Buenos Aires into the Confederation.

But the greatest exile of all was none of these men. When Urquiza marched against Rosas, in the ranks of his army was a middle-aged ex-schoolmaster whose job it was to print the army bulletin on a hand press. His name was Domingo F. Sarmiento. He was probably the greatest man Argentina ever produced.

Sarmiento was from the rocky mountain province of San Juan. His father had been a peon, but after the May Revolution he "got the new idea that came with the Revolution, an unconquerable hatred for the rude and unintelligent surroundings in which he had grown up." [1] The atmosphere was certainly not propitious for intellectual growth, even in the early days when the Rivadavian liberal, Salvador María del Carril, was governor of San Juan. Sarmiento was born the year after the Revolution, and his childhood was spent in the atmosphere that surrounded the campaigns of San Martín, under whom his father served. Those were years of promise for the United Provinces, and the echoes of war reached even remote San Juan and stirred great hopes. Young Domingo was a precocious child, and the elder Sarmiento had great hopes for him: "My son shall never hold a hoe in his hands," [2] he once boasted to a friend.

Sarmiento got what schooling could be had in San Juan, which was almost nothing. He read right through the small private libraries. Then there came the chance his family had waited for. Don Bernardino Rivadavia, who was the minister of Buenos Aires, asked each province to send six children to the capital to be educated at the expense of the state. Sarmiento's father and mother were sure Domingo would be chosen. Did he not stand at the head of the school? Apparently other parents were able to bring more pressure to bear, because Domingo was passed over. In despair the father wrote to Governor Martín Rodríguez of Buenos Aires, begging that his son be accepted, if only as a substitute, so that "in his turn he may be useful to America." [3] One can imagine what would have been the surprise of the governor, if he read the letter—he never answered it—to see that an obscure father in obscure San Juan thought his little boy would some day be "useful to America."

So Domingo stayed in San Juan, and got what further education he could pick up from a clergyman relative of his mother's. When Unitarios and Federales began to tear the country apart, he took no sides—indeed, was quite unaware of the issues at stake. If anything, being a Sanjuanino, he was a Federal. But the civil wars came one day to his own door in the form of a summons to serve in the army of San Juan as a second lieutenant. Absorbed in his books, he wrote the governor an angry protest. Governor Manuel Quiroga summoned the youth. Had he written this? Was this his signature? It was, said Sarmiento. The young second lieutenant began his military service in jail.

In jail, Sarmiento, like a lot of other men since the beginning of history, had an abundance of time for meditation. He put two and two together. Quiroga was a Federal. Quiroga had interrupted his studies and deprived him of his liberty. Therefore, Sarmiento was henceforth an Unitario. When he got out of jail he joined the army that fought the caudillo of La Rioja, Facundo, and he came to hate Facundo passionately. Sarmiento fought with the Unitarios until Paz was defeated, and then emigrated to Chile. He taught school for a while in a remote Andean village. He worked in a mine. Finally, under amnesty from the governor, he returned to his native province, and there he stayed and worked for ten years, teaching school and editing a paper. He loved school teaching, but there came a time when the town of San Juan was too small to hold him and the new caudillo, Nazario Benavídez. Benavídez put the young schoolmaster in jail, and then told him to pack his bags and get out as fast as he could. Once again Domingo Sarmiento learned the hard way what government-by-caudillo meant to Argentina. He went to Chile, but he never forgot.

It was in Chile that Sarmiento's career really began. From the tribune that was the press of Valparaíso and Santiago, Sarmiento began a bitter, unceasing warfare against the "barbarians" that had made his country the most backward in America. Rosas, Quiroga, López, Benavídez, the whole tribe represented to him all that was uncivilized and intolerable. Most of the young writer's ammunition was for Rosas, but not all, by any means. His work, and that of other émigrés, had a powerful orientating influence on the foreign policy of Chile's conservative minister Manuel Montt, who became Sarmiento's friend and patron. Montt made Sarmiento director of the government Normal School, and the young teacher had a chance to see for himself, by the quality of students that presented themselves, how poorly esteemed a profession was that of schoolmaster. He had seen it in San Juan, too, where a man who wanted to make a religious vow of self-mortification promised to spend a year teaching school in some country schoolhouse. In San Juan a political prisoner had once been *sentenced* to teach school as a punishment. But Sarmiento loved his profession. In it he saw the only hope for his wretched, backward country. "An ignorant people," he wrote, "will always elect a Rosas." [4]

In May, 1845, there appeared in *El Progreso* the first installment of an essay on Facundo Quiroga which Sarmiento had dashed off in two months. It was *Facundo; or Civilization and Barbarism*, the most brilliant piece of writing Sarmiento was ever to do, and the most fascinating. As the serialized life of this Riojano caudillo unfolded, chapter by chapter, friend and enemy alike stopped their debates on the personality and character of the author to read this story. As the picture of a country and an age it has not been surpassed. Colored as it was—anything that Sarmiento wrote was colored by that powerful, truculent personality—it was still the best comment that has ever been made on the gaucho mentality. The rude, uncivilized country that was Argentina, its vastness, the uncertainty of its daily living, the cruelty of its caudillos, stood out in red letters for all to read. Overnight Sarmiento was the literary lion of Santiago. But Manuel Montt, trying to keep a precarious peace with his neighbor over the Andes, found *Facundo* embarrassing, and thought the author should leave Chile for a while. Would Sarmiento like to make a trip to Europe, at government expense, to study the primary schools? For Sarmiento, the tactful banishment was the realization of a life's dream.

It was a four months' voyage to Europe from Chile. At the mouth of the Plata he passed close to Buenos Aires, which he had never seen, and he was not allowed to forget that his country was in the hands of Rosas. A wind had whipped up the estuary, and the Chilean captain, half in jest, said: "We are in the river now, and that red is the blood of those they are murdering over there." Sarmiento blushed for his country.[5]

In Montevideo, when he arrived, *El Nacional* was running his *Facundo* in installments, and he was a popular hero. He met Mitre, Varela, Echeverría, Alsina, Vélez Sarsfield, whom he had known by reputation for the common cause they defended. Then he sailed to Rio, and from there to Europe. He travelled through France and Spain, saw the Arabs of North Africa, and then, on a hunch, set sail for the United States to see the world's newest adventure in building a nation. Europe, which had greatly impressed him, was all but forgotten. Sarmiento met Horace Mann, studied the American schools, observed the people, admired their energy, and returned to Chile with the conviction that he had seen the nation that was going to dominate the world. This was the model Argentina must follow. This was the living triumph of democracy, education, and self-government. Sarmiento heaped his scorn on the "tyrants" of Europe and their enslaved peoples, and turned to North America for the example his country must build upon. Twenty years later the fruit of that enthusiasm was to be an Argentine public-school system built by American normal-school teachers on the philosophies of Horace Mann.

At the end, when Urquiza marched against Rosas, Sarmiento was with him. He had presented himself for duty in the uniform of a lieutenant-colonel (self-assumed), and the caudillo of Entre Ríos had accepted him coolly. Sarmiento was allowed to edit the army bulletin. He put his heart into the work, and he and his helpers lugged their heavy iron press the whole length of the march. It was on a hot midsummer day that the ex-editor, ex-schoolmaster, marched into Buenos Aires in the train of Urquiza's army. He was forty years old, and he had never seen his country's capital. He gave himself a pleasure that was better than dreams: he went straight to Rosas' house in Palermo, and there, at the tyrant's desk, and with the tyrant's pen, he wrote a triumphant letter to his friends in Chile.

So the dictatorship was over. Justo José de Urquiza was in Buenos Aires. The terror and pillage that had broken out at the news of Caseros was put down without ruth. Vicente López, author of Argentina's national anthem, ex-president of the Republic (after Rivadavia), and a justice who had served under Rosas, was named governor of Buenos Aires. For the first time in fifteen years the Argentine colors, the blue and white, were seen in Buenos Aires. The hateful scarlet was taken down, the ribbons were torn up. With vast relief and happiness the capital prepared for the victory parade of the 14th of February. Urquiza rode through the streets at the head of his troops. The people in a delirium of enthusiasm crowded the streets and roof tops and shouted. But in his hat Urquiza *was wearing the red ribbon.*

Why was Urquiza wearing the red? This is one of those questions about which every writer has a theory. The Unitarios took it as a mortal affront at once, and decided that Urquiza intended to oust Rosas only to make himself dictator. Acting on this conviction, Sarmiento sadly went back to Chile after less than three weeks in Buenos Aires. Valentín Alsina, who was a minister in the new government, hastened at once to issue a decree that the wearing of the red ribbon was not obligatory. Buenos Aires was stupefied. *Obligatory?* But had there not just been a revolution to end the red ribbon for all time? From Yungay, the home of his mistress in Chile, Sarmiento wrote Urquiza a bitter letter:

"The day of the triumphal entry, Your Excellency enjoyed the delirium of that immense populace crowded on roofs, in windows, in doors, and on sidewalks until it impeded progress. But you will remember, too, that your irritated eyes did not find a single red ribbon, and that the thousands of bouquets of flowers, the flags, the hangings flaunted the colors of our country, and not the red.

"Buenos Aires, that day, then, gave a public, solemn, unanimous vote. It wanted the general and the principles of Federalism, but it did not want a continuation of the farces and violence of Rosas. It wanted the man, but not the system." [6]

Urquiza, for his part, was bitter at the attitude of the Unitarios, who were, as he put it, "trying to claim the heritage of a revolution which does not belong to them." [7] He wore the red ribbon, some apologists have said, to allay the suspicions of his army of Entre Ríos Federales, who were afraid he had sold out to the Unitarios. The porteños, for their part, now became convinced that Urquiza was planning to revive the hated Rivadavian law of capitalization, depriving the province of its government to make Buenos Aires the national capital. Another version of the story was that Urquiza was going to divide the province in two. In any case the temporary union that had brought Unitarios and Federales together in their hatred of Rosas was dissolved, and the country divided into camps. Vicente López and del Carril stood by Urquiza. Sarmiento went back to Chile. And Alsina, Vélez Sarsfield, and Mitre began an active plot to overthrow and kill Urquiza.

BUENOS AIRES SECEDES FROM ARGENTINA

> *On going over the history of the Argentine provinces from their independence from Spain to the present, one is struck by a fact which dominates all others . . .; only it can explain the long and bloody anarchy of which those provinces have been the theater, and in which Europe finds herself entangled without glory for herself or profit for anyone. That fact is none other than the pretension of Buenos Aires to replace Spain in the role and privileges of the metropolis of the states of La Plata.*
>
> —THOMAS MANNEQUIN, *Les Provinces Argentines et Buenos-Ayres.*

On May 31, 1852, the Acuerdo of San Nicolás laid down the bases of the new provisional government. There were to be no more of the transit duties and interprovincial tariffs that had crippled trade. A constituent Congress was to be called, and in the meantime Urquiza was named provisional Director of the nation. The porteño Unitarios set up a cry of "Dictator!" and there were angry debates in the Sala de Representantes, where Mitre made his first great public impression by his speech attacking the Acuerdo. Vélez Sarsfield came out against it. Only Vicente López dared defend it, and when his speech, which was brilliant, was finished, he had to leave the legislature by a side door to escape the mob that wanted to lynch him.

The problem, all over again, was Buenos Aires. Should it abandon its monopoly on the port revenues for the doubtful (to it) advantages of national union? Urquiza's crime was that he was not a porteño, and that he was thinking in terms of the interests of all the provinces. There were, in reality, two factions opposing him in Buenos Aires. One was the group that wished to keep the capital out of the Confederation, with all its old, special privileges intact. Valentín Alsina was its head. And the other faction, led by young Bartolomé Mitre, wanted to unite the nation, but under porteño leadership. These were exactly the same interests of a quarter of a century earlier, and it seemed as though they would never make peace. In any case, they were all porteños, and for them the motto was "Buenos Aires first."

In the ensuing struggle, the psychological factor must not be lost sight of. Otherwise, the behavior of some of the leaders of the time becomes inexplicable. Urquiza stood almost alone in his well-meant efforts to unite the nation, and unless this fact is to redound to the everlasting shame of Mitre and Sarmiento and some of the others, one must find the reason. Was it all just the old Buenos Aires stubbornness? With the porteños, perhaps. But this does not explain the fact that Sarmiento, too, was Urquiza's bitter enemy.

The reason must be sought in the atmosphere of the times. Urquiza, by an odd twist of events, was the man who broke Rosas; but he was a man of the same party and the same stripe. He was a Federal. He was a caudillo. He had been a ruthless dictator, and had probably behaved as badly in Entre Ríos as López had in Santa Fe, or Benavídez in San Juan. Worst of all, his supporters in the provinces were the same caudillos who had made life a hell during the tyranny of Rosas. Sarmiento was not likely to forget that Nazario Benavídez was a collaborator of Urquiza's, and was the man who had exiled Sarmiento from San Juan. It did not matter that Urquiza's motives were of the highest, that he worked intelligently to rebuild the nation, that he represented union, that he had overthrown Rosas. He was a Federal. He had worn the red ribbon on his march into Buenos Aires. Now he wanted to be Director of the nation. The Unitarios agreed that the man was intolerable.

Some of the hysteria against Urquiza may be judged by the paper one enemy prepared as his defense in a libel suit that Urquiza brought against him. "During his rule," wrote the lawyer, "there was in the province [of Entre Ríos] no will but his, no law but that of his eccentricities and hates. He confiscated private fortunes, flogged children and pregnant women, made of his town an armed camp, beheaded hundreds of helpless citizens, disposed of men and things at his whim, without trial and without observing any rule; he proscribed whomever he wished, he had the press in chains, he established the most hateful espionage, he carried prostitution and poverty to the family and he threw over his province the shadow and desolation of death." [8] As if this were not enough, the accusation went on to say that after the battle of Pago Largo, Urquiza had written a letter to his brother boasting of his execution of prisoners, and enclosing the ear of one; that at India Muerta he had killed eight hundred Uruguayans; that in 1842 Urquiza had had only ten to twelve thousand silver pesos, and that now his fortune was worth thirty millions gold; and so on. How much truth there was in all this is hard to say. Probably some truth. Even Sarmiento accused him of being the man "who, since Artigas, Quiroga, and Rosas, has beheaded the most prisoners." But, for a man so monstrous, Urquiza behaved with singularly little personal ambition after the fall of Rosas. Let his record speak for itself.

From the beginning he had the hatred of the Unitarios. Even before Caseros, there fell into Urquiza's hands a letter by Sarmiento in which he spoke of the necessity of getting rid of Urquiza.[9] When the Buenos Aires legislature refused to accept the Acuerdo of San Nicolás, which Urquiza knew was indispensable to the unity of the nation, Governor Vicente López resigned and Urquiza dissolved the Sala. The city was occupied, and Mitre and Vélez Sarsfield were exiled. To the porteños this was conclusive evidence of the caudillo's iniquity. But the best proof that Urquiza was acting in the interest of the country was that he convoked a Constituent Congress to draw up the national constitution, and allowed Buenos Aires freely to elect its two representatives. He was in the city two months, and in that time he organized the municipality, nationalized the customhouse (this was what hurt Buenos Aires), opened the Paraná and Uruguay rivers to navigation, and created a commission to draw up civil and criminal codes for the nation. In November the Constituent Congress opened in Santa Fe, and Urquiza left the city to attend. He set out the 6th of September, and by the 11th Buenos Aires was in the hands of Alsina and his followers. The next month the legislature elected Alsina governor, and Alsina made Mitre his minister of the interior. Once again Buenos Aires had seceded from the nation.

Nevertheless, the Congress met in November, as scheduled, and sat until May of the next year. In those sessions, the guiding spirit was that of Juan Bautista Alberdi, who had written a classic work, *Bases y Puntos de Partida para la Organización Política de la República Argentina* (Bases and Points of Departure for the Political Organization of the Argentine Republic). When one reads the Argentine Constitution in the light of Argentine history, one can see that in reality there have been three major influences in it: one is that of the American Constitution, which served essentially as a model; another is that of the civil wars and all the issues which had been at stake in them; and the third is the ideas of Alberdi on such vital subjects as foreign capital, immigration, and transportation.

"Populating the land," wrote Alberdi, "—that South American need which takes precedence over all the others—is the exact measure of our governments' capacity. The minister of the interior who does not double the census of these peoples every ten years, has wasted his time on bagatelles and superfluities." [10]

"The Federal Government will encourage European immigration," says Article 25 of the Constitution; "and it may not restrict, limit, or tax in any way the entrance into Argentine territory of those foreigners who come to work the land, better industries, and introduce and teach the sciences and arts."

Argentina, wrote Alberdi, must guarantee freedom of religion to its immigrants, or they will not come. "Spanish America, reduced to Catholicism to the exclusion of other religions, represents a solitary and silent convent of monks." [11]

Article 20 of the Constitution: "Foreigners in national territory enjoy all the civil rights of the citizens; they may exercise . . . their religion freely. . . ."

"This America needs capital as it needs population," wrote Alberdi. "The immigrant without money is a soldier without arms." And on the subject of railroads: "The railroads will forge the unity of the Argentine Republic better than all the Congresses. Congresses may declare it *one and indivisible;* without the railroad which draws close together its remote extremes, it will always remain divisible and divided against all legislative decrees." [12]

Congress, says the Constitution (Article 67), "shall provide what will lead to the prosperity of the country, to the advance and welfare of all the provinces and to the progress of learning, dictating plans of general and university instruction, and promoting industry, immigration, the construction of railroads and navigable canals, the colonization of public lands, the introduction and establishment of new industries, the importation of foreign capital, and the exploration of interior rivers, by laws which protect these ends and by temporary concessions of privileges and rewards."

The long, tragic, and futile civil wars left wide tracks in the Constitution. The crippling interprovincial tariffs that had all but broken down trade were forever written off the books. Article 10: "National products are free of duties in the interior of the Republic. . . ." Article 11: "Articles of national or foreign manufacture are free of those duties known as transit duties, as are all kinds of livestock which pass from one province to another, and also carts, boats, and beasts of burden. . . ." Article 12: "Boats going from one province to another will not be obliged to enter, anchor, and pay duties because of transit. . . ." The long fight with Buenos Aires to nationalize the aduana was reflected in Articles 4 and 9: "The Federal Government provides the expenditure of the nation with the funds from the National Treasury made up of the revenues for import and export duties. . . . In all the national territory there will be no customhouses except national ones which shall charge the tariffs sanctioned by Congress."

As for the sheer anarchy that had kept the provinces at war with one another for a quarter of a century, the Constitution made several provisions to prevent its recurrence. Article 109: "No province may declare or make war against another province." In an effort to put teeth into this provision, the Congress wrote into the Constitution two articles which, however wise they may have appeared at the time, were to be the basis of such continual abuse by the executive power that they have nullified all that made the Argentine Constitution federalist. Article 6 said: "The Federal Government intervenes in the provinces to guarantee the republican form of government, or repel foreign invasion, and, at the request of their constituted authorities, to sustain or re-establish them, if they have been deposed by sedition or by invasion from another province." And Article 23: "In case of internal commotion or exterior attack which put in peril the exercise of this Constitution and the authorities created by it, a state of siege will be declared in the province where the perturbation exists and constitutional guarantees will be suspended."

It is easy to understand why these provisions were written in. Before 1853, provinces acted like sovereign nations—which, in fact, they were. In documents of the times, for instance, you find written a man's native province as if it were his native country: "Patria—Corrientes," or "Patria—Buenos Aires." Provinces had their armies, with which they invaded one another. The article permitting federal intervention was aimed at order and unity, but in practice it has been used to interfere with elections before they take place, annul them after they take place, punish political enemies, and reward friends. There is no reason why this provision should have given rise to abuse, for the American Constitution makes the same provision.* But it did, and from 1853 to the present writing, there have probably been a hundred and sixty interventions in the provinces.†

While the Constituent Congress was in session, the province of Buenos Aires had become a battleground of Federal and Unitario forces. A military uprising of Federales unseated Alsina in December of 1852; and the following year the capital was under

* Constitution of the United States, Article 4, Section 4: "The United States shall guarantee to every State in this Union a republican form of government, and shall protect each of them against invasion; and, on application of the legislature, or of the executive (when the legislature cannot be convened), against domestic violence." The Argentine articles forbidding interprovincial tariffs, too, are patterned on similar ones in the American constitution. See Article 1, Sections 9 and 10.

† The number rises from month to month.

siege by land and water. The fleet of the Confederation was led by an American mercenary, John Halsted Coe, who proved too mercenary: in June of 1853, for 26,000 gold ounces, he surrendered his fleet to the porteños, and totally reversed the military situation.[13] Now Buenos Aires controlled the rivers and was unassailable. Urquiza had to make peace. But to insure that the capital would not bottle up the Paraná and Uruguay rivers, and monopolize all the customs, he cleverly made free navigation treaties with England, France, and the United States. "Very few men know when they are no longer wanted," Sarmiento wrote him bitterly from Chile. "Then go right ahead, General, besieging and devastating the outskirts of Buenos Aires, consuming the livestock, regimenting the people, killing your enemies, who, after all, are not Argentines, but *porteños*."[14] Urquiza could afford to ignore the gibes. If Buenos Aires did not want him, the rest of the nation did. The Constituent Congress passed the national Constitution, elected Justo José de Urquiza and Salvador María del Carril the first president and vice-president, called the congressional elections, and dissolved itself. Urquiza and the Congress moved to the small, green river town of Paraná, in the province of Entre Ríos, and began the task of building a nation. Down river, Buenos Aires, isolated from the rest of the country, not recognized by a single major power, kept her riches to herself and pretended that Argentina did not yet exist.

URQUIZA IN PARANA

Paraná was scarcely the city anyone would have picked for the capital of the new republic. But there was nothing else to do. Buenos Aires, alone, was stronger than the rest of the country put together. It was a humble beginning for the Confederation, which was without trained men, without capital, without a decent port, without population: without anything, in short, but a juridical existence, and the timid hope that even without Buenos Aires it could somehow make a go of the experiment. Paraná was a sleepy provincial town, and there were few of the trappings of authority in the new government there. The atmosphere of the times, the real poverty of the times, may be judged by the fact that Vice-President del Carril put up beds for his children at night in the room where by day he received his visitors.[15]

The Confederation started with nothing. The country was depopulated. It had no coinage. Only Buenos Aires and Corrientes had paper notes, and the coins in use were of the most various origins: gold doubloons and Chilean condors; patacoons, Cordoban and Bolivian pesos and half-pesos and reals in silver; copper coins of four, two, and one centavos. There was no transportation except the old, painful oxcart. There was no mint, nor would there have been money for it if there had been. There was no ocean port. There was no army. There were no national schools. But the young Confederation could take pride in the fact that Buenos Aires, in spite of its best efforts, did not succeed in getting diplomatic recognition. England, France, the United States, Spain, Brazil, the Papal State sent their representatives to *Paraná*.

The Confederation did the best it could without resources. The Constituent Congress had founded the Banco Nacional and borrowed six million pesos, of which one-third was alloted to the bank, one-third to administrative costs, and one-third for the building of wharves and customhouses. But within six months the bank closed its doors. Brazil lent the Confederation some money to keep going, but its financial situation looked hopeless. There was no money to coin; and, to untangle the confusion of coins in circulation, the government established the Cordoban peso as national money. But so few were in circulation that it had to be replaced by the Bolivian peso.

The Confederation needed immigration as badly as it did money. Corrientes contracted with a French company to send out two hundred families per year for ten years from the south of France. The government agreed to provide each family with twenty cuadras of land, two bullocks, one mare, one stallion, eight cows, and one bull, besides seed to plant cotton, corn, tobacco, wheat, and sugar cane. Each family was to have a two-room house, and six hundred kilograms of flour for the first year. In October, 1854, the first group of 257 families sailed from Bordeaux. But seventeen children died aboard from smallpox, many adults left the ship at Montevideo, and only 130 souls arrived in Corrientes in March of the following year.[16]

Nothing the Confederation projected seemed to turn out. It needed railroads, badly, and hired an American engineer, Allan Campbell, to survey the Rosario-Córdoba route. He made his survey and estimated at twenty thousand gold pesos a mile, or a total of five million for the whole line.[17] Five million gold pesos! It was cheap enough as railroads go—very cheap, in fact—but the government had neither the money nor any prospect of getting it. Hopefully, however, it authorized one José Buschental to build it if he could, granting land for rails and stations, and half a league on each side of the right of way. Nothing came of the agreement—probably because the government could not guarantee minimum profits—and the matter was dropped.

No money, no railroads, no immigrants, no population. That was the story of the Urquiza government. There was probably less than a million population in the whole Confederation. Buenos Aires had another four hundred thousand or so.[18] In 1857, the first year for which there is any record, the total immigration to the whole country was only five thousand.[19] Argentina was still criollo—still a mixture of Spanish and Indian and negro stocks. Even a decade later, when Sarmiento had the first census taken, only 12 per cent of the population was of foreign origin.[20] Alberdi, who was Urquiza's one-man brain trust, reiterated the need for immigration. "To govern," he said, "is to populate."[21] But you cannot kidnap immigrants, and the Confederation had nothing to offer them.

Urquiza's situation, however you look at it, was hopeless. He could not even find graduate lawyers to be federal judges. In the whole province of Entre Ríos, which is where the capital was, there were only two. Córdoba could produce twenty, all told.

There was no money to pay deputies.[22] Yet in spite of heartbreaking handicaps the government organized primary, secondary, and university education, began the post office, and created a national army. And in 1856, in a desperate effort to stave off bankruptcy and to bring Buenos Aires into the Confederation, Congress passed a law establishing differential tariffs.

The differential tariff had been an old weapon of Rosas. In order to force ships to come directly to Buenos Aires he had established that those that did paid one duty, whereas those that stopped first at Montevideo or any other local port, paid a surcharge. The weapon had worked very well, and now the Confederation proposed to turn it against Buenos Aires. Rosario would be declared the national port, and any ship that did not come directly to Rosario from abroad, but stopped first in Montevideo or Buenos Aires, would have to pay a double tariff. The debates on the bill took place in Paraná in June, 1856, and the project's author stated his case. "The provinces," he said, "continue to be the vassals of the commercial centers existing in Buenos Aires and Montevideo. . . . This law will mean a further step toward the laudable end of bringing to an end the quarrel that separates Buenos Aires from the Confederation; for the loss of the considerable advantages which our dependence on its market gives it, would be a new stimulus to bring it back to the Union." Another deputy attacked bitterly the Buenos Aires monopoly on revenues which should have belonged to the nation. "By what right," he demanded, "by what law of the Constitution or the national organization does the province of Buenos Aires appropriate for itself the revenues from imports and exports? Can it be merely because the aduana is there? Can it be because it is a nation independent of the Argentine nation? . . . Or perhaps because it is a dissenting province? By dissidence, can it claim title to what belongs to the nation?" [23]

The differential tariff had the desired effect. Whereas in 1855 Rosario, the Confederation's port on the Paraná River, had received only two ships from overseas, in the last half of the year 1856 there were two hundred fifty. The port receipts jumped from

870,000 pesos in 1856 to 1,073,389 pesos in 1858. "Events proved once again that commerce is always ready to go where its interests dictate," wrote a French observer. "By the end of a year it was used to the new state of affairs. Great business houses were founded in Rosario, and all the provinces went there to make their purchases." [24]

If Urquiza's government failed, it was not because it did not make heroic efforts to succeed. The Confederation assumed the foreign debt, and this unbalanced its budget. The customs receipts were enough for ordinary government expenditures, but interest on the debt came to around a million pesos a year, and this was exactly the margin of deficit. In spite of the deficit, the government put money into schools, both primary and secondary, and into the improvement of communications. It could not afford the railroad, which was too expensive a toy for so poor a country, but it could and did establish stagecoaches and a national messenger service. A French engineer was hired to study the Mendoza post route and shorten its length: he did, by some two hundred kilometers, and published a report in Paraná in 1857.

The federal government voted an annual subsidy of 24,000 pesos to the company of Rusiñol y Fillol for the founding of a national messenger service by stagecoach. Fillol was made head of the post office, and established a regular diligence service along the routes to Chile and Peru. Posthouses were built for government riders and private travellers, where horses could be had for 30 centavos a league. In 1857, following the example of the United States and Europe, the Confederation adopted the postage stamp, an immense simplification in postal methods.[25]

Public lands came in for their share of study. There were millions of acres. What to do with them? Urquiza did not give with both hands as Rosas had done, but the government established a prize of fifty gold ounces for a memorial on how to classify and distribute the land. The decree that established the prize said in part: "Comparing the vast extension of the Republic's territory, its few inhabitants, its small wealth, with what it could acquire by immigration, the idea of introducing foreign artisans has appeared often among us, but never been translated into action. . . . The government of the Confederation has reason to believe that the obstacle . . . consists chiefly in the present method of land distribution. For that reason it feels the need for a law to correct these mistakes and make it easy to acquire land at a fixed and reasonable price . . . sufficient for each settler to start his own industry." Excellent sentiments, but it was too bad they had not taken root earlier, and in the province of Buenos Aires. What European immigrant was going to the interior of the Confederation, where there was neither train nor boat? The government managed to lure a few artisans from Montevideo by paying their passage.[26]

Urquiza saw the need for advertising. Perhaps if more were known about Argentina . . . It occurred to him that one good book, published in French, in Paris, with all the information that an immigrant could ask, might have an excellent effect. He commissioned Dr. Victor Martin de Moussy to make a three-volume geographical and statistical study. Moussy seems to have been a man of encyclopedic knowledge: doctor of medicine, geologist, geographer, agronomist. His work, "A Geographical and Statistical Description of the Argentine Confederation," aroused wide interest. It is certainly the most complete work ever done on Argentina: a monumental description, province by province, of the history, the soil, birds, beasts, plants, people, cities, communications, customs, society, dress, eating habits—everything one could possibly care to know, and much that one would not. The savant's travels were financed by the public treasury, and his book, in three green and gold volumes, was published under Urquiza's patronage. In spite of this, it is intelligent, objective, and critical. Nowhere is there indiscriminate praise or unwarranted optimism. On the contrary, Moussy was a shrewd and honest observer, condemning much that he saw, and speaking as a European to other Europeans.

To read Moussy is to know Urquiza's Confederation. One sees the smallness and provincialism of Paraná, that makeshift national capital of seven thousand souls, its one-story houses, its unpaved streets, its luxuriant gardens with oranges and pomegranates and figs. Moussy knew Buenos Aires, and includes it as if it were part of the Confederation. Its population was then 120,000, one-third foreign. Streets were cobbled. The houses were not bad, but they were certainly damp, he found. "Today, in all the principal towns, houses are well built, and in the interior brick begins to replace adobe, which is unbaked mud brick dried in the sun, which lasts a long time in a dry climate. The littoral especially has very comfortable buildings and an aspect of elegance, but the ground floor suffers generally from an excess of humidity due to the lack of a cellar. Most of the houses are of one story; a small number have two; and a very few have three. But their principal adornment, above all in Montevideo, is the *mirador*, or belvedere, a kind of square tower which may contain one or two rooms, and from which the view embraces a vast horizon over city and country. On the terraces, which, as in the Orient, form the majority of the housetops, the family enjoys the evening cool; for after hot summer days it is at once agreeable and healthful to be able, without leaving home, to breathe purer air at ease. . . .

"The absence of glass from the windows, and the imperfect closing of the houses' openings, result both from a climate that is remarkably dry part of the year, and from national habits. Half the year is lived outside in the open air: at night, in the middle-class houses, beds are put in the patios, and there people sleep from midnight to five in the morning. In the daytime people sleep the siesta from one to four in order to escape the heat; even in winter some people do it. As for the peon, at the same hours he goes to sleep on a mat or hide, covering himself with a small poncho." [27]

Moussy was distressed by the irregular meal hours. The Argentines, he complained, did not breakfast before noon, no matter how much work they did. Sometimes, if they were busy, they did not eat until nightfall. And when they did eat, it was mostly meat. As for their dress, it had most of the vices of French fashion. "The inhabitants of the tropical zone wear the tight frock coat of the Occident, black trousers with a strap under the heel, and the varnished boot, and they have even adopted the abominable narrow-brimmed hat, in spite of the burning sun." The women "long ago sacrificed that charming Andalusian mantilla which they knew how to wear so gracefully, and have replaced it by the singular little hat which only Paris knows how to make or how to wear. Less bold than the women of Lima, who know how to take from French fashions what suits them and let the rest go, the *élégantes* of Montevideo and Buenos Aires condemn themselves to trailing robes which hide the feet—they have very pretty feet—and surround themselves with those ridiculous and uncomfortable hoop skirts which make a woman look like a dressed-up bell or a pyramid." Moussy was inclined to the belief that this luxury of dress "explains the prodigious amount of women's clothes which hundreds of transatlantic ships bring to the Plata."

Even cosmetics did not escape his critical eye. "Cometics are in great use among the middle-class women and even the colored women. They consume quantities of perfumed waters, pomades, etc., and they generally choose the strongest odors of amber and musk. They also use an immoderate amount of rice powder applied directly to the skin, or even more of manioc flour finely powdered, so that many of these ladies appear in the evening with their faces most strangely floured." [28]

But Moussy, unlike most foreigners who visit Argentina, saw much more than Buenos Aires, much more even than the littoral. He visited the north, where Indians and half-Indians lived in poverty and squalor. He travelled the jungles of Misiones, where the ruined Jesuit plantations of yerba mate, abandoned in the eighteenth century, had reverted to the jungle that surrounded them. The frontiers of the Confederation were uncertain, losing themselves in Indian territory, or in border provinces claimed by neighboring Paraguay and Chile. The Andean frontier was to be under litigation until the end of the century. In the southwest, in a line cutting Buenos Aires, Córdoba, and Mendoza, was a wavering line of frontier forts to hold back the raiding Pampa Indians. The fall of Rosas brought the twenty-year truce to an end, and now there were annual raids against the outlying estancias. Christians were killed, and the women were carried off as prisoners and concubines. In the north the border was under dispute with Bolivia and Paraguay.

There were all kinds of Indians within the Confederation, ranging from the Guayanas of Misiones and Paraguay, who were peaceful farmers and hunters, to the raiding Ranqueles of the pampa. In Río Grande, now Brazil, but then territory claimed by the vaguely defined Confederation, were the Tupís, who were cannibals. But in the Chaco, bordering on Salta, on Santiago, on Santa Fe, were tribes that were beginning to come down to the civilized communities in order to work for the whites. In Salta the Mataco Indians did all the work of the cane fields, coming down at harvest time to gather and peel sugar cane at four pesos a month. They raised their own faggot huts, and in October returned again to the Chaco until the next harvest. The Chiriguanos of the Andes were farmers, planting corn and manioc, sugar cane, vegetables, and fruits. The Quichuas of La Rioja, Catamarca, Salta, and Jujuy raised sheep and llamas, and were Christian converts with a Spanish strain in their blood.[29]

Moussy was impressed by the strange, destructive habit the Argentine farmer had of setting fire to the pampa to burn off the sun-dried grass. These fires were fantastic, one traveller reporting that he had gone two hundred leagues over land burned by a single fire. Once started, only Heaven, or backfires, could stop them. "At night the spectacle is truly extraordinary. In Misiones, between the Trinchera de los Paraguayos and the former estancia of Santo Tomás, we found ourselves thus surrounded by flames, and it is impossible to describe the strange aspect of the countryside, with the silhouettes of cattle and horses fleeing before the fire, the red flush of the sky, and the crackle of the plants twisting in the flames. . . . All the animals fled before the fire; alone, the trapped steer breaks bravely through, while the frightened horse takes refuge in the woods beside the streams." [30]

In Misiones, Moussy saw what was left of the Jesuit missions. The buildings had crumbled, the carefully and lovingly cultivated yerba trees had gone wild. There were no priests left, and the memory of Christianity had all but died out among the Indians.

On the Uruguay River he visited the abandoned mission of La Cruz. "We visited La Cruz one Sunday; the priest had died a year ago and had not been replaced. A young Guaraní sacristan celebrated evening service; an old Indian woman led the chant, which was accompanied by two guitars, a flute, and two violins. The attitude of the small number of Indians and mestizos who filled the desolate church was devout and meditative." The tears came to the Frenchman's eyes when he thought of "the past prosperity of La Cruz and its present poverty, of the faith and resignation of these poor people." [31]

This was the Confederation as Moussy saw it—poor, unpopulated, well intentioned, and half savage, with a man at its head who was too much hated to achieve what had to be achieved if Argentina was ever to be more than this: to achieve, that is, the union with the rich and badly behaved province of Buenos Aires.

CEPEDA AND PAVON

Buenos Aires was not doing at all badly for itself, to the gnawing disappointment of the men of Paraná. The city was prosperous. In its fashion, it was a center of culture, and Sarmiento, who had the provincial's snobbishness about the importance of European culture, could take pleasure in the university, the libraries, and the theaters. Sarmiento had returned from Chile, now that the hated tyrant Urquiza had been banished, and he was the provincial director of schools. He got the school budget enormously enlarged, and began the realization of his life's dream, which was the education of the Argentine people. In his imagination he saw the triumph of culture over barbarism, of the city over the country. It would mean the end of the caudillism he so savagely hated. He frightened the governor with his demands for money, but he built the schools. All over the province, they were opened up, and the serious, intelligent, egotistic genius who had spent half a century in frustration, could at last see the fruits of his life study in these humble one-room buildings. It was a beginning. It was concrete. But his ambition did not stop here.

As cities go, Buenos Aires was not bad. It had a wonderful cathedral with a Corinthian peristyle, worthy at least of Paris. There were two theaters of respectable size: the old Victoria, and the new Colón. Both gave Italian opera, Spanish drama, and French vaudeville. There was a public library, a museum with remarkable bones in it, a high school, and a university. Artists came from Europe to play for Buenos Aires audiences: "The violinist Sivori, the pianist Thalberg, the singer Tamberlik, Mlle. Lagrua, the singer, all artists of a European reputation, have come to be heard in Buenos Aires and Montevideo," Moussy reported.

In the meantime, ex-Rosistas got lynched in the streets, and there were some bloody scenes as the Unitarios settled old accounts. Pastor Obligado, who was governor of the province, conveniently forgot he had been a Rosista himself, and began discharging from government jobs all who had been partisans of either Rosas or Urquiza. His successor, Valentín Alsina, did a further housecleaning. Land donations by Rosas for the Indian campaigns and civil wars were annulled. This caught the small fry, army sergeants, and commissioned officers. The really great fortunes went untouched.

There was a railroad—only ten kilometers long, to be sure, but the first railroad in the country: the "Sociedad del Camino de Hierro de Buenos Aires al Oeste," or Western Railway. The porteños were quick to subscribe but slow to pay up, so the capital was small: 72,000 gold pesos. The company seems to have had odd ideas of locomotion. In 1854, the year the concession was granted, it petitioned the provincial government for release from the necessity of using a steam engine. It preferred, it seems, to employ "the horse, so cheap in this country, instead of coal, which is so expensive. Of course it produces less velocity, but enough. That is, all that the present state of our country could need." [32] In the next year the company brought William Bragg and a hundred sixty expert workmen from England, and began to build the railroad. An investment of 280,000 gold pesos was made by private subscription, the provincial government, and bondholders, and in 1857 the first ten kilometers of track was opened.

Buenos Aires was spared the interesting spectacle of a horse-drawn locomotive, however, by the importation of an old English locomotive which had seen service in the Crimean War, and which the British sold to the company as scrap iron. The locomotive, christened *La Porteña*, and still on display at the Luján museum for all to see, was of Russian extra-wide gauge, and because of this accidental fact, Argentina has had Russian-gauge railroads ever since. *La Porteña* got off to a bad start on her trial run. The day before the line opened, the directors got aboard, and preceded by a man on horseback to shoo people off the track, went chugging up the line. At Almagro *La Porteña* went off the track, injuring one of the directors. Those who had participated in the accident made a solemn pact to keep the accident a secret, for reasons of public confidence, and it was kept so well that the story did not come out until many years later.[33] The first mile or so of track was built like a trolley line down the streets of Buenos Aires, and Hutchinson, who made a trip to Moreno in 1862, described his surprise at "a roaring engine, dragging a train of carriages after it, through streets so narrow that one can almost touch the houses on either side." [34]

The Ferrocarril al Oeste had a magical effect on land prices. Speculators who bought acreage along the right of way and around the new railroad stations saw their investments soar to ten times their original value, and more. The effect of just ten kilometers of track—scarcely more than a suburban railway—gave the clue to what would be the effect on land values if the country were really opened by railroads. Alberdi, who was with Urquiza in Paraná, and could mourn the national government's poverty of capital, wished devoutly that foreign money could be brought in to lace the country with iron rails. Give it any concession you must, he argued, but get the money: "See that the pesos immigrate to these countries of future wealth and present poverty," he had pleaded in his *Bases*. "But the peso is an immigrant that demands concessions and privileges. Grant them, because capital is the left arm of progress." [35]

It was becoming apparent that without Buenos Aires the Confederation would be nothing. There was a sense of injury and outrage in Paraná. The best men, the greatest wealth, and all the port revenues were going to one province. Sarmiento, Mitre, Vélez Sarsfield, Alsina—all the great exiles but Alberdi were giving their services to Buenos Aires. Sarmiento had even descended to a nasty-toned exchange of letters with Alberdi because the latter had given his allegiance to the national government. If it could be of any comfort to him, Urquiza received the blessings and good wishes from overseas of the man he had overthrown. Alberdi, in London as Argentine minister, met the exiled Juan Manuel de Rosas in the house of English friends and had a long conversation with him. It was the first time Alberdi had ever seen the dictator face to face, and he looked at him with curiosity. Rosas spoke very respectfully of the nation and of the national government, and asked Alberdi to tell Urquiza that "he was very grateful for his upright and just conduct toward him; that if he had anything to live on, it was due to him. . . . On seeing him," wrote Alberdi, "I found him less guilty than Buenos Aires for his domination, because it was that of one of those foolish and mediocre men who abound in Buenos Aires, deliberate, audacious in action, and lacking in judgment." They talked of the new government, and Rosas "renewed his words of respect and submission. . . . He says that the government, the sovereign or superior authority that he alludes to, is that of the *Government of the Nation* or *Confederation*, not that of Buenos Aires." [36]

The Confederation was a curious union of provincial caudillos. It was a case of all the best people being against the nation, and the worst people supporting it. This was enough excuse for Buenos Aires to scorn Urquiza's government. But the government was constitutional, representative, and earnest. It was true that Urquiza could not afford to throw out the petty provincial tyrants, because they were his chief support, with Buenos Aires out. A case in point was Benavídez, who had ruled San Juan for twenty years. To Sarmiento he was a gaucho, a barbarian, an enemy of culture. Benavídez had resigned his governorship in 1855, but had gotten tired of his successor two years later and overthrown him. Using its prerogatives under Article 6 of the Constitution, the Paraná government intervened in the province and called an honest election. No sooner was the new governor elected than he threw Benavídez in prison, where he was murdered.

In Buenos Aires the news was received with rejoicing. The monster, Urquiza's henchman, was dead! But in Paraná there was immediate punitive action. The government had been willing to chastise Benavídez when he acted against the Constitution, but that did not give his enemies license to commit murder. Commissioners and troops were sent to San Juan, and governor, ministers, and judges were imprisoned. The commissioners dissolved the legislature and called new elections, and another governor was installed. It was by no means the end of trouble in San Juan. In Buenos Aires the federal intervention had outraged an important group whose leader was the Sanjuanino, Sarmiento. The porteños made political capital of the intervention, and added it to a long list of evidence that Urquiza was a dictator whose only supporters were the caudillos.

For Urquiza the situation was now intolerable. Buenos Aires, feeling its strength, and newly armed, invaded Uruguay, and the Uruguayan government had to appeal both to the Confederation and to Brazil for assistance. Urquiza raised six thousand men, but the invasion was repelled without his help. But now he had to face Mitre, who in 1859 marched from Buenos Aires to see if he could not overthrow the Paraná government. Mitre had the larger army, but at the battle of Cepeda he was beaten, and the triumphant Urquiza continued his march toward the capital. This time the porteños in alarm signed an agreement to enter the Confederation, and Urquiza retired with his troops.

In the period of negotiation that followed, both Buenos Aires and the Confederation elected new executives. In Buenos Aires Bartolomé Mitre, heading the porteño party that came to be called the Autonomistas, was elected governor, and he chose Domingo

Sarmiento as his minister of the interior. And in Paraná Urquiza, having come to the end of his six-year term as president, gave way to the newly elected Santiago Derqui. Mitre invited the general and the new president to come to Buenos Aires for the celebration of the 9th of July, the anniversary of Argentina's independence. The city was in festive mood, and gave Urquiza a great ovation. In September a new Constitutional Convention met in Santa Fe to study and accept Buenos Aires' suggested changes in the Constitution. On October 21, 1860, the assembled deputies were sworn in under the new Constitution.

In the national elections for deputies that followed, a curious thing happened. The Constitution stipulated how many representatives each province should have in the first Chamber of Deputies, and Buenos Aires was allotted twelve. Notwithstanding, the province held its elections in accordance with provincial law, and sent a larger number to Congress. It is hard to imagine what Buenos Aires expected to gain by this strange action. It could scarcely have expected Congress to seat the extra deputies. Congress, of course, did not, and once again, just when everything had seemed settled for good, Buenos Aires broke its relations with the national government, stopped payments of customs receipts to the treasury, and began to arm. In September, the last great battle between Buenos Aires and Argentina took place at Pavón. Mitre headed the provincial troops, and Urquiza the national. The result seems to have been indecisive, because both armies considered themselves defeated and retired. But Mitre rallied his forces and went on to Rosario. Urquiza signed a peace. What did Mitre want? Just two things: first, that the government should be on the basis of the Constitution of 1853–1860; second, that Urquiza should retire to Entre Ríos, where he might do as he pleased so long as he did not try to run the national government.

The peace was a strange commentary on the porteño mentality. If all that Mitre had wanted for the last decade was to obey the Constitution, why the civil war? Was there a single admitted issue that was keeping Buenos Aires out of the Confederation? Apparently not. For Mitre, Urquiza seems to have been the only issue. Once Urquiza was out of the way, and Mitre could be the national leader, he adopted the same policies and turned his best efforts to the organization of the nation. There were still some in Buenos Aires who thought the province was better off by itself with the port receipts, but they were becoming progressively less vocal. Even the porteños saw that their stand was inadmissible. At the end, then, the issue was reduced to whether Urquiza or Mitre should run the country. Even that was no longer an issue: Urquiza, the "dictator," the "bloody tyrant of Entre Ríos," whom Buenos Aires saw as no better than another Rosas, had relinquished the executive power at the end of his term, in strict accordance with the Constitution. So what was the issue? Perhaps that Bartolomé Mitre would like to be president.

The porteños, to the bitter end, saw themselves as the heroes of the national drama. "During this half-century of internal and external struggle," wrote one, "Buenos Aires contributed many times to the conservation of order and of the nationhood. Under its auspices constitutional assemblies met; the first navy was formed; ports were put into shape for commerce; the frontiers were guarded and were advanced southward; the first discount bank was established; foreign credit was initiated with the first loan; it gave its money to found a National Bank; it undertook alone the responsibility of the outstanding debts and national obligations; it founded, at its expense, university, statistical registry, agricultural school, and its share of establishments and institutions of administrative interest or social convenience; it abolished the slave traffic; established its deposit banks; arranged by itself, and at its own cost, the payment of the interest and amortization of the loan of London; constructed customhouses and wharves and the first railroads known in the Río de la Plata." For these contributions Buenos Aires had asked only one compensation: that the national income go to her. But now Buenos Aires had a new role to play. She was to put her culture, her genius, her generosity to work for the nation—all of it.[37]

CIVILIZATION AND BARBARISM

CIVILIZATION AND BARBARISM

The political and social thought animating the Liberal party tended to substitute for the despotic rule of the barbarian caudillos the oligarchic government of the enlightened minorities.
—LUIS H. SOMMARIVA, *Historia de las Intervenciones Federales.*

The porteño Unitarios, the Liberals, the luminaries were in power at last. Mitre had broken the Confederation, and by the victor's right power fell to him and his party.

For almost a year he exercised the governorship of Buenos Aires (legally) and the executive power of the nation (illegally), both simultaneously. His position was something like that of Rosas': he ruled by default. But in 1862 a new Congress was elected, and Mitre was voted President of the Argentine Republic. There was animation in the Liberal ranks. To them the future looked exceedingly bright. The nation was theirs to civilize, to educate, to make great. Sarmiento departed for his native province of San Juan to begin his work of salvation as governor. He would extirpate root and branch the last vestiges of the gaucho mentality, and the memory of that barbarian Benavídez. Almost his first measure was to forbid the wearing of the chiripá. For him, clothes were the symbol of culture. If a man wore a frock coat he was European, and hence civilized at heart. If he wore poncho and chiripá there was no hope for him. So just as Peter the Great shaved his boyar courtiers, Sarmiento put pants on San Juan.

In Buenos Aires the old question of the capital came up all over again. The Law of Capitalization had once broken Rivadavia's government because Buenos Aires refused to have its provincial government suppressed in order to make it a federal district. Mitre was, of course, a porteño to the bone, and therefore there was consternation in the province when this favored son took to

Congress exactly the same proposal Rivadavia had made: to capitalize the province and dissolve the legislature. The project was voted. But under the new constitution, the Buenos Aires legislature had to assent, and this it refused to do. An impasse resulted. To everyone, Buenos Aires was the only logical capital of the Republic. But it was impossible to have conflicting jurisdictions. Nobody saw the solution, and a temporary compromise was reached. For the next five years the national government would be the guest of the provincial government in the capital city. The raising of this old issue heated politics, and brought a split in the Liberal party. Those who followed Mitre were called Nacionalistas, and those who did not formed the Autonomista party under the leadership of Adolfo Alsina, son of that ultra-porteño, Valentín Alsina. In the slang of the time, the Nacionalistas were *cocidos* (*cocido* = cooked), and the Autonomistas were *crudos* (*crudo* = raw). But it soon became apparent that the settlement was not final, and that it was absurd for the nation to be the guest of one of its component provinces.

In the north, there was anarchy. In almost every province—in Córdoba, La Rioja, San Juan, Tucumán, San Luis, Santiago del Estero—opposition to the new porteño government of the nation led to open revolt and warfare. The *montoneras*, bands of mounted guerrillas, terrorized the countryside and laid siege to the cities. The caudillos, who had given their loyalty to the Paraná government, denied it to Buenos Aires. Where once the northern Andean provinces had spoken with fear of Facundo, they now trembled at another name: El Chacho. El Chacho was the caudillo of La Rioja, and his real name was Angel Vicente Peñaloza; but nobody called him anything but El Chacho. El Chacho had an irrepressible itch to invade his neighbors. He invaded San Juan four times, Tucumán three times, San Luis and Córdoba each once—being beaten, it must be said parenthetically, in every battle. This incidental fact did not discourage him in the least.

The porteños decreed war to the death against the caudillos. They had been waiting for years for a chance like this. Sarmiento had written his most brilliant works on Facundo Quiroga and

Aldao, and he did not now spare Peñaloza. But where once his warfare had been confined to an acid pen, now it could take more concrete forms. Mitre write to San Juan and gave Sarmiento authority to direct the war of pacification in the north. "My idea," he said, "can be summed up in two words: I want to make a police war in La Rioja. La Rioja is a cave of bandits who are a menace to their neighbors, and there is not even a government to police the province." Sarmiento replied that he would send So-and-so to do the job. "If he kills some people," he wrote coolly, "be quiet about it: they are two-legged animals of such perverse condition that I don't see what advantage there is in treating them better." [1]

El Chacho was a typical gaucho, except in color (he was blond and blue-eyed). He could not read or write, and signed his name with a mark. Sarmiento could not level against him the charge of ferocity which he had made against Facundo. "Few people have been killed by his order or vengeance," he admitted, "although thousands have died in the disorders he fomented." It did not matter. El Chacho was a barbarian, and away with him. Sarmiento charged him with another high crime: he used bad language, even worse than the ordinarily rude speech of the country people who had lived two centuries in isolation in the interior. "He was the same in dress and manners: seated in postures which the gaucho affects, with the foot of one leg resting on the thigh of the other, dressed in chiripá and poncho, usually in shirt sleeves, with a kerchief tied about his head." As may be seen, these charges were serious in the eyes of the man who had decreed a war of extermination against the chiripá. But this was not all: "Even in Chile, in the house where he was a guest, it was necessary to double the napkins to save the tablecloth where he dribbled when he lifted his spoon to his mouth." [2]

Peñaloza cheerfully assumed the title of "General in Chief of the Reactionary Army" and prepared for battle. To his simple mind he was Urquiza's man, doing as Urquiza would have done—as he probably would do. In fact, he called on the caudillo of Entre Ríos to head the revolt against the despised porteños. He did not understand, any more than the Liberals did, that Urquiza was an Argentine, that his fight had been for national unity, and that he would do nothing to break that unity now that it had been achieved. Urquiza was a greater man than either his enemies or his friends gave him credit for being. To El Chacho's hurt surprise, Urquiza immediately offered his services to Mitre.

Sarmiento was a curious character. That he was a genius, no one can doubt. He was a truly self-made man, without the benefits of formal education or of the polish that comes from life in a large city. He had not seen a city bigger than Santiago until he reached middle age. Perhaps the rudeness of his early surroundings, and the violence of his reaction against those surroundings, can account for the irrelevance and snobbery of some of his ideas about what constituted civilization. Thus, in his letters written from the United States, he stresses again and again that even the most isolated farmers wore *frock coats*; that they had *watches*, and complicated watches at that, that rang bells and played tunes and told when the moon would rise and set. "He loved civilization," wrote Lucio V. Mansilla, who knew him well, "—and was a barbarian in his intransigent partisan polemics. . . . He loved education and was uncultured, in spite of his travels." [3] Sarmiento was a ferocious egoist, too. His genius was more than matched by his good opinion of himself. But fundamentally he was right. Wherever he went, if only on a trip, he founded a school. This was his contribution to that "civilization" he talked about so constantly. If Argentines were educated, all would be well.

The gaucho must be exterminated. To him El Chacho was symbolic, and he had to be wiped off the face of the earth so that his simple-minded followers would remember his end and take the lesson to heart. The pursuit lasted a year. The caudillo never had to use coercion to raise soldiers—in direct contrast to what happened with the national forces. Sarmiento's comment on this phenomenon speaks eloquently of what the matter was: those poor *provincianos* "have few interests to keep them in their wretched houses; the family lives from a fistful of corn or the meat of a goat, and war is life, emotion, hope." [4] The national forces pursued Peñaloza until they had annihilated his scrubby militia, and they finally cornered El Chacho himself. It was in the small hill town of Olta, the evening of November 11, 1863. The caudillo, in shirt sleeves and chiripá, was quietly drinking mate when he was surprised. He offered no resistance. The soldiers tied him, pierced him with a lance, and shot him with their carbines. They cut off his head, and put it on a pike, where the whole town could come to stare at the dead features and white beard of El Chacho. When Sarmiento heard the news, he wrote a happy letter to the President. "If the head of that inveterate rogue had not been cut off and displayed," he told Mitre, "the rabble wouldn't have quieted down in six months." [5] In this way, civilization came to La Rioja.

In 1864 Mitre named Sarmiento Argentine Minister to the United States he so admired. In 1865 Mitre's war against the caudillos was suspended for more urgent warfare: in that year Argentina, Brazil, and Uruguay went to war against the small, tough republic of Paraguay. The Paraguayan war, undertaken lightly, became a nightmare to all concerned before it was through. It started because of Argentine-Brazilian intervention in Uruguay's internal politics. Francisco Solano López, who was director of Paraguay, warned that intervention in Uruguay would mean war. When Brazilian troops nevertheless invaded Uruguay, López marched, and soon everyone was involved against him. The war, for purposes of this story, is not too important, but it was a drain on Argentina's men and resources at a time when the young nation could ill afford it. The fight was without quarter. Paraguay was fantastically outnumbered in men. Its soldiers were no more than barefoot Indians. Nevertheless, the fighting was done, not on Paraguayan but on Argentine soil, and it went on until the Paraguayans were killed almost to a man, and both López and his son were shot. Between 1865 and 1870 the population of Paraguay was reduced from a million and a half to two hundred thousand. Of this remnant only 10 per cent were males.[6] During most of this war Mitre himself was in the field, so that his government's best energies in the end were directed toward a costly and useless war. When his term drew to a close, he had lost much popularity, and the 1868 elections went to the Autonomistas—the Alsinistas (the *crudos*, if you please). In April of that year Domingo F. Sarmiento and Adolfo Alsina were elected President and Vice-President of the Argentine Republic. Sarmiento had reached the culmination of his ambitions.

The Argentine Minister to Washington embarked for Buenos Aires before he knew the outcome of that election. He had been long days at sea when his ship sailed into the Brazilian port of Pernambuco. In the harbor was an American warship that had already heard the news from Argentina. When Sarmiento's ship came in sight the American commodore ordered a twenty-one-gun salute; and this was the way that Domingo Sarmiento discovered he was the President of Argentina.[7]

It was characteristic of Sarmiento that his first act as President was to find out exactly what he was President of. Sarmiento ordered a census, the first census of the Argentine Republic. He wanted to know how many people there were in the country, where they lived, what kind of houses they had, and whether they could read or write. It was the first official count that had ever been taken. (The Argentine Constitution, unlike the American, does not provide for censuses every ten years. There have been only three in Argentine history, the most recent in 1914.* The picture that the 1869 census revealed was not very heartening. There were 1,800,000 people. Exactly one-tenth lived in the city of Buenos Aires. One-third lived in the city and province of Buenos Aires. One-half lived in the littoral (Buenos Aires, Santa Fe, Entre Ríos, and Corrientes). The rest were scattered through the jungles and mountains and desert of ten other provinces and four territories.[8] Of the total population, 88 per cent were criollos, and 12 per cent foreign-born.[9]

Argentines were not well housed. Only one-fifth of the population lived in brick or adobe houses, and almost all of these were in the province of Buenos Aires, which had more than the rest of the Republic put together. Four-fifths of the people lived in huts of twigs, or cane, or straw, with dirt floors, and 78 per cent were illiterate. The most literate province was Buenos Aires, fol-

* The present military government has ordered a new census.

lowed by Santa Fe and Sarmiento's native San Juan.[10] One of the curious features of this literacy count was that considerably more people claimed to be able to read than claimed to be able to write.*

Mansilla has said of Sarmiento that "his politics and government were without plan, like his travels—he saw much, and observed what he could." [11] This is only a half-truth. It is true that his presidency seems almost an anticlimax to the rest of his life. But there was one thing he did for Argentina, and this was the work toward which his whole life had been pointed: he founded its primary educational system, and he introduced a philosophy of education which the school system has never lost. Sarmiento was a personal friend and admirer of Horace Mann. To him, the work of the young American nation in the field of free public education was the most promising in the world, and long before he was President he had observed that education at first hand and returned to Chile to put it into practice. Now that he was President, he would do this for Argentina. Sarmiento chose as his Minister of Public Instruction a young man just turned thirty. His name was Nicolás Avellaneda, and he was short, thin, and feeble. Because Avellaneda used to teeter about on high heels he was nicknamed "Taquito" —Little Heel.[12] Taquito and Sarmiento almost doubled the number of schools in Argentina during their six years in office. The President travelled up and down the country, opening schools. When he left office there were 1,645 public schools with 103,000 pupils, the highest proportion of any country in South America.[13] He founded free libraries all over the country. He brought American teachers to organize normal schools. He opened the Naval School, the Military Academy, the Academy of Exact Sciences, the Schools of Mining and Agronomy. He began the system of school inspection, night schools, the teaching of civics, physics, and physical education. He built the first observatory. He founded the first school for deaf-mutes.

* The number that said they could read was 360,683; 312,001 said they could write (*Primer Censo*, etc., p. xxxvi). This would suggest that the border line between literacy and illiteracy was very tenuous indeed.

During his presidency Sarmiento made his peace with Urquiza. The peace was more of Urquiza's making than Sarmiento's: the President was not popular because he was not a party man, and because he was so disagreeable nobody could get along with him. When Urquiza saw that much that Sarmiento was doing for national unity was misunderstood and attacked by those around him, he wrote the President, assuring him of his support. Sarmiento had never shown the slightest generosity or comprehension when the Entrerriano had been trying to hold the Confederation together. He had conspired against him, insulted him, and attacked him on every occasion. Nevertheless, Urquiza bore no grudges, and when Sarmiento saw that Urquiza understood what he was trying to do, he rather shamefacedly made friends with him. The peace was sealed on February 3, 1870, the eighteenth anniversary of the battle of Caseros, when the President travelled to Urquiza's estancia of San José, in Entre Ríos, to be his guest at a celebration of the overthrow of Rosas. There was a parade of 15,000 militiamen, and relations between the President and Governor were most cordial.

But in Entre Ríos there was a powerful feeling against Buenos Aires among the old Federales, and when they saw this public display of friendship towards the President, whom they considered a damned porteño, there was considerable dissatisfaction. Next to Urquiza, the strongest caudillo of the province was Ricardo López Jordán, a Federal of the old stripe. Opposition to Urquiza centered around him. Just two months after Sarmiento's visit to San José a group of sixty fanatics, followers of López Jordán, broke into the estancia house at night. Urquiza was alone with his family. He was shot in the face and killed. At the same time, in other parts of Entre Ríos, two of his sons were murdered. The provincial legislature then elected Ricardo López Jordán to fill out Urquiza's unexpired term of office.

When the news reached Buenos Aires, Sarmiento knew that his war against the caudillo mentality was not over. As he had persecuted El Chacho to the end, he determined to bring Urquiza's murderers to justice. "Our Constitution," he said, "like all human constitutions of which it is the copy, continuation, and result, does not admit the elevation of the assassin to an office left vacant by assassination." [14] He ordered national troops to Entre Ríos. They went by ship and anchored in the river, staying aboard. But Sarmiento decided that the time had come to disembark them. If they remain in the river, he argued, it will look as if the national forces do not have authority to disembark anywhere in Argentina. It was time to impress on everyone that provincial sovereignty was finished. "The national forces are at home wherever national laws are in force," he declared.[15] The troops were ordered to invade Entre Ríos.

López Jordán raised the provincial militia, and the war was on. There is no doubt he had the support of most of Entre Ríos. "The history of interventions," he said, "is written in blood in the tragic pages of the Argentine provinces. They have served to overthrow governments legitimately constituted; have reviled provincial sovereignty . . . ; have carried disorder and death to once prosperous and flourishing towns." [16] The fight was bloody and bitter. It was hatred of Buenos Aires, not of the national government, that kept it going. "The popular support that López Jordán had," writes Luis H. Sommariva, "is explained by his preaching war against the porteños, not against the federal powers." [17] The caudillo was finally beaten, and in 1871 he fled to Brazil. The backbone of Federalism was broken at last. The feeling took a long time dying—indeed, it is far from dead yet—but there was no fight left in the provinces. Mitre and Sarmiento between them finished the gaucho. It was what they had wanted to do.

It is not a simple coincidence that Argentina's great gaucho epic, *Martín Fierro*, was published in 1872. Like the literature of the American South that wrote of rebellion when it was dead, and glorified an epoch that had been ended beyond resurrection, José Hernández's *El Gaucho Martín Fierro* was the defense of an age that had finished. Hernández had been a Rosista to the bitter end; with Rosas gone, he had moved to Paraná where the Federal Urquiza had his capital; when Peñaloza was killed, he had written a life of El Chacho; when Sarmiento was President he founded a newspaper to attack him; and finally, when López Jordán took to arms, Hernández went to Entre Ríos and fought with him until he was beaten. Down the line, Hernández was a defender of the old order. When physical resistance was put down beyond hope of revolt, he wrote his long poem on the life and sufferings of a gaucho. *Martín Fierro* is widely considered as the best work in Argentine literature. Whatever its poetic merits—they are not beyond dispute—it is a true picture of the life and language, the thought and rather simple wisdom of the nineteenth century Argentine gaucho.

Martín Fierro, like his fellows, is a persecuted man. He is drunk one night in a pulpería when there is a killing, and, because he does not escape in time, the authorities take him prisoner along with an "inglés sanjiador"—an English ditch digger. He is pressed into the army, into the frontier service against the Indians. He escapes and turns *gaucho malo* and is persecuted by the police, who do not understand his love of freedom. "My glory is to live as free as a bird in the sky," he says; "there is no one who can make me build my nest on the ground, where there is so much to suffer, and no one who can follow my flight." Martín Fierro does not consider himself bad: he never fights or kills unless he has to. Finally Fierro takes refuge among the Indians. Thus far, Part I.

But the second part, *La Vuelta de Martín Fierro* (The Return of Martín Fierro), which appeared in 1879, is a very different piece indeed. And here, perhaps, lies the significance of what was happening in that decade. In the second part of the poem, the gaucho leaves the Indians and returns to society, to the life of order and democracy against which he had at first rebelled. Did Hernández have a change of heart? It would appear so. Argentina, and with it the last of the rebels, was coming of age.

Whatever Sarmiento's faults, whatever his inconsistencies, he was a great civilizer. One may be revolted by his pleasure at the barbarous end of Peñaloza. One may reflect that, whatever his admiration for European culture, Sarmiento's greatest writing was about the despised gaucho. One may laugh at his war on the chiripá. One may admit that he was proud, intransigent, and disagreeable. Mansilla said that he did not have nobility of spirit, and even this was true. But no one can deny that he was a great writer, a great educator, and a great Argentine. When all was said and done, he was right: the gaucho was an anachronism. "The day they sound my last retreat," he once said, "you can say with justice: accompany that corpse; you will never again pay equal honors to a more illustrious Argentine." [18] And it was true.

THE CONQUEST OF THE DESERT

> *Sad experience had taught us this inevitable law: civilization and barbarism were two forces which lived invading each other; it was not possible to fix a limit where both would be stationary, facing each other; if one stopped, the other trespassed.*
>
> —Manuel J. Olascoaga, *La Conquista del Desierto.*

Sarmiento's presidential term was drawing to a close. In February of 1874 elections began for his successor in office.

There were two candidates. Sarmiento and Alsina favored young Taquito (Avellaneda, the Minister of Public Instruction), who was only thirty-seven. Bartolomé Mitre, however, presented his candidacy, and he had a powerful party behind him. The elections, like all elections of the time, were violent, fraudulent, and bloody. People were beaten up when they tried to approach the polls. The voting urns were broken open, and the ballots stolen. Possibly because the government candidate had a little more force on his side, when the returns were in, it was announced that he had won. Who really had won is almost a metaphysical question. The electoral mechanism in Argentina in those days was very imperfect. At any rate, though the election was fraudulent, it was no more so than those that had preceded it.

When Mitre saw his ambitions for a second term cheated, he decided to settle the issue by force, and accordingly, a revolution broke out against the Sarmiento government on September 25, just a month before Avellaneda's inauguration was to take place. Mitre escaped to Colonia, Uruguay, and from there he began the direction of a military uprising.

Now it so happened that at this time the Argentine army was chiefly occupied in garrisoning the southern frontier against the Indians who, since the fall of Rosas, had been steadily encroaching. The porteño dictator had pushed the frontier in the west to the Cordillera of the Andes, in the south to Valchetas. He had established forts, and by a system of bribes had kept the tribes at peace. But during the ten-year struggle between Buenos Aires and the Confederation these forts had been abandoned, and the Indians had invaded from the south, burning estancia houses and carrying the whites as prisoners to their camps in Tierra Adentro. Many were the stories of Christian women held as wives and concubines by the Pampa Indians. The stories were true, as testified by the interesting account Colonel Mansilla made of his trip to the Ranqueles during the Sarmiento administration, when he negotiated a treaty of peace with the tribe of Mariano Rosas. Mansilla found many Christians living with the Indians, some as prisoners, some as political refugees after the fall of Juan Manuel de Rosas.

When Mitre revolted, most of his military support came from these frontier garrisons, which meant a further abandonment to the encroaching savages, more burnings, more kidnappings, and more pleas for help from the southern estancieros. To put down the Mitre revolt, Sarmiento called on General Julio A. Roca, who defeated him. Serious as Mitre's offense was, the government pardoned him, and he emerged from the episode with little damage to his fame. "Virtue of seduction, this," wrote Paul Groussac, ". . . which permitted its possessor to salvage his reputation from unheard-of failures . . . only to be raised higher than ever by popular acclaim." Groussac once asked Mitre to what he attributed his prestige, and the General replied: "To the fact that I have never wanted to be a caudillo." [19] Mitre was still the idol of the porteños, and Sarmiento, Avellaneda, and Alsina all lost popularity in Buenos Aires as a result of the fight with him. It was two years later, on July 4, 1876, that the American Minister gave a great ball in honor of the hundredth anniversary of American independence. Avellaneda, now President, Alsina, his Minister of War, and the defeated General Mitre were all present, together with a huge crowd of porteños who were guests at the Ministry. When the people recognized Mitre they began shouting "Viva el general Mitre!" and demanded a speech from their hero. Both Avellaneda and Alsina walked out, followed by the hoots and whistles of the crowd.[20]

The situation in the south was now very serious indeed. The government had been steadily retreating, the Indians steadily advancing. Estancia after estancia had to be abandoned for lack of military protection. Adolfo Alsina, the Minister of War, had been turning over in his mind the idea of establishing a new line of frontier forts. He did not know what this would cost, or how strong an opposition the Indians could offer. As a matter of fact, neither he nor anyone else had any idea how many Indians there were. "A fantastic legend surrounded the interior," wrote one contemporary many years later, in retrospect. "The pampa was still a mystery. It was said there would be no resources of any kind, that the troops would be defeated and would die of hunger and thirst, that the troops of horses would die, and that it would be only with the greatest difficulty that the soldiers could become masters of the territory they invaded." [21] There was a strong newspaper campaign in Buenos Aires against the project of invading the "desert," as it was called.

On October 6, 1875, Alsina wrote a letter to General Roca, who was encamped out on the Río Cuarto, explaining his ideas. "Every day I am more convinced that the present line of the Río Quinto should be advanced . . ." he told Roca. "If nothing extraordinary happens to prevent it, my idea is, the middle or end of February, to advance the Buenos Aires lines in the extreme south as far as Carhué, in the center to Laguna del Monte, and in the west to Tunas or Trenque Lauquen." He then went on to speak of the treaty the Sarmiento government had signed with the Ranquel chief, Mariano Rosas; and it was clear that he contemplated treachery. "The trimonthly ration today costs the nation 15,000 pesos because, though the understanding was to pay them in horses, we have been giving them cows, which cost twice as much. Without for the moment modifying the treaty in this part, it might be wise to make some arrangement so that the Ranqueles could render some useful service, instead of just paying them not to make war, which is not bad business for them. I also believe—perhaps I am wrong—that, since the treaty was made, the tribe of Mariano Rosas, far from increasing, has been weakened by the decimation it has suffered." [22]

When the cacique Rosas had signed his treaty with Mansilla, he had had a presentiment of treachery of this sort. The savage was astute in his own way. Mansilla recounts how one day during the negotiations Mariano Rosas called him to his tent, opened a bag, and took from it a copy of the Buenos Aires newspaper *La Tribuna*. He had marked an article on the project for a great interoceanic railroad to Chile. "Read it, brother," he told Mansilla. Mansilla, who knew the article, told him he knew what it was about. "Then why haven't you been frank with me?" demanded the cacique. Colonel Mansilla was embarrassed, and asked Rosas what harm the railroad could possibly do the Ranqueles. "What harm?" said the Indian. "Why, that after they build the railroad the Christians will say they need more land to the south, and they will want to throw us out of here, and we will have to go to the south of the Río Negro, to other lands, because between these lands and the Río Colorado or the Río Negro there are no good places to live." [23] This was, as a matter of fact, exactly what Alsina was proposing to do, and it was not even a question of the interoceanic railway.

Roca's reply to the Minister of War's letter reads at first as if he were reproving Alsina for his contemplated treachery. "To establish the line at the Cuero," he wrote, "we have to consider as broken our peace with the Ranqueles who, to tell the truth, have kept their promises faithfully in spite of the frontier's having been completely abandoned since the September rebellion. The Indians would look on it as an attack on their rights . . . because they consider these lands theirs, and even those we are already occupying, as can be seen from the claims they have made at different times, and in whose defense they have often taken to arms." This was the beginning of the letter; but it was a long letter, and as Alsina read farther he could discover that what Roca contemplated was not keeping peace with the Ranqueles, but the greatest treachery of all: he would wipe Rosas' tribe, and every other tribe, from the face of the map. Nothing of establishing a new line of forts: it should be a war of extermination.

"In my opinion," he went on, "the best system of finishing with the Indians, either exterminating them or pushing them back of the Río Negro, is an offensive war, which is the same system that Rosas used, and Rosas almost wiped them out. Forts established in the middle of the desert kill discipline, decimate troops, and dominate little or no space. In my opinion, the best fort, the best wall, for making war against the Pampa Indians and reducing them for once and all, is a regiment or fraction of troops of both arms, well mounted, who will constantly patrol the Indian country and fall on the Indians where they least expect it. . . . I could promise, Mr. Minister, to the government and to the country, to do this job in two years: one to prepare, the other to carry out the campaign." [24]

Alsina was not convinced by Roca's promise. He still believed it best to whittle a little at a time; so, paying no attention to the General's ambitious suggestion, he ordered the establishment of the new frontier forts, and took to the field to direct the campaign himself. In the autumn of the next year the line was extended exactly as projected. But Roca had been right after all. In spite of the forts, there was a simultaneous uprising of tribes in the spring that was so well coordinated as to suggest an intelligent secret direction. The savages broke across the frontier in three great waves, from the south, the east, and the north, devastating sixteen hundred square kilometers of settled land, burning, killing, and stealing the livestock. Beating the Indians did no good: they simply melted away into the pampa—abandoning, it is true, their booty. In October the last pampa chief who was not in revolt took to arms. The Indians were intoxicated with success. This last rebelling cacique presented insolent demands to the Argentine government. Abandon the frontier, he said, or pay his tribe an indemnity of 200,000,000 pesos, plus 6,000 head of livestock every two months. He also wanted various gold and silver adornments, and the life salary of general for himself and his chiefs.[25]

A solution to this situation was delayed by Alsina's falling ill while on his campaign. The Minister of War died in December, 1877, without having solved the problem of the frontiers. General Roca was named in his place, and now it was possible for him to carry out his ambitious plan of finishing the Indians once for all. The new Minister prepared his campaign very carefully. He got Congress to vote him an appropriation of a million and a half gold pesos, which was less than the annual cost of sustaining the frontier. He equipped five divisions for the invasion, and sent out four ahead of him in the autumn of 1879. They were to make a clean sweep, and kill or capture every Indian they could find. The campaign proved very easy indeed, and the Indians were rounded up like cattle. As a matter of fact, killing Indians was the simplest part of the battle. More difficult was the problem of getting food, and keeping warm in the bitter winter. Many soldiers died of pneumonia, and the Third Division was decimated by an epidemic of smallpox. Both prisoners and troops died like flies. In April the Minister of War himself, heading the First Division, set out for Tierra Adentro, following the route already taken by the other four divisions. Roca's troops fought no Indians, and the only difficulty which they may be said to have had was that of finding food. After a month they were reduced to eating horse meat. The diary of one of the officers with Roca tells feelingly of how disgusting this food was. "Even the smoke of the fires where it is roasted is insupportable," he wrote. "The special odor it gives off contaminates the whole countryside. It is mortifying to see the impassive way the soldiers eat it. The mate, the coffee, made in the fire where horse meat is roasting, arrive with the same smell and taste. Then there is the moral suffering of watching the slaughter of these animals, which one is not accustomed to seeing killed: because they are such close companions of man, one looks on them almost as friends." [26]

As the First Division advanced, Roca received continuous messages from the preceding troops. The campaign was a total success. Finally, after a month of steady riding, the Minister of War and his men reached the mecca that had been the dream of so many years. On May 24, Julio A. Roca reached the Río Negro. The First Division drew rein, and from the embankment contemplated the green valley. There were rows of willows, and the river was "like a sash of silver, losing itself in the trees, reappearing, dividing, disappearing in the form of successive lakes." [27] Slowly, single-file, the soldiers descended to the water. At sundown they were beside the Río Negro. They followed the river beside the woods, and soon the woods were full of men cutting branches for the fires. That night there was a chain of campfires along the river. The men put on their teakettles of water and brewed the inevitable mate, passing the gourd around in order of rank: the first infusion for the man who prepared it, the second for the sergeant, and so on down the line.[28] And then, in a sad anticlimax, they ate a dinner of horse meat.

Out in the water was the island of Choele Choel, which the Buenos Aires legislature had once so generously offered to Rosas, and which he with equal generosity had refused after considering the possibilities of ever holding it against the Indians. Suddenly someone in the party cried: "There are people on the island!" It was indeed so. It turned out to be a small force of soldiers that had preceded the First. The men shouted back and forth across three hundred yards of river. From the island a voice asked if they had meat. "Horse meat," was the reply. There was a pause, while the men on the island launched a boat, and the commandant rowed over, bringing the carcass of half an ox. Roca ordered it to be scrupulously divided, and there was great contentment among his soldiers. The next morning was the 25th of May, anniversary of the May Revolution, and at dawn there was a solemn reveille. All who were present felt that the moment was historic, that the independence that had begun with the revolt of Buenos Aires had been completed with the Conquest of the Desert.[29]

Across the Río Negro lay the arid, cold Patagonian desert and the southern end of the Cordillera that ended in low hills at the Straits of Magellan. In the next four years Argentine soldiers ended the work that had started in 1879 with the campaign against the Pampas. The Conquest of the Desert was really completed at Nahuel Huapí, that beautiful wooded lake high in the Andes which is today a national park. At San Carlos de Bariloche, in the Swiss civic center overlooking the lake front, stands the statue of Julio A. Roca,—unique among equestrian statues, because the horse is neither rearing nor pawing the air, but standing with drooping head and slack reins, looking very tired. There the bronze Roca can contemplate every day the blue water and red hills that the flesh-and-blood Roca never saw. But the tribute is just. The idea was his.

In after years Roca the Conqueror of the Desert was to be lost in Roca the politician. He succeeded Avellaneda as President for six years, and he served again at the end of the century. Of Roca the politician, a woman who knew him has written: "He had neither talent . . . nor culture. He did not know how to speak in public . . . or to write." He was "a simple politician, with considerable gall and few scruples." [30] Thus, perhaps it is better to remember him for his clearest achievement. As Sarmiento wrote in *El Nacional:* "General Roca saw it, and it is to him in great part that we owe the discovery of a truth—there were no such Indians" as the imaginary hordes in popular legend. There had never been more than two thousand in the whole pampa. "Thinking it over well," said Sarmiento, "one is ashamed that we needed a powerful military establishment and sometimes eight thousand men to finish off just two thousand lances." [31]

THE LAND—II

THE COLONIES: AN EXPERIMENT

We have more than enough land—what we lack is labor and capital.
—NICOLÁS AVELLANEDA, *Estudios sobre las Leyes de Tierras Públicas.*

The province of Buenos Aires was in the hands of the great landholders whose estancias constituted principalities. This was a source of uneasiness to the thoughtful, who saw that Argentina could not be great if it had no population. Unless the land could be given in small parcels, how could it attract European immigrants, small farmers who in Italy or France or Switzerland had had a handful of acres, two or three cows, and a few pigs? They would certainly not cross the Atlantic to work as peons if they had been small proprietors at home.

During Urquiza's government the littoral provinces that were up-river from Buenos Aires, and still half wild and unsettled, such as Santa Fe, Entre Ríos, and Corrientes, decided on their own initiative to contract with European families to settle in small colonies on lands donated by them. This was the beginning of an experiment that was to go on until the end of the century. Each colony was a story by itself: usually of heartbreak that sometimes ended in success, sometimes in failure. Occasionally these European immigrants suffered unheard-of hardships.

The first permanent colony in Argentina was La Esperanza, in the province of Santa Fe. The government of Santa Fe made a contract with Aaron Castellanos to bring out two hundred families from Switzerland, and because the terms of the contract and its results were typical of what was to come, perhaps it would be profitable to describe them. The families, first of all, had to promise to come to the Río Paraná. Castellanos had to advance their passage money of 1,200 francs, and they were to pay him back the capital in three years, plus 10 per cent interest on that money every year for ten years. The government of Santa Fe would advance to each family seven cows and one bull, two oxen, two work horses, flour, seeds and sprouts of potatoes, peanuts, tobacco, cotton and wheat, enough corn for ten cuadras, and a two-room house. Total value, 200 patacoons, to be repaid in two years without interest. The family was to give Castellanos one-third of the harvest for five years.[1]

Now in examining this contract one sees at once that both Castellanos and the government of Santa Fe were very optimistic about the immediate yields of the colony. The colonists were expected at once to begin paying off capital and interest on passage money, capital on livestock and house, besides paying a third of their harvest to the contractor every year. The story of what happened to La Esperanza, to Castellanos, and to all concerned in the project, should have been a warning to future colonizers. As a matter of fact, it was not.

La Esperanza was situated about twenty miles northeast of the town of Santa Fe. At first the colonists were received well by the governor, Don José María Cullen, who had prepared everything against their arrival, and who went out each Sunday to see how things were coming along. But politics intervened to remove the solicitous governor. Cullen was suspected of conspiring with the porteño party against the Confederation, and a few weeks after the colonists arrived he was driven out by Juan Pablo López, brother of the late caudillo Estanislao. López took no interest in the colony, and Aaron Castellanos, who saw his whole personal fortune jeopardized in the venture, appealed to the Paraná government to take it off his hands. The Urquiza government agreed, paying Castellanos the 40,000 pesos he had spent, plus a generous indemnity of 70,000 pesos. If the national government had not done this, there is no telling what would have happened to the colonists—because the government relieved them at once of their obligation to pay a third of their harvest. But even with this help La Esperanza suffered terribly the first four years of its existence. Locusts ate the crops. Some of the colonists abandoned the land for the city. Others, like the natives, went into the woods and began making charcoal.[2]

In the end, perseverance won out. Alejo Peyret, who made a long trip to the interior in the late eighties, visiting and reporting on all the colonies, said that the agricultural wealth of La Esperanza was now valued at 2,000,000 gold pesos. The colonists, who were Italian, French, Swiss, German, with a sprinkling of English, Spanish, and Belgians, had thirteen thousand head of livestock. The town had a hundred and eighty business houses. Over the town hall of Esperanza was a motto symbolic of the idea that had given birth to it: "Subdivision of the Land." [3]

After this start, the colonies multiplied. In the next year several were started in Corrientes, Santa Fe, and Entre Ríos. One of the more interesting was that of San José, which was supposed to have been founded in Corrientes, because it was the government of Corrientes that had contracted with Carl Beck of Basel to bring the colonists out. When the first hundred colonists arrived, however, they were told the contract was no longer valid. Beck, not knowing where to turn for help, presented himself to Urquiza. The President felt that the national government could not undertake this obligation, but he offered the colonists some of his own land to settle on. It was up on the Río Uruguay, in Entre Ríos, and he offered each family a plot six hundred yards square, four oxen, two cows, two horses, and a hundred Bolivian pesos to buy seeds and instruments. No telling what the colonists expected to find in this wild country. Apparently they had been told about the orange groves that grew along the banks of the Uruguay, because, when the boat arrived at the spot where the orange trees were supposed to grow, one old German refused to disembark, "contemplating with fury the jungle trees, so different from the vegetation he expected to find, and striding from one side to another like a caged animal." [4]

At first the colonists lived from game. They shot ostriches and deer, nutria, ducks, and partridges. None of them had ever seen such quantities of wild life, and there was a perfect orgy of shooting. After they were given their livestock and money for tools they planted vineyards and raised chickens. The colony was surrounded by estancias, and since the land was unfenced, the animals invaded it day and night. There was considerable argument over whether it was up to the estancieros to build fences to keep their animals in, or up to the colonists to build fences to keep the animals out. Urquiza liked this experiment of San José well enough to send an agent to Europe in 1859 to bring two hundred more families. The agent was a priest, and he brought only Catholic families from Piedmont.

There were many other colonies. The San Carlos was also contracted for with Beck and Herzog of Basel. Located in Santa Fe, it was successful and flourished. San Gerónimo, like San José, was founded on private lands, donated in this case by Richard Foster, a Santa Fe estanciero. The colony of California was rather different from the others, in that the families were Americans, that they bought the land themselves from the government at 300 Bolivian pesos per square league, and that they brought their own implements. They were the first colony asking no aid from the government. Colonies multiplied so fast that by 1897 in Santa Fe alone there were 335, holding more than three and a half *million* hectares.[5] No one has ever made a thorough study of the colonies, their success and failure as a system of settlement. But one notes immediately the difference between the two agricultural and livestock provinces of Santa Fe and Buenos Aires. Whatever the success of colonies as such, Santa Fe is a very different province from Buenos Aires just because so much of its land is in the hands of small proprietors. Santa Fe, for instance, is the only province in Argentina with a real farmers' union. It has an agrarian party that is progressive, and that has given the country one of the most brilliant figures in twentieth century politics. It is not too much to infer that the reason for this is that not all the land of Santa Fe got into the hands of a small and reactionary class. Santa Fe's early isolation, which made its lands worthless until the building of railroads and river ports, was a stroke of luck for the province.

One of the problems of Argentine colonization has been to keep the colonists on the land. The early difficulties which these settlements often suffered were discouraging to those who had not expected them; and many families gave up and drifted to the cities, where living was comparatively easy. When one reads the story of some of the colonies, one is less surprised at those who gave up than at those who persevered. Among these was the first Argentine Jewish colony, established in the province of Santa Fe.

There were Jews in Argentina before the 1810 Revolution, though they were not recognized as such. They were called "Portuguese," because they had come in from Brazil. A section of northern Brazil had belonged for an interval to Holland, and Holland was the refuge of many Jews persecuted in other countries for their religion: when the whole of Brazil returned to the crown of Portugal, however, and the Catholic Inquisition was reintroduced, the Jews emigrated to the Plata, which was a poor Spanish colony where the Inquisition was of no importance. There the Jews became rapidly assimilated to the population, and were lost as a distinctive community.

It was in 1889, as a result of the pogroms in Russia under Alexander III, that a great stream of Jewish immigration began coming to both North and South America. One group of families bought land from the Argentine consul in Paris, and arrived in Buenos Aires on August 14, 1889, aboard a ship called the Weser. This was the first large, recognizable group of Jewish immigrants in the country. Most of them were city merchants who had never been on a farm in their lives. Nevertheless, with high hopes, they arrived in Argentina, believing they would work the land and found a new life in a country whose Constitution guaranteed the benefits of liberty "to all men of the world who want to inhabit the Argentine soil." [6]

Their first disillusionment came when they were told in Buenos Aires that the land the Paris consul had sold them was gone. Their money was returned to them, and after looking about they made a colonization contract with an estanciero of Santa Fe named Pedro Palacios. Palacios sold them land at 25 pesos a hectare plus 15 pesos for instruments and seeds. When they arrived at the railroad station of Palacios, there was neither food nor shelter for them. They ate wormy flour, and slept in wagons. They were not shown their land, and they were not given implements. As time passed, their situation became truly horrible. Most of the children died in an epidemic, and were buried there beside the station in an improvised cemetery. Many of the colonists returned to Buenos Aires or Santa Fe. Those who remained at Palacios lived from the charity of railroad peons who distributed biscuits to the children. Passengers on trains threw them table leftovers.[7]

There is no telling what would have been the denouement of this tragedy if a wealthy Swiss Jew had not happened to pass through Palacios. During the time his train stopped, he had the opportunity to see what was happening to these wretched people; and he was so moved that he returned at once to Europe and called on Baron Maurice Hirsch, a multimillionaire German-Jewish financier and philanthropist. He also talked to Palacios, and got him to move the colonists to what became the colony of Moisesville. Every family received a canvas tent for cover. The first year at Moisesville, too, was terrible, and many who had survived the stay in Palacios became too discouraged to fight any longer, and moved away. As for Baron Hirsch, he became so interested in the plight of these first Jewish settlers in the Argentine that he founded the Jewish Colonization Association, which in time brought many Jewish immigrants to Argentina.

The roll of colonies, even of colonizing companies, which later became popular, is long, and each project is a story by itself. Colonies were founded in the territory of La Pampa, across the Río Negro. There are colonies even farther south, in Chubut and Santa Cruz. Others have been founded in the grape provinces of San Juan and Mendoza, some in Córdoba and Buenos Aires. There are many who still believe that colonization is the solution to Argentina's population and agrarian problems. But colonization has eventually come face to face with the dilemma: what free lands remain are inaccessible or poor; and those that are good and are close to the railroad have been given out. The best land of all, that of the province of Buenos Aires, has been in a few hands for a century. So where does colonization go from here?

ALIENATION OF THE PUBLIC DOMAIN, 1860–1890

The prodigality with which rights and concessions had been made, without determined location, precise limits, or the definition of conditions, put the state in such a situation that it neither knew what land it had at its disposition nor could it precisely locate the land it had sold or given away.—MIGUEL ANGEL CÁRCANO, *Evolución Histórica del Régimen de la Tierra Pública, 1810–1916.*

The passion for giving away land in great, uneconomic blocks did not, unfortunately, end with Juan Manuel de Rosas.

If one thumbs through the laws and decrees of the seventies and eighties, it almost seems as though the sole function of government was the alienation of public lands. The subjugation of the caudillos, the campaigns against the Indians, the building of the railroads, all opened up vast tracts of territory in the south, west, and north of the new republic. Population was thin, and the government believed that the way to make it grow was to offer lands cheap on the frontiers as they were pushed back. The Homestead Law of the United States provided, too, for the settlement of the public domain, but in small 160-acre lots. In Argentina, where even in colonial times the minimum respectable holding was the Suerte de Estancia of 10,000 acres, the distribution was seigniorial.

In 1876 the Oficina de Tierras y Colonias was founded by an act of Congress for the purpose of registering land laws, concessions, and colonies. National lands, said the new law, were to be settled in sections twenty kilometers square, subdivided into 100-hectare lots. These sections, called *partidos,* were to reserve four lots in the center to be the town; and the other seventy-six were to form the *ejido.* The government was to foment colonization by giving away land, and paying colonists a bonus of ten gold pesos for every thousand trees they planted. The national government would pay the transportation costs of immigrants to the colonies.[8] This, at any rate, was the theory of how public lands would in the future be distributed.

In the next year the government conceded 11,200,000 hectares (some 28,000,000 acres) to a company that promised to settle six hundred families in unexplored Patagonia: one-third in Puerto Deseado, one-third in Santa Cruz, and one-third in San Julián. This company was also given a franchise to exploit whatever coal and salt there might be between the Deseado and Santa Cruz rivers. As a matter of fact, the grant lapsed because the company could not get the settlers; but the concession was indicative of scandals to come.[9] For at that time, 1877, the expedition to the desert had not begun, Patagonia had never been explored, let alone surveyed, and the government had no idea where these lands were, what they were worth, how many Indians there were on them, or whether the coal and salt existed or not. Under these conditions, it had nevertheless given away 28,000,000 acres of the public domain.

In 1878 Julio A. Roca applied to Congress for a million and a half pesos gold to undertake the Conquest of the Desert.

A million and a half pesos was a lot of money in the modest national budget of that period, and Congress probably reasoned that since the end result of the Roca expedition would be the opening of now worthless land to public settlement, there was no reason that this land should not be mortgaged in anticipation of its conquest, and the money used to pay the military expenditures. This, in fact, was what was done. Four thousand bonds were issued at 400 gold pesos, each bond bearing 6 per cent interest, and redeemable in one square league of land after the frontier had been advanced and the country surveyed. Although one bond was worth one league, nobody could buy fewer than four bonds. As a result, every buyer became the potential holder of no less than twenty-five thousand acres, at the cost of six American cents an acre, or sixteen gold centavos a hectare.[10] The curious thing about this bond issue against frontier lands was that the people who bought the bonds thought they were doing the government a favor, and bought them out of charity.[11] This was the first payment in land for the Conquest of the Desert; but before that account was liquidated the Roca expedition was to cost the public domain millions of hectares more, as will presently be seen.

The provinces, in the meantime, were not backward in disposing of what acreage they had. Córdoba sold 350,000 hectares in 1876 for an average price of twenty gold centavos the hectare.* [12] Corrientes at this time controlled the whole territory of Misiones; and in 1881 the provincial government decided to sell it all, disposing of 2,101,936 hectares to twenty-nine persons. The only reason that all of Misiones did not get into those hands was that it had not been properly surveyed and a remeasurement showed it really contained 2,918,183 hectares.[13]

With the conquest of the desert virtually completed, the national government found itself with millions of hectares in the territories. In the year 1882 a new law provided for the sale of land in Patagonia, the Chaco, Formosa, and Misiones. Those who wished to take up livestock raising could buy up to 40,000 hectares (about 100,000 acres) at prices varying from twenty gold centavos a hectare in Patagonia and the Chaco to a little more in Misiones and La Pampa.† Agricultural land sold for 1.50 to 2 gold pesos, and holdings were limited to four hundred hectares.[14] This law was very bad, because the astronomical limits set on grazing lands favored capitalists and speculators, who were just the class that took advantage of these sales. To put it in American measures: for $8,000 one could buy 100,000 acres of land. But Patagonia was far away, there were no railroads, there were no ports, there were no towns, and buyers preferred to hold title and wait for an influx of population to the territories to raise the value of their land. The government no doubt sincerely believed that this law would hurry settlement. But it, and the numberless ones that followed, got so much land into so few hands that holdings in the province

* The Argentine gold peso in the nineteenth century was approximately equal to the American dollar of the period.

† La Pampa is a territory of Argentina, not to be confused with the pampa, which indicates a general region of flat, grassy prairie.

of Buenos Aires are, by comparison, modest indeed, as will presently be seen.

Not content with selling land, the government in 1884 decreed the leasing of public lands in these same territories. Rents were set at 20 pesos (Tierra del Fuego), 30 to 50 pesos (Patagonia), and 80 to 100 pesos (Chaco, La Pampa) for blocks of 2,500 hectares. The same year there was a law authorizing the giving away of land to colonists who wished to raise livestock.[15] At this point it will be noticed that laws and decrees are beginning to follow one another very fast, but that there is no evidence of an over-all plan for the disposal of public lands. Some laws are redundant, and others are simply contradictory. Bear in mind, too, that so far *these lands have not been surveyed.*

In 1885 the Conquest of the Desert was complete, and a grateful nation wished to reward the heroes suitably for their sufferings on campaign. It was decided to give them land according to hierarchy: to the heirs of Adolfo Alsina went 15,000 hectares; to each *jefe de frontera*, 8,000; to chiefs of battalions or regiments, 5,000; to sergeant-majors, 4,800; to captains, 2,500; to lieutenants, 2,000; and to noncommissioned officers, 1,500. Since the lands thus awarded had not been surveyed, and no one knew exactly where they might be, or whether they might not overlap some of the lands already sold to speculators, the awards were in the form of bonds good for so many hectares wherever the heroes wished to settle. By this point in Argentine land legislation, both military heroes and the patriots who had bought Conquest of the Desert, 6 per cent bonds held title to unspecified lands wherever they wished to settle, and certain capitalists and colonists held title to supposedly fixed but unsurveyed lands. Nobody knew whether claims would conflict or not.

It so happened that the Conquerors of the Desert, perhaps because they had seen Patagonia with their own eyes, showed no haste in wanting to settle there, and the situation became very confused when many of them sold their bonds to speculators at twenty centavos a hectare. The government had not foreseen this contingency, and the next twenty years were taken up with new decrees aimed at getting the land out of the hands of the speculators. The transfers of land were not recognized (decree of 1893). In 1894, more land was given out to the heroes. Some of the decrees speak eloquently of what was happening. One for instance invalidates the original General Staff list of heroes of the desert because large numbers of persons who were on it had never gotten beyond the suburbs of Buenos Aires.[16] A corrected list was issued. In the meantime, Heroes of the Desert bonds were fluid as mercury, and in spite of all subsequent decrees, they got into hands that were not intended to have them. They were presented to the government by 541 speculators who took 733,701 hectares in La Pampa, 2,507,870 hectares in Río Negro, 114,570 in Neuquén, 1,218,269 in Chubut, and 5,100 in Tierra del Fuego: a total of over four and a half million hectares.[17]

Alienation of the public domain continued with increased impetus as the booming eighties drew to a close. In 1886, the auction of lands in the Chaco was decreed at the price of thirty centavos a hectare. The minimum lot which any buyer might take was set at 10,000 hectares, the maximum at 40,000.[18]

The greatest sale of all, however, was reserved for 1889, the last year before the great crash of 1890. President Miguel Juárez Celman decided to open land offices in London, Paris, Barcelona, Genoa, Brussels, and Bremen to dispose of 24,000 square leagues (some 150,000,000 acres) in Patagonia, the Chaco, and Formosa. This was very possibly the biggest projected real estate sale in history, and it was launched to save a government that was on the verge of bankruptcy by raising 20,000,000 gold pesos. The plan was too ambitious. It foundered from sheer size, and because European buyers were more wary than Argentine. They not unreasonably wanted to know the location of this land they were going to buy, what its quality was, whether it included pasture, water, and so forth. The government, of course, could not tell them because it did not know.[19] The sale failed, the offices closed, and the government went bankrupt anyway.

And so Argentina reached the crisis year 1890, when the dizzy ride of speculation had finally to be paid for. It is a commentary on these land laws that one of the great problems of the government after the sale or lease of lands was that the buyer or lessor, on seeing what he had bought, frequently demanded his money back because the land was not suited for agriculture or grazing. The limits on landholdings were not respected. Speculators used dummy buyers to get, not 40,000, but often more than 1,000,000 hectares at a time. The damage was done, and no amount of subsequent wisdom served to undo it. The Ministry of Agriculture was founded in 1898. One may judge the real chaos of the land laws by this fact: when the ministry made a study of the status of public lands, it found that, though the government had given away more than 60,000,000 hectares, it had no idea what lands were left, where they were, or what they were worth.[20]

The Republic had far outdone Rosas in generosity.

SUGAR, MEAT, GRASS, AND OTHER MATTERS

> *There is a lack of export of animals on the hoof, which ought to come soon, and with great profit. There is a need to export canned meats for the European markets. Nor are there extract factories, and without doubt these various branches would be of great use and would accelerate the progress of the livestock industry.*
>
> —José Hernández, *Instrucción del Estanciero* (1882).

If land went so fast, it was because there was profit in it. One might raise sheep or cattle in the littoral, or one might turn the land to the newer agriculture. In any case, one made money.

As the century drew to a close, the building of railroads in radiating lines from Buenos Aires brought more and more of the interior within the area where cultivation became economically feasible. The North, which had been moribund since the May Revolution, could now get its sugar and *caña* to market by train, although sugar prices were still not competitive; and there was born the interesting monopoly which was to bring wealth to some, and much misery to many.

Tucumán has always been known as the "Garden of the Republic." It is a small, richly green, mountainous province where rainfall is heavy, and almost anything will grow in profusion. Joseph Andrews, it will be remembered, had commented on the human poverty in this "very garden of the universe" when he visited Tucumán in 1825. Tucumán was, and is, the most thickly populated of the Argentine provinces, reminiscent in its lush greenness of some of the islands of the West Indies. There, in colonial times, the natives grew fruit, vegetables, and corn, and raised cattle. Just four years before Captain Andrews was there, however, a priest named José Colombres, thinking to do his province a favor, brought some sugar cane back from Peru and planted it around his house. In a wooden mill, the first sugar was ground from the cane, and today the Spanish colonial home of José Colombres and the first sugar press have become a provincial monument.

Sugar cane prospered in the humid climate. But the industry as such remained modest, first because the primitive presses, which were three vertical cylinders of quebracho moved by oxen or mules, wasted most of the juice; and also because until 1876 sugar had to be transported in oxcarts at freight costs that doubled the price. The longest shipments were to Córdoba, and sugar was also sent north to Salta and Jujuy. At a time when the price of sugar was three Bolivian pesos an arroba,* freight to Córdoba was two pesos an arroba.[21] There was not even a question of sending it to Buenos Aires. Before the railroad came to Tucumán, there were only 2,000-odd hectares planted to cane.

In 1876 the railroad arrived. Six years later, the sugar fields had doubled in area, iron machinery and generators had been brought in, and sugar was on its way to becoming a major Argentine industry. Generous rainfall, cheap labor, and fast transportation conspired to make sugar a sound capital investment. One could hire a peon or an ox for seventy-five centavos a day. The men and their

* An old Spanish measure equal to 25 pounds.

families lived in grass huts, and were content so long as they could eat and were given caña to drink. It was true, of course, that malaria was universal and chronic, that tuberculosis and trachoma were general, and that ill health made the efficiency of the Tucumano considerably lower than that of the peon of Buenos Aires; nevertheless, the prospective planter could count on certain and high returns for his investment. "Exaggerating the expenditure, and reducing the production to its minimum limits, the result is such that the sugar-cane grower reimburses in the first year all the capital invested, including the costs of planting. This, in the first year. In subsequent years the cash return is *much greater.*" The quotation is from an official publication.[22]

A man who wanted to put up an *ingenio* (refinery), however, had to have rather more capital. The quebracho presses were giving way to modern machinery. The first to install iron mills were the Méndez brothers (Juan M. and Juan C.), who built modern refineries on their plantations of Concepción and Trinidad. These first ingenios were worked by wood-burning tubular generators, and they had a cylindrical iron mill, filters, evaporators, centrifuges, and all that went with them. The new iron age in Tucumán had an immediate effect on the small ingenios that still used wooden cylinders and animal power. Whereas in 1877 there were seventy-three ingenios, in 1881 there were only thirty-four. Those who could not afford the capital investment in machinery, closed their ingenios and became planters. In this way a large-scale modern industry came into being.[23]

In Buenos Aires the cattle industry still paid high returns, but it seemed to have reached the limit of its development. Hides and tallow were its chief profit, and what meat went to Europe was salted at the saladeros. A few blooded bulls had been brought to Argentina, but the importers found there was no market for them. The estancieros were an unimaginative and conservative class, quite content with their hide and wool market. In 1866, however, a small and progressive group of estancieros founded the Sociedad Rural, an organization that was to be the greatest force for the betterment of the Argentine livestock industry. The first president was José Martínez de Hoz, and the vice-president was the first man to put up a fence in Argentina, Richard B. Newton. A decade later the Sociedad was to begin that annual livestock show which has exhibited some of the finest and most expensive pedigreed bulls in the world. The organization represented a small minority of the estancieros: the majority were still in the category of those who believed that all was well so long as their cows calved and their ewes lambed, and their herds did not die of drought or disease. They steadfastly refused to buy shorthorns, arguing that their hides were too thin for leather (which was true), and that their meat was too fat for proper salting.

In this climate of opinion, the Sociedad was received with indifference. In the ninth year of its existence it decided to hold a livestock show to see if interest could not be aroused in improving the breeds. At the corner of Florida and Paraguay, in the heart of Buenos Aires, the first livestock show of the Sociedad Rural opened in April, 1875. It was held on a vacant lot belonging to one of the members, and was poorly installed and poorly attended. On exhibit were 66 horses, 13 bulls and cows, 74 sheep, 16 goats, 11 pigs, 15 dogs, and assorted birds and rabbits.[24] It was true that President Avellaneda opened the show, but it was held like the only livestock show that preceded it, one in Palermo in 1852, in the midst of "public indifference and the surprising silence of the press."[25] The Palermo show of two decades earlier had been a fiasco, and this was almost a failure. First of all, there were few blooded animals to show. The total value of those auctioned was only ten thousand pesos gold, less than the price of a single prize Durham now.[26] In the second place, neither the estancieros nor the public was breeding-conscious. The cattlemen argued, with justice, that they were selling hides, not meat, and what good was a Durham hide?

The Sociedad had little but faith to go on. But even at this time, in England and France, experiments were going on which would vindicate the faith of the Sociedad Rural and revolutionize the Argentine estancia, little as the average estanciero dreamed of it. During the better part of the century inventors had been experimenting with gases in an effort to find an adequate refrigerant. Charles Tellier, improving on earlier English trials, invented a refrigerating machine that used ether as a base, and in 1873 he asked the French Academy to examine a project of his to preserve meat. The experiments, which took place at Auteuil and lasted several months, were evidently impressive, for a company was formed to exploit the invention. A small, 1,200-ton ship was bought in England and converted to refrigeration with the installation of six iceboxes and three motors. It was loaded with meat in Rouen, and on September 19, 1876, *Le Frigorifique*, whose voyage was to make history, and whose name was to become a part of the Argentine language, set sail for Buenos Aires.

The *Frigorifique* arrived ninety-seven days later. Emilio Duportal, president of the Sociedad Rural, congratulated the voyagers in person, and banquets were organized for the first public appearance of congealed meat. Some who tasted it thought it good, others said it was in a state of decomposition. But it was agreed to try the *Frigorifique* again, and seventy-three young bulls, twenty-two wild steers, and two hundred sheep were killed and put aboard. For one reason or another, the boat had still not sailed a month later, and the meat was tried at a public farewell banquet for the crew. Some of it had not preserved too well, but the results were promising.

The second experiment in shipping frozen meats across the Atlantic came in the next year. This time the meat was preserved by another system, designed to freeze it hard as a rock, which it did. The steamer *Paraguay* sailed from Marseilles on August 13, 1877, and arrived a month and a half later with 150 tons of meat, all in good condition. The Sociedad Rural sent back a shipment of its own meat on the *Paraguay*. The voyage was a record seven months long. Proof this time was final. The meat, all of it, reached France in a perfect state of preservation.[27]

One would have thought that the advantages of refrigeration would have been immediately apparent to the Argentine *ganadero*. Such was not the case. Refrigeration was resisted as the shorthorn had been resisted. The average estanciero simply did not see that this technological advance marked a revolution in his industry: that its repercussions would be felt in the value of meat, the value of pedigreed stock, the value of land—in the last analysis, in the economic life of the nation, and in Argentina's capacity to absorb European immigration. The stringy, thick-hided longhorn, the half-wild herds, the slovenly estancias, and the picturesque gaucho were slated to go. A French company, impressed by the *Frigorifique* and the *Paraguay*, built a fleet of refrigerator boats to bring congealed meat from Argentina, but the livestock raisers were so hostile that they influenced the Sociedad Rural to send no more meat.[28] The English were not so blind, and in 1880 they began regular shipments of congealed meat from Australia. Three years later they inaugurated a line with Argentina, and in spite of resistance, the shipments grew, irresistibly. By 1887, 57 refrigerator ships were in regular service between Buenos Aires and English ports. By the end of the century, the number had risen to 278.

It was not long before the idea of a packing plant that used refrigeration followed on the success of the shipping experiments. In 1882 the River Plate Fresh Meat Company was formed in London, and in the next year the first Argentine *frigorífico* was opened in Campana. In 1884 a Frenchman, Eugène Terrasson, followed the English example, founding the frigorífico San Nicolás. Gaston Sansinena opened La Negra. The packing plants multiplied rapidly. Perhaps the Argentine livestock men first saw the point about the importance of breeding when English estancieros, with newly imported Lincoln sheep, outsold them at the frigoríficos. The Argentine merinos, averaging only thirty-nine pounds in weight, used to bring between two and three pesos. In the Smithfield Market in London they were jeeringly known as the "mice" for their size. When the Argentine sheepmen saw that Lincolns outweighed and outsold their merinos, the lesson, being economic, was driven home. Lincolns were imported in ever increasing numbers, until today more than half of all pedigreed sheep in the country are of this breed.[29]

The effect on the cattle market was like magic. The red shorthorns drove the criollo cattle from the pampa. In the International Exposition of 1885, a quarter of the animals shown were pedigreed stock from Europe. It became suddenly important to the estanciero that his cattle be blooded, and that they be fed on tender, fattening grasses. Cattle in this period were still so thin that they were refused by the frigoríficos. "We must confess," wrote José Hernández, author of *Martín Fierro,* "that whether for lack of foresight, because it does not understand the importance of the matter, or for whatever other reason, the truth is that the chief grazing province of the Río de la Plata, which is Buenos Aires, the most fertile piece of soil that exists in the world of all those dedicated to livestock, has not to the present time the smallest official study on the quality and nature of its grasses."[30] Until recently Argentine longhorns had existed on the tough, deep-rooted *pastos fuertes* that had to be burned off from time to time. (This was the origin of those deliberate pampa fires that so impressed visitors to the Plata.) *Pastos fuertes,* with their long roots, sucked water from far down in the earth, and were resistant to drought as other grasses were not. But the cattle that lived on them were lean, and sheep could hardly exist on them.

In the eighties *pastos tiernos* (clover, Indian caustic barley, thistles, foxtail) had largely replaced the older grass except on new frontier lands. These came up with the autumn rains in March and April, and were tender; but hot sun could burn them, and drought make them unfit to eat. It was at this time that two members of the Sociedad Rural, Felipe Senillosa and Emilio Frers, began experimenting with fields of alfalfa, which until then was comparatively unknown in Argentina. The experiments showed beyond question that there was nothing better for fattening cattle, and Frers and Senillosa published two articles on their study in *La Prensa,* which attracted wide and favorable attention.[31]

The Sociedad Rural was becoming fashionable. Whatever pointed to the betterment of the breeds it fought for, against the inertia and indifference of the average estanciero—whatever looked like a threat to the industry, whether higher taxes, higher tariffs, or imported animal epidemics, it fought against. It was the president of the Sociedad Rural, at that time Eduardo Olivera, who first recognized the seriousness of hoof-and-mouth disease when it appeared in Argentina. The year was 1870. Among some of the herds of Buenos Aires appeared symptoms strange to the Argentine cattle breeders: their animals grew thin, without apparent cause, and walked with difficulty; the cows' milk dried up, and the calves got no nourishment; in mouths, lips, and nostrils, were ugly sores. The Consejo de Higiene sent a veterinary to report on the disease, and his report was discouraging. "In the presence of these data, which agree with my first observation," he wrote, "I could without hesitation state the nature of this disease and the diagnosis of aphthous fever . . . characterized by the development of sores in the mouth, the lips, the nostrils and in the base of the nails, as well as in the udder of the female." [32] After this first outbreak, hoof-and-mouth disease, which the Argentines call *aftosa*, disappeared for thirty years, and no more was heard of it until the end of the century.

The early frigoríficos, founded after the first experiments with refrigerator boats showed the possibility of conserving meat indefinitely, went through lean years. This is surprising when one considers the obvious benefits of refrigeration. Such, however, was the case. In 1894 the San Nicolás went bankrupt. The River Plate was saved only because fresh money was poured in. The opening of the packing plants coincided unfortunately with the crisis of 1890, but this was perhaps not the most important reason for the early failure of the frigoríficos. What beat them was the competition from shipments of animals on the hoof. The first shipment of live animals was made in 1874, and the system, almost contemporaneous with the first experiment in refrigerator ships, was more immediately popular, beef on the hoof outselling chilled and frozen meats four to one.

But the frigoríficos were to come into their own. Cattle crowded into ships on long and difficult voyages are prey both to seasickness—which cuts down their weight—and to disease. An epidemic of hoof-and-mouth disease could kill off an entire shipload of animals, or make them unfit to land, and in 1900, after the disease had lain quiescent for more than a quarter of a century, this is just what happened. A serious epidemic in Argentina closed all English ports to shipment of animals on the hoof, and with one stroke killed the frigoríficos' only competitor. The packing houses made 40 and 50 per cent profits. And as if one stroke of luck were not enough, the Boer War broke out in South Africa, and coincided with a bad year for Australian cattle. This brought such dizzy profits to the Argentine meat industry that not only did the frigoríficos recoup all their losses of previous years, but British and American capital poured into the country to build new and bigger packing houses.[33] The war in South Africa ended, but the meat-packing industry did not. In the twentieth century it has been the most important of Argentine industries.

With the fencing of the estancias, the importing of blooded stock, the cultivation of alfalfa, the building of the railroads, and finally the conserving of meats by refrigeration, the Argentine livestock industry had come of age. The Sociedad Rural established its register of Durhams and Herefords. Three-quarters of all the cattle in Argentina today are shorthorns.[34] The prize Durham of a modern Palermo livestock show will sell for 50,000 pesos at auction to the men whose grandfathers said the shorthorn was a bad cow because its hide was thin and its meat was too fat to be salted.*

Refrigeration changed the nation's face. With the solution of the shipping problem, came the rise in value of the herds. As the herds went up, there was incentive to improve the breeds, and there was the capital to do it with. In 1905 the people on the boulevards of Paris gathered before the window of the *Prensa* agency to stare at the photograph of a bull bought in England for 65,000 francs.[35] Running an estancia became the concern of technicians. It is hard to remember what the estancia of 1850 was, even if you set it beside the estancia of 1910. Land had so risen in value that the owner did not bother to work it. He sublet it to a tenant,

* In 1925, Federico Seeger's *Faithful 20* sold for 152,000 pesos, the record to date. The 1944 champion shorthorn was auctioned at 60,000 pesos. Sometimes the runner-up brings more than the Grand Champion. The explanation: buyers may like the pedigree of the second better; and sometimes they just disagree with the judge's choice.

who hired a majordomo to run it for him. The majordomo was a technician, and a man of many skills. He might manage 100,000 acres: do the accounting, run a dairy, breed bulls, raise blooded race horses, make cheese and casein, market milk, and attend to the main business, which was the preparing of yearling calves for market. Profits were still high enough to pay the owner his rent, made a profit for the tenant, and give the majordomo forty or fifty thousand pesos in salary and commission. The land continued to rise. It made millions for the Anchorenas, the Alzagas, the Unzués, the Bosches, the Lynches, the Duggans, and the other families whose names have become synonymous with the aristocracy—or as Oddone put it, *The Landholding Bourgeoisie*—of Argentina. The owners mortgaged their lands and went to Europe, where a generation of playboys came to be known as *les sauvages argentins*. They built themselves French *hôtels* in Buenos Aires and Tudor castles in the country. They educated their children in Paris, and the children grew up to speak French better than Spanish, and be proud of it. The railroad, the refrigerator, the stud farm, and the European immigrant conspired to turn the desert of 1850 into a suddenly rich and wonderful garden. For those whose fathers had had the foresight to buy a share in the land when it cost fifty centavos the hectare, it was a garden where not roses but silver seemed to spring from the ground. In Europe there was a new phrase: "as rich as an Argentine."

BOOM: 1860–1889

THE RAILROAD

Protect at the same time private enterprises for the construction of railroads. Shower them with advantages, with privileges, with every favor imaginable, without hesitating at the means. . . . Is our capital insufficient for such undertakings? Turn them over to foreign capital then. Let treasure, as well as men, come from abroad to live among us. Surround it with immunities and privileges so that it will take out citizenship, and stay. —ALBERDI, *Bases.*

In 1860 Argentina had thirty-nine kilometers of railroad. *La Porteña* did regular service along the Morón route, apparently none the worse for her service in the Crimea, or for the fact that the British who had sold her to the Ferrocarril del Oeste considered her as scrap iron. Argentines could take pride in the fact that their capital —in limited quantities, to be sure—had built the first railroad. Sheepmen along the right of way could get their wool to the Buenos Aires market now for a third less than it had cost by cart. But custom changed slowly, and the majority continued to ship by cart because the driver assumed responsibility for the load.[1]

In the rest of the nation, transport was as slow and dear as ever. The Rosario-Córdoba railroad projected by the Urquiza government had gotten no further than the abortive Buschental contract. The old wagon routes were travelled still by men on horseback, and by ox-drawn carts. One way led through Rosario, Córdoba, Santiago, and Tucumán to the northern frontier with Bolivia. The other went from Rosario to San Luis and Mendoza, and then over the rocky Cordillera by the Paramillos pass to Chile. In the Andes there was only a mule trail joining Argentina to Chile. Trade was as limited as this modest means of transport. A mule could carry three to four hundred pounds, and might make thirty miles in a day. Burros did considerably less, and llamas less still. Over these high, rough passes, troops of thirty and forty beasts, driven by four or five peons and a couple of *capataces*, made the crossing when weather permitted. Between April and November, which is winter, high snows and landslides might block passage and make the crossing dangerous or impossible. At any time of year the traveller had to count on going a week without more resources than he took with him. When cattle were driven over, their feet grew sore from the rocks, and swelled.[2]

This was transportation in Argentina before the railroad. But there was now a project afoot to build the Rosario-Córdoba railroad which had been the dream of the Paraná government. At this time the original survey and estimates of Allan Campbell were in the hands of William Wheelwright, a native of Massachusetts. Wheelwright, as a matter of fact, had the only copy of the Campbell survey. He began negotiations with Mitre's Minister of the Interior, Guillermo Rawson, and got Rawson to grant three miles on both sides of the track to the company building the road. The government guaranteed a return of 7 per cent, and set the cost of construction at 32,000 gold pesos per mile.[3]

Campbell had estimated the cost of constructing this railroad at 20,000 pesos a mile. His estimate was probably correct, because that was about what the Western Railway was costing, and the terrain was the same. So the Rawson agreement was generous, especially in view of the interest guarantee on the authorized capital. To give the promised land to the new company, which was called the Ferrocarril Central Argentino, or Argentine Central Railway, the government began the confiscation of land along the right of way. In the first ninety kilometers, fifty-two proprietors had to be dislodged. The work went on until 1867, when it was suspended for lack of funds. The Central was a British company, the first British railroad in Argentina.[4]

In the same year that Congress authorized the line to Córdoba, a third railroad was being planned to go southward through the province of Buenos Aires. This was the Ferrocarril Sud, or Southern Railway. The F.C.S. was authorized, not by Congress, but by the provincial legislature in May of 1862, shortly before the national Congress met for the first time. This contract was much like that of the Central, 7 per cent being guaranteed on the construction costs.[5] The contract was signed with Edward Lumb, and here, too, the capital was British. When these three lines got underway, one to the north, one to the south, and one to the west, each radiating like a spoke from the hub that was Buenos Aires, the enthusiasm was intense. Alberdi's ambitious plans were bearing fruit at last.

The Southern Railway broke ground for its station on March 7, 1864, and the first dirt was spaded by President Mitre. It was in the Plaza Constitución, then occupied by a battery of cannons. The President of the Republic was there, and the Governor of Buenos Aires. At twelve the president of the local committee of the railroad made a speech, and asked Mitre to move the first shovelful of earth. He took the spade, lifted the dirt, and tossed it into a cart, and then the President, the ministers, the diplomatic corps and the officers of the railroad retired to a great tent where luncheon was set for four hundred guests. In these early days, railroading was a novelty, and people turned to watch a locomotive as children were years later to lift their faces to the sky to see an airplane pass. The *Correo del Domingo* described the luxury of an excursion by train to Chascomús in the first year of the Southern Railway's existence. "Each coach had been provided with a profusion of Havana cigars," wrote the reporter with enthusiasm, "with Eau de Cologne, biscuits, generous liquids, fans. Behind the coaches went a closed carriage. It was a well stocked dispensary for the trip. At each stop this dispensary opened its doors, and iced wines and refreshments were offered to the passengers. . . . Four hours after leaving the station in the city the happy passengers were in the streets of Chascomús. They arrived at the end of the journey dusty, but not tired." [6]

Argentina was eager for foreign capital. In these years no one was more welcome than the man with money to invest. And because the period of Argentina's need was also the period of Britain's surplus wealth, it was British capital that flowed to the Plata, into street railways and gas companies and railroads. At least, it seemed to the Argentines then that it was British capital coming in. In later years, when the flush of enthusiasm was gone, and the Argentine had learned to grudge foreigners their profits, there were many who went back over the history of the period and proved that things were not what they seemed: that it was Argentine money that had worked the wonders, that had paid for the railroads, and that the so-called "British capital" was a fiction. How could this be so? In order to understand the bitterness and the mutual recriminations that were to come, it would perhaps be profitable to follow the financial transactions as they took place. What was the source of the "British capital invested in Argentina"?

Let us take up the story of the Ferrocarril Central Argentina, whose line was suspended in 1867 for lack of money. In that year the company books showed that it had put 1,300,000 gold pesos into the railroad, although on closer inspection one could see that some of this capital was in the form of gratuitous issues of stock to directors and therefore was not investment. The Argentine government rescued the company with 1,700,000 pesos, so that now more than half of the capital was the government's. With this help the Central reached Córdoba. In the year of its completion it was far from making the 7 per cent it had been guaranteed: more money was granted by the government to make up the total, and by now, between the payment for the original study, the expropriation of land, the guarantee, and the stock it had bought, the government had spent almost the sum that Campbell had estimated the railroad would cost. Campbell had estimated four and a half millions gold, and the government had spent three. This, by 1867.[7]

In 1870 a curious situation arose when the British government began to discount income tax on the railroad shares held by the Argentine public and government. The British argued that the company was incorporated in England, and therefore owed income tax. But Sarmiento, who was President, issued a decree forbidding its payment.[8]

By 1880 the boom that had gripped the nation was bringing

the Central the highest profits of any railroad in the country.* Under terms of the government contract, when the profits exceeded 15 per cent, the railroad should use the excess profits to repay past government guarantees. The Central instead wrote up its capital so as to show low returns. Its recognized capital was more than twice the Campbell estimate. Raúl Scalabrini Ortiz, who is one of the Argentine muckrakers, in his study of the Central claims that if the capital had not been puffed, the gains of the company in 1883 would have been 17 per cent and in 1884, 21 per cent, and the company would have had to lower its rates by half.[9] Some of the accounting by which Scalabrini Ortiz arrives at this conclusion is doubtful. The real watering began later, as will presently be seen. The point is that in this early period of railroading Argentina could afford to wink at what was going on, because the benefits the railroads brought so far outweighed all other considerations.

In 1890 the Central bought the Ferrocarril del Norte. The Norte was thirty kilometers long. The Central claimed it cost 6,585,000 gold pesos. This would make it worth 219,500 pesos per kilometer, just ten times the Campbell estimate. With this purchase the Central in 1890 declared a capital of 34,000,000 pesos; in 1891, 50,000,000. The growth in capital bore no relation to the growth of the railroad, at least not to the length of the track, as may be judged by the following figures:

Year	Length (km.)	Capital (gold pesos)	Costs per km. (gold pesos)
1884	396	8,143,230	20,560
1888	396	13,508,000	36,630
1891	1,147	50,688,497	44,190

In this way the company was now showing pitiful returns: 1890, 2.71 per cent; 1891, 0.89 per cent.[10] The English stockholders were

* Comparative profits of railroads in paper pesos per kilometer:

National Railroads		*Private Railroads*	
Oeste	1,693	Sud	1,667
Andino	595	B.A. & Rosario	2,363
Central Norte	1,499	Central Argentino	4,238

(Raúl Scalabrini Ortiz, *Historia de los Ferrocarriles Argentinos*, B.A., 1940, p. 129.)

being cheated as badly as the Argentines. Where was the money really going?

But the watering had just begun. In 1902, the Central was sold to the Buenos Aires & Rosario, keeping its old name, and the capital was written up further. In 1906–1907, the capital was inflated 11,000,000 gold pesos without the building of a single kilometer of track. The capital was written up 22,000,000 with the building of 49 kilometers of track.[11] The railroad rates were now so high in Santa Fe that the mills and storehouses were shutting down because they could not pay them.[12] The F.C.C.A. said it had invested 223,000,000 gold pesos between 1908 and 1930; the Dirección de Ferrocarriles investigated and allowed 148,000,000. There had been an almost 40 per cent inflation by paper manipulations. The extra gains were not paid to the stockholders in England—who thought, and continue to think, that Argentine railroads are a bad investment, and that in some dim way the Argentines are to blame for the fact. This money went into special funds—"renovation," "accidents," "cost of exploitation"—and much of it was invested in Argentine bonds. Between 1908 and 1930, these funds totalled 155,000,000 gold pesos, or more than the sum invested by the F.C.C.A.[13] Is this where "new capital" was coming from?

There would be no point in raking up old scandals—after all, is the history of American railroading any better?—were it not that the claims of British capital, and the counterclaims of the Argentines, were to lead to such rancor in the last few years. At the same time that the conviction of unfair treatment has grown among English stockholders with investments in the Plata, the conviction of foreign exploitation has grown among Argentines. In later chapters the recent phases of the controversy will be studied at length, for their bearing especially on modern Argentine foreign policy. Indirectly, the repercussions have hurt the United States, too. But it is well to bear in mind that in the nineteenth century foreign capital was still welcomed and defended in Argentina, and that it is only in the last decade that anyone has cared about the watering of capital so many years ago. While the watering was going on, there were no voices to protest. On the contrary, the

Argentine government was so anxious to attract the foreigner with money to invest that even such successful ventures in national railroads as the Ferrocarril del Oeste were sold to the British for no better reason than the conviction that the government should stay out of business.

The case of the Oeste is a curious one. The railroad belonged to the province of Buenos Aires until 1889, and averaged better than 7 per cent profit during these years. When Máximo Paz, who was governor of the province, sent his message to the legislature to urge the sale of this most successful investment, his stated grounds were that the government should stay out of business. Buenos Aires could use the sale money for public works, he said: irrigation, roads, sanitation, pavements, etc. (There was a frenzy of investment in public works at this time.) Furthermore, the low rates of the Oeste gave farmers along its route an unfair competitive advantage over those along the Sud, who paid more.* The legislature voted the alienation of the Oeste, and the next year it was bought by H. G. Anderson for the British Western Railway for £8,134,920, two-fifths being paid in cash, and the rest representing the assumption of the railroad's debts. Thirty days after buying the Oeste, Anderson, who was a director of the Western Railway, turned it over to the Western for £1,150,000 more. The Western paid him the £150,000 in cash, and the million in free stock. In this way, a month after its sale, the Oeste's capital had been watered by more than a million pounds sterling. But that was not the end of this curious transaction. To pay the Buenos Aires government the £3,000,000 it owed in cash, the Western Railway sold half of the F.C.O. to other companies for £3,000,000. In this way the British company acquired the Argentine railroad without paying anything, and the capital figured in London as "British capital invested in Argentina." [14] The following figures on costs of the F.C.O. per kilometer in gold pesos, and profits per kilometer required in order to make 10 per cent, will give some idea of why British railroads in Argentina show almost no profits:

* "Would this not be a good reason to expropriate the other railroads, rather than to sell the Oeste?" asks Scalabrini Ortiz (*Historia de los Ferrocarriles,* p. 49).

Year	*Kilometers*	*Capital*	*Costs*	*Required Profits*
1884	779	15,442,855	19,823	1,982
1887	1,022	25,195,707	24,650	2,465
1890 *	1,057	41,000,000	38,789	3,878
1890 †	544	34,796,000	47,022	4,702
1891 ‡	544	47,638,861	64,376	6,437

* Price of sale, June, 1890.
† According to decree of Sept. 27, 1890, after sale of half the line.
‡ According to *Memoria* of Western Ry., June, 1891.

In this way, private capital came to Argentina. The men who made government policy defended what they were doing. In a debate in the Chamber of Deputies Ezequiel Ramos Mexía, who was the Minister of Public Works, defended foreign capital in unequivocal terms. "I say: if we wish to be sincere and serious, we have to give tangible proof that the purpose of the national government is to respect this capital, once it has reached the country, and to defend it, as I defend it, exposing myself to irresponsible accusations or insinuations that I am paid by such enterprises. I am proud of having made myself their champion, because I believe that I have done my country a great favor. . . . I believe, and I will always reiterate it, that the executive and the Congress ought to respect private capital, and should protect it, because it is ruinous business to a nation that foreign companies should come here with a great deal of capital and lose it." [15] This was the argument of maintaining the nation's credit rating; and that it has been the keystone of policy is shown by the fact that Argentina heads the list of responsible South American countries in the investment capitals of the world. Perhaps Argentina has bought its good name at a price. At least, that is what Argentines now argue.

Whatever the source of capital, whatever its real value, the railroads were built. The nation that had had just thirty-nine kilometers of track in 1860, had more than seven thousand in 1889. Lines laced the country, bringing to market the wool and hides and meat that had once been carried by cart. Wherever the railroad went, land rose in value, and the estanciero became rich. The country was in a fever of speculation and prosperity.

IMMIGRATION

In America, to govern is to populate.—ALBERDI, *Bases.*

"The Argentine peon," wrote Moussy critically, after studying the criollo character, "does badly and unwillingly, even lazily, if you will, what he is not used to doing. . . . He is essentially routine, reasons little about what he does, has no desire to better his condition, and that is, in our opinion, his worst fault. He is also too stubborn, too indifferent to his own welfare, and without doubt the mildness of the climate contributes to his lack of wants. So long as he has a hide to sleep on, a tree or shelter of branches to cover him, he asks nothing more. His nourishment will be a piece of meat roasted in the open air, without bread and often without salt, or corn boiled in water with a little grease, and that only once a day, in the evening; some gourds of mate will help him down this meager meal, and there you have his life. A glass of wine—and above all, caña, from time to time—a meat pie called an *empanada*, will be the biggest addition, especially because afterwards he will have the pleasure of listening to a guitar and dancing. . . . Children, they have been reared in the same environment: adults, they continue in it, and their children will live exactly like them." [16]

When Moussy studied the country, it was still Indian-criollo. There was an infinitesimal number of foreigners, and these lived in Buenos Aires. As Samuel Haigh had said, "the rank and file are such a mixture of white, Indian and negro, that it is difficult to tell their origin." [17] In the interior there were provinces that had not seen a foreigner. In 1860, the number of immigrants was a shade over five thousand. There seemed little fulfillment of Parish's prophecy that the colored population must "ere long be entirely lost in the rapid increase of the white population and the continual immigration of fresh settlers from Europe." [18] But the conviction existed that an influx of Europeans was what the country needed most. This is what Alberdi had stressed in his *Bases*. Sarmiento had felt keenly the ignorance and poverty of the criollo in contrast to the foreigner in his midst. The German and Scotch colonies which he had seen in the south of the province of Buenos Aires had impressed him: "The cottages are painted, the front yards always neatly kept and adorned with flowers and pretty shrubs; the furniture simple but complete; copper or tin utensils always bright and clean; nicely curtained beds; and the occupants of the dwelling are always industriously at work. . . . The town inhabited by natives of the country presents a picture entirely the reverse. There, dirty and ragged children live, with a menagerie of dogs; there, men lie about in utter idleness; neglect and poverty prevail everywhere; a table and some baskets are the only furniture of wretched huts remarkable for their general aspect of barbarism and carelessness." [19]

It has become fashionable in these recent years of nationalism for the Argentines to attribute all virtue to the country's ancient stock, and all evils to the foreigner. In popular legend the *verdadero criollo* was strong, brave, hardy, honest, patriotic, and so forth. The Italian and Spanish emigrant, on the other hand, brought vice, disorder, and a grasping commercial spirit. This is a charming myth, and is the source of the Argentine's mental portrait of the old, uncorrupted criollo: he is a Martín Fierro kind of character, sitting under an ombú drinking mate, and prepared to fight quixotically with daggers at close quarters, poncho rolled around the arm for protection. Political and commercial advertising portrays this imaginary Argentine. He is drawn with the floppy felt *chambergo* on his head, and bombachas, and mate, just as the Average American of the billboards is a ruddy-cheeked, handsome husband with ruddy-cheeked wife, and two ruddy-cheeked children, all of them either seated in a fast automobile, or gathered around a gleaming white enamel icebox. The fact that neither hygiene nor comfort enters into the Argentine myth is significant: he has the heroic qualities, and the American the hygienic. In this sense the gaucho legend has survived. Sarmiento, one imagines, would not be pleased. He and Alberdi had a different ideal, and it was, if anything, the American. Neat front yards and bright pots and pans entered into it, and if Sarmiento were living today, it would probably include bathtubs, window screens, and frigidaires.

That the immigrants brought the commercial spirit is all too true. The immigrant brought commerce, industry, and the savings account to Argentina. Francis Clark Ford reported in the sixties that, of every 100 depositors in the Banco de Buenos Aires, 30 were Italians, 13 Spaniards, 13 Basques, 9 French, 4 English-Irish, 4 German, and 9 miscellaneous Europeans. The remaining 18 were Argentine.[20] Yet foreigners totalled only *12 per cent* of the population. The more one thinks about it, the more extraordinary this becomes. Since there have been statistics on the subject, foreigners have out-numbered Argentines in commerce and industry. The criollo is traditionally a landlord or a peon. The middle class are immigrants and the sons of immigrants.

Italians, Spaniards, Basques were small shopkeepers and artisans: they were pulperos and brickmakers, bakers and tailors. The immigrant had the drive that the criollo lacked, and starting humbly he often built a fortune on trade. Ebelot tells of a Basque he knew who worked as a peon when he first came to Argentina. Because the man was literate his employer gave him money to start a small pulpería in the campo, the two dividing the profits fifty-fifty. The Basque as pulpero bought the wools and hides from the estancieros of the district, advancing them the money on what they expected to have. If the price went up, he made money; if it went down, he lost. In this way he might make a small fortune for himself. If the speculation turned disastrous, the solution was easy: he could take his tropilla of horses and skip out for other parts.[21]

The English and Irish were more ambitious. Like the Argentine gentlemen, they settled on the land and built their fortunes on herds and flocks. Indeed, the Irish came to form the bulk of the sheep-farming community, and one is amazed in reading the roll of the largest landholders in Buenos Aires to find that in this period the English, Scotch, and Irish numbered fully a third, though their number in the whole population was negligible.[22] The Englishman did not immigrate to the Plata to work with his hands. The Italians and Spaniards did. For decades the Italians were harvest hands, commuting annually in steerage from Europe, and returning when the harvest was over. The Argentines called them *golondrinas* (swallows). A large percentage of the golondrinas stayed, particularly as the mechanical harvester replaced them, and in time they formed the backbone of the middle class.

The encouragement of immigration was government policy during the nineteenth century. It started modestly in 1856 when a group of private citizens presented a memorial to the government of Buenos Aires of a plan to help "the foreigners who arrive in the country looking for work, and who frequently find themselves abandoned without knowing where to offer their services." These individuals called themselves the Philanthropic Association,* and they rented an asylum where immigrants were received for the first four days of their stay. The Philanthropic Association lasted until 1862, when the government took it over. Its funds had come about half from private subscription and half from the municipal and provincial governments. During its five years of existence it had lodged 1,647 immigrants, a modest number.[23] It was not until the next decade that the nation created a hotel for immigrants, which included an employment bureau that received requests for workers from all over the country. It was located in Buenos Aires, in the Dársena Norte, and train tracks for all parts of Argentina passed through the hotel itself.[24] In this way, without effort on their part, immigrants could find employment and set out for it directly without getting lost, strayed, or stolen.

The majority settled in Buenos Aires, in city or country, and there were many who went to Santa Fe. To the grape province of Mendoza, to cultivate the vine, went Italians and Spaniards, especially Italians, who had had small vineyards in their own country, and who understood wine making. There had been wine presses in Mendoza from colonial times, but the European immigrants came to predominate in the industry: indeed, it would be

* The predominance of wealthy estancieros among the members would seem to suggest that one of the aims of their philanthropy was to encourage an influx of cheap, good, European farm labor.

no mistake to say they created the industry as it is today. The criollos, of whom Moussy had said they were unambitious and routine, sank to the peon level, and immigrants and the sons of immigrants predominated in the province. "The criollos of Mendoza and Cuyo," said one Mendozan, "who did not have the spirit of enterprise, gave valuable help to the workers who disembarked from transatlantic ships and were scattered through the interior. Unfortunately, they received no recompense. Their conditions of life got worse, in spite of the progress of the wine industry, which was reflected only in the foreign population. Our criollos were definitely the victims of this stage of development in Argentine capitalism." [25] Curious, this inability of the criollo to defend himself. That it was true, that it is still true, can be seen by the most casual visitor to the provinces: the criollo, whose dark skin proclaims the admixture of Indian blood, lives little better than an Indian, in the most wretched and filthy of huts, working only the minimum necessary to feed himself; and the son of the Italian and Spanish laborer who came to Argentina to better his condition has a house and car, and sometimes he is a wealthy industrialist. The criollo legend is perhaps an attempt to explain this failure in heroic terms: the criollo was too noble, too disinterested to meet the immigrant on equal terms. He was the victim of exploitation, as the cited quotation suggests. Of course, he was also the victim of exploitation under the criollo landlord, but the legend does not extend to landlords, and it also does not face the obvious question of why the poor immigrant, who competed, in the final analysis, on unequal terms with the natives, was so easily able to rise above their level. What is the answer?

As the sixties drew to a close, as the reputation of this new nation spread across the seas to Europe, immigrants came in increasing numbers. Five thousand came in 1860, forty thousand in 1870. But it was the eighties, the decade of frenzied prosperity, of railroads, of booming land values that saw the real rush of immigration. The number was 109,000 in 1885; 121,000 in 1887; 261,000 in 1889.[26] Some of these were golondrinas, and went back to Italy, but the balance was still stunning. That a nation whose first census shows only a little more than a million population should in just one year absorb two hundred thousand immigrants was something even Alberdi could not have dreamed. Italians headed the list, and just behind came the Spaniards. The two races accounted for almost three-fourths.[27] This was a different kind of Spanish immigration from the Andalusian adventurers that had gone out from Spain in the sixteenth century as mercenary soldiers and would-be gentlemen. These were peasants, most of them from the province of Galicia, sober, hard-headed and hard-working. There were so many from Galicia that Argentines call all Spaniards *gallegos*, without distinction. The expression is affectionate, and a little contemptuous at the same time. *Gallego* in Argentina means porter, servant, or small groceryman. The *gallegos* were not gentlemen, and for that reason they were excellent immigrants.

After Italians and Spaniards came French, Belgians, and English-Irish, in the order named. None of them was numerically important, the British least of all. But the financial standing and the moral influence of the British community were out of all proportion to its size. Most of its members had bettered their position by far when they came to the Plata, the Irish in particular. At home they might have been small clerks and tradesmen, or poor sheep farmers; but in Argentina they represented the Empire, they had standing in the community, and they were gentlemen. They behaved like gentlemen: *palabra de inglés* (word of an Englishman) became synonymous with absolute reliability. They took up land, they married into the aristocracy. The generations passed, and the Anglo-Argentines clung with tenacity to their language and customs. They spoke Spanish with an English accent, and English with a Spanish accent, and their English broke down, and became odd, deformed. The Argentine language absorbed Anglicisms from the British community, together with the football, golf, and tennis that the British brought. "It may appear surprising," wrote Michael Mulhall, who edited an English newspaper in Buenos Aires, "that in a continent twice the size of Europe, where the total number of English residents is hardly equal to the population of Chester or Carlisle, and does not reach one in eight hundred of the inhabitants, the English element has in a few years been able to make its impress felt in a greater degree than any other foreign nationality. This appears mainly owing to the influence of British capital and trade." And Mulhall allowed himself a prophecy which was fulfilled to the letter: "Whatever may be the fortunes of South America during the next fifty years, one thing seems certain, that its development in the arts of peace will be in a great manner identified with the growth of its relations with Britain." [28]

In this way Italians, Spaniards, French, Belgian, British, Germans, and Swiss came to Argentina in its years of growth and prosperity. They took up land, they opened small shops, they bought property, they saved their money. By the end of the century they were the most stable element in the community. Only 10 per cent of native criollos were property owners, but 12 per cent of the foreigners held property. In commerce and industry the foreigners outnumbered the criollos three to one. Two and a half times as many foreigners had restaurants and hotels as did native Argentines. In the clothing industry foreigners predominated four to one. In medicine they outnumbered Argentine doctors five to one.[29] They predominated in the construction industry, in transport, in whatever was not the care and feeding of cows and harvesting of crops. They went even into agriculture, not as holders of enormous latifundia, but as small tenant farmers raising grains and fruits. In Mendoza they took over and built up the wine industry. The immigrants were the middle class, and when the crash of 1890 brought economic crisis to Argentina, the new political movement that was to come out of it was the expression of their demand for a voice in the destinies of the nation. Argentina, its mentality, its economy, its physiognomy, were changing fast.

BUENOS AIRES

Buenos Aires, the capital city, was the barometer of change. At mid-century it was still the squat, dreary town of the revolution, without a port, without pavement, without gas, without streetcars. Houses were of one story, rarely two. There were great swamps in the center of the city that sometimes occupied blocks. Pedestrians circled by the most devious routes to avoid the seas of mud left by the rains. Doctors left their horses at peril's edge and walked the necessary blocks to their patients' houses, "taking advantage of the path which some charitable neighbor or some interested pulpero had improvised with the help of bricks, pieces of tile, etc." Marshes were filled in with garbage. They gave off a horrible odor and attracted thousands of flies which invaded neighboring houses. Sometimes one would see a dead dog or horse trapped in these marshes. Houses were still colonial, with window bars to keep out thieves on summer nights when shutters were open. Pilferers foiled the bars with long poles that had loops or hooks on the end, and sleepers awoke on occasions to see their clothes or gold watches moving silently out the window.[30]

Buenos Aires was a small town, with the small-town mentality. Society was a closed circle of acquaintances. It was fashionable to promenade in carriages downtown, in the narrow Calle Florida, which was—and is—the shopping center of Buenos Aires; or out in Palermo, where the former estate of Rosas was still to be seen.[31] Great families knew one another intimately, and married into one another's ranks, children preserving the names of both father and mother when the names were eminent. Thus the landed fortunes did not move out of the circle. Below this top stratum came the great middle class of Spanish and Italian shopkeepers whose family names were anonymous, and whose children already aspired to the university and the professions. The town was carefree, as only a small city can be, and the annual pre-Lenten carnival was celebrated with streamers and confetti and small bombs of perfumed waters. There were breakneck races on horseback, and *comparsas* —masked or black-face bands of celebrators, all dressed alike, who toured the city and played pranks. Humor tended to the barbarous, and there was nothing so funny to the porteño as to throw a bucket of water from a second-story balcony and ruin the costume of a passing pedestrian. Next to this in wit came the squirting of perfume in somebody's face, with blinding effect.

Streets were narrow and quiet, lighted with horse-oil lamps until the coming of the first gas company in 1853.[32] Night watchmen made their nightly rounds. They were called *serenos* because they habitually cried, "Las diez han dado y sereno" (Ten o'clock and the sky's clear). The English-language *Standard* chronicled a street fight between two serenos in the winter of 1863. One, who was crying, "Eleven-thirty and the sky's clear," met another who was simultaneously shouting, "Twelve o'clock, and cloudy." The disagreement terminated in a fist fight.[33]

For amusement one could go to the theater. The Teatro Argentino, at the corner of Cangallo and Reconquista, put on Spanish and Italian drama. The Victoria gave plays and Italian operas. The Colón, which was begun in 1855 by the French engineer, Carlos Pellegrini,* was inaugurated the following year with a masked ball. There, entertainment was catholic, and one could see anything from Spanish drama and Italian opera to Hermann and Linsky, the magicians. Hermann's tour de force was to make an omelet in the hat of a spectator and turn it into a wreath of flowers. Even acrobats passed through the Colón. The old theater was located on the Plaza de Mayo, on the site now occupied by the austere Banco de la Nación. The modern Colón, on the Plaza Lavalle, is the Metropolitan of Buenos Aires, a respected institution dedicated to symphony concerts and grand opera. And finally, the list of nineteenth century theaters would not be complete without the Politeama, which was a circus until 1879. After that it turned serious, and Eleonora Duse, Adelina Patti, Sarah Bernhardt, and many other notables played the Politeama. Regina Pacini, the

* Father of President Carlos Pellegrini (1890–92).

Portuguese light opera artist who scandalized porteño society by marrying Marcelo T. de Alvear, a favored son, and who as the Sra. de Alvear was to become First Lady of the land, made her Argentine debut at the Politeama in 1900, just before the historic old theater was torn down.[34]

Buenos Aires was a dusty city: dirt that in spring was mud was turned in summer to a fine powder by passing winds. The city was sometimes gray with dust storms, as provincial cities still are, and no amount of good housekeeping would keep furniture clean. There were plazas, but these were squares of earth where oxcarts gathered. The Plazas Once de Septiembre and Constitución were the great wool markets of Buenos Aires, and what is now the Plaza de Mayo was two plazas, the Victoria on the west and the 25 de Mayo on the east, separated by an ancient colonial arcade called the Recoba Vieja (Old Market).

In the fifties and sixties gas lighting came to Buenos Aires, together with horse-drawn streetcars, and a small attempt at running water. Gas illumination had begun in 1853, and by the end of the century it lighted fourteen thousand lamps in the city. The first tram line was built in 1868 from Retiro to Rivadavia. The following year Mariano Billinghurst inaugurated another line from the Recoleta, where the North Cemetery was, down to the Plaza de la Victoria and across to Plaza Constitución where the Ferrocarril Sud had its terminus. This decade saw, too, the first pipes for running water, built by the Ferrocarril del Oeste to bring water from the river to fill its locomotives. In 1868 the service was extended to private subscribers, but the system was limited.[35] What perhaps showed most urgently the need for an adequate water supply and drainage was the terrible yellow fever epidemic of 1871.

That was a year which nobody then living was ever likely to forget. Yellow fever was not uncommon in Buenos Aires in this period, because no one had yet guessed that the disease was mosquito-spread, and because the marshes of the city and stagnant muddy banks of the Plata were ideal breeding grounds for the *Aëdes aegypti*. The first case appeared in midsummer, in late January of 1871, and the epidemic reached its peak in April. In January there were 6 cases; in February, 298. In alarm government officers, judges, clergy, even medical men, began to abandon the stricken city. It was the presidency of Sarmiento, and Sarmiento was one of the first to go. With both national and local authorities in full flight, government offices closed, and the city had to name a Popular Commission to keep some kind of order. March, 4,895 cases. The Exchange shut down. In outlying towns rents reached fabulous levels. So many people were dying, there was no place to put them. The North Cemetery was filled, and a new cemetery, the Chacarita, was opened to receive the dead. April, 7,535 cases. With extraordinary heroism, men of all social classes, and especially of the leisured aristocracy, took over the government, opened hospitals in their homes, even dug trenches in the cemeteries to bury the victims. On April 10, when word came to the Commission that there were six hundred unburied corpses, the men held a solemn meeting in the patio of the University. At eight o'clock that night they put on their hats and adjourned to the Chacarita, where by torchlight they helped to bury the dead. The epidemic had reached its height, and in the following months it declined slowly. There were many porteños who wore gold medals in after years for the courage they had shown in these fearful days, and there were many who never lived down the reputation for cowardice, especially among the government officers who had abandoned Buenos Aires. The porteños did not forget that their President had gone, that the provincial government had gone, that the municipal government had gone. They also determined that such an epidemic should not happen again, and although they did not know its real cause they felt that the water supply had something to do with it. In that same year the city took over the pipe system from the F.C.O. and began extending it to the whole city. In 1874, the first sewers were dug in Buenos Aires.[36]

The seventies were years of progress. New tram lines crisscrossed the city, and extended to the suburbs, to Flores, to Belgrano. Rosas' estate of Palermo was made into a great public park, and the dictator's home was taken for a Military and Naval Academy. Four hundred miles of railroad radiated from Buenos Aires outward into the pampa. Fifteen lines of ocean steamers called regularly at the port from overseas. There were hotels, banks, and newspapers. The city was "well lighted with gas," and was being rapidly provided with water and drainage. Italian truck gardeners in the suburbs brought their fruits and vegetables to the city's markets, and the new railroads carried in partridges, ducks, and domestic poultry, butter and eggs. Basque *lecheros* on horseback ladled milk from tin cans that hung from their saddles.[37] The city imported French manners and modes, and children of the upper and middle classes learned the language. "Buenos Aires is becoming more and more French," wrote one visitor. "Paris fashions are the only ones adopted; French is the fashionable language, and in general whatever comes from France enjoys special favor."[38]

In 1880 came the last phase of that historic battle which was Buenos Aires against the nation. The national government of Avellaneda had been the city's guest since Mitre's administration, under the compromise which was the Ley de Residencia. The old issue of the capital entered once more into the picture when Avellaneda's term came to an end, and the two chief candidates to succeed him were General Julio A. Roca and the Governor of Buenos Aires, Carlos Tejedor. So deep was the agitation before the elections that secret corps were formed in the city for practice in the use of firearms. Tejedor called up the National Guard, and Avellaneda, in alarm, called out the army. The situation was so threatening that Tejedor resigned his candidacy, expecting that Roca would do the same; but the Hero of the Desert did not. A shipload of arms arrived for the province, and Avellaneda ordered it seized, but instead the provincial forces captured the intercepting naval vessel.

Everyone thought that civil war had come again to the nation. The President, followed by half of the Chamber of Deputies, and all of the Senate and Supreme Court, left Buenos Aires for near-by Belgrano, and troops were called up from the provinces to save the national government from the porteños. The two forces battled on the outskirts of Buenos Aires, and the national forces finally took the city. A new Congress settled the capital question by federalizing the city in September, 1880, and the next month Julio A. Roca was sworn in as President of the Republic.[39] The province of Buenos Aires had lost the city of Buenos Aires for good, and it had to build a new capital down river a few miles, at La Plata.

In the eighties Buenos Aires entered into the building fever that had taken the country. Torcuato de Alvear was named mayor of the city, and in his brief four-year term he did more to change its face, to make it the Paris of South America, than any mayor in its history. French tastes were already rooted, but they had not found outward expression, and Buenos Aires still looked Spanish-colonial. Alvear wanted to make it beautiful and European. The Plazas Once, Lavalle, and Constitución, which had been no more than empty acreage for bullock carts and street markets, he ordered to be planted with grass and trees and flowers. The Plazas Victoria-Mayo were made into one park by the removal of the dividing Recoba, and the new Plaza, on which bordered the colonial Cabildo, or Town Hall, the Casa Rosada, or presidential mansion that was under construction, the University, and the Congress, was renamed simply the Plaza de Mayo. The most expensive project of Alvear was the Avenida de Mayo, a wide, tree-planted boulevard running thirteen blocks from the Plaza de Mayo to what is now the Plaza del Congreso. The idea was Alvear's, and he had no sooner taken office than he called in the architect Juan Buschiazzo to make the plans. A national law was voted, authorizing the Avenida, which had to be cut through the heart of downtown Buenos Aires at vast expense. Thirty meters wide, thirteen blocks long, it cost 14,000,000 pesos and took ten years to complete.[40] When it was finished, when the trees were planted and the French Second Empire style buildings had been constructed the length of it, it looked for all the world like a boulevard in the heart of Paris. There were even sidewalk cafés to add to the illusion. Today, cheap movie houses and intruding functional façades in the taste of another period have tarnished the ancient splendors of the Avenida de Mayo; but in its day it was the pride of Buenos Aires, and the most fashionable and admired boulevard in the city.

In 1889, Argentina thought prosperity had come to stay. A new

British company had bought most of the city's tram lines and was now known as the Compañía Anglo-Argentina de Tranvías. The city had a fashionable Jockey Club, copied after the one in France, and there were two big race tracks where porteños gambled 35,000,000 pesos in 1889. At important auctions that year race horses had gone for fifteen and twenty thousand apiece. The *Prensa* was printing letters from Paris on fashions, the theater, interesting crimes. Congress had put up for sale 50,000 square kilometers of land, more than the combined territories of Denmark, Holland, Belgium, Portugal, Switzerland, Greece, Serbia, Bulgaria, Bavaria, Saxony, and Baden.[41] It was a boom the like of which Argentina had never seen. *La Prensa* was printing Cassandra-like editorials against public extravagance, but the President, Dr. Miguel Juárez Celman, was spending money with both hands and making public statements that prosperity had come to stay. Argentina was represented at the Universal Exposition in Paris. The Argentine pavilion was one of the most pretentious of a pretentious Exposition: it was a large, domed Byzantine building on the Champ de Mars, near the Tour Eiffel. The pavilion was a demountable iron frame whose different parts screwed together, and it was filled in with mosaics, porcelain, glass, and varnished brick. On the four corners were angels with trumpets. Here the visitor could see woods, cereals, wool, and hides from the Río de la Plata. Sansinena had an exhibit of frozen meats from its frigorífico "which has served for instruction and aroused great curiosity." Looking at photographs of Buenos Aires the Parisians stopped in surprise and admiration. "Why, look," they were heard to exclaim, "there are trams and plazas and parks just like ours!"[42]

Argentina was proud of its Byzantine pavilion at the Paris Exposition of 1889, where its products won six hundred prizes. The President and the nation could take satisfaction in nearly eight thousand completed kilometers of railroad, in fifty thousand more conceded, and under construction. Argentina's livestock was worth a staggering 458,000,000 pesos. It had two and a half million hectares under cultivation.[43] The nation was building bridges in Buenos Aires, Entre Ríos, Corrientes, and the Chaco;

ports in Rosario, Concepción del Uruguay, and Buenos Aires; a dam in Córdoba; irrigation projects in Salta. In Buenos Aires the Casa Rosada, the presidential mansion, was already partly occupied. Under construction were the police department, post office, military hospital, normal school, medical school, and maternity hospital. In Córdoba the government was building a clinic; in San Juan, an engineering school. Eleven hotels for immigrants had been constructed in the provinces. There was a competition for plans for a new Congress. La Rioja had new waterworks. The Río Gualeguaychú was being dredged, and in Buenos Aires the Riachuelo was being channelled to accommodate transatlantic steamers. Juárez Celman looked about and concluded that things were good, and could be better. "The 7,706 kilometers of existing railroad lines in operation are not enough," he told Congress in his opening message. "Millions of tons of freight are piled in the stations for months on end, awaiting shipment. . . . The country needs 20,000 kilometers of railroad if it wishes to be an agricultural nation of influence in the foreign market, and if immigration is to save the littoral and penetrate into the interior." He reviewed the prodigious building effort and concluded: "Everything goes up: the value of land, of livestock, of agriculture, of industry, commerce, credit, the accumulation of capital, public and private incomes. . . . For this I congratulate the country and I congratulate you, *señores diputados y senadores*."[44]

The next year Argentina entered the worst economic crisis in its history.

THE NOVENTA

THE GOLD CRISIS

The country moved toward the inconversion of paper money, the inevitable course, and discredit abroad. But there were few who saw clearly, and many, on the contrary, who benefited from the situation: the landlords, cattlemen, and farmers first of all.

—EMILIO FRERS, *Cuestiones Agrarias.*

During the booming eighties there arose a financial situation that was to bring about a complete cleavage of interests between the estanciero of the country and the tradesman of the city. This was the depreciation of the paper peso, a downward spiral that started in 1884 and brought the country to bankruptcy in 1890.

Now it so happens that printing-press money is an old Argentine device for getting loans out of the public. In the seventies there were hundreds of millions of pesos of inflationary notes in circulation, unbacked by gold or by anything else. The Roca government tried to bring some order by tying pesos to gold and silver in 1881, and issuing uniform currency. Before this, coins and bills of the most diverse kinds circulated in the provinces, some Chilean, some Peruvian, some Bolivian, some issued by the Banco Nacional and provincial banks. A Mendocino merchant, for instance, who had his money in Mendoza and wanted to buy in Rosario had to transact his exchanges as follows: (1) change Mendozan money into Chilean condors, the only coins circulating in quantity; (2) change these into pesos; (3) in Rosario change pesos for bolivianos and buy his merchandise; and (4) sell his goods in Mendoza for local paper.[1]

In 1881 provincial pesos were called in for exchange against gold notes, and for the first time in the history of the republic a peso was convertible to gold at par value. Money was sound and uniform, and bore the national seal. Conversion lasted through

1883–1884; then the government stopped converting, and the paper peso, slowly at first, then with increased momentum, dropped in value against gold. What was happening?

These were the years of national expansion, and the country was in a boom that had been touched off with the opening of the new lands in Buenos Aires and Patagonia. The roll of public spending, which the President called each year in his opening message to Congress—dams, bridges, ports, government buildings, parks—got longer and more ambitious with each year of prosperity. The government was spending more money than it had, and was borrowing abroad to do it. And at the same time imports exceeded exports year after year by wide and dangerous margins. In order to cover unfavorable balances of trade abroad, it became necessary to ship gold; and as gold reserves shrank the peso could be kept at par only by reducing the notes in circulation. In other words, the remedy was deflation. But instead of deflating, the government did the opposite. It issued new notes, at first openly, then secretly, flooding the country with paper. The result was that the peso began to drop. In January of 1884 it was at par: 100 pesos paper bought 100 pesos gold. In January, 1885, it took 120 paper pesos to buy 100 pesos gold. In January, 1886, the figure was 144.[2] The inflation was on, and no one cared to stop it.

In order to understand the financial suicide on which the Argentine government now embarked it is necessary to realize that inflation hurt some interests, but that it was very welcome to the estancieros and farmers of the littoral. The agricultural class was selling meat and grains abroad for sound British pounds and French francs. As the peso dropped, the pounds and francs the estancieros had were worth more and more. They were holding foreign money, not Argentine, and each year that money rose in value as against the declining peso. If the government restored sound money, if it deflated, this lucrative speculation would stop. Their pounds and francs would drop, and they would be the losers. The Roca government and, above all, the government of Miguel Juárez Celman represented the grazing interests of Argentina, and were afraid to stop the inflation when it was once started. On the contrary, the policies of Juárez were aimed at keeping the inflation going.

At the same time that inflation benefited the estanciero, it hurt the middle-class merchants of Buenos Aires who imported Scottish woollens and French linens and wines and olive oils to sell in the Argentine market. Their situation was the reverse of the estanciero's: they were on the other end of the seesaw. The goods they imported had to be paid for in pesos; and, as the pesos dropped, those goods got costlier to them and to their customers. Inflation meant ruin to the merchant class, and they watched the spectacle of government spending and irresponsible finances with despair and frustration, for they had no voice in public affairs. It was an estanciero's government, and they were middle-class small-business men, in large part Italian and Spanish, immigrants and sons of immigrants.

It was in this period that *La Prensa* made its reputation for economic wisdom. *La Prensa* represented then—as it still does—the grazing interests of Buenos Aires; but the editor saw that the vicious circle of unfavorable trade balances, paper issues, and unlimited foreign borrowing would in the long run lead to disaster for the estanciero as well as the merchant. It could not keep up indefinitely. Accordingly, the newspaper began running a series of warning editorials, trying to impress on an unimpressionable public mind that a crash was coming. *La Prensa* hammered at Juárez Celman to no effect. The President seems to have had no idea what he was doing. Millions were put into railroads, and still Juárez was able to complain to Congress in May of 1889, when disaster was already upon him, that the country needed not eight but twenty thousand kilometers.

The national government not only issued paper money but practically forced the private and provincial banks to do the same. Juárez felt, and told Congress so, that there was not enough money in circulation in the provinces. Private banks were urged to buy government gold bonds up to 90 per cent of their effective capital: against these they were authorized to issue money. In this way, 196,000,000 pesos were issued in less than three years. At the same time unfavorable trade balances continued in a pronounced degree, and the public debt grew from 117,000,000 pesos in 1886, when Juárez Celman took office, to 295,000,000 in 1889.[3]

Money was spent like water—on land, transportation, insurance companies, banks, commerce, industry. There was a frenzied speculation in land, encouraged by the Banco Hipotecario (Mortgage Bank) of Buenos Aires, and the Banco Hipotecario Nacional Credit was far too easy. Anyone could borrow money on land up to almost 100 per cent of its value, because the mortgage banks were so sure the inflation would continue and values would rise. Their *cédulas* (bonds) were common on foreign exchanges. Both banks were dominated by political camarillas, and many of their loans went to friends, or politicians, or anyone with the right connections.[4]

By 1889 it was evident that the structure could not hold up. Interests on old debts had for several years been paid only by borrowing more money abroad, and there came the moment when the services due on foreign debts were larger than the new loans. Gold jumped from 158 in May to 233 in December. On the floor of the exchange, merchants read the gold quotations and burst into tears.[5] President Juárez issued a statement: "In my opinion, the depreciation of paper money . . . does not depend on the amount of emission, nor has this any importance . . . in the present painful situation. Let us avoid complicating these grave financial questions with unnecessary conflicts and these inexplicable efforts to hurry the government." Said *La Prensa:* "Dr. Juárez lacked all notion of when to say things. His statements had not the slightest repercussion or influence in the direction of public opinion, and even less in the direction of business." [6] Said a contemporary: "A revolution goes about the streets looking for someone to lead it." [7]

Rumor was—and time was to prove the rumor all too true—that the Juárez government was making secret emissions of paper money, hoping thus to maintain the inflation without destroying public confidence in the peso. The head of the Oficina Inspectora de Bancos Garantidos (Office for the Inspection of Guaranteed Banks) resigned, and the story ran about Buenos Aires that he had refused to give the Banco Nacional 2,000,000 pesos because the bank had secretly launched into circulation 18,000,000 that were supposed to have been burned.[8] The story was neither confirmed nor denied, but it caused much excitement in Congress, and in the press, which by now was in full hue and cry after Juárez. It was certainly true in the President's case that whom the gods destroy they first make blind. What he hoped to accomplish by his financial prestidigitation was not clear then, and is not clear now. His actions were not even those of a desperate man trying to keep one step ahead of ruin: apparently he was the least worried man in the government, even though every sign pointed to collapse. Shipments of gold abroad, which in 1888 had come to only 4,500,000 gold pesos, in the first nine months of 1889 reached 25,000,000.[9] Exports in 1889 were 90,000,000 paper pesos; and imports, 165,000,000.[10] The consolidated debt stood at 309,-000,000.[11] April 9, the quotation of gold was 292; April 12, it was 305, 310.[12] April 13, the cabinet resigned en masse.

The new Minister of Finance, Francisco Uriburu, got a cool reception in Congress when he was called in to report whether it was true that the government had been making clandestine emissions of money. It was May 29, and Uriburu was facing Senator Aristóbulo del Valle of Buenos Aires:

Uriburu: The Senator said, accusing the government of extravagances which had brought us to the crisis that the emissions were—

Del Valle: Had contributed.

Uriburu: —one of the main reasons for the present difficulty, and that he demands the sacrifice of this tax. Mr. President, people have talked so much about the secret emissions that as soon as I became minister my first idea was to find out what was known about this. I went to the office created by law, but unfortunately the office did not have its books in order, and it wasn't the Executive's fault.

Del Valle: I suppose it was mine.

Uriburu: This office has been headed by outstanding citizens of our country, and through their fault I have not been able to get trustworthy statistics on this matter, which is so exaggerated, but which, I may say, has little foundation.

Del Valle: Clever, clever. To be sure.

Uriburu: The investigation isn't finished yet. Government agents are now in those provinces which have been accused of secret emissions. Until now the only thing I have been definitely able to find out is that it is mainly a question of old issues of the provincial banks, issues which, for a number of reasons which we should not now try to judge, it has been impossible to withdraw from circulation.

Del Valle: And has not the minister found any traces of *new* emissions?

Uriburu: Yes, sir, I have found traces, and I am going to bring them before Congress, and with all responsibility, with all the honor that the Senator has done me the favor of recognizing, I must say that I approve the measure.

Del Valle: I never!

Uriburu: I should, sir: not only should I approve it in the name of the Executive Power, but also as a man of conscience, as an honorable citizen who approves a saving measure, an indispensable measure.

Del Valle: A secret emission is a falsification of money, and there is no human reason which obliges a man to sanction the falsification of the national seal.[13]

The government was in too deep now to save itself or the country. Business houses suspended payment, and banks closed. In Buenos Aires the merchant class, looking about for a political party to represent it, and finding none, decided that the time had come to create one.

CIVIC UNION: A REVOLUTION

This is not the meeting of a party, nor even a coalition of parties. It is an association of healthy wills, a condensation of live forces responding to imperious necessity.

—Bartolomé Mitre, April 13, 1890.

It was in August (midwinter) of 1889 that there was a banquet of young Juaristas to express their unconditional support of the President's political policies. On the same day that the banquet took place, there appeared in *La Nación* an article by Francisco A. Barroetaveña entitled "Tu quoque juventud!" in which he bitterly attacked the attitude of the young Juaristas for their approval of the *unicato*, the one-man government of Miguel Juárez Celman.

The article was widely read and commented. It seems to have appeared just at the moment when middle-class indignation was strongest and least vocal, because within twenty-four hours the young author had received a stream of condemnations from groups representing the agricultural interests, and congratulations from those representing the merchants of Buenos Aires. The day after "Tu quoque juventud!" appeared, visitors crowded into the Barroetaveña home to tell him, as he wrote, that "they and many friends of the Exchange wanted to give me a banquet for my political stand." [14] Barroetaveña made the counter proposal that the banquet be a great protest meeting of young university men, and so it was arranged. Among the personal friends who came that day to congratulate Barroetaveña and stayed to plan the reaction against Juárez Celman were Juan B. Justo, a brilliant young doctor who was later to found the Argentine Socialist party, Tomás Le Breton (in later years Minister of Agriculture), and Marcelo T. de Alvear, son of the ex-mayor of Buenos Aires, and future President of the Republic. All of them were under thirty—young men who were to form an unforgettable generation.

The article had appeared August 20. On September 1 the great banquet of protest was held in the Jardín Florida with an attendance of more than two thousand people. The organizers got the support of the two outstanding leaders of the political opposition: Aristóbulo del Valle, Senator from Buenos Aires and the greatest speaker in Congress, and Leandro N. Alem, the best known unknown in the city, a man who had for years been a ward politician of the old Alsinistas, or Autonomistas. Del Valle was black-haired, with a wide face and puffy eyes, and a curly beard. His had been the fiery speeches against Juárez on the floor of the Senate, and the scornful interpellations of the cabinet ministers. Alem was a man of a different stripe. He had a beautiful, a sad face, with deep-set eyes and a gray beard that fell almost to his waist. He was an intellectual and an introvert, a man whose youth had been lonely and persecuted because his father was killed as a

Rosista during the Unitario reaction in Buenos Aires. In the university, where he studied law, professors and students had been cruel. "I was the son of the man who was hanged," Alem wrote bitterly. "In my examinations a rotten vengeance was taken on me. Many of the professors had come back from exile with a blind rage against all that smelled of Rosas. I was the son of the hanged man. I was the son of the *mazorquero* Alén." * [15]

Alem had grown up in porteño politics, first as an Autonomista, then as a member of a split party called the Partido Republicano which Aristóbulo del Valle founded. (Oddly, Del Valle later walked out on his own party, leaving Alem behind.) At the time of the Jardín Florida banquet everybody had heard of Alem without quite knowing who he was. The great dailies of Buenos Aires had given favorable attention and publicity to the meeting, and there was excitement in the city. At the meeting Alem spoke, and many others, and it was decided to form the Unión Cívica de la Juventud (the Youths' Civic Union). Alem was elected president of the executive council by acclamation. When the meeting was over, there was a procession down Florida to the Plaza de Mayo, where wreaths were laid on the statue of the revolutionary hero Manuel Belgrano. From the second-story windows of Florida an enthusiastic populace showered flowers on the heads of the demonstrators.

The movement did not bog down, as so many do, but gathered momentum as the Juárez government headed for financial disaster. Propaganda commissions were created, and parish clubs sprang up around the city. The movement spread to the province, where it got support from small tenant farmers and shopkeepers. The middle class had found a spokesman for its discontent, and rallied to it. The President obstinately refused to see the revolution that was gathering about him. On January 4, 1890, there was an army fiesta in the woods of Palermo, and Juárez Celman gave a speech. "I count on the army," he said, "to maintain my policies against the small group that sees everything through political prejudice, spurred on by an irresponsible press." [16]

* The original family name was Alén. Leandro changed the spelling to Alem.

In April, the gold quotation reached 300, and there was panic on the exchange. The Unión Cívica de la Juventud announced a gigantic meeting in the Frontón Buenos Aires at which the chief speaker would be General Bartolomé Mitre, long retired from public life, but the figure with the greatest prestige in Buenos Aires. Mitre was almost eighty, a white-haired, slender, aquiline-nosed figure dressed habitually in a black frock coat and black *chambergo*. His support had been enlisted in the campaign to break the Juárez government. The meeting was scheduled for April 13. On April 12, gold reached 310. On April 13, the cabinet presented its collective resignation to President Juárez, and the revolutionary forces met in the Frontón Buenos Aires to hear Mitre, Barroetaveña, Alem, and Del Valle. Enthusiasm was tremendous, and the crowd burst from the hall and paraded to the Plaza de Mayo with Mitre at the head. Again, flowers were showered from the balconies. The next day the three outstanding official candidates to succeed Juárez Celman in office, Vice-President Carlos Pellegrini, ex-President Julio A. Roca, and the Post Office Director, Ramón J. Cárcano, all wrote to the President saying that under no circumstances would they accept the presidential nomination to succeed him.[17]

At the meeting of April 13 a new organization, the Unión Cívica, came into existence. Mitre was the figurehead, Leandro Alem the real leader. The men had nothing in common. Mitre was almost accidental in the movement, and the younger man realized uneasily that he could not be counted on. Alem, in his political life, had never been a Mitrista. There were here all the elements of disunion, including the mentality of the old General, who had been a politician too many years not to be willing to compromise with the enemy if necessary. Alem, whether he realized it or not, was bringing a new idea into government. The platform of the Unión Cívica was free suffrage and honest elections, which meant, in other words, a chance for the great, inarticulate middle class to make itself felt against the estanciero minority that had the government in its hands. Alem asked for honest elections, and prepared for revolution, for honest elections did not exist. Only force could dislodge the Juaristas. And force meant the army.

It was then that two distinct movements came together to create the revolution of 1890. Certain elements in the army were dissatisfied with Juárez on their own account. Even before the September banquet in the previous year, thirty-three junior officers had secretly met to discuss the possibility of an uprising against the government. By April, 1890, their number had grown to sixty, and included generals as well as younger men. Four days after the mass meeting of the Frontón Buenos Aires, these officers offered their support and their services to Aristóbulo del Valle. Their leader was General Manuel J. Campos. The conspirators agreed that if the revolt were successful, Leandro Alem would be President. They enlisted the support of some sixteen hundred men of the army and navy, and planned the outbreak for July 21. The city and even the papers were full of rumors, and someone betrayed the conspirators, for on the 20th the Minister of War arrested the leaders and ordered the revolutionary regiments to the Chaco.

The revolutionists, thrown off balance, did not know whether to go ahead with their plans or not. It was finally decided to strike before the revolutionary regiments left for the Chaco, and accordingly the revolt began on July 26. The revolutionists gathered at the Parque de Artillería, and the President and Vice-President took refuge in the barracks of Retiro. The original plan was to attack the Retiro, and the failure to do this lost the battle to the revolutionaries. The next day they were out of ammunition, and asked for an armistice. On July 29 the armistice was signed: the rebels were not to be punished; the revolting corps were to be conducted by their chiefs to their quarters to await the government's orders; they were to put down their arms. In the moment of failure Leandro Alem lost his nerve. Lisandro de la Torre, a young lawyer from Rosario who was leader of the Unión Cívica in that city, and who worked intimately with Alem, many years later passed the following judgment on him:

"Dr. Alem was a man of proven personal valor, but not of rapid action in confused circumstances. From the moment it was necessary to parley he gave the impression of a sleepwalker, and delegated everything to Del Valle. One only heard him repeat, 'We are to blame. . . .' "

"The members of the revolutionary government and the extinct junta began retiring from the park," De la Torre went on. "Alem stayed to the end. When he walked out on the sidewalk on Talcahuano Street heading south, a second lieutenant, who came from the direction of Lavalle, told him that around the corner were soldiers of the revolting 5th Regiment, still in arms, shouting death to traitors, and if he tried to cross the intersection they would almost certainly fire on him. Alem went on his way, heedless, as if obeying the fatalism of his race, followed by the officer. At the corner of Talcahuano and Lavalle half the street was blocked by a streetcar overturned the first day of the revolution to serve as a barricade. Alem crossed the street, the guns of the soldiers were aimed. The second lieutenant gave him such a violent push that it made him fall headlong under the streetcar. Shots sounded, and the lieutenant fell dead, pierced by the bullets." [18]

The brief revolution was over; but Juárez Celman was finished. Congress decided to ask the President for his resignation. They waited, and he temporized, obstinate to the end. On the 5th of August his entire cabinet resigned, and the next day he reluctantly stepped down from the presidency. His successor was Vice-President Carlos Pellegrini, son of the French engineer who had built the Colón Theater. Pellegrini was popular and handsome, a dark-eyed man with chestnut hair and a short beard. He took office the 8th of August, and he said: "My most fervent wish will be to descend from the government as I have ascended—in the arms of the people." [19] There was a general amnesty for the revolutionists. In their first test of strength they had failed; but, as Dr. Manuel Pizarro said on the floor of the Senate: "The revolution, Mr. President, is beaten. But the government is dead!" [20]

HIPOLITO YRIGOYEN: THE RISE AND FALL OF THE RADICAL PARTY

MITRE BREAKS THE CIVIC UNION

Dr. Leandro N. Alem was the Don Quijote of Argentine politicians. —A. R. ASTENGO, *Hombres de la Organización Nacional.*

Leandro Alem had a nephew whose name was Hipólito Yrigoyen.*

There was only ten years' difference in their ages, and the men were more like brothers than uncle and nephew. Hipólito's grandfather, the father of Leandro, was Leandro Antonio Alén, a man of modest means who had belonged to Rosas' Sociedad Popular Restauradora, and who, in the reaction that followed the downfall of Rosas and expulsion of Urquiza from Buenos Aires, was shot dead by the Unitarios and then strung up as a public example. Alén's daughter Marcelina in 1847 married an illiterate Basque named Martín Yrigoyen, who was either a baker's deliveryman or a blacksmith, or both. They were the parents of Hipólito Yrigoyen.

Yrigoyen was a strange, silent child, dark, almost Indian-looking. He finished secondary school, and at the age of twenty, through the influence of his uncle Leandro, was appointed as a police *comisario* (district head). Six months later he was suspended when a young married woman accused him of having called her husband to the police station, and while he was detained there, of having sent her a love note by a negro servant. The charge was not proved, and Yrigoyen was reinstated.[1] It could well have been true, for Yrigoyen, who never married, nevertheless had various affairs and several illegitimate children. His first child was by a servant girl, and he kept her always with him. She was beside him while he was President—indeed, all her life, for she never married.

* Yrigoyen wrote his name with a Y instead of the *I* that modern Spanish orthography makes standard, possibly to distinguish himself from Bernardo de Irigoyen, who was no relation. Nevertheless, obstinate government printers changed the Y to I on all his published documents.

As a district comisario young Hipólito learned much about people and about politics. A silent man always, introverted, uncordial, he was a shrewd observer; and he used his knowledge to good effect. He joined the political club of the Autonomista party, in which Leandro Alem was chief of a ward, and he never abandoned back-room politics until he had reached the presidency of the nation. In 1874 he entered the Facultad de Derecho (Law School). Alem was already a graduate lawyer, with the degree of doctor, but there is no reason to suppose Yrigoyen finished the Law School. The records show he completed one year of a six-year course.[2] Nevertheless, he always claimed the title of doctor, and this particular vanity of his was the butt of many jokes in later years. It seems to have been one of Yrigoyen's few vanities, for he was a quiet and unpretentious man.

In 1878 Yrigoyen was elected to the Buenos Aires legislature. The election, like most elections of the period, was dirty, and the newspaper *La Libertad* accused him and two other deputies of obtaining their seats by fraud. The other deputies resigned, but Yrigoyen kept his mouth shut and held his seat. At this time he was a member of Del Valle's Partido Republicano, a division of the Autonomistas. Neither he nor Alem ever had any truck with Mitre's party, possibly because he was the heir of the Unitarios who had hanged Leandro Alén. This curious Rosista strain in the political segment that was one day to emerge as the Radical party has never been adequately studied, and it may be of some significance. Again, perhaps not.

In the eighties Yrigoyen became a teacher. He taught civics and Argentine history in a girls' normal school. This was the time, too, when he discovered the rather confused philosophy of the German philosopher Krause, who was then much in vogue in Spain. Krause's theories were a mixture of rationalism, idealism, and spiritualism, and they had a profound influence on this ex-comisario of police, whose culture and education were thin: too thin, at any rate, to make him a very critical reader. The most lasting impress of the German philosopher on Yrigoyen was on his language. To his death he spoke and wrote in a foggy metaphysical prose that was all but impossible to decipher.

When Alem headed the Unión Cívica, Yrigoyen was beside him. Had the abortive 1890 revolution triumphed he was to be chief of police. Of his behavior during the actual fighting Lisandro de la Torre wrote: "He did not demonstrate a single quality, he did not expose himself personally at any moment to the enemy's fire." [3] Perhaps this is true. Yrigoyen was never at the front of anything, but was a born behind-the-scenes worker. Those who hated him hated him intensely, and those who admired him admired him uncritically. There has never been a character whose motivation was more obscure, or whose personality was more secretive. In dealing with Yrigoyen one may choose between the White Legend and the Black Legend. There are no grays in the picture. Without being intelligent, he was almost unfathomable.

Yrigoyen became the political caudillo of the province of Buenos Aires, and that was his great strength. When the July revolution was put down, the Unión Cívica persisted; and in January of 1891 the party convention nominated Bartolomé Mitre for President and Bernardo de Irigoyen, who had been minister under Roca and Avellaneda, for Vice-President. Mitre had been in Europe, and he landed in Buenos Aires the day after his nomination. The city gave the eighty-year-old general the most uproarious welcome in its history. He was the hero of the hour, and his followers looked to his prestige to break the Unión Cívica's only opposition, which was the Partido Autonomista Nacional, headed by Julio A. Roca. Both Roca and Mitre had long since left their military careers behind them and were masters of the more artful dodges of politics. The two put their heads together and made a political deal: they would unite their forces instead of fighting it out at the polls. Mitre could have the nomination for President, and a Roquista would be Vice-President.

When Mitre's betrayal became known, from the most popular man in Buenos Aires he became the most unpopular. The uneasy fears of Barroetaveña and the young idealists of the Unión Cívica were realized. Mitre had not been with them after all, but only using them. The new party split down the middle: out of it walked all the men who had been the moving spirits of the revolution: Alem, Del Valle, Bernardo de Irigoyen, Hipólito Yrigoyen, and the younger men like Marcelo T. de Alvear and Lisandro de la Torre. What had once been Civic Union became disunion. Those who went with Mitre called themselves the Unión Cívica Nacional, and those who went with Alem called themselves the Principistas, but Mitre's followers nicknamed them the Unión Cívica Radical. The name stayed, and the party continued to be known as the Radical party. The U.C.N., which, in the last analysis, was only another personal party like all those that had gone before it, quickly vanished from the political scene. But the U.C.R., the Radical party—which stood for suffrage, for honest elections, and for the participation of the urban middle class in the national government—continued to grow until it became the biggest movement in Argentine politics.

Mitre's deal with Roca was fatal to his candidacy. Had he stood by the Unión Cívica he would almost certainly have been president. But now the sense of betrayal was so strong in Buenos Aires that Mitre and Roca had to find another man to head their ticket. In this confused political situation there arose another candidacy, that of Roque Sáenz Peña, a relatively young man who had been the Argentine delegate to the First Pan-American Conference in Washington in 1889. Roque Sáenz Peña looked too strong to Mitre and Roca, who, casting about for a way to get him off the political scene, hit on a most diabolic and effective scheme: they would nominate his father for President, and family loyalty would of course dictate that Roque withdraw in favor of his parent. Accordingly the two politicians got the party to nominate Luis Sáenz Peña, who was a very old and manageable candidate. The result was everything hoped for. Roque withdrew his candidacy in favor of his father, and in March, 1892, Luis Sáenz Peña was elected President of the Republic.

Luis Sáenz Peña was an unfortunate President. He had inherited the virtual bankruptcy of the nation's credit. The gold premium had risen to an unprecedented 384.[4] The nation's external debt was 412,000,000 pesos,[5] and the London firm of Baring Brothers, which had lent millions to Argentina since the time of Rivadavia, went down with the ruin of Argentina's foreign credit. To economic complications were added political ones. The President showed an ungrateful unwillingness to take advice from Roca and Mitre who, having put him in office, expected also to dictate his policies. When the old gentleman proved unamenable, Mitre and Roca turned Congress against him, and cabinets came and went in crisis after crisis. Furthermore, the movement which was Radicalism was getting strong and dangerous. In Buenos Aires the silent, mysterious Hipólito Yrigoyen managed the provincial party. "A more absolute rule, or a more personal work, have never been seen," said Lisandro de la Torre. "He decides, he orders, he makes and unmakes. He is president, treasurer, and secretary, all at once. He surrounds himself only with men who obey him and whom he can manage at will." [6] Yrigoyen built up the strength of Radicalism in the province; and in the capital Alem headed the national party. Alem wanted to try another revolution as the only possible means of getting power. Yrigoyen said no. Uncle and nephew began working at cross purposes, and Alem felt uneasily the increasing power of the other. Yrigoyen was so taciturn it was impossible to argue with him. Most of the party, with Alem, wanted to make a revolution, but they were helpless without the province, and Yrigoyen, steadily refusing to explain, avoiding party meetings, keeping to himself, held the balance against Alem. Why did he hold out? Nobody knows. Lisandro de la Torre, who despised him, said it was because of ambition: "If the Radical revolution had triumphed in 1892 or 1893, Dr. Alem would have taken over the government, and this thought did not attract him. He preferred to destroy Alem even at the cost of postponing the revolution for a long time, so that the day it came it would be for his benefit." [7]

De la Torre was a man of strong opinions, young, brilliant, acid. He, like others, was to leave the Radical party because of Yrigoyen's dictatorial methods. In these days he was the youngest outstanding figure in the group. Yrigoyen was already in his forties, a politician of experience. What De la Torre despised in Yrigoyen was precisely what made him a successful politician: clever, effective, not necessarily clean work in building up a party machine in the province of Buenos Aires. De la Torre was to be in his day the most intense figure in Argentine politics. His intelligence and intransigence were unmatched. But he was a magnificent failure in public life, and what his honesty would not let him do, Yrigoyen's singleness of purpose accomplished. In the final analysis the machine politician, the caudillo, inherited the Radical revolution, leaving Alem, Del Valle, Irigoyen, and the rest behind in the wreckage.

When Alem needed his help, Hipólito Yrigoyen retired quietly to the province and abandoned him. The revolution was postponed. In the meantime the aged President, helpless in the face of a Congressional revolt that would not let him keep a cabinet, turned to Aristóbulo del Valle. Del Valle agreed to form a Radical cabinet for Sáenz Peña, and he took for himself the portfolio of the Interior, a key cabinet post because it controls provincial intervention. The Radicals, with Del Valle in the ministry of the Interior, were in a position to make a revolution from above. There were outbreaks in San Luis, Santa Fe and in Buenos Aires, and the Buenos Aires revolutionaries, headed by Yrigoyen, took La Plata, which was the capital of the province, and installed their own government. At the same time the Radical Minister of Finance announced he would investigate the administrative acts of previous governments. Carlos Pellegrini persuaded President Luis Sáenz Peña that the first person investigated would be his son Roque, who had been Minister of Foreign Affairs in the Juárez government, and in alarm the old man put the Radicals out of the cabinet and intervened in the revolting provinces. A rebellion in the army in Rosario and Tucumán was crushed by General Roca, and Radical leaders went into exile. When Congress voted amnesty for the rebels, the President refused to sign, and he was forced out of office, being replaced in January of 1895 by his Vice-President, José Evaristo Uriburu.

After the '93 rebellion, the heart seems to have gone out of

Leandro Alem. He had been a failure. In 1896 Del Valle died. Shortly afterwards Leandro Alem, who had been too much of an idealist, too much of an intellectual for his own good, ended his life by suicide. "The man who silently watched the failure and downfall of Dr. Alem was his nephew, Hipólito Yrigoyen," said De la Torre. "Underneath his black clothes and taciturn manner, underneath his repeated disclaimers of all personal ambition, underneath even his easy and frequent tears, he was intriguing, deceitful, ambitious." [8] With Alem gone, with the tactics of this "Quijote of Argentine politicians" in disrepute because they had led only to failure, the party gravitated inevitably to Yrigoyen. Alem had made a frontal attack on conservatism and failed. Now Yrigoyen could try his own methods, which were less direct.

ROQUE SÁENZ PEÑA

> *There is not an article of the electoral law whose violation has not been converted into an honorable act; the falsification of signatures, the stealing of public registers, the usurpation of name and estate, and even the dishonesty of magistrates. . . . In the Argentine Republic there is only one thing dishonorable in the matter of elections, and that is to lose them.*
>
> —JUAN BALESTRA in the Chamber of Deputies, September 10, 1890.

Argentina came slowly from the crisis of 1890 to a new and growing prosperity. During most of the decade amortization of the national debt was suspended, and the peso fluctuated annoyingly; but as the century closed Argentina once again resumed payments on her foreign debt, and the peso was tied to gold at the rate of 44 gold centavos per paper peso. The Conversion Law had been the outcome of a bitter fight between the hard-money men, the importers and city merchants, and the estanciero group which favored inflation. The government had compromised: the peso was not pegged at the old par rate, but it was pegged, thus combining monetary stability with a minimum of deflation.

Bad as the crisis had been, the country continued to grow and to build. Immigration, which had finally reached a minus quantity in the depression year of 1891, climbed quickly back to the level of the previous decade, although it was far from reaching 1889's quarter-million peak. In 1894 the Avenida de Mayo was opened, and Buenos Aires began to look like Paris. Railroads grew and spread. The nation's second census, in 1895, showed that half the population could now read and write, where a quarter of a century before nearly 80 per cent were illiterate. It was an improvement, even if it was far from the ideal. The same census showed a new and important fact: one-fourth of the population of Argentina was now foreign-born. This group had commerce in its hands. It outnumbered native Argentines in all that was not agriculture. But it had no voice in the government, and the revolution that was to have given it that voice had failed.

Government was the government of the "enlightened minority," a group that represented the estanciero class, the free-trade philosophy, and the great latifundia. The philosophy of the ruling class could be summed up as a profound distrust of the lower classes, which included the immigrants and sons of immigrants. The criollo peon had never been a threat to oligarchy, but the foreign-born brought new, disquieting ideas from Europe which the government could keep submerged only by limiting the suffrage. The struggle of 1890 had revolved about the issue of free suffrage. Juárez Celman had been forced from office, but Carlos Pellegrini, for all his popularity, for all his statesmanship, was a man of the conservative mentality where the vote was concerned. "This has been the great fault of Pellegrini," wrote a woman who knew him, "—his absolute neglect of, not to say contempt for, the exercise of the suffrage. Did he think the people lacked sufficient culture to vote? It was a handy pretext for those that favored force. A fragile pretext. . . . President Pellegrini by his indifference helped check the political evolution of the Republic." [9]

His successors were to be no better. The next term was filled out by Luis Sáenz Peña and José Evaristo Uriburu, both men of the same stripe. For the 1898 elections Roca announced his candidacy to be President a second time. Roca was the essence of conservative politics, with all its fraud, and force, and political chicanery. Even Mitre, whose deal with Roca had broken the Civic Union, could not quite swallow this candidacy, and the aged general tried again to re-form ranks with the Radicals. Just as his activities in 1891 had split the Unión Cívica, so now his new maneuvers were to divide the Unión Cívica Radical. There was a party convention to consider Mitre's proposal of a united front against Roca. Bernardo de Irigoyen,* who had nominally inherited Alem's leadership, was to be candidate for President. The majority accepted the ticket, but the provincial committee of Hipólito Yrigoyen walked from the convention, and when the elections came the U.C.R. abstained from voting. Roca was elected President as the only candidate running.

It was an estanciero's government par excellence. Policies were aimed to please the Sociedad Rural: easy money, no tariffs, low land taxes. The pedigreed bull became a national symbol. The Sociedad Rural, from the days of frantic speculation in land and money, had declined in membership and prestige during the worst days of the depression, and the Palermo livestock shows had had to be suspended. But they started again in 1895, and by the end of the decade were more brilliant than ever. On the eve of Roca's election the Sociedad issued a manifesto defining its stand on protective tariffs, which was virtually the liberal free-trade position of Great Britain. "To high tariff barriers," it said, ". . . the countries consuming our only articles of export reply by raising tariffs on livestock and agricultural products. . . . We do not ask the absolute abolition of protection to existing industries and those that may be created in the future; we only ask that it be less absolutist, that its methods not bring us the reprisals of countries consuming our products." [10] It was the voice of the Revolution unchanged, the policy that had driven the provinces to rebellion. But now it spoke almost without opposition, for colonial indus-

* No relation to Hipólito Yrigoyen.

try had been ruined beyond revival, and there was no manufacturing to demand protection. The city merchants were free traders, too. The only group that asked a tariff were the sugar men of Tucumán, who found that their sugar could not meet foreign competition. But they were still without importance in the economic balance, and the free-trade chorus was almost unanimous.

If the immigrant commercial class was in agreement on tariff policy, it was not in agreement on a government from which it was excluded by the electoral mechanism. The vote was not limited by legal means, such as property qualifications, but it was limited by naked force. The opposition did not get to the polls because police or army barred the way. What fraud did not accomplish, intervention in the provinces did. Article 6 of the Constitution, which had been aimed at rebellious provincial caudillos, was coming to be the weapon by which the party in power perpetuated itself. The article said that the federal government might intervene in the provinces to guarantee the republican form of government. The phrase "republican form of government" proved elastic. In effect, the republican form of government was considered to be jeopardized when the opposition won an election; and a federal interventor was sent to call new elections and guarantee that they went the way the President wanted. Intervention could be voted by Congress when it was in session, or decreed by the President when it was not.

The Argentine President has much more power than the American, for Argentine "federalism" has nothing in it of the spirit that created the United States. Spanish colonial government was highly centralized, and the executive by tradition was strong. Provincial federalism had for a moment arrested the tendency, but under the reunited Republic power gravitated to Buenos Aires and to the executive. Under the Argentine Constitution presidential orders must be countersigned by the minister in whose jurisdiction the order falls, but the ministers are the President's men, responsible to him, not to Congress. In practice it has become customary for the executive to rule by decree. Expenditures not allowed by Congress are agreed on in cabinet meetings and made. Decrees, which in theory can only amplify or regulate the provisions of the laws which are voted by Congress, are in fact legislation by themselves, independent of any control.

In this way it was possible for a strong executive to rule the country as he wished, and to make and unmake elections. By intervention, by fraud, by declaring a state of siege and suspending constitutional guarantees when it seemed convenient, the conservative landholding aristocracy ruled Argentina even when the democratic majority was against it. The nucleus of opposition to the status quo was the Radical party led by Hipólito Yrigoyen, who believed that Radicalism would never triumph at the polls, but would some day come to power by revolution. It was this belief that determined party tactics: at every election, the Radicals abstained from voting, to emphasize the illegality of minority suffrage, and to protest against it.

Yrigoyen was a political boss, a caudillo of a new, nonviolent kind, none the less autocratic for being a tactician instead of a provincial bandit. He ruled the Radical party by the force of his personality, which must have been extraordinary to command such fanatic loyalty. But there were already some who did not like dictatorship, even when it was in the name of democracy. One of the first to rebel against Yrigoyen's personal leadership was the young Rosario lawyer Lisandro de la Torre. De la Torre mistrusted Yrigoyen for his ambition. He confided to a friend his suspicions that Yrigoyen was deceitful and intriguing, and the friend would not believe him: "Hipólito couldn't be like that," was the reply.[11] Yrigoyen's pose was that of a man without personal ambition, altruistic, idealistic. His followers believed in him, and that was a source of great power. Whatever he did was for the party. For himself he sought nothing. This was the legend. Nevertheless, De la Torre asserted that Yrigoyen was two-faced and self-seeking. At the Radical convention of 1897 in Santa Fe, De la Torre, presented his resignation, and from the platform told his reasons. "The Radical party, from the beginning," he said, "has nourished a hostile and perturbing influence which has impeded its progress, has diverted its best intentions, and has converted all patriotic impulse into a debate compounded of personal prejudices and ambitions. This influence has been Mr. Hipólito Yrigoyen, a hidden and persevering influence both before and after the death of Dr. Alem, a negative but terrible influence, that with cold premeditation made the revolutionary plans of 1892 and 1893 come to nothing." [12] In Argentina, a challenge like this is mortal, and Yrigoyen demanded a duel. The two men fought, cutting each other. There was no reconciliation afterwards, because Yrigoyen refused it. It was the first challenge to his leadership, but it was not to be the last.

Young Dr. Juan B. Justo, too, left the party. In the days of the July revolution, while De la Torre had stood sentinel at the door of the Parque de Artillería, Justo had been inside, in the hospital, tending the wounded.[13] He was intelligent, serious, and of unquestioned personal integrity, like Lisandro de la Torre; but he left the party less for personal reasons—he had no quarrel with its leaders—than out of conviction that it was not far enough left. In 1894, Juan B. Justo founded the Argentine Socialist party; and he was its leader until his death. Socialism, even more than Radicalism, was an immigrant movement. Its earliest beginnings the decade before had been in a German club called "Vorwärts," founded with the objective of "cooperating in the realization of the principles and ends of socialism." [14] In many ways the party never lost its Germanic impress: in organization, it followed that of the nineteenth century German Socialist parties; and its leaders, men like Justo and Nicolás Repetto, have been men of an un-Latin concreteness of mind, and of a passion for facts and statistics. In the late 1880's, Vorwärts lent its clubrooms to striking workers (although these were few in those early days); and when the Paris International of 1889 designated May 1 as an international labor day, Vorwärts organized a mass meeting of more than three thousand workers for May 1, 1890. From that meeting grew a workers' union.

The movement was clearly of foreign impetus. At its meetings, speeches were in Italian, French, Spanish, and German. Committees were called "Internationals," and the organization published a paper, *El Obrero* (The Worker). The gold crisis struck as hard at the workers as it did at the middle class. Inflation meant the lowering of real wages, and suffering for the laborers who even in normal times lived at the margin of decent existence. One of the important strikes of 1891, for instance, was at the yards of the Ferrocarril del Sud because the workmen demanded that the company keep to its contract about devaluated money. The revolutionary movement of the Unión Cívica had the wholehearted support of the labor groups, because both workers and merchants had a common grievance against the speculating estancieros; but after the initial failure the workers went their own way. It was at this time that Juan B. Justo joined the Socialist movement, and that for the first time the party was organized with Argentine membership.

In 1894 appeared the paper *La Vanguardia,* and in the next year the central committee resolved that only Argentine citizens, born or naturalized, should be party members. The resolution had the important effect of getting the immigrant working classes to take out citizenship papers and get the vote for themselves, so that they might have a voice in the government. In 1904, to the surprise of everyone, Socialists included, the party elected its first deputy to Congress from the national capital in the person of Dr. Alfredo L. Palacios.

Like an amoeba, the Radical party underwent various divisions in the early years of its history. Justo left to found the Socialist party on Marxist principles. Lisandro de la Torre retired to his native province of Santa Fe to dedicate himself to the agrarian interests of Rosario. His first political activity was in a purely local question, which was the dominance of the capital city of Santa Fe over the younger but growing Paraná River port of Rosario. De la Torre founded the Liga del Sur, or Southern League, a farmers' party. He himself was a wealthy farmer in those days, although he was later to lose his fortune. But there were other, less important divisions in the Radical party. In the first years of the twentieth century two new groups split off, leaving Yrigoyen's "Blues," as they were known, in a decided minority. Yrigoyen's stronghold was the province of Buenos Aires, where he was the most important political boss. Radical politics was carried on in an atmosphere of conspiracy. Yrigoyen still thought that the only possibility for triumph was in armed rebellion, and acted accordingly. The party regularly abstained from elections. In 1905 the Yrigoyenistas broke into active revolt in Buenos Aires, Bahía Blanca, Santa Fe, Mendoza, and Córdoba, but the would-be revolution was suffocated by the government.

The country, in the meantime, was once again on the economic upswing. The twentieth century brought new prosperity to agriculture, and land began to rise in value. One of the significant trends was away from livestock to agriculture, especially in Santa Fe, which was beginning to rival Buenos Aires in the wealth it produced. Where in 1888 the total land planted in Argentina had come to only a little over 2,000,000 hectares, in the twenty-two years from 1888 to 1910 the number increased by 17,000,000. In the same period the value of livestock exports doubled.[15] The trend to agriculture was the making of the river port of Rosario in the south of Santa Fe. This was the heart of the grain belt, and there was every reason why grain should be moved from here and not from Buenos Aires. The national Congress passed a law authorizing the government to let a contract for the building of a real port in Rosario, and in 1902 the French company of Hersent et Fils, Schneider et Cie. was awarded the right to build the installations and exploit them for forty years.

It is said that the Port of Rosario in its heyday was one of the two or three most successful enterprises in the world, falling only a little behind the Panama Canal. The government made its contract with the Schneiders on an estimate that the maximum traffic the port would reach would be 2,500,000 tons a year, and that this limit would not be reached until 1930. As a matter of fact, 2,500,000 was reached in 1905, just three years after the contract was let.[16] Rosario became the leading grain port of the world, and the second city of Argentina. Port of Rosario shares that had sold originally for 500 francs reached a quotation of 35,000 francs on the Paris Bourse.[17] This meant stunning profits for the company, but it was also the index of the agricultural growth and prosperity of the Argentine cereal zone.

Argentina was still a country of great landholdings, with more than half of the land in parcels of over 5,000 hectares. In the 1914 census, 506 owners held 29,000,000 hectares between them.[18] The landed aristocracy had the country's economic wealth, and the government represented them and their interests. The small tenant farmers of Santa Fe, the importers and small-business men of Buenos Aires, the working class of city and country might have other interests; but their voice was not heard, nor was there the legal mechanism to make it heard. Labor meetings and strikes were broken up by the police. The Radicals, by their own free choice, abstained from voting. The provinces, which nominally had their own governments, were in fact ruled from Buenos Aires by intervention. The government was conservative and aristocratic, and was determined to hold on to present advantage. Yrigoyen, surveying the scene, calculated that successful revolution was the only solution. Juan B. Justo wryly estimated that if the present trend continued, he would be elected to the Chamber of Deputies in 1940.

It was at this point that Roque Sáenz Peña, whose way to the presidency had been barred by Roca and Mitre when they made his aged father candidate, was elected President of the Republic. When Sáenz Peña was inaugurated in 1910, he had behind him a career as deputy, delegate to the First Pan American Conference of Washington, and Minister of Foreign Affairs in the cabinet of the unfortunate Juárez Celman. He was a man now in his sixties, and ill. "There is no doubt," wrote Paul Groussac, "that the first and only premeditated plan that Sáenz Peña brought to the government was the reform of the electoral law as a means to the end of bringing the abstaining parties to the polls." [19] The new President was a Conservative, like all that had gone before, a man representing the same minority and the same social class. But it is to the everlasting credit of Sáenz Peña, and of his Minister of the Interior, Indalecio Gómez, that they believed in the free suffrage of the Argentine people. The President was troubled at the spectacle of a party that year after year refused to go to the polls in protest at the fraud and force employed in elections. Within a year of his election, he and Gómez drew up a plan of electoral reform which was passed by Congress in 1911, and has been known always as the Sáenz Peña Law. Under the new law, voting and military service were tied together. A young man at eighteen had to register for military service, and when he registered, was given the Libreta de Enrolamiento, or enlistment book. His Libreta was his ticket of entry to the polls, his enlistment inscribed him on the register of voters. Voting was secret and compulsory for all males over eighteen. The law also created the incomplete list, by which the majority party in each province was given two-thirds of the deputies elected, and the minority party one-third. Thus, in a province which has nine seats in the Chamber, the winning party will elect the six candidates from its list which have the highest number of votes; and the party that runs second, no matter how many or how few votes it has polled, will send its three most-voted candidates.[20]

The Sáenz Peña Law was the magic Open Sesame to the government for Hipólito Yrigoyen's Radical party. The first elections under the new law, in April of 1912, gave an overwhelming victory to the Radicals. For the Socialists, who were strong in the Federal Capital, the Sáenz Peña Law was an equal salvation: in 1913, the Socialists captured the majority representation of the city of Buenos Aires.* In Santa Fe, Lisandro de la Torre organized a new political party called the Partido Demócrata Progresista. In the first elections held under the new law in Santa Fe he had won a minority seat in the Chamber of Deputies, and two years later he organized the new party, looking toward the 1916 presidential elections.

The 1916 presidential elections were the focus of attention. For the first time in its history the nation was going to have a President that represented the popular majority. In their hearts, all parties—Conservatives, Radicals, Socialists, even the Partido

* The city of Buenos Aires, under the 1880 Law of Capitalization, is represented on a par with all provinces by senators and deputies.

Demócrata Progresista—knew what that meant: the next President of the Republic would be the caudillo, the political boss, the conspirator from Buenos Aires, Hipólito Yrigoyen. For years Yrigoyen had been building his machine all over the country. For years he had worked as a back-room politician who was seldom heard and seldom seen, but always felt. Yrigoyen said he had no personal ambitions, and refused to discuss his candidacy. His enemies believed that he was a hypocrite, and that only a miracle could prevent his being the next President of Argentina. The great middle class adored him. Lisandro de la Torre said that he represented the *reacción gauchesca*—the gauchesque reaction.[21] The Conservatives did not care what he represented, but trembled for their lost power.

Yrigoyen was a tall, swarthy, heavy-set man who exercised an almost hypnotic fascination over his followers. It is hard to know what his power was. He was not an orator. He was introverted, silent, almost morose. But there was an aura of religious mysticism about him. When he called his followers in for personal interviews one by one—he always interviewed people alone—he gave them the impression of wonderful wisdom and power. To say that he was worshipped is not to exaggerate. There is no reason to believe the man was intelligent. Nor had he any culture: nobody took seriously his claim of being a doctor. But in his own curious fashion he was a leader of men and a consummate politician.

When 1916 came, all eyes were on Yrigoyen. The Partido Demócrata Progresista had proclaimed De la Torre its candidate. The Conservatives were disconcerted and uncertain what to do. With the elections scheduled for April, the Radicals held their convention in March and nominated Yrigoyen for President. Since Yrigoyen had repeatedly proclaimed his lack of personal ambition, he refused the nomination, and the convention had to ask him again. Upon being urged, he accepted. The next month, in the first free, representative presidential election in Argentine history, Hipólito Yrigoyen received the majority vote by 150,000. But by one of those quirks to which the system of presidential electors is subject, Yrigoyen did not quite have a majority of electors in the

Electoral College. The balance was held by a group of dissident Santa Fe Radicals who had announced they would never vote for Hipólito Yrigoyen.

Between the election and the meeting of electors, there was frantic work behind the political scenes. The Conservatives felt that if they could get De la Torre and the P.D.P. over to their side, and agree on a candidate, they could stop Yrigoyen. At first De la Torre lent a sympathetic ear, willing to make the coalition and sacrifice his own candidacy if the Conservatives were willing to come out with a clean slate and constructive program. But a few conversations with Conservative politicians made it amply clear that they had no more in mind than the old, discredited politics that had always been theirs. In anger, De la Torre said that if he had to choose between the Conservatives and Hipólito Yrigoyen, much as he mistrusted and disliked Yrigoyen, he would choose him. "Are you not aware," he wrote to one Conservative politician, "that I always felt aversion for the politics of General Roca, founded on the systematic usurpation of the suffrage? Are you not aware that I was always the enemy of Pellegrini, not even his great services as a statesman saving him in my eyes from the inherent evils of his lack of democratic principles? . . . Why, then, in my hour of defeat, should I join in policies which have never been mine? . . . To have gone down . . . with the *traditional* banner of governments I had been fighting for twenty-five years would have been disastrous and shameful for me."[22] And so De la Torre, another politician in the great quixotic tradition of Leandro Alem, would not lift his hand to defeat the popular will. The Electoral College met, the dissident Santa Fe Radicals threw their votes with the Radical majority, and Hipólito Yrigoyen became the President of the Argentine Republic.

That October 12th when he took his oath of office, Buenos Aires gave him the most fervent and happy demonstration in its history. When he left the Congress, neither the police nor the Grenadier Guards could clear a way for him through the tremendous populace that had gathered in the Plaza del Congreso. Somehow the tall, dark, unsmiling man got through to his carriage.

When the carriage began its march, the people unhitched the horses and pulled the carriage with their own hands. "Colonel," said Yrigoyen to the officer of Grenadiers beside him, "how can you permit such an act?" "Sir," the Colonel replied, "we could only avoid it by using our swords." When he heard this, Yrigoyen gave orders to let the people alone, and they pulled his carriage down the Avenida de Mayo. They were so delirious with enthusiasm that the President stood up in his carriage and made signals with both hands for them to be quiet.[23] A curious personality! The enthusiasm brought no smile to his face. But it was a great triumph: for him, for the middle class that had created the Radical party, and for the great mass of the Argentine people, who had at last had a voice in the election of their own chief executive.

PRESIDENT YRIGOYEN

> *Yrigoyen was always a politician of democratic pretenses, and nevertheless it was he who was the cause of the discredit into which democracy may have fallen in our country. . . . Yrigoyen is the man who buried democracy. Social legislation, however, is another question. I have always recognized that his government became more humane, and that that evolution took place in spite of the Conservatives.*
>
> —LISANDRO DE LA TORRE, August 2, 1938.

The new President was not a man to inspire lukewarm enthusiasm. "Tall of stature," wrote one admirer of Yrigoyen, "as if to see above the crowd and be seen by them, his head energetic, manly, the true head of a Roman emperor, rests magnificently by means of a well proportioned, robust neck, on shoulders that are wide, cyclopean, made to bear the weight of a great nation. His glance is piercing like the eagle's, to scrutinize from head to foot, and to see at great distances, where the sight of mortals cannot reach. His forehead is wide and high like a mountain summit. One sees that behind it, like the granite deep in the Andes, the ideas are firm, well rooted."[24]

This was Yrigoyen as his followers saw him. To the ordinary observer he was merely a large, dark-skinned man who habitually wore a bowler hat, whose face was stern, and whose speeches to Congress sounded metaphysical and confusing. Nobody could deny that he had inherited the government at a difficult moment for the nation. Europe had been at war for two years, disrupting world economy and, with it, the agricultural economy of Argentina. The outbreak of hostilities had found the country unprepared, and in a serious business depression. From 1912, gold had been steadily draining from the country, because of unfavorable balances of payments. When war broke out at the end of July, 1914, there was panic in Buenos Aires, and on August 2nd the government had to close the Gold Conversion Office and the banks and financial houses. Nobody knew how world war would affect the country, whose life was foreign trade. The British blockade stopped all trade with the Central Powers. It meant a diminishing list of peacetime goods that could be bought abroad as the industrial nations of the world turned their plants to war production. Argentina had bought everything in Europe: shoes and hats, wines and olive oils, woollens, silks and linens, telephones, copper wiring, electric-light bulbs, trams and locomotives, coal, iron, hardware, machinery, dishes. All that was not food came from abroad. But now, suddenly, the life line was cut. What would happen to the grains piling in elevators, to the meats stocked in the frigoríficos, to the estanciero who lived from his produce, and to the city merchant whose business was importing? That was the great question mark in 1914.

By the time Yrigoyen came to power, the question had been largely answered. It could be read in trade figures. Under the first shock of war, both imports and exports dropped sharply in 1914. In 1915, exports were higher than the peacetime average, but imports were low. And this balance was to last during the war years, and through 1919. Exports continued to climb, imports were low, sometimes as low as half the exports. The explanation was that England and France were buying heavily in the Argentine market to supply their armies with food, but they had nothing to send in return. The greatest profit was in meat. Agriculture, whose products had outstripped livestock in the prewar years, lost its lead and fell behind as the Allies bought all the beef and mutton and hides the Argentine could send. Actually, the physical volume of exports scarcely moved during the war period. Rather it was the values that had gone up, bringing great profit to the country. From 1915 to 1919, values rose 64 per cent. Wheat that had sold for 8.60 pesos the quintal * in 1913, was selling for 16.13 pesos in 1917. Two-year-old steers in the Liniers market that had sold in 1912 for 125 pesos, reached 172 in 1917, 224 in 1919. Wool tripled in price from 1912 to 1918. But land, curiously enough, was almost stationary in price. Estancieros were renting fields instead of buying, uncertain how long the war would last.[25]

The war brought high profits to some; but all classes felt the pinch of scarcity when no goods came from abroad. The great profits from agriculture, combined with a lack of things to buy, brought serious inflation, and the cost-of-living index climbed from 92 in 1914 to 157 in 1918, and to 1920's high of 172.† [26] In short, the cost of living almost doubled. Argentine wool and meat might be bringing fancy prices, but so were the cheese and olive oil and kerosene that came from abroad and were necessities of life to the people. Cheese that had cost 37 cents per pound in United States money in 1914, cost $1.47 in 1918. A quart of olive oil that had cost 20 cents in 1914, cost 70 cents in 1918.[27] And not only imported products but domestic meats were high, because the English and French buyers had been bidding the price up.

And so it was Yrigoyen's fate to be a war President. He proclaimed his government's neutrality, and stuck to it even when the sinking of Argentine merchant ships by German U-boats brought great popular indignation against the German Empire. Feeling in Argentina was strongly pro-Ally, and German businesses and newspapers and clubs were smeared with tar and had their windows broken. The British government blacklisted firms suspected of being German, but the blacklist was circumvented somewhat by

* A metric quintal is 100 kilograms, or 220 pounds.

† On a basis of 1933 = 100.

dummy Turkish firms that sprang up during the war and made great fortunes selling to the banned houses.[28] Yrigoyen resisted the strongest public pressures for Argentina to join the Allies as the United States and Brazil had done. The popular attitude was summed up by Luis M. Drago, who had been Roca's Foreign Minister, and was a distinguished Pan American statesman who had enunciated the Drago Doctrine against armed intervention in the American Republics. Since Drago's opinion on the war was almost word for word that of the United States, and that of those Argentines who favored belligerency in the succeeding war, it is worth quoting:

"My opinion has been from the first," he said, ". . . that we should accompany the United States when it cut its diplomatic relations with the German Empire. The submarine blockade, and the intimidation with which it menaced us . . . would have amply justified that attitude. Today the situation is worse. The United States finds itself at war with the German Empire. The struggle has presented itself as President Wilson's message says: democracy *vs.* absolutism. How could an American nation withdraw from the conflict and remain neutral without denying its past, and at the same time compromising its present and future? Brazil hurries to join the belligerents. . . . Can Argentina, breaking its bonds of solidarity with its Latin brothers, and its traditional policy, maintain itself in an isolation which nothing justifies, and which, in addition, is full of danger?" [29]

But Yrigoyen was determined to keep his country out of war, and keep it out of war he did. He very prudently concluded that if Argentine merchant ships got sunk, the nation being neutral, far more would be sunk if the nation were belligerent. Neutrality was good business for the country. The economy boomed, and gold balances piled up in Argentine embassies abroad, where they were kept until shipping was safe again. Yrigoyen's record of severe correctness toward Germany was fittingly crowned in 1920, when he took Argentina out of the League of Nations because the Central Powers were not allowed to enter. On one occasion after the war, when the Argentine President's name was mentioned on the floor of the Reichstag, the assemblage rose and cheered him.[30]

When the war was over, and passions had subsided, even Yrigoyen's enemies, who were many, concluded that his neutrality had been a good thing. From 1916 to 1919, the peso had been quoted above every major currency in the world.[31] Argentina was, for the first time in its history, an international creditor to whom both England and France owed money. After 1920, however, when new imports came from abroad to redress the unbalance of the war years, the peso began to decline, and the country returned to its normal situation as a debtor nation. This was inevitable. But Argentina could thank its neutrality for the fact that it suffered so little, and profited so much, when the rest of the world was at war. And the shutting off of supplies for five years had one good permanent effect, which was to stimulate the creation of light industries where none had existed. When the war ended, Argentina was manufacturing many of the things it had always bought abroad, and with the ending of hostilities, the industries remained. The country would never again be caught in the situation of 1914, when it had been dependent on Europe for the smallest of necessities. Industry was embryonic, but at least it existed.

It was for his internal policies that Yrigoyen was most criticized. This is understandable. His was the first non-Conservative government the country had had. This was the triumph of the revolution that Alem had begun a generation before. There were many who lamented the Sáenz Peña Law becacause it gave the vote to the politically immature—or to those that the Conservatives judged politically immature. According to these critics, the people were not ready for self-government. The law was commendable, well intentioned, of course; but it was not realistic. Does a half-illiterate peon, they argued, have the judgment of a university man? Could you take a drunken Indian from a Tucumán ingenio and expect him to elect his own government? And what of the 35 per cent of the people who were frankly illiterate, as the 1914 census showed? What of the foreigners? In the years prior to the war immigration had been annually in the two hundred thousands, a number that frightened those who wanted to keep Argentina creole, who were afraid of the new, dangerous un-Argentine egalitarian ideas that immigrants brought with them. As for the urban middle class that the Radicals claimed to represent, that too was foreign and un-Argentine: two-thirds of all the people in commerce—in food, clothing, building, furnishing, education, transportation, medicine, banking—were born abroad.[32] Yrigoyen, then, represented the illiterate, the ignorant, and the foreign-born, and for this calamity of a government Argentina could thank Sáenz Peña.

This was the Conservative view. There was also a non-Conservative opposition to Hipólito Yrigoyen: Juan B. Justo and his Socialists, who sniffed at Yrigoyen's halfhearted labor reforms; Lisandro de la Torre, who said that Yrigoyen represented the gauchesque reaction, that he was a caudillo, that his democratic pretenses were insincere. Now that the Radicals were in power, friend and enemy could watch their performance and judge for themselves. And what was the record?

Well, it was true that the Radicals made some attempt at social reform: laws were passed that established retirement funds for employees; work in the home was regulated. Yrigoyen sent Congress messages and projects on arbitration, collective bargaining, housing projects, Sunday rest. Labor unions were allowed a freedom of activity they had never had before. This was the period, too, of the great University Reform that for the first time opened the doors of higher education to the lower middle class.

The Reform—it is always written with a capital letter in Argentina—is a phenomenon which can be understood only if one understands Latin university education. Argentine universities, in the first place, belong, all of them, to the national government, and are in the highest degree political institutions. The President of the Republic can intervene at will in the university administration, discharge university authorities, change the rules governing the organization. The university, too, is a professional school. A student studies his chosen profession six years, whether it be medicine, law, engineering, or philosophy and letters. Courses are not elective. One may study nothing but one's profession. And one has to take the prescribed courses, from the prescribed professors, whether one wishes to or not.

The Argentine university, traditionally, is a miniature battleground of national politics. Students strike, riot, and stage political demonstrations on the slightest provocation. They picket their professors, barricade themselves in the buildings, throw bombs at the police, print partisan handbills. Between the political intervention from above, and the political disturbances from below, education gets somewhat less attention than it should. The professor is a man who earns his living outside, and teaches one or two courses at the university. He is usually a lawyer or professional man of some kind. His appointment is largely a matter of political influence. Whether he has any interest in teaching, or in his students—usually he does not—he has no time to devote to them outside class because he has to earn a living. He is neither a scholar, in the sense of being a research man, nor a teacher, in the sense of being a friend and guide to his students.

Before the 1918 Reform, the situation was even worse. Given the combination of political appointments, and the helplessness of the students who had to take from prescribed professors, it was possible for teachers to fail their students on political grounds, or make education difficult for them. The universities were staffed with incompetents, whose only claim to their positions was that they had friends in the government. Education was backward and bad. In 1918 the students of the University of Córdoba, the oldest and most traditional university in the country, went on strike against an interventor that Yrigoyen had sent to the school. The following month, the First National Congress of University Students met in Córdoba to plan for a thoroughgoing university reform. The Congress voted for the creation of a "University Republic," in which students, alumni, and professors should each have an equal say in university government. The reformers wanted to break the small governing oligarchy "which impedes healthful development." [33]

The movement spread to the universities in Buenos Aires, Santa Fe, and La Plata. In Buenos Aires the Law School was assaulted. In La Plata, too, there were attacks on the university.[34] The movement lasted for more than a decade, and many of the reforms demanded were realized. Students were given representation on university councils, and a voice in the appointment of professors. A university education came within reach of classes that had never before been able to aspire to it. Yrigoyen's part in the movement was, to say the least, negative: it was his intervention in Córdoba that set off the whole movement. But on the other hand, without the general atmosphere of liberalism which Yrigoyen had brought to the government, without the declarations of democratic principles, the Reform would have been unthinkable.

It was in the Radicals' methods of government that Yrigoyen's enemies found the most legitimate causes for complaint. The Radicals had come to power in the country's first representative presidential election, with a platform of free suffrage and political democracy. They had complained long and bitterly of fraud and intervention, of high-handed methods in government. Yet Hipólito Yrigoyen was the man who, after Urquiza, intervened in the greatest number of provinces. In his first administration, there were twenty interventions in a nation with only fourteen provinces.[35] In some provinces there were as many as three interventions. All that Conservative Presidents had stood for in the way of excessive centralization and illegal methods was represented in exaggerated form by the man who claimed to be the spokesman of democracy. Lisandro de la Torre was not surprised: it was what he had always prophesied. If Yrigoyen was a tyrannical caudillo within his party, who could expect him to be democratic in his government? It became evident that the new President had no concept of the delegation of authority. He intervened everywhere. His government was personal in the highest degree. He did not understand that only Congress had the right to vote appropriations, and he spent money not authorized by the budget. When Congress called him to account in interpellations, he replied that no one had the right to criticize what the government did with "its own resources." Questioning revealed that these "resources" came from public offices which Yrigoyen left vacant, but which still figured in the national budget.[36]

No one has ever been able to accuse Yrigoyen of personal dishonesty or bad faith. He died as he had lived, a poor man. But not so the run-of-the-mill Radical politician. The country was treated to an orgy of spoils politics, in which ministers lined their own pockets and found employment for their family and friends, and in which men who were mediocre and less than mediocre filled all the offices from schoolteacher to chemist. The Conservatives had, at any rate, a number of intellectual luminaries in their ranks; and the nineteenth century aristocrat had been a man, for all his mistrust of the mob, with a feeling of noblesse oblige. The Radicals had no organization beyond the discipline of Yrigoyen's personal leadership, as was to be amply proven the day Yrigoyen died. They had in their ranks a few men like Tomás Le Breton and Marcelo T. de Alvear who were men of the Noventa, and whom everyone respected. But the rank and file were political hangers-on with no interest beyond their personal gain. The intransigent men, the idealists, the men of the caliber of Justo and De la Torre, had been sacrificed to Yrigoyen's dictatorial leadership, and were lost for good. And the day was coming when Alvear and the rest who were decent would go, too, and Lisandro de la Torre's harsh judgment would be justified: "Yrigoyen is the man who buried democracy." [37]

The saddest failure of Yrigoyen's presidency was his attempted conciliation of labor which ended with the labor massacre of January, 1919, in the so-called *Semana Trágica* (Tragic Week). Reading about it after the lapse of a quarter of a century, it is hard to visualize what happened. The Semana Trágica cannot be divorced from its context, which was that of a world that had just seen the finish of the greatest war in history and its aftermath, which was hunger and revolution. The porteño who opened his *Prensa* or *Nación* in the summer mornings of 1919 could read United and Associated Press dispatches of Communist riots in Berlin and Munich, of mass murder by the Russian Bolsheviks, of thrones that had fallen, and nations that had broken apart, and frenzied peoples that were taking their revenge on their old leaders. To the comfortable Argentine middle classes it looked like mass insanity. To the submerged labor movement, it seemed the beginning of a new socialist order. It was in this atmosphere of fear and unrest, complicated by a suffocating Buenos Aires summer, that there occurred a harmless-looking strike in the Vasena metal works, a British plant in the city's suburbs.

The strike at first attracted no attention, but on January 3rd the picketing workers fired on a group of policemen who were conducting wagonloads of metal to the Vasena works. Two days later a police sergeant died of his wounds. On January 7 an unrelated event took place: the maritime workers of the port of Buenos Aires voted a general strike for better hours and wages. That same day, at the Vasena metal works, the police, who had laid a trap of cleverly planned crossfire, fought it out with the striking workers when they tried to stop a load of metal escorted by the police. The battle was fought with revolvers, Mausers, and Winchesters, with a toll of five workers dead and twenty wounded.[38]

The next day, Wednesday, there was an ominous quiet in the city, as the waterfront strike began, and all ship movements, and loading and unloading, came to a stop. Thursday was the funeral of the five workers that had been killed by the police, and on that day all hell broke loose in Buenos Aires. A hundred and fifty mourners in procession, some of them armed, followed the funeral coaches, and as they went they turned aside for attacks on objects of their anger. They burned an automobile along the way. When they came to the station of the Lacroze, a British tram company, they attacked the building. Then they broke into the convent of the Sacred Heart, at Yatay and Corrientes, and set the church on fire. As they were attacking a store the police caught up with them, fired into the procession, and killed and wounded some of the demonstrators.

But it seemed now as though the mob were loose all over the city. Groups overturned and burned streetcars, until by noon traffic was paralyzed. They plundered sports shops and carried off the guns. At three in the afternoon three thousand people stormed the

Lacroze station. Congress was in session, and the deputies, who had to walk blocks, sometimes miles, in the fierce January sun to reach the Chamber, could see in all the streets the evidence of the general rioting and destruction. They met in an atmosphere of short tempers, and instead of taking action, they threw their notebooks at each other and said things which had to be deleted from the *Diario de Sesiones*. Fire trucks, streetcars, automobiles were overturned and burned in the streets. The funeral procession met a suburban train at a railroad crossing and broke every window in it. At the Vasena works angry crowds pushed garbage wagons against the doors to break them down and get at the British directors who were besieged inside. The British Minister appealed to Yrigoyen for help. The President seems to have given the police the order to shoot to kill, because they fired indiscriminately on everyone in the streets; and as the toll of dead and wounded mounted, the mobs became more frantic and destructive. That night the Federación Obrera Regional Argentina (Regional Argentine Workers' Federation) met to consider police action and voted a general strike for twenty-four hours throughout the city of Buenos Aires.

On Friday the city awoke to find there were no newspapers, that markets and stores and hotels and bars were closed, that there was neither food nor transportation nor communication, for telephone lines were down. In the absence of information on what was going on, there was panic in Buenos Aires. The streets were full of soldiers and sailors, and troop trains from all over the country were coming into the city. In every quarter there was shooting. The riots were taking an ugly turn, and for the first time one noticed that it was no longer the angry workers, but cruel and irresponsible mobs who were running the streets, shouting death to the *Rusos*, the Russian Jews, who were somehow identified in the popular mind with anarchists and Bolsheviks.* The Jewish sections were invaded, and the terrified Jews dragged from their homes and beaten and shot and killed. Some escaped by pleading

* Much of the later phase of the Semana Trágica was instigated by the Liga Patriótica (Patriotic League), a proto-fascist organization of the period, which hated communists, labor, and the Jews.

they were Italians. Fire trucks full of armed police ran through the streets shooting to left and right. A mob stormed the police department. There was no food in the city, and eggs that were selling for 90 centavos in the morning reached 3 pesos by evening. The railroad union voted to stop trains all over the country in a sympathy strike. The Socialist party issued a protest at the police massacres: "Men who have no military organization or means of repelling violence from above cannot forever protest with folded arms," said its manifesto. "It is the government which has proven itself afraid and inferior, and has from the beginning assumed an attitude at once brutally repressive and exaggerated in its senseless determination to stamp out for its own ends so spontaneous and justified an explosion of feeling." [39] That evening a de luxe restaurant of the Calle Florida, which was serving its old customers behind locked doors from an amply stocked icebox, gave an index to the prevailing confusion. Diners who knocked at the door were covered by revolver as they entered, by a doorman who in normal times was employed to bow ladies and gentlemen from their carriages.

It is hard to account for what was going on except on the theory that Yrigoyen was in a panic. Much of the killing was being done by the police, and most of the victims were bystanders who had no part in what was going on. By Saturday the Federación Obrera realized that there was a new element in the massacres, which was the Jewish pogrom that was bringing an ever growing list of dead and wounded Jews to the newspaper columns. The union ordered its members back to work, and issued a statement disclaiming all responsibility for Friday's killings. The papers were full of the list of dead and wounded, but it was impossible to tell the number of victims because the government would issue no statements. The streets of Buenos Aires by now stank with uncollected garbage and refuse, and the city presented a scene of desolation. Electric cables were lying in the streets, together with wrecked vehicles. Trains did not run in any part of the Republic. No ships entered or left the port.

The week ended on a note of farce. Saturday the Montevideo

police had informed the authorities of Buenos Aires that they had uncovered a Communist plot to seize both sides of the Río de la Plata with the taking of the capitals of Argentina and Uruguay. On Sunday the porteño police solemnly informed the Buenos Aires press that they had broken into a private apartment where forty persons, all of them Russian Jews, were in session as the "First Soviet of the Federal Republic of Argentine Soviets." [40] This was too much even for the newspapers, who, now that the city was again becoming quiet, refused to be alarmed. The worst of the crisis was over, and the column of dead and wounded for the first time in days was growing shorter.

When the week was over, all sides took stock of the government's acts and concluded that they had been bad. The middle and upper classes felt that the police had added to the confusion instead of controlling it; and the workers were angry and resentful at the brutality with which their strike had been broken, and their fellows senselessly murdered. Perhaps the most sensible words spoken on the subject were those of the Socialist deputy for Buenos Aires, Dr. Nicolás Repetto, in the Chamber of Deputies.

"The Radical government," he said, "has believed that one treats the labor movement with exquisite amiability and formal concessions, and that to this one adds promises which are never fulfilled, and which the government does not even know can be fulfilled. With these tactics the present government has not solved a single labor conflict; every time it has thought one solved, there was already in it the germ of a new and graver one, and that is why an insignificant strike like the Vasena one has developed into a conflagration.

"The first fight was a completely useless slaughter of workers by the police. The deputies can visit the place for themselves and see how the police arranged their forces so as to concentrate fire in determined places, even shooting into private houses. . . . The conflict was started by the imprudence of the police, enormously aggravated the following day when they fired on the funeral procession. . . . Before taking violent measures against the labor movement we should ask ourselves what we have done to solve the labor problem in this country." [41]

Yrigoyen did not deserve all the blame, though. With a world in revolution it is not surprising that the echoes of great events penetrated even to the Río de la Plata. Yrigoyen, like most of Buenos Aires, merely mistook the echo for the terrible event itself.

SEPTEMBER, 1930

The revolution of September 6th ends in the return to the country's most ominous electoral past. It will probably constitute one of the most sterile and dismal episodes of Argentine history.
—LISANDRO DE LA TORRE, Córdoba, October 18, 1931.

When Yrigoyen's term drew to a close, in the summer of 1922, the Radical caudillo looked about him for a successor—under the Argentine constitution no President may serve two successive terms—and decided that it should be Marcelo T. de Alvear, his ambassador in Paris.

Alvear was the aristocrat of the Radicals. A porteño, son of the mayor who had changed the face of Buenos Aires in the booming eighties, Alvear had name, fortune, land—all that could possibly lend luster to a party that some thought less than respectable. He had been among the first organizers of the Unión Cívica de la Juventud in 1889. Most of his life had been spent abroad, for he was one of the *niños bien*, the moneyed playboys who had adopted Paris as their spiritual home. There was, in Yrigoyen's eyes, no political taint in the man. He was safe, ornamental, and manageable. Accordingly, the President told the Radical convention to nominate Alvear, and it did. Alvear returned from Paris with his wife, Regina Pacini, the Portuguese singer that porteño society had snubbed, to be the second Radical President of the Argentine Republic.

The Alvear presidency shone for its prosperity. Land was worth so much, especially in Buenos Aires, that the aristocratic fortunes were reckoned in the millions. A hectare in the province of Buenos Aires which had cost 38 pesos in 1903, reached 257 pesos in 1921, and was worth 260 the year after Alvear left office. Good cereal land was at the staggering average of 373 pesos.[42] The estancieros mortgaged their estancias and built châteaux in the country, in the city, and in France. To mortgage the estancia was an old custom: money was easy to get from the Banco Hipotecario, and paying the mortgage was no problem when land doubled in value every few years. But already families with aristocratic names, whose grandfathers had owned large parts of Buenos Aires, were losing their fortunes, and the number was to grow. A mortgage for improving the land is one thing—a mortgage to build châteaux and buy diamonds is another; and many a millionaire, suddenly faced with a bad year, found himself unable to meet interest payments. Multimillion-peso fortunes began collapsing when war prosperity ended.

On the whole, though, the twenties were prosperous, even brilliant, for Argentina. Not only did the landed aristocracy spend most of the year in Paris, but even the middle class could afford the luxury with the decline in the franc. This was the period when majordomos could be making 40,000 pesos a year, and spending their vacations abroad. Buenos Aires was as French as assiduous imitation could make it. Buildings were in the style of the Second Empire. The Avenida de Mayo had its sidewalk cafés, like any Paris boulevard. The theaters gave French plays, the bookstores sold French novels, and French philosophers and pseudophilosophers filled the Sunday supplement of *La Nación*. The Paris fashions of November appeared on the streets of Buenos Aires in April, almost as chic as the originals. The gay songs that Maurice Chevalier and Mistinguett were making popular in the Casino de Paris or the Folies-Bergère were sung in the *boites* of Buenos Aires. Gallic intellectuals lectured to eager porteño audiences, and wrote articles for literary magazines dedicated to the spreading of European culture. Cultured porteños, gathering at five o'clock tea or cocktails, spoke in French. The average Frenchman, in the meantime, continued to confuse Buenos Aires in his mind with Rio de Janeiro, and could not have told whether Buenos Aires was the capital of Argentina or Brazil.

Alvear was the symbol of a Gallicized Argentina whose heart belonged to Paris. Alvear was a large, bald man, with a face that was froglike in caricatures. He was amiable, respectable, and very much a gentleman. Buenos Aires society did not like his wife—she had sung in public and could not possibly, therefore, be a lady; but Regina Pacini conducted herself with dignity, and it was difficult to snub the President's wife. Alvear would not go anywhere without her. When he had married her, he had bought up all records she had made and taken them off the market. She had of course had to retire from the stage, because she was the Señora de Alvear. But, now that all this was behind her, she was his wife, and a lady; and the President imposed her on Buenos Aires society until it accepted her without reservations.

Yrigoyen was at first pleased with his hand-picked President, whose government he intended to run. But there were soon symptoms of difficulty between the two men. Alvear proved (in Yrigoyen's eyes) ungrateful, and refused to take orders, and in less than two years President and ex-President had broken relations. The rupture became public at the opening of Congress in June, 1924, when Vice-President Elpidio González, an Yrigoyenista, did not preside. In September of that year Alvear took his followers out of the Radical party and organized the U.C.R. Anti-Personalista to challenge the dictatorial management of Hipólito Yrigoyen. The Anti-Personalistas joined the Conservatives in the 1928 elections to try to keep the Radical caudillo from becoming President the second time. But Yrigoyen was still the idol of the people. In March of that year he was again voted to the highest office in the land, and there began the most disastrous presidential term in Argentine history.

Yrigoyen was in his eighties. His mind was failing. As the months passed it became evident that he had no business in office, because he could not understand what he read, and nobody could understand what he spoke. He was painfully and publicly senile. Of him, as of the aged President von Hindenburg of Germany, it was said that if you left the electric-light bill on his desk he would sign it. The nation's finances became a tangle as a parasitic host of Radical politicians robbed the public treasury. The senile President made hopeless, impossible appointments of incompetent people to offices that were not authorized by Congressional budget. There was robbery in the Post Office, the State Railways, the Aduana, the national lottery—in every branch of the government where money was to be stolen. It was a tragedy for Yrigoyen, who had no idea what was going on, and who was a poor and honest man. In the Aduana there were 3,500 employees unauthorized by law. In one office of the State Railways there were 300 employees where the budget authorized six.[43] A government like this would have been intolerable under the best of circumstances; but it unfortunately coincided with the New York stock market crash of 1929 that set off the world economic depression of 1930. The peso, too, was in a precarious situation, because foreign lending, which had kept it up, was suspended in 1928, and gold was flowing out of the country so fast that the government closed the Conversion Office in December, 1929.[44]

Argentina urgently needed a government that could cope with this crisis. Yrigoyen's incapacity was sadly evident. As depression deepened in 1930, as exports dropped, and the peso dropped, and the spectacle of political plundering continued without abatement, there were growing rumors of a military revolution against the government. They were spoken of publicly, in the press, and on the floor of the Chamber. The only ears they did not reach were Yrigoyen's—if they did, the aged President was too foolish to heed them. On August 9th, forty-four Senators and Deputies signed a petition against the government, protesting interventions in the provinces and extravagant expenditures. On August 19th the Anti-Personalistas made a declaration against the government.[45] There were public meetings of protest. On August 26th, Lisandro de la Torre, who had retired from public life to an estancia in Córdoba, received a call from an old friend of his, General José Félix Uriburu,* a professional soldier whom he had known since the revolutionary days of 1890 when Uriburu had been a young lieutenant with the revolting troops. Uriburu's Radical days were far behind him, and he was, like all the Argentine army officers, of the most conservative and clerical opinions. Nevertheless, he and De la Torre were personal friends, and Uriburu admired the austere, honest, and intelligent Santafecino. The General told Lisandro de la Torre that the army was going to make a revolution against Yrigoyen, and that he was going to form the provisional government. He offered De la Torre a portfolio in the cabinet. "I suppose you know," he said, "that if I decide not to allow a definitive government, this revolution will go to you." [46]

De la Torre was surprised at the offer, but he did not nibble. He knew Uriburu too well. "The program of Uriburu was a greater menace to the country than the misgovernment of Yrigoyen," wrote De la Torre. "The program of Uriburu led to civil war, even though he did not suspect it. He wanted to implant a *military dictatorship* of the worst kind, and he even disdained the title of Provisional President. He wanted to be called *Dictator*." [47]

Buenos Aires, on the verge of revolution, was full of rumors. On September 1st the Minister of Agriculture, when he went to Palermo to open the annual livestock show of the Sociedad Rural, was greeted with whistles and catcalls and had to leave precipitately. On September 3rd the Minister of War resigned, saying: "I am not a politician, and I have been sickened by the intrigues I have seen around me. Your Excellency," he told Yrigoyen, "is surrounded by few loyalties and many interests." [48] That same day police fired into a crowd of demonstrating law and medical students from the University of Buenos Aires, and killed one of them. On September 5th, Dr. Alfredo L. Palacios, Socialist ex-deputy, now Dean of the Buenos Aires Law School, asked Yrigoyen to resign. That same day Yrigoyen sent Congress his resignation in favor of Vice-President Enrique Martínez. But by now nobody

* General Uriburu is not to be confused with President José Evaristo Uriburu (1895–1898).

wanted Martínez or anyone who had had any part in the Radical government.

On September 6th, the city awoke to the drone of military airplanes, and the people knew that the revolution was on. They poured into the streets to greet the column of military cadets, and troops from the Campo de Mayo, as they filed into the city with Uriburu at their head. The column paused at the Medical School, and General Uriburu was personally greeted and congratulated by the Dean. Along Callao the soldiers were cheered. It was in the Plaza del Congreso that they met the first resistance, when the Guardia de Seguridad fired into the crowd, killing seventeen people and wounding a hundred and eighty. Mobs sacked the Confitería del Molino, across from Congress, where Radical deputies had often gathered for tea, or for cups of coffee during late night recesses. They attacked the Hotel España, in whose dining room Radicals gathered for lunch and dinner. They sacked the houses of the Radical ministers, and invaded Yrigoyen's wretchedly poor apartment and threw his iron cot out into the street. The President, aged and ill and trembling, almost too sick to move, was bundled by friends into an automobile and driven out of the city to the provincial capital of La Plata. And there the brief democratic experiment came to an end. Radicalism had risen and fallen with its caudillo, Hipólito Yrigoyen.

The new Provisional Government of José F. Uriburu had popular support, but it faced a crisis that was not Argentine but worldwide. The peso was dropping, and there were no foreign loans to hold it up. There were rumors that American bankers would not renew their 50,000,000-peso loan, and the government sent frantic telegrams to New York. The rumor was true. The Americans did not trust the new government, and the current depression did not put them in the mood to lend money. The provisional government managed to amortize the loan only by taking gold from the Caja de Conversión (Conversion Fund).[49]

It became quickly apparent that the new government was the old Conservatives in a militarized and more brutal form. Under pretext of punishing old frauds, the Uriburu government discharged Radicals from public office down to the most minor postal employee. In the provinces, in small towns, men who had belonged to Radical clubs were called into the police stations and beaten. Many of the Radical leaders were exiled, and some were sent to the Federal Penitentiary of Ushuaía, at the farthest end of cold, barren Tierra del Fuego, above Cape Horn. Conservatives were put into every public office on the basis of friendship or family relation. Lisandro de la Torre, who saw the turn events were taking, wrote to General Uriburu. "Sensible opinion," he said, "will never accompany a reactionary government, and the revolutionary party which you hope to see formed, will never be; your government, little by little, is going to fall under the influence of the reactionary parties." [50] As usual, the Cassandra prophecy of De la Torre was to be realized.

The first elections under the provisional government were scheduled for April 5, 1931, in the province of Buenos Aires. As it did not occur to anyone that anybody would vote for the discredited Radicals, the government did not bother to work the usual electoral frauds. It was not that the government believed in free suffrage: on the contrary, what Uriburu wanted most to do was to abolish the Sáenz Peña Law and replace Congress with a Corporative Chamber representing the various classes, along the lines of the Italian Fascist state. The only reason he had not carried out the plan was that the navy refused its support.[51] The April elections in Buenos Aires were honest because the Conservative victory looked so certain. But when the returns were in, Uriburu was taken aback: just seven months after the Radical government had been ousted in disgrace, the Radicals got 56 electors, the Conservatives 49, and the Socialists 9.

Uriburu was so surprised and disconcerted he did not know what to do. It was true that the Radicals did not have an absolute majority in the Electoral College, but the Socialists were more likely to vote with them than with the Conservatives. What should he do? To permit the return of the Radicals was to admit the revolution was a failure. He suspended the meeting of the Electoral College, and cancelled scheduled elections in Santa Fe,

Córdoba, and Corrientes. There was a rebellion in Corrientes which the government suffocated. Using the rebellion as an excuse, Uriburu forbade further political activity by the Radical party, and exiled Marcelo T. de Alvear, who was not an Yrigoyenista, but showed symptoms of returning to the party now that Yrigoyen was out. Uriburu did not want a leader of this caliber in the opposition. Alvear went across the river to Montevideo, and from there he issued a statement: "The ethic of the authorities who call themselves revolutionaries is to investigate with much noise the small thefts of the administration, but to consider it legitimate to defraud openly the will of a people, expressed in an undisputed election."[52] For an answer, Uriburu annulled the Buenos Aires elections. The Radical party decreed that in the November presidential elections, they would abstain from voting.

In the meantime, the April elections had been a blow to Uriburu's prestige among the group in power. His strongest rival among the ruling camarilla was a retired general and ex-Minister of War named Agustín P. Justo. Justo was an Anti-Personalista Radical of the kind that had gone over to the Conservatives in 1928 and stayed with them. Justo had presidential ambitions, and he was an excellent politician, a jovial man with a pleasant personality. Justo saw that the military dictatorship of Uriburu was not popular, and that it would be well to return to the forms, if not the substance, of constitutional government. He wanted to be President. Uriburu knew this, and fought him as best he could; but Justo was strong enough to force Uriburu to give the key post of Minister of the Interior to a Justo man. The Minister of the Interior regulates elections, and if he is disposed to fraud there is no legal way to stop him. Uriburu, sullen and helpless in the face of what was happening, agreed to call a presidential election for next November, but he told De la Torre: "I will not help Justo's candidacy in any way."[53]

Uriburu would probably have liked to see De la Torre President. Had the quixotic Santafecino been disposed to the transaction, the matter could have been arranged. But once more Lisandro de la Torre renounced personal ambition, to do what he thought was the right thing. He decided to fight Uriburu and Justo openly, democratically, at the polls. The Radicals were dispersed and disorganized, but there still remained his Partido Demócrata Progresista, and the Socialists. Socialists and Demócratas Progresistas agreed to a united front against the Conservatives in November. De la Torre was nominated for President, and Dr. Nicolás Repetto, since the death of Juan B. Justo the leader of the Socialist party, was nominated for Vice-President. Repetto, like De la Torre, was a man of unquestioned personal integrity: austere, serious, a successful Buenos Aires surgeon who had left his practice when he was elected Socialist deputy for the Capital in 1913. Lisandro de la Torre was no longer the young man of the Noventa. He was in his middle sixties, a handsome figure with blue eyes and white hair and beard.*

The campaign, as far as Repetto and De la Torre were concerned, was fought on an exceptionally high plane. Speeches were trenchant, intelligent, and devoid of the bombast of usual political oratory. Both men came to grips with the issues. For the Argentines of democratic sentiment, they were the only hope. It is related that, one day during the campaign, Lisandro de la Torre was travelling on the train between Rosario and Buenos Aires, and went into the diner for lunch. When he asked for the bill, the waiter shook his head. "When Dr. de la Torre travels on the railroad," he said, "the railroad workers have the honor to pay the small expenses of the trip as the union's contribution to his presidential campaign." [54]

Toward the end of the fight, De la Torre realized that the anonymous, democratic mass of the people would not get to the polls. The Conservatives had learned a lesson in April, and the November elections were a return to the politics of the nineteenth century, with new refinements in fraud that were destined to circumvent the Sáenz Peña electoral mechanism. The police confiscated Libretas de Enrolamiento, the dead rose and voted, known Radicals were denied access to the polls, signatures were falsified, stamps and seals forged, ballot boxes broken open, fake ballots

* It is said the beard was grown to hide the saber cut Yrigoyen gave him.

printed, and interventions made in provinces where necessary. Agustín P. Justo was elected President of the Republic, and Argentina got a foretaste of what "constitutionalism" in government would henceforth mean. The forms of voting were to be observed. As for the substance, it may be judged by the story of the village priest in a small provincial Buenos Aires town who went to the polls to cast his ballot. The president of the reception table, who was a Conservative, said to him: "You have already voted. You may leave now." The curate protested that he had just entered the polls, and got the same reply. Finally he said: "I've been the priest in this town now for twenty years, but this is the first miracle I ever saw." [55]

Lisandro de la Torre could have been President, but he would not accept the presidency from a *dictator*. His was the dilemma of the man who is too honest for his own good. The country needed him, and he condemned himself to political failure. In his case opportunity had knocked twice, and the most quixotic of Argentine Quijotes had twice said no.

THE STRUGGLE FOR ECONOMIC SOVEREIGNTY

THE BRITISH "OCTOPUS"

> *Argentine enterprise and British capital provided this country with its all-productive system of communications; British enterprise and Argentine capital provided Argentina with her stock-raising industry; . . . British money controls the tramways. Unfortunately, there is an ever-increasing chauvinistic opinion that the shareholder is ipso facto an exploiter, a blood-sucker, and a person for whom no consideration should be shown. "Octopus" and "interloper" are the least offensive terms applied to the humble citizens and the widows who have invested their savings in public utilities in the hope of obtaining a little better rate of interest than would be the case were they to entrust their money to the British government at 4 per cent.*
>
> —Buenos Aires Herald, November 23, 1932.

In prosperous 1928, the British claimed an investment in Argentina of £420,000,000, on which they were receiving an interest of 5.6 per cent. In 1933, with an investment they valued at £436,000,000, they were getting an average of 2.4 per cent. Their railway shares were bringing them (so they said) only 1.7 per cent in 1933.[1] They, who had been so generous with Argentina when that young country needed money, were now, in hard times, being discriminated against in every way. British tram lines were saddled with unjust taxes. Their railroads were not allowed to charge enough to make both ends meet. Britain was not only the country that had invested most money in Argentina, it was Argentina's best customer. It bought almost half of all that country exported—90 per cent of the exported meat.[2] What it got in return was 2 per cent. Was this Argentine gratitude?

The British recalled that it was they who had made the first loan to the struggling young Republic back in 1824, when nobody would have thought of risking money in so unlikely a part of the world. They remembered the young Irish and English sheep farmers who had gone to the Plata and built up great estancias, and taught the Argentines all they knew about animal husbandry. They had sent the first pedigreed bull, Tarquin, to that land when its herds were bony, half-wild longhorns that were worth no more than the hides and grease they gave. They had sent the Lincoln sheep. An Englishman had put up the first wire fence on the pampa. They had built the first railroads. What would Argentina have been without the British railways? without tram lines, the electric-light companies? Yet the Anglo-Argentine tramway company of Buenos Aires was now losing 25 per cent of its passengers to the new microbusses that were springing up around the city, subject to no legal control.[3] The least the municipality could do would be to forbid these wildcat vehicles that endangered life and limb, and that gave most unfair and unequal competition. Altogether, the situation for the British investor in Argentina was very bad.

The peso was dropping. That meant that Argentine dividends brought fewer and fewer pounds in London. The situation was such that most of the British companies left their peso profits in Buenos Aires to await transfer at a more favorable rate. This was fortunate for Argentina: its balance of payments was unfavorable, and the involuntary loan somewhat cushioned the shock.[4] But to the investor in the British Isles it meant no return on his investment. In the House of Commons the government was angrily called to task for not doing or saying something. In Buenos Aires *La Nación* replied: "It must be said once again that these matters of an internal nature will be solved without the necessity of suggestions from abroad." [5]

World depression, bringing losses both in Argentina and in England, had shortened tempers, and the two nations who had always been the best of friends, whose economic ties were of the strongest, for the first time exchanged hard words across the Atlantic. The generous British investor who had brought his capital to the Plata was now a Shylock asking for his pound of flesh. So it seemed to the Argentines. Suppose the British were losing money. So were the Argentines. As one paper, of nationalist tendencies, put the matter: "Today foreign capital, just as respectable as our own, exists among us with the losses or natural gains of any investment. We have absolutely no reason to accord it preferential treatment over our own, or over the general interests of the Republic. . . . We have already said that this foreign capital gave impulse to our progress. It would not have done so if it had not intended to get rich returns. Now we are in hard times. We suffer from them ourselves, and the rest will have to suffer along with us. Or shall we resign ourselves never to have a network of roads throughout the country because British capital built the first rails and maintained an absolute monopoly in transportation for more than half a century? And are we going to resign ourselves not to have subways, or elevated or bus lines, because the Anglo-Argentine brought us the first electric cars?" [6]

The answer to these rhetorical questions, so far as the British were concerned, was Yes. The British did not want the Argentines to start bus lines or build roads. The country had never had automobile roads. Why should it start now? Had not the British railways proved perfectly satisfactory? If the government wanted to build roads, it could build feeder lines to the railway stations, but certainly there was no point in running roads alongside the train tracks. Automobiles and trucks were dangerous and unsatisfactory, as every nation that had mistakenly built roads could testify. The ten most important railroads presented a memorial to the Argentine Government protesting the fact that money taken from them in taxes was put into highways.* "This is no exaggeration, Mr. Minister," they said. "The automobile and the truck constitute a serious preoccupation to the statesmen of all the nations with a good road system because of the complications they bring in transportation, and Argentina is feeling every day more menacingly the competition with the once normal traffic of the railroads, in spite of the sensible deficiencies of its land routes. From this one can infer what will happen when the roads that run along the railroad

* The railroads: F.C. Buenos Aires al Pacífico, FF.CC. de Entre Ríos y N.E. Argentino, Cía General Buenos Aires, F.C. Oeste, F.C. Central Argentino, F.C. Sud, F.C. Central Córdoba, F.C. Santa Fe, F.C. Rosario a Puerto Belgrano, F.C. Central de Buenos Aires.

tracks have been paved, as is even now happening in many places by action of the national and provincial governments. It is not groundless to conjecture that the chaos produced could result in a destruction of economic forces with perhaps catastrophic effects on the general welfare. . . . Competition has no reason for being and is absurd in the case of companies or persons dedicated to the public service." [7]

The Argentines, on the other hand, felt that a little "chaos" of the competitive kind was overdue. The train coaches they had to ride in for lack of any other means of transportation would have been scrapped in any other country. Cumbersome, built of wood, without any ventilation except that afforded by open windows, they dated from the turn of the century—on some lines, from the nineteenth century. The Argentines saw similar ones occasionally in Wild West movies; but in Argentina they were not movie props or museum pieces, but the best available means of transportation. Passengers were covered with dust and smoke, and in the diner soot lay heavy on the food.

As for the Anglo-Argentine tram company, anybody in Buenos Aires could tell you about that. The streetcars averaged a quarter of a century in age. They were slow, rough, and noisy. It took an hour to get downtown from Belgrano, and during rush hours passengers hung on the steps, or clung to the rear cowcatcher. When there was no more room of any description, they did not ride. The floor boards sagged with age. It had been a salvation when some enterprising taxi drivers in 1928 had put a sign "Colectivo" in the windows of their cars, and filled their taxis at ten centavos a head with people who were left waiting on street corners by the Anglo-Argentine trams. The colectivos had become an institution. The drivers had new special bodies made for their cars so that they could seat a dozen people, and these had grown into colored microbusses that covered in ten minutes what it took streetcars half an hour to do. Lines sprang up all over the city, and colectivos followed one another at three-minute intervals—in rush hours, one-minute intervals. Working people who had had to live downtown in tenements because they could not get to work on the streetcars, moved out into the suburbs to little houses with gardens, and rode into town every day on the colectivos. Whole new sections of Buenos Aires were built up where before there had been open fields. And they would still be open fields if it had not been for the colectivos.

Also, the colectivos were Argentine. They belonged to Argentine chauffeurs. Argentines were tired of running their country for the benefit of foreigners. All the British cared about was their profits. Their streetcars and trains were so broken down they did not deserve any returns. So said the Argentines.

The British investors, on the other hand, had not seen either the trains or the trams; but they knew they had invested their money in good faith and were not getting a cent. They knew about exchange losses, because every time they collected dividends—when they did—their dividends were worth less and less in pounds sterling. They also knew that out of £276,000,000 of their money invested in Argentine railroads, £167,000,000 returned not a penny in 1933.[8] Their companies had told them about their unfair tax loads, of how the 3 per cent government tax was being used to build competing highways, of how they were not allowed to raise rates or cut their employees' pay. The British government promised to look into the situation and make representations to the Argentine government. The British were in a good bargaining position, as they well knew. They bought much more from Argentina than Argentina bought from them. Britain was Argentina's best customer. If it suddenly stopped buying Argentina's meat, who would buy it? It was embargoed in the United States because of hoof-and-mouth disease. Without the British market, where would Argentina sell its beef and mutton? Perhaps if Great Britain let it be known that it would buy no more beef the Argentine government could be persuaded to take a more lively interest in the problem of the British investor.

In the year 1932, with the world in the trough of a very serious depression, the British Commonwealth of Nations held a conference in Ottawa, Canada, to consider giving imperial preference in trade. It was the beginning of the Buy British movement, a reflection of the economic nationalism which, under the pressure of closing markets, was beginning to attack every country. So far as Argentina was concerned, what was of immediate, alarming, and vital interest in the Ottawa Conference was the agreement England made with Australia and Canada to give their farm products preference in the English market. England promised not to lower its tariffs on foreign meats, or allow more than a specified quota to enter. The measure was aimed at Argentina. Lest there be any doubt of it, the threat of closing the British market to Argentine meats, which were 16 per cent of Argentina's total exports,[9] was accompanied by representations in favor of the Anglo-Argentine tram company of Buenos Aires. The Argentine ambassador in London sent a telegram to Adolfo Bioy, Minister of Foreign Affairs. The Duke of Atholl, said the telegram, asks "your good offices in the immediate solution of the matter of the Anglo-Argentine with the municipality of the Capital." A month later there was another telegram: the British Foreign Secretary, it said, asked the *urgent solution* of the Anglo-Argentine question; and also the London *Times* had published an editorial complaining of Argentina's unjust treatment of the British tram company.* [10]

The government of President Justo was in a quandary. Its financial situation was bad. Since the signing of the Ottawa agreements, Argentine meat exports to England had begun dropping off at the rate of 5 per cent a month.[11] Argentina at first thought to invoke the most favored nation clause in its 1825 treaty with England; but the British let it be known that they considered the Dominions not as sovereign nations, but as a part of the Empire, and the clause did not apply.[12] Whether it did legally or not, the Argentines were in no position to argue the point: the British held all the cards. England was Argentina's best market, and this was depression. Argentina decided to negotiate, on Britain's terms. It sent Vice-President Julio A. Roca to London to talk with the British government's representative, Walter Runciman, President of the Board of Trade.

* A "British company," however, whose control is in Belgian hands, by one of those strange quirks of international finance.

Runciman's main point in his talks with Vice-President Roca was that Great Britain had a consistently unfavorable balance of trade with Argentina. Year after year it was the same: Britain bought more in Argentina than Argentina bought in Britain. The balances in favor of Argentina were in the hundreds of millions of pesos.[13] Why should Britain continue to buy such excessive amounts in Argentina, when Argentina, instead of buying from Britain, bought from the United States? What did the United States buy from Argentina? Almost nothing. It certainly admitted no Argentine meats. Yet Argentina had a consistently *unfavorable* balance of trade with the United States, an unfavorable balance just as large as Britain had with Argentina. The British motto henceforth would be: Buy from Those Who Buy from Us.

To bolster his argument, Runciman could produce statistics. Argentine chilled beef was selling in London for 25 centavos a kilogram: at so many kilograms, there was such-and-such an amount of sterling exchange available to Argentina. The Argentines looked at these statistics with some surprise, since their own government figures showed that far from 25 centavos a kilo, they were being paid 18. There were other talking points that may or may not have occurred to Roca. One was that England had many invisible exports that it had not counted in. What about the millions of pesos Argentine companies paid to British ships for transport every year? As for the favorable balance Argentina had with Britain, and the unfavorable balance with the United States, a great part of that came from the fact that Argentine dollar bonds were held by Englishmen, but since they were payable in dollars, this was a drain on the dollar exchange, and showed up in unfavorable balances with the United States. Probably at least half of all dollar bonds were held in England.[14] When one considered these items, not to mention British investments in American companies operating in Argentina, it was just possible that not England, but *Argentina*, had the unfavorable balance of trade.

Whether Roca used these arguments, we do not know. The Argentines were in too weak a position to make a good bargain. In May, 1933, the Roca-Runciman pact was signed, and the victory went to the British. Argentina agreed to leave all her sterling exchange to service the debts to England. She agreed to give 85 per cent of her meat business to the foreign frigoríficos, and the remaining 15 per cent only to Argentine companies that were non-competitive, and non-profit-making. She agreed to reduce her tariffs on British goods to 1930 levels, and leave coal on the free list. In return, Britain agreed not to limit chilled beef to less than that imported in the three months ending June 30, 1932. There was a significant protocol to the treaty: "That the Argentine government, valuing the benefits of the collaboration of British capital in the public service and other enterprises . . . proposes to accord such enterprises . . . a benevolent treatment tending to assure the greatest economic development of the country and the due and legitimate protections of the interests connected with such enterprises." [15]

In London, the newspapers showed themselves far from pleased at the British victory, which they insisted on viewing as a defeat. The *Daily Express* headlines of May 1 were: "Britain Tricked into Pre-Tariff Plight—The Argentine Trap Today . . . A Farewell Banquet to the Argentinos Who Pulled Off the Agreement Will Be Given Tonight." But the *Daily Mail* was perhaps more exact in its appreciation of the real situation. Its comment was: "These pacts are the first fruits of the tariff which was put into force in Great Britain last year. For the first time in the last seventy years, *British statesmen have been able to negotiate with foreign powers upon even terms.*" [16]

THE BENEVOLENT TREATMENT

There are still some months before the present convention terminates. . . . While it has served the useful purpose of tiding over a difficult period and has taken us some distance towards a balancing of accounts . . . we are in duty bound to ask for more; and if I add that on the whole we have not been specially favored or shown preference, it is with an eye to the wide difference separating us, which both countries agree should be adjusted.

—S. G. IRVING, Commercial Counsellor to the British Embassy, 1936.

In Argentina, the first flush of relief at the signing of the Roca-Runciman Pact gave way to a feeling of anger and injustice. The price Argentina had paid for Britain's promise not to reduce meat quotas was high: not only did British goods get most favored nation treatment, which did not matter, but the country had undertaken a moral obligation to give more favorable treatment to British companies in Argentina. The protocol was not specific, but everyone knew the Argentine government had made verbal promises with regard to the railroads and the Anglo-Argentine tram company. Just how far the commitments went, the average person did not know. There were all kinds of rumors. Had Argentina undertaken to build no more motor roads? Was it going to buy the bankrupt railroads? Was it going to buy the Anglo-Argentine? The extreme left and extreme right began a public campaign against foreign capital: groups like the Socialists, the Communists, the Argentine nationalists, the Hispanists—all who were not believers in the capitalist system or classic liberal economics. The Conservatives kept quiet.

At first President Justo could not have taken too seriously his moral obligations under the new treaty, because, although the matter of the Anglo-Argentine was referred to a special commission for study, nothing came of it. As for the complaint of the railroads that Argentina was paving its highways, with possible disastrous economic effects, it was Justo who founded the Dirección Nacional de Vialidad, the National Highway Commission, and began building more roads than Argentina had ever seen before. Old highways were gravelled or macadamized, bridges were thrown across rivers and streams, and roads were blasted out of the mountains in the Andean provinces where there had been only trails before. This meant a great increase in automobile traffic, and made possible the growth of truck and bus lines in competition with the old, slow, expensive railroads. It is to the Justo government that Argentina owes its modern road system and road-mindedness. Comparative figures will illustrate the change. Whereas Argentina had invested 3,000,000 pesos in highways in 1920, and 18,000,000 in 1930, it invested 33,000,000 in 1940.[17] The road budget doubled in the decade 1930–1940. By the end of the Justo administration, Argentina had 17,000 kilometers of all-weather roads, and 393,000 kilometers of dirt roads.[18]

The British government was displeased by what it considered the indifference of the Argentine government to its moral undertakings under the Roca Pact. The Anglo-Argentine's gross receipts were down to almost half of their pre-depression highs.* The company, according to its own claims, represented a British investment of 242,000,000 pesos.[19] The Anglo-Argentine was loaded with taxes and street assessments. In the meantime the colectivos paid only a hundred pesos a year to the city, and were subject to no regulation. It was no wonder they were taking the business from the streetcars.

The debate got hot, and the whole question of foreign companies, of railroads, trams, electric-light companies and telephones, became the subject of public furore. There were investigations, private and public. Argentine nationalists published "exposés" of the companies, showing that their stock was watered, that they lied about returns, that they kept books in a way no other country would permit, that their service was bad, and that they were

* In 1928, 46,000,000 pesos; in 1938, 30,000,000 (Great Britain Department of Overseas Trade, *Report on Economic and Commercial Conditions in the Argentine Republic*, Nov. 1929, p. 83, and June, 1939, p. 122).

exploiting Argentina. The Justo government got investigating commissions to issue reports that, on the contrary, the foreign companies gave good service, and that they deserved and needed consideration from the nation. Senator Alfredo L. Palacios studied the capital structure of the martyred Anglo-Argentine and came out with some surprising discoveries. If the Anglo-Argentine, he said, had the costs of the Canadian streetcars per kilometer, then its real capital was not 242,000,000 pesos, but 127,000,000, or just about half. But the Canadian trams were modern and efficient, and the Buenos Aires trams, as everyone knew who had to ride on them, were turn-of-the-century museum pieces.

Palacios went very carefully into the company's books. He went back to 1909. In that year there were some interesting transactions: 320,000 shares of £5 stock at 10 per cent were changed to 640,000 shares of £5 stock at 5 per cent, increasing the capital from £1,600,000 to £3,200,000, or just double. On what authority was this done? None. But it was convenient, because the company now showed only 5 per cent return on its investment where before it had had 10 per cent. Then Palacios went into the details of purchase of other tram lines. A large percentage of the company's declared capital investment came in this category. He compared the declared purchase price that the Anglo-Argentine had on its books with the purchase price as notarized before the national notary Pedro Zamit, and discovered there was a falsification of £1,516,847. Then Palacios looked into other items in the declared capital of the Anglo-Argentine. The company did not amortize its trams, he discovered, yet charged renewal of rolling stock to capital; and, most amazing of all, the money it paid in taxes it listed as "invested capital." * [20] What kind of accounting was this? His verdict: the company was watered, and recognizing this inflated capital could lead to no good either for it or for the city of Buenos Aires.

The British wanted the Argentine government to create a municipal street-railway system to be called the Corporación de Trans-

* In the case of paving taxes, this would be justified. Palacios did not specify what taxes were charged to capital.

portes. Into this company would be taken all the big tram, subway, and bus lines, at their capital value. The city would charge no more taxes, and in lieu of taxes would be given stock in the Corporación to the capitalized value of the taxes. This corporation would have an exclusive monopoly for fifty-six years. It would be guaranteed 7 per cent on its investment. And it would have the right to confiscate all the independent colectivos in the city at the value it wished to assign them.[21]

When the Buenos Aires public realized what the proposal was —that Argentine private colectivos would be confiscated, that the British would now have a monopoly of all city transportation at a guaranteed 7 per cent return on *watered capital*—there was an angry outcry. But the government determined that the law should be voted, because in 1936 the Roca-Runciman agreement came to an end, and the British let it be known they were thinking of not renewing it. Not only did the Argentine government have to do something concrete about the tram lines; it had also to buy the weak Córdoba Central railway as the price of renewal. Competitive road building must stop. The plight of the railroads, which had done so much for Argentine progress, would have to be considered by Argentina.

The debate on British railroads went on while the Anglo-Argentine was under discussion. What was the real situation of the railroads? The British knew the situation of railroad stocks. None of them had paid dividends since 1930. Taking the decade 1928–1938, with 1928 as 100 per cent, the Central Argentino's stock was at 9 per cent, the Sud's at 10 per cent, the Pacífico's at 4 per cent, and the Oeste's at 8 per cent. As for returns of all kinds from British railroads in Argentina, they averaged 1.7 per cent.[22] That, to be as brief as possible, was the situation of the British railroads. So said the British.

The Argentine government investigated the capital structure of the railroads, and made some downward revisions. The capital, the government said, was watered. Others who studied the railroads, but did not have the government's international obligations of courtesy, estimated the inflation of values at considerably higher than even the government. They went back to the nineteenth century, and studied the railroads step by step. They showed how free stock figured as capital, how declared capital was increased by millions without the building of a line of track, how small lines were bought at fantastic figures. And then there was this item of "exchange losses." Half the total profit was deducted as "exchange losses." What did that mean?

Investigation showed that whenever the sterling exchange rate fell below 11 pesos to the pound, the British deducted the difference as losses. The Argentines argued that these were national railways, that the national money was the peso, and that pounds sterling had nothing whatever to do with the matter. They could show that when the railroads were being built the peso was continually on the rise, without the railroads' noting exchange *gains*. And what about 1918–1920, when the peso was above par? Did the British make the adjustment there? Not at all.[23] Then why should they deduct exchange "losses" and show a 1 per cent profit when they were making twice that much even on the watered capital value? If the capital had not been watered, no telling what their real interest return would be. And finally, if further proof of inflated capital value were needed, Argentina need go no further than the fact that any business organization with a good accounting system is capitalized on the basis of its interest returns, and not vice versa. If the British railroads could not show 5 per cent, then their total value was certainly not £276,000,000, but something far, far less.*

As for the Argentine public's share in this debate, all they knew was that the Anglo-Argentine's trams had *not* been able to carry the city's passenger load before the colectivos came, and that the colectivos were far more rapid. The trains were dirty, slow, old,

* By their own figures the British showed a capital investment in 1928 of £251,000,000, in 1933 of £276,000,000. Yet in 1928 the return was 5.5 per cent, and in 1933, 1.7 per cent. And in 1928 only £3,000,000 were in default, and in 1933 £167,000,000 were in default. On what basis could they raise the capital value £25,000,000? They had built no track. Their trains were getting older. And railroad stocks were selling at one-tenth what they had sold for in 1928. (These are figures in the *South American Journal*, quoted in *The Standard*, Apr. 8, 1941.)

and inefficient. The railroads had been taking money from the employees' retirement funds for years, until there was not enough money to pay pensions. As even President Justo admitted, when he asked Congress to take over the weak Central Córdoba railroad from the British: "The Executive Power has had occasion to observe that in the frequent conflicts that have arisen with the employes in the privately-owned railways there is a growing difficulty in finding reasonable solutions of the differences between the parties, because the mass of workmen regard themselves as being exploited by foreign capital, the profit-seeking ambitions of which they blame for their economic situation; and owing to the hardships they have had to suffer for years past they have no disposition to attempt to overcome differences in a reasonable manner. It is felt amongst the workers that shareholders have no right to any dividend, and there is increasing resistance to contribute in any form, at the expense of wages, to the companies' fixed charges." [24]

The Argentine nationalist viewpoint on the foreign capital debate was summed up in *Crisol:* "What has happened is that the big enterprises have not adapted themselves to circumstances. For example: the railroads did not believe that some day we should adopt a wise railroad policy, that we were going to introduce, logically, competition with their services; the packing houses, that we were going to think of regulating and arranging the meat industry for ourselves; the oil developments, that we were going to have a powerful state company; and, not to prolong the enumeration, the tramways, that colectivos and busses were going to appear. In short, foreign capital invested in these businesses in a time of absolute lack of competition and control, did not prepare itself for the growth of the country, and with it for the very just anxiety for improvement and for economic independence, not on the former bases, but on those which sovereignty itself imposes." [25]

This was the general feeling. Foreign capital had done its job, and made its profits. As even the British *Financial News* had admitted: "There are British capitals invested in South America which have been amortized twice over in a period of forty years, and which nevertheless continue to charge amortization services." [26] The Argentines felt that it was time to declare their economic independence. It was not their fault that trains got old when the years passed and nobody renewed rolling stock. It was not their fault the automobile had been invented. It was not their fault the British had watered stock in the early years of railroading and weakened their capital structures. It was not their fault that microbusses were faster than trams, and that the Anglo-Argentine's trams were twenty to thirty years old. Progress did not stop for old, unwieldy companies, and the British should be satisfied that they had taken their profits out long ago. Why should the Argentine public be made to continue guaranteeing them 7 per cent on money they had not invested?

This is what the public said. But the government knew that 1936 meant the termination of the Roca-Runciman Pact, and that the British had it in their power not to renew. They decided to be reasonable. Congress was asked to pass the law creating the Corporación de Transportes. The only party that refused to vote it was the Socialist party. It was voted in the Chamber of Deputies at midnight, September 25, 1935. The Socialists rose from their seats, and their Chamber leader, Américo Ghioldi, told the president his party was going to walk out in protest at what was about to be done. "It hurts us deeply to take this stand," he said. "We retire en masse, and we want all the moral force of the Socialist party—recognized by friends and enemies alike—to bear on this project which will remain as a stain on this legislature." [27]

THE ROCA-RUNCIMAN PACT AND THE UNITED STATES

The Roca-Runciman agreements of 1933 and 1936 determined Argentina's commercial relations not only with Great Britain but also with the United States. By signing these treaties Argentina served notice on the world that she was abandoning the principle of multilateral trade, and was henceforth going to Buy from Those Who Buy from Us. That meant she was going to buy more from England and Germany, and buy less from the United States. Argentina's unfavorable balance of trade with the United States runs anywhere from 150,000,000 to 350,000,000 pesos every year. Her favorable balance of trade with Britain is just about the same size. With Germany her trade is normally well balanced. So, at least, Argentina's official figures show. But these figures do not stand up well under analysis, as will presently be seen.

What does Argentina import from the United States? First of all, machinery—automobiles, farm machinery, factory machinery. Argentina normally buys four times as much machinery in the United States as she does in England. Secondly, petroleum. Her imports of petroleum are high, but about equal in value to her imports of coal from England. In the third place, chemicals. Argentina also buys chemicals in England, to about the same value. In the fourth place, great quantities of wood, which she cannot buy in the United Kingdom. Finally, iron. Argentina also buys iron in the United Kingdom to more or less the same value.

In return, what can Argentina export? Her most important export, ranging from 17 to 20 per cent of the normal total, is wheat. It is perfectly evident that since in normal years the United States has more wheat than it knows what to do with, the United States is no customer for wheat. Her second most important export, normally 13 per cent in value of the total, is chilled and frozen beef, and the United States has a sanitary embargo on Argentine beef.* Argentina's third most important export is linseed, and here the United States is the best customer, buying great quantities. The American duty on linseed is 57 per cent. Argentina's fourth most important export is unwashed wool. The United States buys wool, but there is a 95 per cent duty on it.[28] To put the matter in the simplest terms, American and Argentine economies in agriculture are competitive. But the United States has

* In 1935 the United States signed a sanitary convention with Argentina to permit the entry of beef from areas free of hoof-and-mouth disease, but the Senate refused to ratify it.

industrial products which Argentina needs and uses. Since in return, Argentina has nothing to sell but wheat, meat, wool, and linseed, she cannot pay for them.

Argentina bought more from the United States than from any other country. She sold more to Britain than to any other country. These two facts gave Mr. Runciman an excellent talking point when the first agreement was signed in 1933. Shortly before the treaty came up for renewal, the argument broke down, however, because in 1935 Argentina had a favorable balance of trade with the United States. Accordingly, an "equilibrium" clause was written into the 1936 agreement: "The contracting governments agree that if either of the two governments is of the opinion that any measure undertaken by the other government is likely to alter the equilibrium resulting from this agreement, the latter government will give sympathetic consideration to the representations and proposals which the other government may make.[29]

The devices by which the Argentine government began slicing down imports from the United States were many and varied. In the first place, Argentina reckoned her dollar exchange by a peculiar system for evaluating exports, called the "aforo" system. Under the aforo system, the average previous month's price of a commodity is listed as its value. Since the United States buys high-quality goods in Argentina, their real price is greatly undervalued. In 1941, Argentine understatement as compared with United States invoice figures was as follows: hides, 23 per cent; wool, 11 per cent; flaxseed, 9 per cent; quebracho, 4 per cent.[30] In this way Argentina tried to prove that the United States buys less than it does.

In the second place, in 1933, the year of the first Roca pact, Argentina initiated preferential exchange rates for those countries which buy more from Argentina than Argentina buys from them. Argentine business houses which wished to buy English goods could get pounds at a special cheap rate, the "A" rate. But those who wished to import from the United States had to buy dollars on the free market. The difference amounted to 20 per cent in favor of England, and this extra edge made it possible for English firms whose prices were really higher than those of American firms to make lower bids on contracts.[31] It made British goods cheaper to Argentines, and it meant a progressive rise in the cost of American machinery, especially automobiles and typewriters.

A third device for keeping out American goods was that of quotas. Quotas were used to exclude American automobiles, and in 1939 the number of automobiles was cut to 70 per cent of the 1938 figure.[32] The combination of giving unfavorable rates of exchange for the purchase of automobiles, and establishing quotas, so reduced imports that in 1940 they were less than a third of the 1929 figure.[33] In 1939 Argentina put 103 tariff classifications of imports from the United States, which had formerly been on the free list, under complete embargo.[34] It is evident that these actions were contrary to Argentina's treaty obligations with the United States, which included most-favored-nation clauses. The United States did not retaliate in kind. The Argentines, however, claimed that the sanitary embargo on Argentine beef was really a tariff in disguise, and that it was discriminatory.

In 1937 Argentina had accumulated so much dollar exchange by these devices that it was decided to repatriate 225,000,000 pesos' worth of bonds held in the United States. This, of course, cut the dollar exchange even further. But there was a joker in all this for the Conservative governments of Argentina, which thought they were outwitting the United States. The joker was that when war came, shutting down every source of iron, steel, and machinery, Argentina had gold reserves, and it did not have trucks, automobiles, steel, machines, or replacements. The result was that instead of starting the war years with a good stock of these necessities, it started them with a less-than-normal supply. And as year after year went by without new machinery coming, streetcars and trucks and automobiles went out of service, building construction got less solid and more expensive, and there were no replacements for textile machines, or oil drills. Typical of the government's obtuseness was its refusal before the war to permit the import of machinery to distill alcohol from corn. When war came, bringing a shortage of fuel, Argentina was unable to distill fuel from its huge grain supplies. Corn had to be burned in cakes to heat houses and furnish electricity, a most wasteful use of its potential calories.

The outbreak of war did not bring any change in government trade policies with regard to the United States. To show how little Argentina realized what war would mean to its normal European sources of supply, one may read the circular of the Exchange Control Office of the period: "It is, then, necessary for the sake of our exports that in fulfilling our import needs we take particular care to satisfy the same from normal sources of supply and avoid unnecessary diversions to other sources or countries, since this could bring ulterior complications which it is convenient to guard against in advance." [35] In other words, Argentina still had no intentions of buying in the United States. The fact, of course, was that it had to, and that there came a time when the Argentine government had to send a very humiliating note to the United States begging for replacements.* It took Argentina several years of war to discover one cannot burn gold or drive dollars.

MEAT

> *The report which I have signed reveals a discouraging picture. The most genuinely Argentine industry, the livestock industry, is largely in ruins because of two factors: the extortion of a foreign monopoly, and the complicity of a government which permits it to act, and at other times directly protects the action of the monopoly.*
>
> —LISANDRO DE LA TORRE in the Senate, June 18, 1935.

Argentina signed the Roca-Runciman Pact for one reason, and one reason only. That was to protect its meat industry. Meat represented 16 per cent of the country's exports, but there was more in it than the economic factor. The estancia, the Palermo livestock show, the pedigreed shorthorn champion, represent a way of life

* The Storni note of 1943.

and a way of thinking. In what country but Argentina would cabinet ministers be proud of being photographed with a Durham bull? In what country but Argentina could one imagine the President of the Republic and Grenadier Guards parading around a show ring dedicated to the exposition of Holstein cows, Aberdeen Angus and Shorthorn bulls, Percheron horses, and Lincoln sheep? In what other country would national feeling be wounded to the point of sulkiness because foreign markets accused its animals of carrying hoof-and-mouth disease, when they certainly do?

The Argentine estancia is a national tradition. It does not matter that agriculture has largely superseded the raising of livestock, and that new industries are superseding both. The point is that the one field in which Argentina has been able to take first place among the nations of the world, is the breeding of cattle. No one would think of Argentine hats and shoes as the best in the world, or of the Argentine landscape as particularly admirable, or of the nation as militarily and economically powerful; but anyone who has seen the parade of shorthorn champions at Palermo will grant Argentina the honor of producing some of the finest pedigreed bulls in the world. This is a matter of national honor and pride, and not only the estanciero and the member of the Sociedad Rural, but the city merchant, the industrial worker, and the government bureaucrat identify their country's prestige with its livestock. For Argentina, therefore, the possible closing of the British market to Argentine meats was as much a moral as an economic blow. Furthermore, the Justo government, like all the Conservative governments, represented the estanciero above all. That is why it was willing to make a bad, even a shameful, bargain if by doing so it could keep open the only market for Argentine beef, which was the Smithfield Market in London.

The Smithfield Market (London Central Market) comprises five great shedlike buildings covering several acres in the heart of the city, near the General Post Office, and bounded on the east by Lindsay Street, the north by Charterhouse Street, the south by Long Lane and King Street, and on the west by Farringdon Road.[36] To the Smithfield market goes Argentine chilled beef from Armour,

Smithfield, Wilson, Swift, Sansinena, Anglo, and the British and Argentine, the great foreign-owned frigoríficos of the Plata, and also in small quantities, beef from the Argentine frigorífico Gualeguaychú. The Smithfield is a wholesale market, furnishing meats to the butchers of London. At Smithfield the highest-priced beef is freshly slaughtered meat from Scotland, which goes to the upper-class tables; and next in price and quality is Argentine chilled beef, selling for two-thirds as much, and the staple diet of the middle-class consumer. It is the English middle class, then, that is the great market for Argentine chilled beef. The steps by which an Argentine steer becomes a British roast beef involve the whole livestock economy of Argentina. In 1934–1937, two investigations were independently conducted to determine whether the meat industry was being run for the benefit of the Argentine seller or British buyer: one was by a committee of the Argentine Senate headed by Dr. Laureano Landaburu; and the other was by a mixed Argentine and British committee which held hearings both in Buenos Aires and in London. The second, in a sense, grew out of the first, and followed it in time.

There are two main divisions of cattle raising. One is the raising of calves until they are weaned at eight to ten months; and the other is the fattening of the animals for their sale at two to three years. The first does not require exceptional land. But fattening needs good pasture. The fattener, or *invernador*, when his animals are ready for market, calls in a buyer from the frigorífico and sells them on the estancia. The biggest frigorífico is Swift La Plata and next comes the Anglo. As specified in the Roca agreement, 85 per cent of the meat exporting business is in the hands of the six great foreign frigoríficos, which have a monopoly on the business. They work together and assign quotas of space aboard the transatlantic refrigerator ships.[37] The question that arose between Great Britain and Argentina was as follows: does this monopoly work for or against the best interests of the Argentine estanciero, or for that matter, of the British estanciero in Argentina? The mixed commission took pages of interviews on all aspects of the meat business. This was the testimony:

Question: To what degree is the raising of livestock a remunerative business?

Answers, London, April–July, 1935

MAJOR E. DUKE MOORE, for Las Cabezas Estancias Co. Ltd.: A few years ago we made almost nothing. Now we begin to pay dividends again. . . . Our situation is different. There is no doubt that the business is unremunerative *for those who have bought their lands at high prices.**

ASSOCIATED ESTANCIAS LTD.: At present prices and at the free market rate of exchange, the best prices you can obtain for Durham, Hereford, or Aberdeen Angus calves is £7. This does not leave much, after paying taxes in Argentina and Great Britain, for the owner who is a resident of the United Kingdom or stockholder of a British company.

MR. J. S. FAIR: *If we had to pay rent for the land, I do not believe we could make a profit* at present prices. . . . We are owners of the land. . . . We can make a profit if climatic conditions permit. You cannot count on a regular return.

MR. J. LIDDON SIMPSON for the Australian Mercantile, Land and Finance Co., Ltd.: With an adequate extension of land, well-administered, and *without the inflation of land values,* it is possible . . . to operate with a fair margin of profit.

Answers, Argentina, August–September, 1937

CONFEDERACIÓN DE ASOCIACIONES RURALES DE BUENOS AIRES Y LA PAMPA: The economic situation of the producer has not varied very much and continues to be bad, but with a brighter outlook. This bad situation is due to the rise in rents, provoked by the profits to be made in cereals. . . . As for the *invernador,* his economic situation has been and is satisfactory because he can regulate the price of his purchases and in this sense nothing prevents him from buying according to what he can sell for; and leaving sufficient margin between the two prices to pay him for fattening the calves, he does not have to worry about the costs of production which fall entirely on the *criador.*† [38]

Question: Is the system of sale of livestock satisfactory?

Answer, Argentina, August–September, 1937

SOCIEDAD RURAL: The way in which the cattle have been habitually negotiated is not satisfactory. . . . The different situations

* Italics in this testimony are mine.

† The man who raises the calves for sale at eight to ten months.

of seller and buyer result in the dispersion of offers in the face of a demand concentrated in the hands of a few.

Question: Is there real competition between frigoríficos in the buying of livestock?

Answer, Argentina, August–September, 1937

CONFEDERACIÓN DE SOCIEDADES RURALES DE BUENOS AIRES Y LA PAMPA: The prices are fixed by the packing houses, putting the producer in the situation of accepting or not; in this latter case he can send his meat to the Liniers market for public sale or private sale through a consignee. If the producer prefers to offer privately to another plant, the chances are it will not look at his animals because there is a kind of agreement to respect customers. . . .[39]

Perhaps the final word, however, on the position of the estanciero in the face of the packing-house monopoly may be read in the profit-and-loss accounts of company estancias and the leading frigoríficos, according to their own figures. Here are the average profits (per cent)[40] for 1929–1936:

Year	*Estancias*	*Frigoríficos*
1929	8.49	10.8
1930	4.9	13.65
1931	2.29	13.13
1932	3.7	12.22
1933	1.5	11.46
1934	1.9	14.12
1935	3.5	5.75
1936	3.6	7.21

The report of the mixed commission on the livestock industry showed: that land prices and rents were too high for what meat was bringing; that cereal lands were worth more than those devoted to cattle, and that livestock men were finding it profitable to convert to agriculture; that the packing industry was a monopoly with price-fixing agreements, against which the estanciero was relatively helpless; and finally that, when depression struck, the losses were borne not by the packing houses but by the estancieros.

I have purposely considered the report of the mixed commission before that of the Senate committee which preceded it, because the debate, the most sensational—and in the end, tragic—of which the Senate chamber has ever been the scene, is not comprehensible unless one understands all the economic problems at stake. The situation was this. Argentina had signed the Roca-Runciman Pact to safeguard its English market for beef and mutton. The agreement had placed a monopoly of the packing business in British and American hands; and the Argentine estanciero, for whose interests the pact had ostensibly been signed, was not benefiting but suffering under the monopoly. If, as the figures showed, the estancias that were stock companies were making less than 2 per cent profit in the depths of the depression, what of the small cattle man, the man who leased his land from an owner at very high rents? What must his situation have been? Land values were inflated, rents were too high. The independent estanciero was facing ruin. It was under these conditions that the Argentine Senate voted an investigation in 1934. Senator Laureano Landaburu was the committee head, and one of the members was Lisandro de la Torre, now in his old age the senior Senator from Santa Fe. The other two chief actors in the drama about to unfold were: Luis Duhau, Minister of Agriculture and multimillionaire estanciero; and the Minister of Finance, Federico Pinedo, an ex-Socialist who had become a corporation lawyer, and director of two of Argentina's largest companies. The Senate committee investigation went on for a year, and when the time came for a report it was announced that Lisandro de la Torre dissented from the majority and was going to present a report of his own. It was with mild interest and expectation that in June, 1935, the public began to watch a Senate debate that was going to lead to a duel, to murder, and to the fall of two cabinet ministers.

The report of the majority was read by Landaburu, and the general picture it represented was one of cooperation and good will between frigorífico and estanciero. Prices were fair, the commerce was well regulated, and all was well. So said Senator Landaburu. On June 18, De la Torre took the floor. He was a magnificent old man, still in the full vigor of his physical and mental powers. He held the floor, and the public attention, from June 18 to July 23. His first words on the meat industry were those quoted at the beginning of this chapter: "The report which I have signed reveals a discouraging picture. The most genuinely Argentine industry, the livestock industry, is largely in ruins because of two factors: the extortion of a foreign monopoly, and the complicity of a government which permits it to act . . ." [41] And then De la Torre went on to present the results of a year's investigations which he had carried on with the help of professional accountants.

The majority report had given the impression that the government and the frigoríficos had cooperated in the investigation of the meat industry. Such was not the case. "The lack of cooperation from the Executive Power has been lamentable. . . . The committee has encountered only difficulties, ill will, and evasive or inexact answers on the part of the ministers and the chiefs of administrative divisions. . . . Thus, for example, the statistics presented by the Minister of Agriculture were full of errors which were not unknown to him, but which were given to the committee without the slightest warning of their mistakes and deficiencies. And when the investigation, in the part referring to the payment of income tax, proved evasions that were *prima facie* evidence of fraud on the part of some of the frigoríficos, the Minister of Finance, after two months' delay, refused to let us examine the books with the sworn declarations, and did nothing to help the clarification the committee was trying to make. And as for the bookkeeping irregularities of the frigoríficos, in violation of the commercial code, you will see, too, how the Minister of Justice was asked to intervene . . . and how all that was achieved was that an inspector presented himself one day in the committee's headquarters, chatted for ten minutes, and never returned." [42]

As for the frigoríficos, the majority had hidden their books. The Anglo had tried to smuggle its books out of the country, putting them into twenty-one boxes labelled "corned beef" and hiding them aboard the British freighter *Norman Star*.[43] Fortunately, the fraud had been discovered in time, and the books seized. The companies had been dishonest with the Argentine government. They reported one cost to the customs, and showed another in their own records, the object being to evade Argentine exchange controls and keep money for negotiations in the free market and abroad.[44] By this time the attention of the country was on the Senate debate, and the galleries were packed with people to hear Lisandro de la Torre.

De la Torre showed that the frigoríficos had lied not only about the real amount of sterling exchange they had, but about their profits as well, so as to avoid high income taxes. The Dirección de Réditos charged the frigoríficos much less income tax than they should pay. Profits were enormous: in five years Swift's made 91,000,000 pesos on an investment of 45,000,000. Swift International lost money in Australia, New Zealand, and Brazil, and made up for it with the profits of Swift La Plata. Yet it paid a higher price for inferior Australian meat than it did for top-flight Argentine chilled beef. And the Dirección de Réditos allowed Swift International to deduct losses abroad from gains in Argentina, and show a loss, so that it did not have to pay taxes.* Also the government allowed the foreign packers to keep as high as 25 per cent of their foreign exchange for their own private use, a privilege allowed to no other exporters, not even to the Argentine frigorífico Gualeguaychú.[45]

By now De la Torre had made so many accusations of government complicity in the irregularities of the foreign frigoríficos that there was great tension in the cabinet. He had not finished, however. His most sensational charge was that of the subornation of the Minister of Agriculture, Luis Duhau. How was it, he wanted to know, that Swift's regularly paid Duhau per steer thirty pesos more than the market price? (Duhau was a wealthy estanciero, as well as Minister of Agriculture.) What did Swift's get in return? The charge was very serious, as Duhau well knew, and he tried to refute it by showing that other individuals were paid as good prices

* Swift International, incorporated in Argentina, is a holding company for the Swift packing houses all over the world. As Minister Federico Pinedo pointed out in rebuttal, when Swift International made money in Australia and New Zealand, it paid taxes to the Argentine government; so that it was only just that when it lost abroad it be allowed to deduct the losses.

for their cattle as he. But De la Torre, in great scorn, read from the reports of the company, and demolished Duhau's statistics. The Minister of Agriculture had been paid an exceptional price, and he still had not explained why. Duhau was reduced to shouting after every charge De la Torre made: "We shall see about that!" But it was evident that both Pinedo and Duhau were frightened. The galleries were now daily packed with curious visitors, and nobody spoke of anything but the Senate debate. It was De la Torre's tour de force, and so sensational were his charges that by July 22 there were ugly incidents in the Senate. An exchange of words between Pinedo and De la Torre had to be expunged from the record. Tension was at the breaking point, but De la Torre showed no evidence of having run out of material.

On July 23 it was almost impossible for the debate to get started, such was the anger of both parties. The stenographic report of that day was suppressed from the *Diario de Sesiones* for a long time, and was only added weeks later when it had been toned down to the point of printability (Lisandro de la Torre had the fiercest vocabulary in the Senate when he was aroused). After a few moments the following exchange (expurgated) took place:

DE LA TORRE: I have already told you that you are as insolent as you are cowardly.

PINEDO: The Senator from Santa Fe reaches at this moment the highest note of his histrionic clowning. [*De la Torre abandons his seat and comes toward Pinedo.*] He accuses me of insolence and cowardice! The Senator from Santa Fe, Mr. President, is capable of provoking me to a duel because he knows that on account of my convictions I do not fight.

At this point the *Diario de Sesiones* says that "there occurs a personal incident between the Minister of Agriculture and the Senator from Santa Fe." The personal incident was that as De la Torre started toward Pinedo, Duhau pushed him over a desk into the aisle. Enzo Bordabehere, the junior Senator from Santa Fe, started forward, and at this moment a pistol shot rang out, followed by two others in quick succession. Bordabehere dropped in his tracks, mortally wounded.[46] At the same instant, Duhau threw himself to the floor. The murderer backed toward the door of the chamber, his gun still pointed. Outside, he was seized.

The shooting of Bordabehere was never satisfactorily explained. The murderer was one Ramón Valdez Cora, an ex-comisario of police who had been tried for swindling and for extorting money from prostitutes. He had been in the Senate every day of the debate on the meat industry; and on the day of the murder he had been admitted to the floor when absolutely nobody else could get near the chamber, which indicated that someone of influence had gotten him admitted. Had he intended to kill Bordabehere? Or was it De la Torre he was after? It was shown in the investigation that Valdez was a hanger-on of the Minister of Agriculture, and a henchman of the Conservative politicians.[47] Duhau denied ever having seen him, but it was proven that he was a frequent visitor to Duhau's office and even his home, and that on the day of the murder Duhau had greeted him in the lobby of the Senate. From these facts to the conclusion that the thug had been sent to murder De la Torre before he said any more, was a leap that the public imagination made; but such was the sensational nature of the case that the matter was hushed completely. The assassination stopped the debate on frigoríficos. De la Torre was deeply shaken by the death of his young friend, and worse shaken by the Senate's refusal to go into the case. He had made his most brilliant debate, but it was the end of his career. The heart went out of him. The Ministers of Agriculture and Finance resigned "to give the President a free hand in the reorganization of the Cabinet." [48] Pinedo and De la Torre fought a duel. And the Argentine and British governments appointed a mixed commission to get at the bottom of the meat question. The commission's report, published in 1938, was in part whitewash, but it was a useful study of the industry. Needless to say, the matters of the exchange irregularities and the prices paid for Sr. Duhau's steers were not brought up again.

DEFEAT

The incapacity and vacillation of the Radicals has completely enervated popular feeling, and the present situation exists because of them, who refused a united front of the democratic forces.
—LISANDRO DE LA TORRE, July 23, 1937.

As the Justo administration progressed, the Radicals who had been in exile or in prison began returning to political life. Justo himself was an Anti-Personalista Radical. The Anti-Personalistas, who had joined the Conservatives, made up part of the Conservative governmental bloc which went by the name of the Concordancia (Concordance). In the opposition were the Radicals, now headed by Alvear, the Socialists, headed by Nicolás Repetto, and the Demócratas Progresistas, whose leader was Lisandro de la Torre.

The Radicals were demoralized. Had public opinion been allowed to speak freely, they would even now have been in power, as they knew, and as the country knew. The Radicals had spent twenty years trying to get into power—years during which their leader had been Yrigoyen, and during which they had developed a technique of their own to protest against fraud. That technique was to abstain from voting. It had served them well at one time—or so they thought; but it must be emphasized that not conspiracy and not abstention, but the passage of the Sáenz Peña law by the Conservatives was what had made possible their rise to power in 1916. Nevertheless, they felt that the most effective weapon against fraud was not to go to the polls. Now that they were again in the situation of their early years, they returned to the old tactics. But this time they did not have their picturesque and popular caudillo, and there was evidence that without him the Radicals were less a party than a disorganized agglomeration of personal interests and vague democratic sentiments.

The Justo government was a dictatorship, and it was not popular. The mass of the people knew that their will had been defrauded by dishonest elections. They were shocked at the spectacle of public corruption in the Conservative government, and at the unjustified and inexplicable concessions that Justo and Pinedo made with both hands to great foreign corporations. Government offices had been cleaned of all who were not Conservatives, friends of Conservatives, or hangers-on of one kind and another. Young people graduating from the universities found every avenue of advance shut to them. They could not be teachers, or government engineers, or college professors unless they had friends among the camarilla in power. It did not matter what degrees they possessed, or whether they had studied abroad, or whether they were intelligent, or what their qualifications were. The only question asked of a man looking for employment was: "And who is recommending you?" Engineers were given positions teaching English, biologists were put to work in the post office, and lawyers improvised in all kinds of positions. And during the years the Conservatives held power (1930 to 1943) an entire generation of young people was submerged. They did not enter either politics or the professions. Leaders in all parties grew old without young men coming in to take their place. The intelligent young for the most part stayed out of politics and were lost in the anonymity of private life; and those that went into politics joined either the extreme left, the Communists, or the extreme right, the nationalists and fascists.

These were years, too, when public opinion was becoming more and more opposed to the granting of unfair advantages to foreign capital. Yet there has not in modern Argentine history been an administration that made more concessions to foreign corporations than that of Agustín P. Justo, especially while the ex-Socialist and successful corporation lawyer Federico Pinedo was his Minister of Finance. Some of the Justo-Pinedo contracts were so detrimental to Argentine national interests that there is no explaining them. Such, for instance, was the Port of Rosario contract of November, 1935.

The early history of this remarkable business concession has been already briefly sketched. The Port concession was granted on the basis of a national law, No. 3885, passed by Congress in the year 1899. In 1902 the executive power had signed a contract with Hersent et Fils, Schneider et Cie, authorizing the company to exploit the Port of Rosario for forty years, at the end of which the Port, and all its improvements and installations, was to pass to the national government without charge. In other words, Schneider had forty years to amortize the investment. The contract was generous in the extreme, allowing the company to keep 40 per cent of its gross income for "administrative expenses," and guaranteeing it at least 6 per cent on its investment. The concession proved fabulous, and on a port which cost 10,000,000 francs to build, the company made a gross of 265,000,000 pesos,[49] between 1902 and 1939. In the twenties the 500-franc shares of the Port were quoted at 35,000 francs,[50] and in 1929 one share was sold on the Paris Bourse for 41,000 francs.[51]

It is clear, then, that the company was not losing money on the Port. However, 1942 was approaching, and in that year, by law and by contract, the Port had to be turned over intact to the national government, with all installations and improvements, and without charge. It was in this situation that in November, 1935, the Justo government signed a new contract with the Schneiders. If, said the contract, there remain any company bonds which have not yet been amortized by 1942, *the company shall remain in possession of the Port until the bonds are paid off.* And another article so defined the gold peso (by law a gold peso is 2.27 paper pesos, no matter what the value of paper) that the 40 per cent of gross income going by law to the company began to rise spectacularly, and so did the bonded indebtedness. The whole maneuver is complicated in the extreme, and is still in litigation in the Argentine courts, so that it is manifestly impossible to explain it here. Suffice it to say that by means of the 1935 contract the Port of Rosario, which by law should pass to the state free of charge, was to be kept in the hands of the company, and the Government admitted owing the company millions of pesos. That the contract was illegal, there is no doubt, for the executive had no authority in the matter of the Port of Rosario beyond that granted by the law of 1899, and the law was explicit: at the termination of the 1902 contract the Port was to go to the Argentine government without any charges whatsoever. But the 1935 contract gave the company grounds for long and expensive litigation, by which it was hoped to keep the Port in private hands for a few years more while the lawsuit was on. As a matter of fact, when the concession expired in 1942, President Castillo simply had the government move in and take over the Port, and the protests of the company were ignored. What nobody has ever satisfactorily explained, however, is why President Justo signed the 1935 contract.

The Justo administration was rich in cases of this kind. Another was the question of the C.A.D.E. concession. The C.A.D.E. was the Compañía Argentina de Electricidad, the big power company of Buenos Aires. The company had a fifty-year concession, granted in 1907, expiring in 1957. As in the case of the Port of Rosario, the installations were to pass free to the hands of the municipal government at the expiration of the contract. In 1936, the Consejo Deliberante (Buenos Aires City Council) voted two ordinances: by one the C.A.D.E. concession was extended until 1971; and by the other the city obligated itself at the expiration of the contract to *buy* all the company's buildings and property and installations. The newspapers openly spoke of how much the councilmen had been paid for their votes by the C.A.D.E., a company which seems to be owned in Belgium, although it was originally German. According to the Socialist newspaper *La Vanguardia* the councilmen received from 60,000 to 120,000 pesos each for their votes.[52] The day the ordinances passed, the council chambers were packed with spectators. After the vote, a man who had been among the visitors strode to the center of the room and stood accusingly before one of the councilmen. "Sold!" he screamed. "You have dishonored our father's name! You grafter!" It was the councilman's brother, and a member of the same political party.[53]

To the Argentine people, the discouraging aspect of the situation was that in the face of such a government as this the Radicals did nothing but quarrel among themselves. "The vacillating attitude they have adopted in the Chamber of Deputies," wrote

Lisandro de la Torre to a friend, "shows how little is to be expected from them. The public spirit cannot be returned to normal with such leaders as these." [54] In 1937 a historic low in politics was reached by the Argentine Congress. In that year the legislature passed only three laws: one authorized the Chamber to spend more money, and the other two permitted the President to leave the city of Buenos Aires on vacations. Although the executive got its budget to Congress on time, the finance committee did not even get around to meeting until the end of the session. The Conservatives would not attend Congressional sessions, and the Radicals spent their time in interminable minority wrangles. And when the Conservatives were there, the Radicals were absent in protest at fraudulent elections. This was the Argentine government in 1937, the last year of the Justo administration.[55]

The year 1937 was an election year, and Justo chose as his successor Dr. Roberto M. Ortiz, a corporation lawyer who had been Alvear's Minister of Public Works, and who in the Justo administration had succeeded Pinedo as Minister of Finance. Ortiz was an Anti-Personalista, like Justo. He was a large man, already ill with diabetes. Apparently the Radicals were quiet in 1937, refusing all efforts of the other opposition parties to make a united front against the Conservatives, because they had a secret understanding with Justo that he would make Ortiz President, and with Ortiz that if he were elected he would help the Radicals back into power.[56] The general public did not know this—in fact, still does not know this—and continued to watch the behavior of the Radicals with frustration and disillusionment. To the average Argentine, Ortiz was another corporation lawyer who had served foreign interests all his life, and that was all. As for the Vice-President to be, Dr. Ramón S. Castillo, everyone knew his reputation as the most reactionary man in the Buenos Aires Law School, of which he was dean.

The 1937 elections went as prearranged. Ortiz defeated Alvear, who was the Radical candidate, by the generous use of fraud and intimidation. On February 20th of the following year Ortiz and Castillo took office. Argentina could count the harvest of the September Revolution and see nothing but evil in it. The national interests had been betrayed at every step. The Roca-Runciman Pact had delivered the meat industry to a foreign monopoly, and the municipal transportation to the Anglo-Argentine. The country had been defrauded on the Port of Rosario, and the city of Buenos Aires on the C.A.D.E. The government was the rule of favoritism and corruption. Elections were as bad as they had been before Sáenz Peña. The Radicals, on whom all hopes were centered, did nothing. There was no hope of peaceful change, and there could be no revolution without the army. But the army, reactionary to a degree, was solidly behind the Conservatives. Public opinion was disorientated, and the country was sullen and apathetic.

In Congress the great liberal Lisandro de la Torre had made his last fight. He surveyed his life, and saw that he was a failure. He could speak out in the Senate, but the great Conservative press would not publish what he said. His friend Bordabehere was murdered on the floor of the Senate, and the Senate hushed the investigation. Everywhere he saw indifference. Neither Radicals nor Socialists would make a united stand against the government. "I have fought in the Senate for five years, without having behind me either the Unión Cívica or the great papers," he said. "I have fought savagely, attacking all the serious abuses that came up, despite the conspiracy of silence of the important dailies and the absolute lack of solidarity of the opposition parties, the Radicals and the Socialists." In the middle of his term, Lisandro de la Torre presented his resignation to the Senate, and retired to private life. "I have retired from the Senate because I could not keep quiet there," he said, "and the time has come to keep quiet. . . . The country now is interested only in how much wheat is worth. The hour of repentance will come, and then there will be many voices that speak." [57]

He was nearing his seventieth birthday, and the idea of death came more and more to fill his thoughts. "The best and surest prospect for man," he wrote to a friend, "once his consciousness is extinguished by death, is the scattering of the atoms of his body in nature. This way he may remain in ignorance of what was the object of his stay on earth, but what necessity is there for him to know it? Does, by any chance, the tree that grows and dies know it? Or the bird that sings in the branch, or the ant that carries his burden? Let man be satisfied with being only a small, sad aspect of nature." [58]

As 1938 came to a close, and his friends prepared to celebrate his seventieth birthday, the old man went home one day to his small apartment on Suipacha where he had lived for most of his adult life, alone—for he had never married—and surrounded by his books. He sat down and penned a letter to his friends: "One should not give too much importance to the final unravelling of a human life," he told them. "If you do not mind, I wish my ashes to be scattered to the wind. It seems to me a good way to return to nothingness, to become a part of all that dies in the universe." [59] And Lisandro de la Torre, the great fighter who had lost every battle, took a revolver and put a bullet through his heart.

WAR

THE ELEMENTS OF DISUNION

> *Recently there has been officially instituted the Fiesta of the Race —in the singular,* The Race, *which we interpret as the Spanish race. . . . The concept of race has not been revived in the Río de la Plata to make us love more those who supposedly belong to the same race, but to make us hate more those who supposedly do not. The Spanish aristocrat who never created in any part of the world institutions designed to bring love among men, had to announce his spiritual reconquest of the Río de la Plata by making notions of race and race hatreds reappear in mid-twentieth century.*
>
> —ROBERTO KURTZ, *La Argentina ante Estados Unidos.*

On September 1, 1939, Germany invaded Poland, bringing general war to the world for the second time in twenty-five years. President Roberto M. Ortiz, with the example of Yrigoyen's successful neutrality in mind, declared on September 4th that Argentina would again be neutral. Throughout the Americas the determination not to mix in the European war was firm and unanimous. Like the United States in the north, Argentina in the extreme south of the hemisphere took a spectatorial attitude toward the struggle, in the meantime wondering whether this war would bring the profits of the last. At the same time, the conflict of ideologies which was convulsing Europe reflected itself in minor scale in Argentine life.

If the psychological attitude of the Argentine people could be summed up, it would be found to be very similar to that of the Americans in the same period. In the first place, the average mind had been conditioned against Nazism by the press, which subscribed to the great American news services, the United and the Associated Press. For several years Buenos Aires, like New York and San Francisco, had been reading atrocity stories from Germany in the daily papers. The vast majority of Argentines were unsympathetic to the Axis governments, and after the fall of France this dislike became almost a personal grievance, for France had been Argentina's spiritual mother. But at the same time that all this was true, there was another thread running through popular feeling: long and unacknowledged resentment against the English, which had been brought to a head by the Roca pacts and the Anglo-Argentine question. Dunkirk gave secret satisfaction to the Argentines because it humiliated the British. And it was the first time in Argentine memory that the British had not appeared self-assured and superior to the world. The Argentines had really believed in British imperturbability. That (as they conceived it) icy front which the English gentleman showed to the world was something they had respected while they envied it. They recalled that even after three generations in Argentina, the English colony was still inbred, and Englishmen who married creole women were considered to have lost caste. They knew that Anglo-Argentines whose grandfathers had been born in the Río de la Plata still travelled on British passports for fear they would be considered Argentines. They had always accepted this as connoting an inherent Anglo-Saxon superiority. Now that the fall of the Empire looked imminent, and the Englishman's pedestal had been knocked out from under him, they were suddenly very glad, and gloated at his downfall.

Thus the reaction to the war was complex. Ideologically, the average Argentine did not like the totalitarian governments. The great newspapers of Buenos Aires were unanimously pro-Ally, and what they published of foreign news was simply American dispatches in translation. However, in Argentina as in all countries, there is a large, inert segment of public opinion that goes where the sun shines warmest; and for the first two years of the war it looked to all observers as though the Axis were going to win. A small body of opinion was frankly pro-fascist, and it influenced to a large degree a greater body of opinion which might be summed up as: "Well, if the Axis is going to win, let us not be on bad terms with the winners." Or, as the saying in Spanish is, "Let's stay on good terms with God and the devil."

Fascism appealed to a certain mentality in Argentina, and

attracted various elements into a nucleus that was not homogeneous, but hung together. One group was that of the impoverished sons of ruined estancieros whose ideals were reactionary, but who had neither economic nor political future. In this class were also a few *niños bien.* But for the estancieros as a whole—those that were still selling their meats and making money—self-interest dictated that they be pro-British. In this group, which might be called the Jockey Club group, the salient characteristics are a lack of intelligence combined with good family name, reactionary social views, and extreme clericalism.

A second category was that of the disgruntled intellectuals, who were usually young people who had passed through phases that included communism, but who ended up by taking the extreme nationalist position. Most of them had suffered disappointments of one kind and another. Many had been submerged in the last ten years of Conservative government. All of them were frustrated, and their frustration manifested itself in a hatred of foreign capital, or of the Jews, or of democracy. Members of this second group were called fascist in the real sense, for they were not conservative but revolutionary. They wanted a strong, independent Argentina with an army strong enough to invade Brazil and take its iron and coal deposits. They were against capitalism and economic liberalism, and they wanted a docile working class, at the same time wishing to better its working conditions.

A third group was that body of opinion in the army which liked fascism because it glorified the military virtues. Since most of the Argentine army was German-trained, and since many of the officers had lived in Germany, served with the German army, and spoke German, it might be said that as a class they favored an Axis victory, and that they would also look favorably on the establishment of a fascist government in Argentina in which they would have positions of importance and control. The army group, however, was quite independent of the other nationalists, and was a segment apart.

A fourth element was the Argentine clergy. A large proportion of the priests in Argentina were Spaniards, and they were pro-

Franco and anti-communist. The clergy wanted to see something like a corporate state in which the church had a share of control, as in the government of Francisco Franco in Spain, but with the clergy more powerful. They perhaps subconsciously feared the kind of anticlericalism that swept Spain during the Republic, and thought a fascist state would be a bulwark against leftist ideologies. In Argentina this group worked through a lay organization called Acción Católica, which was ostensibly nonpolitical. Actually, its members were indoctrinated by the rightist clergy with their ideals. Members of Acción Católica were militantly anticommunist, sympathized with General Franco, considered Russia as the worst enemy of civilization, and believed that the limits of social change were those laid down by Leo XIII in his encyclical *Rerum Novarum*. The most intelligent spokesman for the fascist Catholic clergy was Monseñor Gustavo Franceschi, editor of the magazine *Criterio*, and a notable orator.* The outstanding leader of the Catholic left wing in Argentina was Monseñor Miguel de Andrea, probably the outstanding figure in the Argentine church. De Andrea, who held the titular bishopric of Temnos, was a very handsome old man with white hair and blue eyes. He was a great public speaker, an organizer of unions for working girls, and a spokesman for the democratic cause. De Andrea would have been the cardinal-archbishop of Buenos Aires if it had not been for the bitter opposition of the rightist clergy and the landed aristocracy. He and Franceschi represented the two opposite poles of opinion within the Argentine church. On the whole, however, the clergy were ultraconservative, and the medium of the confessional was used by them to warn their parishioners, especially the women, against the reading of Karl Marx and the acceptance of dangerous social doctrines.† From the pulpit, too, the clergy exerted great

* As a result of a lecture by Lisandro de la Torre in the Colegio Libre in 1937, he and Franceschi entered into a long and very interesting polemic—Franceschi through the medium of *Criterio*, and De la Torre in the columns of *La Vanguardia*. De la Torre's articles have been published in book form under the title of *La Cuestión Social y un Cura* (B.A., 1943).

† I do not make this charge lightly, but know from personal experience and that of close friends that it is true.

influence. In Santa Fe they made a long campaign against De la Torre and the Partido Demócrata Progresista. In Buenos Aires they attacked the Socialists, spreading stories that their leaders were owners of tenement houses, etc. In matters of international politics they attacked the Spanish republic, and favored the Nationalist victory.

In general, the Argentine nationalists agreed on a body of doctrine. They were, as they said, *antiliberal*. They did not believe in freedom of the press, in economic laissez-faire, in capitalism, or in any of what went to make up nineteenth century liberalism. In this the fascists shared the opinion of the Catholic Church, which believed that intellectual liberalism was dangerous because it assumed that all doctrines were equally true and equally deserving of propagation. It had been the Catholic viewpoint since the initiation of the Inquisition and the Index that some ideas were so dangerous they must be suppressed.

The Argentine fascists on the whole were Hispanists, which means that they believed in the rehabilitation of Spain in the popular mythology. After the revolution against Spain there persisted in the former colonies what is known as the Black Legend: that all that Spain had done as a colonizer was bad, that the conquistadores had been cruel and ugly, and that their ideals were false. The Black Legend came in with the liberal revolt, and it is therefore logical that a movement which was professedly antiliberal should be Hispanist. According to the Hispanists, there must be a return to the ideals of the Spain of the sixteenth century, the Siglo de Oro (Golden Century). Since the Siglo de Oro was characterized by a worship of the cross and the sword in about equal measure, Hispanism fitted in nicely with both the clerical and the militaristic aspects of Argentine fascism. Hispanism was also the rallying cry of those who did not like Pan Americanism because there was too much of the Anglo-Saxon in it: in short, it was the rallying cry of those who hated the Yanquis and wanted Spanish America to unite in spiritual resistance against ideas which they considered to be cheap and false, and propagated by the United States (divorce, the emancipation of women, and so forth).

Hispanism antedated General Franco by many years, as did the custom of celebrating Columbus Day as the Día de la Raza, or Day of the Race—presumably the Spanish race. (The fact that Columbus was an Italian does not enter into the picture.) Hispanism in its earlier phases was obviously directed against the United States. However, with the fascist triumph in Spain, it became something more. Now it stood for a concrete kind of society: for a government of soldiers and priests, in which the church was the spiritual and intellectual leader, and the army did the ruling. It must be emphasized that Argentine fascism, like Spanish fascism, had little in common with Nazism beyond its intolerance. It was strongly clerical, as Nazism was not, and it was backward-looking rather than revolutionary. The ideal of the sixteenth century was a society without any commercial interests whatever. It was full of the kind of misplaced heroism which Cervantes so brilliantly satirized in his *Don Quijote*, and full of the bigotry of the Spanish Inquisition.

The Argentine nationalists were *Rosistas*. They made a martyr of the porteño tyrant, and they wore red ribbons in their buttonholes because red was his color. They sang the Federal Hymn of Rivera Indarte, and they glorified Rosas as an Argentine patriot who successfully resisted the Anglo-French intervention in the Río de la Plata. They liked him because he would not allow foreign capital to enter Argentina and develop the country. They liked him because he was a strong dictator, and because he ruled by the Mazorca. One of the nationalist papers, although an unimportant one, was called *El Restaurador*. Inasmuch as Argentine nationalism hated the foreigner and was against capitalism, and did not believe in democratic government, Rosas was a logical hero for the movement. The modern Rosistas preached against Mitre and Sarmiento and Alberdi because they "sold the country to the foreigner," and because they taught false democratic ideals.

The Argentine fascists were imperialists. They believed in a strong army, and wanted to "reincorporate" all the territory of the Viceroyalty of the Río de la Plata, which would include Uruguay, Paraguay, and Bolivia. They also favored war against Brazil, because they saw in Brazil their greatest rival for the leadership of Latin America. They aspired to lead the Spanish American world, not only spiritually but economically and politically.

They were against Great Britain and the United States. The United States was the Yankee Peril. The American movies represented their idea of the United States. It was a country without religion, interested only in making money. The Americans had no feeling for the sanctity of the home. Divorce was current, and their women acted like streetwalkers, going out without chaperons, earning their own living, going to night clubs, getting drunk, and in general, behaving shamefully. The Catholic Church in Argentina considered the American movies as a menace to young womanhood, and was much concerned at the evident influence they had on the behavior of the younger generation. The nationalists said that these cheap and false ideals must be combated if Spanish America were to be saved for its great tradition. As for Great Britain, it was the octopus that had all the country's wealth in its hands, and until all its enterprises had been confiscated and put into Argentine hands, the nation would never be truly sovereign.

The fascists were anti-Semitic, and wished to expel the Jews from public office, from the normal schools and universities, and from the professions. But anti-Semitism was really the least important element in the movement, and was more a reflection of European events than anything else.

In short, Argentine nationalism was a mélange. It really had two component parts which had little or nothing to do with each other historically. One was reaction of a very Spanish and indigenous nature. This included the religious fanaticism and the Hispanism and the impossible Siglo de Oro ideals. This phase had deep historic roots in Latin America, and there have always been classes of the population—usually the most aristocratic—that have represented it. The other component part was modern revolutionary nationalism of the German sort. This included the hatred of capitalism, the imperialism, the ideal of the totalitarian state, and the anti-Semitism. It just happened that both these movements in this historic moment coincide in being *against* the same thing.

They were against capitalism, liberalism, and democracy. Hence the union of forces. All the nationalist groups would have agreed on the establishment of a corporate state along the Italian lines. Even those nationalists who were indifferent to Catholicism would have no objection to letting the church play an important role, in return for its support. The religious apparatus, as they saw it, would be an important element of stability.

Now, as for the groups themselves. They were many and various, and each published a small paper or magazine of limited circulation. They were in contact and in sympathy with one another. They gave themselves names like *Renovación, Recuperación, Afirmación*. Numerically the most important, as well as the least intellectual and least aristocratic, was the Alianza de la Juventud Nacionalista, which claimed 10,000 members in all parts of the Republic. The Alianza was headed by a retired army general named Juan Bautista Molina, and was organized along Storm Trooper lines. Some of the members, especially in small provincial towns, were simply the town rowdies. They considered themselves to be *mazorqueros,* and occasionally beat up people of whom they disapproved. Their program included the establishment of concentration camps for deputies and democratic politicians, and ghettos for the Jews. The Alianza was really an aggregate of various nationalistic groups, and one of the component organizations was a group with the initials J.M. de R.O.S.A.S.* The motto of the Alianza was also Rosista: *Restauración o Muerte* (Restoration or Death).

The most important nationalist publication was *El Pampero,* a newspaper founded in 1939 and subsidized by the German Embassy. *El Pampero* was, until 1942, the only nationalist newspaper in Buenos Aires that pretended to compete with the popular dailies. In 1942, however, Manuel Fresco, ex-governor of Buenos Aires, and one of the most vociferous nationalists, founded *Cabildo,* which featured racing and sporting news in the hope of

* Juventudes Militarizadas de la Restauración Orgánica de la Sociedad Argentina Sindicalizada. This name, which is obviously constructed to spell "Rosas" at the cost of making good sense, may be translated the Militarized Youth of the Organic Restoration of Syndicalized Argentine Society.

getting a popular following. *El Pampero* was strictly war-inspired, and was more an agent of Nazi foreign policy than a real Argentine newspaper. Nevertheless, in domestic policy it was nationalistic, anti-British, and Rosista. (On anniversaries of Rosas' death, and any other days of sentimental interest to the Rosistas, it published appropriate poetry and mottoes, and toasts to the *Restauración*.) In nationalism it is evident that the Nazi propagandists found a ready-made tool. The use they have made of it will be discussed at greater length in the next chapter.

The oldest nationalist daily was *Crisol* (Crucible), which was founded shortly after the Uriburu revolution. Like *El Pampero*, *Crisol* used Trans-Ocean news service, furnished by the Germans. Another morning daily of less importance, which also grew out of the Uriburu revolution, was *Bandera Argentina*. *Bandera Argentina* was not exactly fascist, but represented rather the extreme right wing of the Conservative party. It used Trans-Ocean and Stefani news services. There were numerous other small publications of limited circulation. Some were highly intellectual, like the literary magazine *Sol y Luna*, which was Hispanist and Catholic.

These nationalist groups did not represent one class or one tendency. On the contrary, there were important differences. Some were aristocratic, and some, like the Alianza, were not. Some were intellectual. Some were clerical. Some were revolutionary in a social sense, and others clearly reactionary. In any case, they did not believe in liberalism, capitalism, or communism, and this put them on the Axis side of the fence. They were important as agents of Axis propaganda, in organizing and spreading a hate-the-British and hate-the-Yankee campaign. The Argentines had experienced in their own daily living what imperialism and capitalism in the worst sense could mean. They had seen their foreign policy respond to the pressure of another nation because it bought their meat, and they had seen foreign-owned public utilities buy their own government. Without experiencing American imperialism themselves, they knew other Latin countries that had. Out of the Argentine people's normal resentment the Axis forged its most powerful weapon of propaganda. The British and Americans, it said, were not fighting for democracy. They were fighting for their empire and their monstrous capital. And there was just enough truth in the allegation to make the Argentines uncertain.

But there was one certain test of sincerity in the antiforeign capital campaign. The groups that were seriously against the abuses of foreign corporations, that had not been using the issue for the benefit of Axis propaganda—the Socialist party, for instance—unanimously called off the hue and cry until the war was won. Their attitude was: The British and Russians and Americans are fighting for what we believe in. Let's not draw red herrings across the trail. When the war is won we can go back to our campaign for economic independence. Even such bitter enemies of the public utility companies as Alfredo Palacios kept quiet on the issue so as not to play into the hands of the fascist forces. It is interesting in this connection to note that the extreme left and the extreme right saw eye to eye on the abuses of foreign capital. The difference was that the right tried to turn this hatred against the whole cause of the United Nations, and the left called a truce until fascism should be beaten.

THE GERMAN CAMPAIGN

The Nazi propaganda campaign in Buenos Aires was directed and paid for by the German Embassy. Its funds came from trade balances in Argentina which could not be liquidated through the regular trade channels because the war stopped all commerce with Germany. In 1940 the Embassy asked the Minister of Foreign Relations if it might use some of this money to pay for the internment of the sailors from the pocket battleship *Graf Spee*, which was scuttled in the Río de la Plata to keep it from falling into British hands. The *Graf Spee* seamen were interned in various parts of the Republic, in Córdoba, in Santa Fe, on the island of Martín García. The Argentine government consulted the Banco

Central, which said that "the cited balance was to be used by Germany only for the acquisition of Argentine products, but that, for the moment, there did not exist the possibility that exports could be sent from the country." Accordingly, the Ministry agreed to let the Embassy draw on these balances: it was granted 884,600 pesos for normal expenditures, and the Argentine government took 752,000 pesos to pay for the internment of the *Graf Spee* seamen.[1]

In addition to this money from the trade balances, the German Embassy had other funds. There was 4,600,000 pesos from the accounts of various Berlin banks in Buenos Aires banks, and there was 3,000,000 in an account which was under the control, but not the name, of the Embassy. Since the Embassy's normal expenditure was 800,000 pesos, and this was now being released to the Embassy by the Argentine government from the trade balances, that left a considerable sum for other purposes. In one year the German Embassy issued 2,000,000 pesos' worth of checks made out "to the bearer" (*al portador*)—which required no endorsement from the persons cashing them. Some of these checks were for as much as 200,000 pesos; others were small. German Embassy expenditures began to rise notably over the prewar averages: 1938–1939, 850,000 pesos; 1939–1940, 3,397,600; 1940–1941, 5,983,100.[2]

Where was this money going? As a matter of fact, much of it was hard to trace, because the checks did not require endorsement. It is possible, however, to infer the destination of much of this money by a correlation of facts. For instance, from July 1 to August 13, 1941, propaganda sent out from Buenos Aires by mail compared as follows: German, 502 packages totalling 4,394,850 kilograms; British, 127 packages totalling 729,905 kilograms. These pamphlets and papers were destined for the interior of Argentina and the whole of South America.[3]

An investigation of the Axis news agencies and pro-Axis newspapers shows that much of this money must have gone to them. The Axis-dominated news agencies were first of all Trans-Ocean, which was German, and which furnished news free to seventy dailies and sixty periodicals of the interior. In Buenos Aires it served without charge *El Pampero, Bandera Argentina, Crisol,* and the foreign-language newspapers *Deutsche La Plata Zeitung, Il Mattino d'Italia,* and *Diario Español* (pro-Franco). In addition, Trans-Ocean used three radio stations for news broadcasts. Since by the admission of the director, Walter von Simons, Trans-Ocean received less than a third of its budget from the sale of news and photographs, 70 per cent came from the German government. Trans-Ocean, said von Simons to the investigating committee of the Chamber of Deputies, did not have a fixed charge, but "takes into account the economic status and needs of the press." [4]

Other Axis-dominated news services were Stefani, Andi, and Havas-Télémondial. Stefani was an old Italian bureau closely connected with the Italian Embassy in Buenos Aires, and gave free service to the papers. Andi was a syndicate of Axis bias. As for Havas-Télémondial, after the fall of France the old Havas agency changed directors and added "Télémondial" to its name. It received a subsidy from Andi, and served *El Pueblo* (a Catholic paper with 50,000 circulation), the *Diario Español,* and *La Fronda* (semiofficial organ of the Conservative party, circulation 1,500).[5] Although the important dailies of Buenos Aires, with a total circulation of a million and a half, subscribed to American and British news services, the Axis agencies had an advantage in the interior where small papers could not afford the charges of Associated or United Press, and welcomed the free services of Trans-Ocean and Stefani. The element of cost must be borne in mind in understanding why so many little provincial dailies and weeklies subscribed to Axis news agencies.

The porteño daily which most certainly was subsidized indirectly by the German Embassy was *El Pampero,* which was founded in the year the war broke out, and was official Argentine spokesman for the Axis in foreign policy, and for the Rosistas and nationalists in internal policy. Nobody knew the exact circulation of *El Pampero,* which was estimated between 15,000 * (probably too low) and 80,000 (probably too high). In any case, investigation of *El Pampero's* checking account in the Banco Central showed that in the last six months of 1940 the paper had a 40

* Estimate of the United Press Mailer Service, Dec. 18, 1940.

per cent deficit, which was made up somehow. Part of the subsidy was traced to Enrique Vollberg, head of the Office for the Promotion of German Commerce in Argentina, who gave more than 100,000 pesos to *El Pampero* in two months.[6] Where did Vollberg get the money? Probably the Embassy. Rich fascist sympathizers also helped *El Pampero*.

Other outlets for Axis propaganda were furnished by publishing houses like Tor, and by the two or three Buenos Aires movie houses which showed fascist newsreels, and pictures made by the Franco government in Spain to glorify such achievements as the defense of the Alcázar during the Civil War. These theaters showed documentary films and newsreels from Germany (UFA), Italy (LUCE), Spain (NO-DO), and Japan. There was a larger number of newsreel theaters showing American films, and they had the advantage of being more entertaining and less grim, notably because of the Disney pictures and other animated cartoons. The Axis newsreels suffered from being too serious and not very amusing. They showed battles, the sinking of merchant ships, military reviews, and historic moments in the lives of Hitler and Mussolini. The UFA "culturals" were deadly bores, being occupied with such subjects as the circulation of the planets, the behavior of heavy water, and the making of textiles from ground-up fish. The only pictures with artistic value were the films made in Japan, which cleverly emphasized the cherry-blossom and silk-kimono aspects of that country. Occasionally the German documentaries were very beautiful, a case in point being a picture on the training of naval cadets aboard a sailing ship. Most of the porteños, however, still preferred to spend an hour with Donald Duck, Popeye, and the Florida bathing beauties. For every Argentine that saw an Axis picture, two hundred saw an American movie. In the final analysis, the influence of Axis propaganda through the moving picture was of no importance whatever. On the other hand, the influence of Allied propaganda through American pictures was incalculable.

As a matter of fact, weighing the matter well, one may say that the direct action of the German Embassy in subsidizing media of expression, like the pro-Axis papers, the movies, and publishing houses, was of no real importance in influencing Argentine public opinion. It gave Argentine democrats a chance to fuss, and made sensational reading in some American magazines. The real weapon against the democracies was furnished by the democracies themselves, and that was the record of coercion and dissimulation by their interests in Argentina. There is no doubt that the actions of giant British and American corporations in Latin America have left a profound residue of ill will toward both the United States and Great Britain. As one Argentine said to me, sneering at the Rockefeller Foundation's contributions to tropical medicine: "Yes, the Rockefellers have done a noble work in exterminating mosquitoes. For every mosquito they exterminate, they drill an oil well: one mosquito, one oil well—one mosquito, one oil well." The Argentines know what imperialism is, because they have experienced it.

THE DEMOCRATIC FRONT

The war brought mobilization not only to the Axis forces in Argentina, but to the democratic ones as well. When the imminent surrender of France in early June, 1940, brought home the realization that democracy was on the defensive, and that it was facing disaster, one of the first groups to be organized was Acción Argentina, which signed up 300,000 members almost at once. This was just thirty times as many members as the Alianza de la Juventud Nacionalista ever claimed. The movement for the formation of Acción Argentina, in the first months of its existence, had all the aspects of a crusade. It held two and three mass meetings a week, broadcast almost daily, and sent speakers to tour Argentina in special trains. By the end of the year it had founded three hundred branches all over the country, and was publishing a paper *Alerta* which claimed a circulation of 35,000.

Acción Argentina was pro-British, but not even after the entry of Russia into the war did it become pro-Russian. It represented midde-of-the-road democratic opinion, and included on its governing committee such men as Dr. Federico Pinedo, who had been Justo's Minister of Finance, Dr. Marcelo T. de Alvear, leader of the Radical party, and Dr. Nicolás Repetto, leader of the Socialist party. There were many Conservatives in Acción Argentina. But the organization slowly began to bog down from natural inertia; and from the Argentine tendency to show more enthusiasm for starting a movement than persistence in keeping it going. After the entry of Russia into the war, Acción Argentina showed a notable coolness toward groups of a more communist bias, although when the United States became involved it supported the American war effort.

Groups in which communists took a leading role showed far better organization than Acción Argentina. They were on the whole less spectacular, but they had staying power and did not peter out after the first flush of enthusiasm had passed. One of the most successful of these was the Junta de la Victoria, whose president was Ana Rosa Schlieper de Martínez Guerrero, a woman very prominent in Pan American affairs, and president of the Inter-American Women's Commission of the Pan American Union. Sra. de Martínez Guerrero was not a communist, but other officers of the Junta who were less decorative, and even harder working, were known communists, as were most of the leaders of the provincial branches. The Junta sent bandages, sweaters, and medical supplies to Russia, China, England, and the United States, according to the wishes of the giver. Since most of the members were Russian sympathizers, most of the shipments were to Russia. But the Junta was absolutely impartial in sending any donation to the country indicated by the person who made that donation. Its attitude was that all the United Nations were equally involved in the war, and that it did not play favorites. Neither the British nor the American Embassy looked on the Junta with favor; nor would they cooperate with it in any way—considering it a "communist front." Yet in truth it must be said that there was no better organized or more intelligently conducted group than this. The Junta, along with Acción Argentina, was suppressed by the Ramírez government in 1943 as "communistic." The leaders of the Junta must have smiled at having Acción Argentina included in its company.

Among the political parties, the Socialists and Radicals were clearly pro-Ally, as was even the majority of the Conservative party. The Communist party was for the United Nations after the attack on Russia, although previous to that it, and its chief newspaper, *La Hora*, had taken the line that this was an imperialist war, and that Pan Americanism was Yankee imperialism in disguise. Once Russia was in the war, however, center and left were strongly united against the Axis. The Conservative party was in a somewhat anomalous position, which will be explained at greater length later. The Conservatives, as representatives of the landholding class, favored a British victory, but did not favor the Pan American movement. The right wing of the party shaded off into nationalism and extreme reaction, and among this element there was a fear of the possible social changes that an Allied victory would bring. On the whole, however, the Conservatives were pro-British, anti-American, and anti-Russian.

Thus, it will be seen that among those favoring the Allied cause there were as many complexions as in the fascist opposition. Some favored the United Nations because they thought Russia was the hope of the world. Some favored them because they believed in representative government, and considered that the Anglo-Saxons were the greatest defenders of democratic institutions. Others wanted the Allies to win because they were selling their meat to Great Britain, and did not want to lose a good customer. Still others were advocates of Pan Americanism, and considered that the attack on the United States by the totalitarian nations was an attack on all the Americas. And others just did not like fascism.

The Allies in reality had almost a monopoly on the avenues of propaganda in Argentina in the present war. The newspapers with the greatest circulation all subscribed to the American press services. The theaters showed American movies. Most of the American atrocity books about Germany were immediately translated into Spanish and given wide circulation. Business houses put up posters furnished by the British Ministry of Information. The Spanish edition of the *Reader's Digest* had the widest circulation in Latin America. The result of this monopoly on the channels of information was to condition the Argentine mind to see fascism as the democracies saw it: as a tyranny of the human mind and spirit that must be broken at any cost. This influence was strongest in Buenos Aires, and diminished as you moved into the provinces. In the provinces many newspapers were too poor to subscribe to the United or the Associated Press, and movie houses often could not afford American pictures, showing Argentine ones instead. In the interior, too, there was much less interest in the war, and much less awareness of the issues. Part of this came from the isolation of distant communities, and part from the high illiteracy and ignorance of much of the population.

The Chamber of Deputies committee investigating anti-Argentine activities showed that the German Embassy was spending twice as much as the British and American Embassies combined. But, even if this was true, it gave a totally false picture of the relative propaganda efforts of the two sides. The moving pictures alone did more to condition Argentines to a hatred of fascism than all the nationalist papers, books, magazines, and newsreels put together accomplished in winning them to the other side. The influence of the American motion picture on attitudes, customs, and beliefs cannot possibly be exaggerated. The Buenos Aires movie houses that showed American pictures—the majority—sold out night after night. Audience reaction was all that Hollywood could hope for. Heroes who escaped Nazi villains and made resounding speeches against their tyranny got loud and generous applause. President Roosevelt was almost always applauded, and the applause was accompanied with comments like "Qué simpático es!" (How charming he is!) In a subtler way, the moving picture influenced customs. The young Argentine girl, noting with envy the freedom of the American movie heroine, put considerable pressure on her family to allow her more personal liberty. Coiffeurs tried American hair styles on their customers, and dress shops appeared with the latest Hollywood fashions. It is also true, of course, that the American moving picture industry has never understood the responsibility inherent in such a situation, and was largely responsible for the spreading of very false ideas about the morals of the American people. Along with the impression of the American woman's freedom which was conveyed by the movies, went an impression that bigamy and divorce were standard family relations in the United States.*

The press, too, helped mold public opinion. The important Buenos Aires newspapers carried not only news dispatches by American and British correspondents, but political cartoons by Low and American comic strips in which the villains were frequently Japanese and Nazis. The porteños read the standard American funnies: "Bringing Up Father," "Winnie Winkle," "Flash Gordon," "The Katzenjammer Kids," "Popeye," "King of the Royal Mounted," "Tarzan," "Terry and the Pirates," "Donald Duck," and all the rest. Virtually all of them appear in one paper or another, even in such august sheets as *La Nación*. When their heroes were not engaged in sinking German submarines or foiling spies, the story usually revolved around rationing, the buying of war bonds, and other situations of the United States at war. It is true that some of the translations and situations could not possibly make sense to the Argentines, but these difficulties did not discourage comic-strip fans. On the contrary, *Crítica*, which published colored comics two nights a week and charged double price on those nights, always sold more papers then than during the rest of the week.

Another powerful weapon of the Allies was economic. Great Britain and the United States were Argentina's only customers during the war, and the United States was virtually the only source of goods of any kind. Thus the American and British blacklists of firms that dealt with the Nazis were able to exert almost irresistible

* One of the most curious examples of Hollywood influence I have ever seen was in an Arab café in Biskra, Algeria, where it was evident that some of the younger Ouled-Naïl dancing girls had been strongly influenced in their ideas of what an Arab dancing girl should wear by American harem movies which they had seen.

pressure. The frequency with which companies were taken off the blacklist would indicate that many were willing to see the point and accept what was inevitable. The pro-Nazi press suffered from an American embargo on newsprint, and there was a period when *El Pampero* appeared only in bulletin form for lack of paper. The Argentine Ministry of Agriculture, however, made paper available to this and other pro-Axis publications by a special decree, and *El Pampero* returned to circulation.

It may be said in general that commerce and industry—the former for its dependence on imports, the latter for its need of machine replacements—were strongly in favor of good relations with the United States, and believed that the government should cooperate in the Pan American movement. They disapproved of the Conservative foreign policy which tended to alienate the United States, and they supported the Ramírez revolution in the belief that it meant a change in foreign policy. At the present time the United States has a virtual embargo on shipments of any but the most necessary medical and health supplies to Argentina. Business is beginning to feel the pinch, and will feel it even more severely in the future, as more and more machines go out of use for lack of parts. The pressure exerted by the industrial element in Argentina is for conciliation and cooperation with all the American nations, and it is at the opposite pole of opinion to the estanciero group, who have been responsible for Argentine foreign policy in the past. There is every reason to believe that if this group gains the ascendant, Argentina's international position will change most radically.

What weighed perhaps most of all in the balance of public opinion about the war were the Allied victories which made it evident that the Axis was finished. That mass of inert opinion which tends to go with the victor abandoned the Axis and went over to the Allies. People who once gloated at German victories, and spoke as if Germany were going to dictate the peace, now gloated at Allied victories and applauded the fall of Italy and invasion of Europe. Many Argentines undoubtedly were in this category. Their response, of course, was quite human. Nothing succeeds like success, as the saying goes.

THE TRAGEDY OF DR. ORTIZ

I see, in all the country, with the force and push of an ideal on the march, the necessity of recovering the popular sovereignty.
—Roberto M. Ortiz, March 2, 1940.

It fell to the lot of Roberto M. Ortiz, as it had fallen to the lot of Hipólito Yrigoyen, to be the President of Argentina during a great world war. Both men declared the neutrality of their country, and kept to it. But here the likeness ended, for Ortiz was not the least bit like Yrigoyen, nor was the Argentina of 1939 like the Argentina of 1916. Ortiz was a successful corporation lawyer who had been fraudulently elected by the Conservative minority. Yrigoyen was a great political caudillo, and the first popularly elected President Argentina had ever had. The Argentina of 1916 had been one of a new democracy, and high hope for the future. And the Argentina of 1939 was apathetic and demoralized after nearly a decade of unpopular minority government.

Marcelo T. de Alvear, now almost an old man, was the leader of the Radical opposition. He knew, and the country knew, that if tomorrow there should be untrammelled elections, his party would be in power. Alvear had been beaten by Ortiz and Castillo because elections were managed. But the Radicals did not fight very hard, and Lisandro de la Torre had said it was because they had a secret understanding with Roberto Ortiz. Ortiz had once been Alvear's Minister of Public Works, and had followed him out of the Radical party into the camp of the Anti-Personalistas. Alvear, after 1930, had gone back to the party, but Ortiz had stayed with the Conservative coalition, and had been Minister of Finance under Justo. The public expected nothing from him, and his inauguration was received with indifference if not hostility.

But what happened afterwards would indicate that De la Torre's hunch had been right. For Roberto M. Ortiz, like Roque

Sáenz Peña, went to the presidency with an *idée fixe*, which was to end minority government and restore honest universal suffrage to the people. The first indication that this was so came in August, 1938, on the eve of an election in La Rioja. President Ortiz directed a letter to the governor of that province in which he said that he wanted the secrecy of the vote respected. The letter aroused mingled hope and skepticism. But when Ortiz intervened in San Juan and annulled a fraudulent vote, and when he sent special federal missions to Santiago del Estero and Catamarca, both the Conservatives and the Radicals realized that when he had said he wanted the vote respected, he had meant it. The Conservatives were in a panic when they realized that the man they had elected intended to put an end to their minority rule. And the Radicals, and the vast body of public opinion that followed them, felt that the chance had come at last to put an end to the state of affairs that had begun with the September Revolution.

All the hopes of Argentina were centered now on the man whom everyone had considered just another corporation lawyer. In February, 1940, there was to be a gubernatorial election in the province of Buenos Aires, now the stronghold of the Conservative machine as it had once been the stronghold of Yrigoyen's Radical machine. The governor of Buenos Aires was a right-wing Conservative named Manuel Fresco, who represented the extreme nationalist segment of the party. The two candidates for governor were Obdulio Siri, a Radical, and Alberto Barceló, the Conservative boss of the industrial city of Avellaneda, on the edge of the Federal Capital. Barceló was a man who had started life as a peon —he was even yet considered semi-illiterate—and who, although he had never dedicated his life to anything but politics, was now a multimillionaire. The election took place on the 25th of February, and was one of the most fraudulent in the history of a province that had seen a lot of fraud in its day. With Fresco managing the election, people were forced to vote not in secret booths but out in the middle of the street, and the Radical representatives were not allowed at the reception tables. So bad was the election that Ortiz, who was vacationing at the seaside resort of Mar del Plata, returned that same night to Buenos Aires, where a street demonstration marched to the Casa Rosada, yelling for intervention in the province.[7] On March 4th newspapers all over the province began publishing denunciations of fraud, and three days later Ortiz ordered intervention in Buenos Aires and put Manuel Fresco out of office. This, to the Conservative party, was like a declaration of war. Two of Ortiz's cabinet ministers resigned in protest. They were Conservatives: Manuel R. Alvarado, Minister of Public Works, and José Padilla, Minister of Agriculture.

The moment was serious. Eleven provinces were to have their elections in March. On March 2 Ortiz had talked to the nation by radio, speaking the words at the head of this chapter: "I see, in all the country," he had told the people, "with the force and push of an ideal on the march, the necessity of recovering the popular sovereignty." The 1940 elections were honest, and did much to redress the balance in both chambers. But the renewal was only partial. In the Senate the Conservatives still had the majority. In the Chamber the balance tipped in favor of the Radicals. The U.C.R. now had 76 deputies. The Concordancia had 73. And the Tucumán Radicals and the Socialists had nine. This meant that the democratic bloc had 85 votes against the right's 73. This was the situation when fate intervened to reverse the political picture suddenly and unexpectedly.

In April, 1940, the wife of President Ortiz, whom he apparently loved very much, died, and the President's health and morale began to decline perceptibly. Ortiz was not a well man. He was diabetic, extremely overweight. In the middle of 1940, when the new Congress was in session, he began to go blind, and so precarious was his general health that the doctors refused to take a chance on a cornea transplantation, which might have saved the President's sight. By July he could not even see to sign government documents, and in that month he turned over the reins of government to Ramón S. Castillo, his Vice-President, and an arch-Conservative.

All that Ortiz had done in two years to restore the suffrage to Argentina was undone. Vice-President Castillo appointed a new cabinet, and every one of Ortiz's ministers was put out. Into the

Ministry of Foreign Affairs went Julio A. Roca, the man who had signed the pact with Runciman. Into the Ministry of the Interior went Miguel J. Culaciati, one of Justo's men. Federico Pinedo became Minister of Finance. In short, there was no doubt of the stripe of this government. Castillo began intervening in province after province to ensure Conservative victories, and interventors were sent to Santa Fe, Mendoza, San Juan, Buenos Aires. The people reacted almost numbly. In a twinkling they were back where they had been before, their will circumvented, the Radicals disorientated. Alvear was a sick man, living in virtual retirement, and in any case his leadership had become passive. In the Chamber the Radical majority tied legislative functions into a knot by refusing any cooperation to Vice-President Castillo. Nothing could be done because the Conservatives held the Senate. What passed one house would not pass the other. The Radicals refused even to pass such necessary measures as the budget. And in his great house on Suipacha President Ortiz lived in twilight, and refused to see anyone.

This was Argentina to the end of 1941. In December there were fraudulent elections again in Buenos Aires. In the Capital one group of angry voters went to the steps of the Casa Rosada, and there they tore up their *libretas de enrolamiento* and threw them into the doorway. The police arrested them. A group of students from the University of Buenos Aires went to the base of the statue to Roque Sáenz Peña, on the Diagonal, and laid a wreath of flowers. The police beat them, and took them to jail, for of course to pay homage to the man who had given Argentina the vote was to protest against the party that had taken it away. When Vice-President Castillo, a small, glum, ungracious man,* appeared in public, there was no applause, only silent hostility.

* Glum as he appeared in public, in private Castillo was said to be affable, and he was popular with the newsmen who interviewed him.

RIO DE JANEIRO, 1942

Outside problems should not disturb us, simply because Argentina is not and could not be other than Argentina. Everything else is another question; another ideal; another interest.

—Ramón S. Castillo, Rosario, October 7, 1941.

On December 7, 1941, the Japanese attack on Pearl Harbor, Hawaii, brought war to the American hemisphere.

In Buenos Aires the news was received with shocked incredulity. *La Prensa* blew its siren, a siren that blows for good news or bad news, but only the most important news. *Crítica* ran a front-page editorial: "The first bombs have fallen on American soil. . . . Aggression against any part of the American continent—it has been said more than once—automatically means aggression against the twenty-one republics of the continent, sisters in origin, in development, and in their common destiny of freedom. For that reason we proclaim that the Axis has wounded us as well. We should be blind if we did not comprehend this, if we obstinately believed ourselves providentially on the margin of catastrophe, with an optimism which now has much of suicide in it."[8]

Vice-President Castillo saw in this new phase of the war an excellent excuse to suspend constitutional guarantees and put an end to the violently anti-Axis tone of the press. On December 16th he declared Argentina under a state of siege. That night at midnight the police walked the streets of Buenos Aires, breaking up groups of more than five people with the order to "move on." It was henceforth forbidden to sing the national anthem without previous police authorization, possibly because the words contained subversive expressions about tyrants, liberty, and the breaking of chains. Mass meetings which had been scheduled in homage to the United States and to President Roosevelt were suspended. To the newspapers went a police order forbidding them to make any more comments on foreign affairs, or to comment on the state of siege itself. The state of siege, said Vice-President Castillo, had been declared to preserve the "moral unity" of the nation, and to prevent "inconvenient modes of expression." Furthermore, the obligations of Argentina under Pan American agreements imposed "the safeguard of her neutrality and of the continental defense." Said *Crítica:* ". . . Disconcerting. And so it seems that in order to defend democracy it is necessary to begin by suppressing individual guarantees, freedom of opinion, the right of assembly." [9]

The Castillo government was beyond doubt hostile to the United States. Enrique Ruiz Guiñazú, who was now Minister of Foreign Affairs, had a personal dislike for that country, as did a number of high people in the government. Many elements seem to have entered into the hostility. One was that it was an estanciero's government, and the estancieros as a class felt that their natural orientation was toward Great Britain. There was much Catholic sentiment, too, which in Argentina tends to be Hispanist and anti-Pan-American. Ruiz Guiñazú felt that the United States was a nearer and bigger menace to Argentina than Germany was. And at this time, too, the war was going badly for the Allies, and the Castillo government seems to have believed that the Axis was going to win. All in all, the feeling in the Argentine chancellery was such that when Chile suggested a consultation of American foreign ministers, which it was decided to hold in Rio de Janeiro in January, 1942, there was good reason to believe that Argentina was going to make trouble.

In 1940 Argentina, along with the other American republics, had signed the following declaration in Havana: "That any attempt by a non-American state against the integrity or inviolability of territory, against the sovereignty or political independence of an American state, will be considered as an act of aggression against the states signing this declaration." These states, the declaration further stated, would in case of such aggression "consult among themselves to agree on the measures which should be taken." [10] It was under this latter clause that Chile had asked for a consultation of foreign ministers. The Rio conference was planned so quickly that Argentina did not have time to talk things over previously with those nations it believed might follow it politically, instead of going with the United States; but inasmuch as the Chilean, Paraguayan, and Peruvian foreign ministers had to pass through Buenos Aires on their way to the meeting, Ruiz Guiñazú was able to have last-minute conversations in private with them.

It became evident even before the conference opened that Argentina's policy was to form a southern bloc of nations to counteract the northern bloc that responded to the United States. On January 7th Dr. Ruiz Guiñazú gave a luncheon at the chancellery for the three foreign ministers that were then in Buenos Aires, and in a speech he spoke of the "sisterhood of southern republics." But he was rather pointedly rebuffed by Juan B. Rosetti, the Chilean foreign minister. "In America," said Rosetti, "there is no room for distinctions between North, Central, and South. There is only one sisterhood: that of all the American peoples." [11]

In reality, then, Ruiz Guiñazú went to Rio with no support from the other republics for what he was going to do. He embarked with his delegation on the American steamer *Uruguay*. The Buenos Aires newspapermen were also aboard the *Uruguay*, with the exception of reporters from *El Pampero*, who were refused passage by the captain. Interviews with the various delegates on the way to Rio gave a suggestion of what was in the wind. Rosetti, in a special interview to *La Nación*, said that Chile had a long unguarded coastline to think of, the implication being that Chile was not in a position to break with the Axis should a break be recommended. Argentina, then, had hopes of taking Chile along with her in a refusal to break relations. Little Uruguay, across the Río de la Plata, a nation smaller than the province of Buenos Aires, was sure to do whatever Argentina did not do, because not the Colossus of the North, but the Colossus of the South, was Montevideo's biggest bugabear. It has been Uruguay's historic policy to cultivate the friendship of the United States as a guarantee against any ideas which Argentina might get about "reincorporating" the old territory of the Viceroyalty of the Río de la

Plata. It was, of course, an almost historic certainty that in Rio, as in Havana, Buenos Aires, Lima, Washington, and all the other conferences, Argentina would get in a few words about its "sovereignty." Perhaps Alberto Guani, the Uruguayan Foreign Minister, had this in mind when he gave an interview to *El País* of Mondevideo on the eve of the Rio conference. "People are always speaking of solidarity," he said; "but they will never understand the scope of this term in international law if they do not realize that when a country establishes solidarity with another or others, it is necessary to abolish absolute national sovereignty for the solidarity to make sense." Did Dr. Guani mean to imply, asked the interviewer, that an American sovereignty should be created with each state ceding part of its sovereignty? Yes, replied Dr. Guani, that in effect is what happens in international conferences.[12]

It was evident at Rio that the majority was prepared to vote the rupture of relations. Many of the republics had already broken relations with the Axis, several having declared war as soon as Pearl Harbor was attacked. All the Central American republics, and those bordering on the Caribbean like Colombia and Venezuela, were in the line of danger, and were certain to be with the United States. Even Mexico, which in the last war had been a focus of German activities, was now with the United States, and it was the Mexican delegate, together with those of Venezuela and Colombia, that presented the first project for a united break with the Axis. Uruguay proposed that the allies of the United States be declared nonbelligerents, and be allowed to use all American harbors for the refuge or repair of war vessels.

To the United States, the project for rupture with the Axis was the most important question on the agenda. A moral issue was at stake: whether the United States, in the hour of attack by the totalitarian nations, could show the world that the hemisphere vas spiritually united behind her. If even one nation should refuse ts support, it would be a bitter diplomatic defeat. All the republics knew this. Argentina had never been in such a good position to frustrate American foreign policy, as Ruiz Guiñazú well knew. He represented a government that considered the United States as a menace to its sovereignty, and a class that feared the economic interests of the United States as a threat to their meat trade with Britain. Ruiz Guiñazú believed that there was more fear than love behind the solidarity of many of the republics with the United States; and he believed that it was the aim of the United States to build up Brazil into the greatest economic and military power on the continent. Argentine-Brazilian enmity went back to the day in 1493 when Pope Alexander VI had drawn a line down the map of the newly discovered America, granting all lands on one side to Portugal, on the other to Spain. The two nations had fought a war in the nineteenth century. They had had a boundary dispute which had been settled in Brazil's favor. They were rivals in the buffer states of Paraguay and Uruguay. And each looked on the other with misgivings, and suspected the other of imperialistic designs. In certain military circles in Rio and Buenos Aires, the idea that some day the two nations would go to war had become almost an obsession.

All this, and much more, must have been in Ruiz Guiñazú's mind at Rio. Colombia, Mexico, and Venezuela had presented a project for the rupture of relations with the Axis which read: "The American Republics manifest that, by reason of their solidarity, and to the end of protecting and preserving their liberty and integrity, none of them may continue having political, commercial, or financial relations with the governments of Germany, Italy, and Japan." [13] Neither Argentina nor Chile was disposed to accept this resolution. As a matter of fact, Argentina's Foreign Minister did not have the slightest intention of breaking with the Axis, nor did Vice-President Castillo; what was bothering both men was how to achieve nonrupture without stating publicly and frankly what their aim was. On the 18th of January Dr. Castillo granted an interview to the Associated Press in Buenos Aires, and when asked to state his position replied evasively that "the instructions which the delegation of our country has received are not rigid. These instructions have a certain degree of elasticity." When asked whether Argentina was disposed to employ its naval forces to convoy merchant ships to the United States, he said only that "this is a delicate problem." On the general question of solidarity, so long as it was not defined in precise terms, however, he stated that Argentina was disposed to sign any agreement in the safeguard of common American interests.[14] In short, he would not define his position.

In Rio it was a sweltering summer, and as there seemed to be no possibility of getting Argentina to sign a common declaration on the rupture of relations, tempers grew strained, and there were more or less dramatic moments in the assembly, as when Foreign Minister Ezequiel Padilla of Mexico shook his fist under Ruiz Guiñazú's nose. The pressure on the Argentine minister was intense, and Ruiz Guiñazú showed signs of faltering. There was a premature announcement in the papers that an accord had been reached, which was quickly denied, possibly after consultation with Buenos Aires. More than a week went by without a formula's being reached, and finally on the 24th a definitive text was voted which showed the Argentine hand in its drafting. Instead of saying, like the original project, that the American republics, in view of the Axis aggression, could not continue to maintain political, commercial, or financial relations with Germany, Italy, and Japan, the final resolution said that the rupture of relations was *recommended*. The change seemed innocuous enough, but what Castillo and Ruiz Guiñazú had in mind was very clearly expressed that same day by the Vice-President in an interview granted to *Noticias Gráficas*: "The optional rupture approved at Rio," he said, ". . . has given me logical satisfaction. . . . We said clearly at the beginning and maintained at all times *that Argentina would not go to war nor break off relations*, but was disposed to accept, in consequence of its never absent American sentiments, whatever formula for the future reaffirmed continental solidarity and unity, and at the same time left each country free, *in the exercise of its sovereignty*, to adopt the special resolutions which the particular situations and circumstances of each country made best in each case."[15] In short, on the same day that Ruiz Guiñazú in Rio voted the recommendation to break relations with the Axis, the Argentine Vice-

President in Buenos Aires publicly declared Argentina would not break relations. The new wording of the resolution left a legal loophole of escape, for, as anyone could see, it only *recommended* the rupture of relations. It was not a promise that the recommendation would be followed.

There is no doubt that the Rio conference was a diplomatic defeat for the United States. In his anxiety to achieve outward unity of the republics, Sumner Welles had sacrificed the whole substance, the whole sense of the resolution. There can be no doubt he knew this perfectly well, but did not see a way out. Perhaps he thought that Argentina would break some day, and that the important thing was to show the Axis that the American front was united. There is little reason, however, to suppose, that the Axis was misled. Nobody was misled. The American front was not united.

MORAL CRISIS

From December 16, 1941, to June 4, 1943, Argentina was officially in a "state of siege." The constitution permits the executive to declare a state of siege only when Congress is not in session; and when Congress meets, it may lift the state of siege by a vote of both houses. This was where the curious division between the Senate, which was Conservative, and the Chamber of Deputies, which was Radical, served Castillo well. Congress could not muster the vote to lift the state of siege.

Death relieved Dr. Castillo of two of his most important opponents. Early in 1942, Marcelo T. de Alvear, who had long been in ill health, died, and the Radical party was virtually without leadership. Alvear's funeral was the occasion for a great civic demonstration in Buenos Aires. Crowds jammed the Avenida de Mayo and Callao, where the procession had to pass, and lifted the coffin from its gun carriage. There were shouts of "Viva la democracia!" The Grenadier Guards and police were helpless against the mobs, who were taking this occasion to make public their repudiation of the Conservative government. The pro-Allied press, too, gave much space to the Alvear funeral, and by innuendo made it the occasion for attacks on fraud, on minority government, and on the Axis sympathizers.

In reality, the Castillo control of the press was never very strong. The papers were not really afraid of Castillo, even though occasional indiscretions were punished by a paper's being suspended for several days. The original ban on comments on international affairs was later extended to comments on internal politics as well, on the ground that discussions of politics "perturbed the public order." But the press, especially the popular press, used every device known to human ingenuity to circumvent the state of siege. One paper, for instance, on the day the decree went into effect, published the most horrible pictures it could find of Hitler, Mussolini, and the Japanese premier with a caption saying that, because of the state of siege, it could no longer tell what treacherous, murderous, perverted tyrants these men were. Later someone sent a quetzal from Guatemala—known as the *Pájaro de la Libertad* (Bird of Liberty)—as a gift to the Buenos Aires Zoo. On the day of its arrival that paper printed a drawing with the caption: "Bird of Liberty arrives in Buenos Aires. Can it survive our climate?" Day after day the progress of the quetzal was followed. There were photographs of the bird puffed up and looking miserable, with a bottle of medicine and a teaspoon beside it. The stories reported the sufferings of the Bird of Liberty in Buenos Aires, and were at once so malicious and so impossible for the government to censor without being ridiculous that they provided amusement for many days.

This tongue-in-cheek attitude was typical of the popular press. *La Nación* and *La Prensa,* which had their dignity to consider, were more magisterial but no less hostile to the Castillo government even though both were very conservative. Neither paper approved of the government's foreign policy or its electoral fraud. The nationalist press continued to support Argentine neutrality because it served the interests of the Axis; but it would be a mistake to say that it approved very heartily of Castillo himself. One nationalist magazine probably expressed the attitude of that political sector when it called the Vice-President "the best of this system of government, that is, the best of the worst."[16] Even the Conservative party was not united behind him. All segments supported him out of self-interest. To have done otherwise would have meant that they would be put out of office, together with all the brothers, uncles, and cousins whose government jobs depended on them under the spoils system. But more than half of the party was pro-Ally, and the extreme right wing was pro-Axis. There was the fundamental division. The body of Conservative opinion that represented, as always, the meat interests, wanted England to win. And the nationalists wanted the triumph of fascism.

In May the foreign policy of Dr. Ruiz Guiñazú, if it had not been clear enough before, became quite explicit. On May 1st, which is celebrated by the labor unions and the Socialist party as the international labor day, the Alianza de la Juventud Nacionalista organized a counter demonstration. While thousands filled the Diagonal Roque Sáenz Peña to hear the Socialist leaders urge all-out aid to Russia, England, and the United States, the young nationalists gathered in another part of the city to hear an address by the Foreign Minister, whose son was one of their number. In this way Ruiz Guiñazú identified himself not only with neutrality, but with Hispanism and all the other characteristics of the nationalist movement.

Ruiz Guiñazú was a Hispanist. At the end of that same month he gave a banquet in the chancellery for an economic mission sent by General Franco to Buenos Aires. "For the first time," said the Argentine Foreign Minister in a speech of welcome to the Spanish mission, ". . . the fortunes of a war without quarter threaten to cut all communication and all solidarity between Europe and the American continent. . . . In Europe is the center of our religious faith, Europe is the home of our culture, from Europe we receive many products that we cannot easily replace. And on the other hand Europe needs, and will probably for a long time continue to need, our essential raw materials. . . . Not long ago, on a visit to a neighboring country, I had occasion to say that in the present state of the world those nations who do not wish to perish at the hand of coalitions more powerful than they, have the obligation to join the others who have the same mission and the same parallel interests." [17] Here were all the elements of what went to make up Ruiz Guiñazú's foreign policy: the Catholicism ("In Europe is the center of our religious faith"), the admiration for European culture ("Europe is the home of our culture"), the interest in selling meat to Britain ("Europe needs . . . our essential raw materials"), hatred and fear of the United States ("coalitions more powerful than they"), and the Hispanism ("the same mission and the same parallel interests").

Two days after delivering this speech, Ruiz Guiñazú had to face an interpellation on foreign policy in the Chamber of Deputies, by Dr. Nicolás Repetto, the leader of the Socialist party. Ruiz Guiñazú refused to speak except in secret session. He would not even allow stenographers to be present, so secret and so explosive (he said) was the information he had to give the Chamber. Repetto presented his interpellation on May 29th, and nearly two months went by in wrangling over whether stenographers would or would not be admitted to the session. It was finally agreed that they would not. The secret session took place on July 19th, and such is Buenos Aires that by the next day rumors were all over town about what had happened. The story was that Ruiz Guiñazú had presented what he said was absolutely trustworthy information that the United States was planning to conquer all of South America, including Argentina. To prove it he read from American books describing the coming conquest, and showed maps of how the United States was going to divide the continent. After the session was over the Foreign Minister gave an interview to the press in which he said that his defense of his foreign policy had been so triumphant that, if there had been a vote of confidence, practically the whole chamber would have voted with him. At this the Radicals and Socialists, who had the majority in the lower house, went into an uproar. The Foreign Minister, they said, had violated the secrecy of the session on which he himself had so long insisted. Furthermore, his statement was not true. Neither the Radicals nor the Socialists would have voted for him. Repetto asked the chamber to let him publish his speech of the secret session to refute the arguments of the Foreign Minister, but the Chamber refused. And there, after quite a tempest, the matter remained.

Death, in the meantime, had intervened to relieve Dr. Castillo of his second possible rival, the stricken President Ortiz himself. Ortiz had apparently never given up hope that his sight might be restored. His mental and moral suffering, shut up in the silence of the great house on Suipacha, and helpless in the face of what was happening, can only be imagined. In June a famous Spanish eye specialist, Dr. Ramón Castroviejo, was sent by President Roosevelt to Buenos Aires to see if an operation might restore the President's sight. Castroviejo spent much time with the ill man, and also with his Argentine physicians, who insisted that a cornea transplantation could not be attempted in the precarious state of the President's general health. Finally Castroviejo and the President's physicians signed a joint report. The verdict: no operation. Castroviejo flew back to the United States.

It must have been only hope that had kept the sick man alive, for, within a week of hearing that his blindness was incurable, Ortiz resigned the presidency and died. His death ended the last hope that popular government could be restored by legal means, and the country mourned for him, and for the hope that had died with him. President Castillo would not declare a public holiday for the Ortiz funeral, remembering what had happened at the Alvear funeral, so that neither schools, government offices, nor private businesses were closed. This had the effect of keeping away large numbers of people who would otherwise have attended. This time the Grenadier Guards shielded the coffin so well that the crowds did not get near it to carry it on their shoulders, and those that tried were run against the wall by the mounted guards. Nevertheless, there was a repetition of the popular demonstration that had taken place at Alvear's funeral. This time the people shouted not only "Viva la democracia!" but "Presidentes, sí! Dictadores, no!" (Presidents, yes! Dictators, no!) The chant was taken up in the streets as the mobs, in angry mood, followed the cortège. Near the Recoleta cemetery the popular procession was detoured by the police, and the coffin and carriages of flowers arrived at the cemetery with no accompaniment but the Grenadiers, and the soldiers and sailors that lined the avenues. Criollo wits were now saying that Castillo was a funeral director, he was burying so many of his opponents.*

The year 1942 was one of deep moral crisis in Argentina, none the less deep for being so quiet on the surface. People were angry and dissatisfied, but helpless. Congress did nothing constructive to help matters. The Minister of the Interior, Miguel J. Culaciati, had to face an interpellation in the Chamber on his restrictions on the press and on Acción Argentina and other democratic groups. The Radical deputies greeted his speech with hoots and catcalls, and Culaciati finally became so angry that he stalked from the Chamber with his portfolio under his arm, and refused to go back. But there was little constructive legislation in Congress, and much senseless obstruction that brought discredit on the parliament at a time when parliamentary institutions everywhere were on the defensive. The Radicals were undergoing a "reorganization"; but, so far as anyone could see, no decisive leadership had come out of it. The Conservatives were hanging on to power by the police force and the backing of the army. In public office there was venality and favoritism. One could not even get a job as clerk without *cuña* (pull—literally, wedge). There were stories that the Minister of Agriculture was robbing everything in sight. In the provinces, elections were fraudulent. When they were not, the President intervened and "rectified" them.

A case in point was Tucumán. The elections held there late in the year were normal and perfectly honest. However, it became

* Before his term of office was ended by the June Revolution, Castillo had buried two more dignitaries, ex-President Agustín P. Justo, and ex-Vice-President Julio A. Roca. All in all, 1942–1943 was a year of many and impressive state funerals.

evident that in the electoral college the local Radicals were going to have a majority, slim but none the less real. Under the circumstances the Conservative electors decided to walk out of the college, thus preventing a quorum and the election of a Radical governor. They climbed into automobiles and drove to the neighboring province of Salta, where they installed themselves in the new and luxurious tourist hotel and prepared to sit the matter out. In the meantime the Conservatives sent a letter to President Castillo asking for an intervention in the province to "restore electoral normality." Whatever abnormality there was, was of their own making; but the executive had long since ceased bothering to pretend that interventions were to restore republican government, as the constitution said they were. The Minister of the Interior intervened, and called new elections.

If the Castillo government had determined to make itself unpopular, it could not have gone about this more directly. It proceeded now to the last stage of the salvation of the Anglo-Argentine tram company, which had become part of the legally created Corporación de Transportes. The time had come to confiscate the colectivos, so that the twenty-five-year-old streetcars would not have to compete with fast motor transportation. This, as Américo Ghioldi said in the Chamber of Deputies, was the "stage of spoliation." [18] The government ordered all the colectiveros in the city of Buenos Aires to turn their microbusses over to the Corporación de Transportes, which would pay for them in due time. The chauffeurs, whose only capital was their colectivos, and who had no say in the valuation the Corporación would set on their cars, simply went on strike. They drove the colectivos out into the province of Buenos Aires, and went into hiding. The thousands of fast colored microbusses that had been the backbone of Buenos Aires transportation for nearly fifteen years disappeared from the streets. What happened was the best demonstration that the Anglo had never been able to cope adequately with the urban transport problem. Whole sections of the city were left without transportation. Where streetcars ran, they became so crowded with passengers at the rush hours that the riders hung from the buffers and windows, and the vehicles sagged with their weight. There were sporadic acts of violence against rolling stock of the Corporación. Trams were attacked and burned. The Castillo government forbade the newspapers to print any more about the strike of colectiveros because it came under the "perturbation of public order" clause. The porteños sided unanimously with the chauffeurs, and made admiring comments to the effect, "*Che*, these colectiveros are anarchists, but brave devils."

The Buenos Aires public was always willing to believe the worst of the Corporación de Transportes, which had become a kind of Public Enemy No. 1 in the popular mind. Typical of the attitude toward the Corporación was the story that went around during the nickel shortage early in 1942. The nickel shortage was one of those fantastic occurrences which seem to happen only in Argentina. It has not yet been satisfactorily explained.

One day porteños who boarded streetcars, or went to vegetable markets, or tried to buy theater tickets, discovered that neither they nor the party with whom they were dealing had anything but paper money. Change had disappeared from circulation overnight, without a trace. Nobody had change. When one boarded a streetcar, one gave the conductor a peso, and he wrote an I O U for ninety centavos. In the early mornings, merchants with bags over their shoulders in search of nickel coins formed a queue a block long in front of the Central Bank. The bank had none, and so released to circulation copper two-centavo pieces by the thousands. So it came about that purchasers of ten centavos' worth of vegetables received forty-five copper two-centavo pieces in change. Nobody in Buenos Aires talked of anything but the nickel shortage.

Where had the money gone? And how had it disappeared so fast? It was known that two boatloads of nickel from the United States had been sunk by German submarines, and that the government could not mint any more nickel coins. But what had happened to those that were in circulation? Some people said everyone was hoarding them out of fright. Others said that the nickel was worth more than the face value of the coins, and that speculators were melting the coins and selling them to Spain to be shipped to Germany. But the best story of all was the one that the colectiveros spread about the city: The nigger in the woodpile, said they, was the Corporación de Transportes.

This was the colectiveros' story. Within a month the Corporación had to get together millions of pesos to buy the colectivos. As everyone knew, the financial situation of the Corporación was such that it lacked the money, and lacked sufficient credit to borrow the money. So, ran the story, the Corporación had hit on a diabolic scheme to force a loan from the people of Buenos Aires: for several days it withdrew from circulation every coin that came into its hands. Since it ran the subways and streetcars, this took almost all the nickel out of circulation in three days. When the crisis came, nobody had any coins, so that every passenger boarding a streetcar had to pay not ten centavos but one peso, receiving in return an I O U for ninety centavos. Within a week the Corporación had, in effect, obtained a gigantic forced loan, raising the money to begin the confiscation of colectivos.

If this story was true, the man who hit on the idea was little short of a genius. If it was not true, whoever invented the libel was something of a genius. The fact is that the story gained credence, and conductors refusing change were often cursed and threatened by the passengers, who shouted, "We know who has the nickel."

Whoever had the nickel, the crisis passed as suddenly and mysteriously as it had come. One day there was change for everyone in Buenos Aires: the Central Bank began issuing new brass coins and fifty-centavo notes to relieve the shortage; and, whether it was this measure or a restoration of public confidence that brought the nickel out of hiding, or whether the Corporación really *had* had the coins all along, the shortage came to an abrupt end.

The strike of colectiveros did not achieve its aim. Sooner or later the drivers brought their cars in. In hiding, they were making no money. If their cars were confiscated, they could go to work for the Corporación as chauffeurs. It was a living, at any rate, and these men were not rich. Gradually, all the microbusses passed into the hands of the Corporación; some were painted red and returned to service, and others were left in vacant lots because the Corporación did not have the money to run them. Service throughout the city got worse, and there was only ill will for the municipal street railway monopoly that had been created to solve the financial problems of the Anglo-Argentine. The Corporación, from any point of view, was a failure. It had run with a 3,500,000-peso deficit in the previous year, in spite of having to pay no taxes. It could not even pay its electric bills, and had a debt of more than 40,000,000 pesos. It could not put any money into its employees' retirement fund, and owed the fund millions. Three-quarters of all its trams were over twenty years old, and the average age was twenty-five. Service was worse than it had ever been, worse even than the service of the old Anglo-Argentine which the transport law had been designed to save.[19]

The cost of living was going up. Great Britain was buying so much meat for her soldiers that the domestic price of meat reacted by rising until it became difficult for the working classes to buy meat. The Castillo government allowed a rise in the price of sugar, which everyone knew was already too high, and would benefit nobody but the big ingenios of the north and the sugar trust of Buenos Aires. High-quality textiles were disappearing from the market because imports had ceased. Cheap Argentine and Brazilian materials were fetching any price the manufacturer cared to ask, and would fall apart almost at once when they were worn. Rents were rising perpendicularly. But wages were not responding, and the situation of the hundreds of thousands of people who were living on family incomes of 100 to 200 pesos became more difficult with the passage of time. Speculators were cornering potatoes and other necessities, and creating artificial scarcities. The government crop-buying policies launched new emissions of paper into circulation, making the inflation more acute, and the condition of the working classes almost desperate.

People saw no hope for a change. Early in 1943 the Radical party began conversations with the Socialists, who had suggested a united front against the Conservatives in the coming presidential elections. But everyone knew that an electoral majority was no guarantee of winning the election. The only hope was revolution, and the army was far to the right of center—farther right, even, than the Castillo brand of Conservatism. Without the army, no change was possible. And after all, what leadership could the Radical party offer? That was the rub. The Radicals had not even been able to carry the Federal Capital in 1942. The majority representation had gone to the Socialists, as it always did when the Radical party could not present a ticket that commanded respect. The public feeling was one of the most complete frustration, and it showed itself in political apathy. The Conservatives, who controlled the electoral mechanism, were in the meantime playing politics among themselves, to see who should succeed President Castillo. Governor Rodolfo Moreno of Buenos Aires had aspirations, which ended quickly when Castillo intervened in the province and put him out of office. The story gained ground that the President had already decided on his successor: it would be Robustiano Patrón Costas, the President of the Senate.

Patrón Costas was known to the Argentine public as the *dueño de Salta* (owner of Salta). He was the greatest landholder of the sugar-supported north; his holdings ran over a million hectares, and he was known in his province as "that *negrero.*" Patrón Costas stood for all that was hateful in the sugar monopoly: the traffic in Bolivian Indians, the shipping of peons in cattle cars, the company stores that kept laborers perpetually in their debt, the poverty, the filth, the disease that were the price of great individual fortunes. Patrón Costas had had a political debt with the Banco de la Nación estimated variously at anywhere from 20,000,000 to 30,000,000 pesos.* Now he no longer had the debt, having placed it elsewhere, evidently because, if he were to run for President, the existence of this loan would be a political handicap. The question was, however, Who had taken over the debt? Had it

* The Banco de la Nación has always lent money to politicians with insufficient security as a kind of courtesy. The Banco, however, does not publish the details of these loans, or the losses it incurs in making them. Private financiers also lend to politicians on insufficient security, as a kind of political insurance. The Patrón Costas debt was well secured, but it was at the same time in the category of a political loan.

been absorbed by the sugar trust, and, if it had, what did the sugar trust expect to get from Patrón Costas? Or had it been taken by a private *consorcio* like the Bembergs? In any case, was the government being mortgaged in anticipation to powerful private interests?

Unpopular as Patrón Costas was with the mass of the people, there was a fatalistic attitude that he would, willy-nilly, be the next President of Argentina. Important business and diplomatic representatives of the British colony gave the President-select a banquet at the Plaza Hotel, and there was toasting of Anglo-Argentine good will. Patrón Costas was considered to be more strongly pro-British than the Castillo wing of the party. It was probably this factor that finally determined the nationalist military revolt against the government. Castillo's neutrality was welcome to the nationalists, but they feared that his prospective successor was a different kind of Conservative. In any case, the Patrón Costas candidacy did not really please anyone but old-time Conservatives. Under the threat of such a government, the movement for a Democratic Union of the opposition went forward hastily. The Radicals, the Socialists, and the Partido Demócrata Progresista of Santa Fe were the three parties going to make it up. The question was, What ticket could the Democratic Union present for the coming elections?

For weeks the papers were full of rumors of dissension. It was agreed by all three parties that the candidate for President would be a Radical, and the most likely man for the job was Honorio Pueyrredón, who had been a cabinet minister, and later Argentine Ambassador in Washington under Yrigoyen. Pueyrredón had the advantage of carrying an aristocratic name, and of being an old Yrigoyenista. But the real fight was over who should be candidate for Vice-President. Both the P.D.P. and the Socialist party wanted to have this post. In April and May of 1943 there was little union in the Democratic Union. The essential weakness of the democratic parties in Argentina showed up all too clearly. There was a constant tendency toward atomism, impelled by personal ambitions, and by a total failure to understand the spirit or meaning of cooperation. Now was the time of all times when personal differences should have been subordinated to the fight ahead. But in the moment of crisis, instead of disappearing, they grew, and got worse. One can only conjecture where the Democratic Union would have ended had it not been for the June Revolution; but the conclusion is inescapable that it would not have ended in the Casa Rosada.

1943: ARGENTINA ON THE EVE

THE WORKING CLASSES

The Buenos Aires of 1943 was a beautiful city for those who had money. There were the moving picture theaters, showing the latest American films. There were *confiterías*, a typical porteño institution, half tearoom, half bar, where the middle and upper classes gathered at five o'clock to drink tea, and at seven-thirty to drink cocktails, to the accompaniment of American jazz and Argentine tangos. There were good restaurants serving the world's best beefsteaks, as well as roast chicken or duck or partridge. There were the night clubs. These fell into two categories, the boites, where one could take the family, and the cabarets, where one could not. There were great public parks—some, like Palermo, covering acres, with trees and lakes and rose gardens.

But to amuse oneself in Buenos Aires, one needed time and leisure, and a certain—not exorbitant—amount of money. To live in the fashionable Barrio Norte, in the marble-fronted chrome-and-glass-trimmed apartment houses required a considerable amount of money, for rents were high. To own an automobile one had to belong to the upper middle class at the least, for a Ford or Plymouth or Chevrolet cost two years of a white-collar worker's average wage. In short, like all cities, Buenos Aires was built for the well-to-do.

One saw surprisingly little of what could be called slums in the city, although until a short time ago the squatters' shacks along the mud banks of the Plata might have come in this category. The city was built of brick and plaster, and since it had never had heavy coal-and-oil-burning industries, it was clean-looking. Old houses were a light gray, and new ones cream-colored. In the heart of the fashionable apartment-house district, like the filling of a sandwich, were two-story buildings twenty and thirty years old that were like human hives. These were the *conventillos*, the tenements of Buenos Aires. Inside there were patios, and around the patios one-room apartments where working families lived. Anywhere from two to a dozen people might live in the same room. And even, surprisingly, on the tops of luxury apartment houses whose tenants paid 200–400 pesos a month in rent for an unfurnished apartment, the owners rented space to the poor, who put up metal and wooden sheds to sleep in. Thus, a resident in the heart of the swank Barrio Norte might be next door to his laundress, who lived in great poverty.

In the last normal year before the outbreak of war brought the inflation of living costs, the National Labor Department calculated that the average porteño family of five needed 147 pesos a month to live decently. As against this figure, the average white-collar worker made 128 pesos, and the average laborer, 78.[1] How did the family make up the difference? Usually it had to be made up by the woman of the family, who might work as a servant or take in laundry. As a servant, she would work from seven-thirty in the morning until nearly midnight (for Argentines eat at nine o'clock and sometimes ten), and would earn 40 to 60 pesos a month. This would be enough to bridge the gap. If the man was working in industry, he would be averaging forty-four hours a week.[2] Both for women and for men these were the best wages and hours in the country. A servant in a small provincial city would make only 20 pesos a month. As a result, there was a drift to Buenos Aires from all parts of the country, especially from the wretched northern provinces. .

It was in Buenos Aires, too, that labor was the best organized. The largest union was the Confederación General del Trabajo. In 1940 it claimed * 311,000 out of the 473,000 workers belonging to labor unions.[3] The labor movement was not as militant as in the United States, nor had it the legal protection which American unions have. Strikes were still not respectable, and they were usually

* The unions probably pad their membership figures to make it appear that they are stronger than they are. The CGT, like the AFL, is a union of many unions.

suppressed without ruth. The Socialist party had a large membership in the Capital and its outlying suburbs, principally unskilled laborers. The Socialists in recent years had usually had a majority in Buenos Aires elections. The party was organized along democratic lines, consulting the rank and file on all matters of elections and policy. It published a newspaper, *La Vanguardia*, and maintained a library and classes in general and political subjects for its members. The leaders were intelligent and respectable but mostly, like Repetto and Palacios, in their seventies: the youngest man among them, the leader in the Chamber of Deputies, was Américo Ghioldi, a schoolteacher. Young Argentines were not attracted to Socialism. They considered it unexciting.

Outside Buenos Aires, on the estancias, or farther north, on the sugar plantations or *yerbatales*, where yerba mate is grown, there was a precipitate drop in the standard of living, and in the intelligence and organization of the workers. The peon of the estancia lived better than any non-urban worker, but his condition was only a little above that of a century ago. He probably lived in a kind of barracks, sleeping on the wooden floor with his head on his horsegear. For food he was given two kilograms of meat a day, all the yerba he wanted, *puchero* (boiled vegetables and meat), and *galleta* (a kind of hardtack). The meat ration will seem surprising to the non-Argentine, but it must be borne in mind that Argentines each consume an average of 136 kilograms per year—where Americans consume 59, and Frenchmen 40.[4] The peon did not have a house to live in, and he did not make enough to support a wife and children. This perhaps explained the Argentine illegitimacy rate, which for the whole country was 28 per cent in 1938. The lowest illegitimacy was 11 per cent in Buenos Aires (the city). In the provinces of Buenos Aires, Santa Fe and Córdoba it was 10 per cent,[5] still better than the national average.

On the estancia the peon was paid by the month, and his wages were probably 50 pesos, although careful studies and statistics are not available on this point. A puestero was a grade above a peon, and lived in a small house of two or three rooms, with his wife and children. Many estancias had a rule that if a puestero had more than two children he would be discharged, for the estancia had to furnish food for the family. The arrival of a third child was a tragedy that ended sometimes in abortion, but more usually in the discharge of the unfortunate father. Some estancias limited the children of the majordomo, as well. Majordomos of 1943 were only a grade above a hired man, and were far from receiving the princely salaries of twenty years ago. One on a company estancia made about 500 pesos a month, with house, cook, and food furnished. The only advance he could make was to be appointed administrator of all the company's estancias, in which case he might make a commission as well as a good salary.*

In agriculture, conditions were somewhat different. Work was seasonal, and paid by the piece, or by the day. During the summer and autumn plowing, the peon got up at three-thirty or four in the morning. He returned to the house at eleven to rest and eat, and went back to work at one or one-thirty. The afternoon work was short, especially when horses were employed, so that the sweaty animals would not catch cold at night. (The animals were very well cared for.) Work was over at five or six, so that the day averaged twelve hours. During the harvest, workers labored from four in the morning until ten at night, and made four to six pesos a day. They had half-hour rest periods morning and afternoon, when they were given mate and galleta, and sometimes roast meat.[6] This was in the grain belt, in the rich provinces of Buenos Aires and Santa Fe.

To the north of the littoral provinces, however, is a very different and unsuspected Argentina. A few hours by train from Santa Fe is Santiago del Estero. Santiago is a desert like parts of Arizona and Nevada, dry, dusty, full of bushes and quebracho trees, where the people live in mud huts. The Río Dulce that runs through the province periodically goes dry, bringing a desperate situation to the Santiagueños that live from fishing, and have no drinking water but what is brought to them by water trains—where

* The data are my own, gathered from owners, majordomos, and puesteros. Since my conversations with these have been limited to Buenos Aires and Patagonia, I do not claim the figures are average.

there are water trains. Their livelihood was the cutting of quebracho, and was miserably paid. A muleteer who made one round trip a week between the capital city, Santiago, and the woods, might get ten pesos for the trip; and this included the rent of his wagon and mules. The woodcutters were the victims of company stores, to which they usually went in debt. In one of the forest concessions along the Ferrocarril Central Argentino was the following sign: "Any worker who works in this establishment and who does not spend 60 per cent of his salary in provisions, will be immediately discharged." The woodcutter (*hachero*) was paid four to five pesos per thousand kilograms, and in sixteen hours could average about five hundred kilograms. In a month he made some 50 pesos, working from four in the morning until six or seven at night.[7] The people were largely of Quichua stock. They slept on beds made of leather thongs, covered with blankets woven by the women. The huts had dirt floors. Food seemed to consist of berries, mashed-up corn meal, and whatever small animals and rodents they could trap, or fish they could get from the river. The most desperate necessity of Santiago was water, and after that came food, for there was always hunger.

Tucumán was called the Garden of the Republic—usually, now, in irony. It was the great sugar province, where twenty-eight ingenios had a monopoly on the refining and made good profits from a state-fostered situation of privilege. There, malaria, tuberculosis, leprosy, trachoma, rheumatism, mange, and impetigo were so common as to pass without comment. The peon who worked in the sugar fields gathering and peeling cane made 1.50 to 2.50 pesos a day, according to the Labor Department of Tucumán. About half the school children in the province had trachoma, and perhaps nine-tenths had malaria, for the anopheles mosquito breeds in the wet climate.[8] The housing for the laborers ranged from the adobe cottages of the semiskilled workers in the refineries, to the cane huts of the seasonal harvesters. Drunkenness was common, and was apparently even encouraged, for it has been common practice to pay sugar workers part of their wages in caña. Ill health, malnutrition, and drink combined to make the Tucumán peon a poor and unsatisfactory laborer. Tucumán is the most densely populated province in Argentina, with twenty-one people to the square kilometer, as against Buenos Aires' sixteen.[9] Its illegitimacy is neither the best nor the worst in Argentina, but halfway between. About half of the children born in the province are illegitimate.[10] Tucumán is green and beautiful, with mountains richly covered with vegetation, and rainfall is such that the province could grow almost anything. But it has been the victim of monoculture, which benefits two dozen millionaires and the sugar trust of Buenos Aires, and breeds only misery for the small grower and the peon.

Salta and Jujuy lie farther north still, against the Bolivian frontier. Here the workers were almost totally recruited among the Bolivian Indians, smuggled across the border by contractors called *negreros* who took 10 per cent of their wages in commissions.[11] These, too, are sugar provinces, and conditions have been far worse even than in Tucumán. The peons were transported in long trains of cattle cars of the Ferrocarril del Estado.[12] They were packed in and the doors locked until they reached their destinations. The cane workers lived in huts full of lice, and were fed coca and alcohol by their employers until they were in a state of stupefaction. Nicolás González Iramain, who was sent in 1942 to Jujuy as interventor by President Castillo, and who resigned in horror after three months, told of the terrible conditions he had seen. In the schools were "children who come without breakfast, on foot, over rough mountain roads, without shoes, and who return this way uphill to their houses after eight hours; and teachers who pass the entire morning talking continually in school for five hours without even so much as a cup of coffee." [13] Senator Alfredo Palacios, who made a trip through the northern provinces, told of one school he saw in Jujuy where the children stayed overnight all week because they lived so far away. The school fed them on *tulpo*, which is corn prepared with mutton grease; and even this wretched fare was furnished by the director out of his own salary. In one hut in the woods of Salta, Palacios talked to a fourteen-year-old girl. He asked her if she were an Argentine, and she replied that she was a Salteña. Then he showed her the Argentine colors, which are blue and white; but she did not know what they meant.[14]

In the northeast corner of Argentina, like a wedge between Paraguay and Brazil, lies the junglelike territory of Misiones, from which comes the Argentine yerba mate. Yerba was once imported exclusively from Paraguay, where it grows wild in the forest (it is a tall tree whose leaves are picked and roasted), but in this century experiments were begun with its cultivation, abandoned since the eighteenth century when the Jesuits had a monopoly. Now there were *yerbatales*, or yerba plantations, throughout Misiones. Workers were recruited by *conchabadores* (contractors) for delivery to the plantations. Since their traffic was illegal, they worked not out of the city of Posadas, but across the Paraná River in the Paraguayan port of Villa Encarnación. They were usually small grocerymen who would advance money to the workers during the off season, which these had to promise to work off during the harvest. Peons were contracted for by the conchabador, and then shipped upstream in the holds of river boats to the ports where they were to disembark. These were company ports, and a peon could not disembark unless he had a contract. His Libreta de Enrolamiento was confiscated by the company when he landed.[15]

Wages were so low that the whole family had to work to make enough to eat. The family—father, mother, and children—might make 3 to 3.50 pesos a day, most of which had to be spent in the company store, where prices were twice the prices in the nearest towns.[16] The worker would finish the season without anything, and then return to the conchabador of Posada or Villa Encarnación to start the cycle of debt all over again. The traveller on the Paraná could see these poor men, in tatters, with gunny sacks on their heads, loading yerba onto the river barges, or being unloaded from the steamer in small rowboats at the plantations. They were thin and wiry, and their skin was burned black; and in their baggy pants and canvas slippers they looked like pirates.

These, then, were the workers of Argentina in 1943. In most

cases they lived at the margin of existence. But there were some people in Argentina with money. Who were they, and where did their money come from?

PRIVILEGES IN CONFLICT

A study of the highest incomes of Argentina in 1941 reveals a significant change in that country's sources of wealth. Of the one hundred persons paying the most income tax, ten were estancieros, four were cereal brokers, and *thirty-five were manufacturers and industrialists.* The highest declared income was 3,650,000 pesos, from the making of textiles. The second highest was 2,367,000, also from textiles. The third highest was 2,249,000, from metallurgy. There were four sugar ingenio owners on the list, and three newspaper owners (including the owners of *La Prensa* and *La Nación*). There were beer barons, casino owners, importers, financiers, movie magnates, mine operators, radio station owners, and manufacturers of bags and shoes among the richest men in Argentina.[17] This was the Argentina of 1941, in contrast to the Argentina of 1841. The political implications of the new situation must not be overlooked.

In the first place, it was evident that Argentina was not now living from cows and wheat alone. In 1941, there were 829,000 people employed in industry, an 18 per cent increase over 1939.* [18] This was larger than the number employed in cattle-raising and farming. It is true that the greater part of Argentine industry was engaged in the elaboration of what its farms produced—sugar, wine, cotton, meat, and so forth. But is also true that not the farmer and not the estanciero, but the packer and distiller and refiner were making the profits. And it is also true that the laborer in industry was making better wages than the peon on the estancia. Economic

* The term "industry" includes meat packing (the most important), baking, dairies, and wine making as well as manufacturing.

power was changing hands, and no longer belonged to the estanciero. But government policy was still in the same minority hands, and the Roca-Runciman Pact proved that the free-trade theories of the nineteenth century cattlemen prevailed in the Conservative government. The country acted as if it had no future beyond furnishing raw materials to England and buying manufactured goods in return: the same policy that once brought on the civil wars between Buenos Aires and the provinces.

To understand the conflict of interests that was involved in free trade and the acceptance of a colonial position, it is necessary to see who benefited from free trade, and who wanted tariff protection. First and foremost, of course, the estanciero and farmer were free traders. They represented the landed wealth of Buenos Aires and Santa Fe in particular. The frigoríficos were also for free trade, because they lived from meat. The historic position of these people was: if we build industries and supply our own needs for manufactures England will no longer be able to sell her textiles and machinery here, and buy our meat and grains. It will mean ruin for the estancias. It will be the end of the frigoríficos. The historic spokesman for this opinion was the great Conservative daily, *La Prensa*. But in the face of present conditions the free tradesmen found little reason for hope. First, as England said, Argentina was buying not from England, her best customer, but from the United States, which imported much less from Argentina. This unbalance led to the Roca-Runciman Pact, and has still not been redressed. In the second place, industry was growing by leaps and bounds—especially the textile industry (of the thirty-five manufacturers on the list of one hundred highest incomes, seventeen were manufacturers of textiles). One of England's chief exports to Argentina has been woollens. The present situation meant a shutting down of the market for British textiles, to exclude all but high-quality goods. In other words, the complementary economies of Argentina and England, so perfectly harmonious in the nineteenth century, were becoming progressively less complementary in the twentieth.

Against the agricultural interests stood a formidable array of groups that wanted and needed protection. There were the wine men of Mendoza, who wanted the country to keep out Chilean and French and Italian wines. There were the sugar refiners of Tucumán and Salta and Jujuy, who needed protection to compete against Cuban or Javanese sugar. There were the yerba growers, who wanted Argentina to shut out Brazilian and Paraguayan yerba. And finally there was the new and rising industrial class, whose future depended on protective tariffs. Of all the economic groups struggling for power, some had privileges and some had none, but all wanted them. Let us consider the groups one by one, and see what was their actual situation.

First, the farmers and estancieros. As is evident from the balance sheets of estancias which were stock companies, they were not making large profits except under unusual war conditions. Agriculture during the war was kept alive only by a program of government buying, although meat was selling for high prices. The land problem was the same as it had been for many years: land cost too much, and was in too few hands, and small farmers and immigrants who wanted to settle could not find good land. The prices of grazing and cereal lands went down during the thirties because of world depression, but not as fast as farm income. Thus, land that was worth 260 pesos a hectare in Buenos Aires in 1929, was worth 228 in 1937, the year of the last agricultural census. In the same period, average prices per hectare dropped from 185 pesos to 123 in Santa Fe, from 66 to 38 in Tucumán; and in Mendoza the average rose from 43 to 44.[19] Obviously there were different factors at work in these provinces. Santa Fe is chiefly a cereal province; Buenos Aires, livestock and cereals; Tucumán has the sugar industry, and Mendoza the wine industry. Therefore the last two are in a different category.

The testimony before the Argentine-British mixed commission seemed to show that land was overvalued during the thirties. Of course it must be borne in mind that this was a decade of depression. The situation changed with the outbreak of war, and will change again when the war is over. But the price of land was inflated, and this had a paralyzing influence on attempts at breaking up the latifundia and at making it possible for small farmers to compete. The reason for the inflation of land values both in Buenos Aires (the city) and in the littoral provinces was that the Argentines preferred this type of investment to any other. Industry was constantly handicapped by the fact that an Argentine with money to invest would rather buy government securities and land than put it into industry. The stock exchange in Buenos Aires dealt in government securities, not industrials. The papers did not carry stock quotations. On the other hand, one could buy or sell an apartment house in one day, and nothing was more liquid than land. The *Prensa* and *Nación* carried pages of land and building auctions in city and country, and one would see advertisements like this: "I want to buy thirty apartment houses at once. Will not accept intermediaries." In any other city than Buenos Aires such an advertisement would have made one rub one's eyes. There were two reasons for the extraordinary preference for what is called *bienes raíces,* or real property. One was tradition, and the fact that land in the past had always risen in value, so that it seemed to be a sure speculation. The other was periodic fear of inflation, which in 1943 was of great importance. The result of the preference for land was that land values were badly inflated; and the mortgage banks, which were too eager to make loans, helped the inflation along. There was good reason to believe that the bubble was some day going to be badly punctured: perhaps when the drop in prices after the war brought a crisis in agriculture. Given the situation of the Banco de la Nación and the Banco Hipotecario Nacional, it was evident this would entail a banking crisis as well.

Land was not as concentrated as it had been. The 1937 Agricultural Census, however, took pains to conceal the real status of the latifundia by classing together all holdings of over five thousand hectares. One significant fact shown by that census is the growth in company estancias as opposed to privately owned ones. There were nearly twelve thousand in Argentina. Some of these were in the hands of banks, schools, and religious groups.[20] But the real significance of the stock-company estancia was that the aristocracy had discovered a device to keep death from dispersing their holdings. The children of an estanciero, instead of dividing his estate, formed a company with anonymous shares. These companies helped in the evasion of death duties and income tax, but above all they kept land concentrated in the same few hands. A study by the Dirección General de Rentas of the province of Buenos Aires in 1942 showed that 272 individuals and companies held 5,000,000 hectares (12,500,000 acres), or one-sixth of the entire province. Governor Rodolfo Moreno proposed an extra tax ranging up to 14 per cent on holdings over 10,000 hectares; but the Castillo government deemed him unsatisfactory as governor for this and other reasons, and intervened in the province to put him out of office.[21]

In the national territories, the landholdings were even more seigniorial. There are no good modern studies, but Jacinto Oddone, who published an interesting study in 1930, showed that in the territories 1,804 persons owned land equal in area to Italy, Belgium, Holland, and Denmark—countries supporting 60,000,000 people. Two companies owned as much as Switzerland and Belgium combined.[22] For cattle and sheep, the latifundium is economically feasible. For agriculture, however, it is not. Intensive farming on small farms is more productive than running an estate of 50,000 hectares. Argentina's yield per hectare of wheat, corn, and potatoes was very low in comparison to that of peasant farming countries like Germany and France. In part it was because intensive farming was not practiced, and in part because the Argentine was so proud of his rich alluvial soil that he was stubborn about using fertilizer. Most Argentines would have been surprised at the following figures published by the League of Nations, showing yields in quintals per hectare in 1938: [23]

	Wheat	*Corn*	*Potatoes*
United States	8.9	17.8	83.5
Argentina	11.8	15.0	83.9
France	18.6	14.9	110.6
New Zealand	21.5	30.2	159.6
Germany	27.4	29.5	191.5

These figures reveal that the only good argument for the latifundium in agriculture—that its size makes exploitation economical—is not true. Germany in each case produced at least twice as much as Argentina, and in Germany farms were tiny in comparison. As for the social consequences of the latifundia, those are too well known to need reiteration.

This, then, was the economic situation in 1943 of the class that traditionally ruled Argentina. Its importance was rapidly diminishing, but its influence was still strong in Argentine foreign policy. The landowning aristocracy had the highest social standing in the country, even though many families of aristocratic name had lost their fortunes through foolish mortgages and sudden bad years. Conservative government policies were directed to benefit these people. What kept the government from making any serious study of mineral deposits was the fear that coal and iron, if they were found in quantities, would make a heavy industry inevitable; and that heavy industry would end the political predominance of the landowning class.* The Roca-Runciman Pact was the expression of the politico-economic interests of the estanciero, even though it did not benefit him as much as it did the English and American frigoríficos.

In opposition to the free-trade doctrines of the estancieros, however, there were the protectionist interests of other groups all over the country. The next case to study is that of the sugar monopoly, which was protected by law and was one of the most bitterly debated privileges in Argentina. It was created by the Saavedra Lamas Law of 1912, which provided absolute protection against foreign sugar up to 41 centavos a kilogram.[24] The protection was so high that the ingenios could not help making money, however inefficient their refining methods. The internal Argentine market was secure. In Tucumán there were twenty-eight ingenios (refineries) whose margin of profit was secure year after year.

* Known deposits existed, but were economically uncompetitive on the world market. The present military government is attempting to develop them through subsidies in order to achieve autarchy, even though deposits are small and production costs almost prohibitive. The effort appears doomed to failure.

Below them came the class of cane growers. There were eighty-six big planters that made profits; but the medium and small growers were at the subsistence margin, and did not benefit from the sugar monopoly.[25] The growers were permanently in debt to the ingenios, to which they mortgaged their crops. As for the workers, they lived in unbelievable filth, poverty, and ill health. The sugar protection meant profit for twenty-eight ingenios and eighty-six major growers. In return, the country paid twice as much for Argentine sugar as it would have paid for foreign sugar delivered in Buenos Aires.

The Tucumanos who benefited from the monopoly argued: "For the simple mentality of the man in the street in the littoral and especially of that conglomeration of bureaucrats that is Buenos Aires, what matters is the price and nothing but the price. . . . Buying sugar abroad, even at a lower price, means to the country an important drain of millions of pesos from our economy which influences our balance of payments unfavorably." [26]

The littoral agricultural interests, which did not benefit from the monopoly, argued: "For those of us who have sustained the inconvenience of prohibitive tariffs, which are something quite different from protective tariffs, sugar, the sugar industry of Tucumán, represents the Bastille. . . . I believe, sir, that an industry which has to live for thirty years or more, protected by a tariff of 100–140 per cent—which is what the protection of sugar has amounted to on more than one occasion—is an industry harmful to the very state that cultivates it. . . . For many years we have, I believe, been able to receive in Buenos Aires foreign sugar for half of what Tucumán sugar costs us." [27]

Said a Tucumano who did not benefit from the monopoly: "If this protection does not realize the welfare of all the social classes that reside in the sugar zone, the industry *has no right to be protected at the expense of the entire population of the nation.*" [28]

In the meantime, it was impossible to get the real figures on how much profit the ingenios made, because the companies would not open their books to government investigators. They argued that they could not compete with foreign sugar because their wages were so high (*sic*), and that if they had not been in competition with the sweated labor of Cuba and Java, they could have made a good profit without protection. This was not true, because the yield of sugar cane in Argentina per hectare of cultivated land was the lowest in the world, being a third as high as Peru's and less than a quarter as high as Hawaii's. Argentina was at the very bottom of the list. Even the continental United States did better.* In the meantime, sugar was a highly profitable business for a few monopolists and for the middlemen in Buenos Aires who went to make the Sugar Trust. Prices were set, production was limited, and there was a permanent shortage of sugar.[29] The public paid a high price. The almacenero did not make any profit on selling sugar, and most almacenes would not sell a housewife a bag of sugar unless she made another purchase, too. As for the hundred thousand peons of Tucumán, their standard of living could be seen by anyone who would take the trouble to leave Buenos Aires and visit the sugar fields.

Yerba mate was in somewhat the same situation as sugar, but the protection was not so high. Until the beginning of this century the yerba consumed in Argentina was imported from Paraguay, whose major industry was the picking and roasting of the leaves. There was a myth among yerbateros that the tree could not be cultivated: that it would not germinate, that it would not grow leaves, that if it did grow leaves they would be inferior and bitter, and so forth.[30] The persistence of this legend is hard to explain in view of the fact that the Jesuits in Misiones in the eighteenth century had great plantations from which they derived good profit. They

* Yields of sugar cane in quintals per hectare (Institut International d'Agriculture, *Annuaire International de Statistique Agricole* (1938–1939):

Country	*1928–1932*	*1936*
Argentina	281.4	297.8
United States	337.2	500
Cuba	385.8	—
Peru	1,080.6	—
Java	1,308.8	1,884.0
Hawaii	1,349.4	—

were expelled in 1769, and their missions fell into decay, until by the middle of the nineteenth century they were in the state which Moussy describes. The Argentines continued to drink mate, but it was imported from Brazil and Paraguay. In 1903 the first modern experiment in domestic cultivation was tried out near the ruins of the Jesuit mission of San Ignacio, in the territory of Misiones. Its success led to emulation, and by 1930 the industry was worth some 150,000,000 pesos.[31] But it was not, and is not, prosperous, as company balance sheets show. The yerba companies want higher tariff protection so as to exclude all Paraguayan and Brazilian competition. The argument against higher protection is that the industry in the first place should not have been permitted to grow up, because yerba is one of the few things Argentina can import from Paraguay, and unless Argentina can buy from Paraguay, it cannot sell there. Fostering a redundantly competitive business behind high tariff protection would hurt Argentina and would ruin Paraguay. In view of the marginal existence of the yerba plantations at the present time, this argument is cogent. The plantation workers certainly do not profit from their labor in the yerbatales. In 1941, at least half the companies that published their profits were in the red; and none of the others made more than a very modest return.[32]

The wine industry of Mendoza is a third industry requiring protection. Mendozan wines, perhaps from a lack of aging, are mediocre, and would not monopolize the home market if the excellent Chilean Rhine wines and the French Burgundies and Spanish sherries were permitted free entry. In the free-trade days of the nineteenth century, when government was by and for the estancieros of Buenos Aires, Mendozan wines were sold only in the neighboring provinces where transportation costs favored them. The national capital drank the best Europe had to offer, at a low price. But since that time, especially since the Italian and Spanish immigrants built up the wine industry in Mendoza, there has been increasing government protection. And during the depression the industry came to be regulated, as well, to prevent overproduction.

Unlike the sugar and yerba industries, the wine industry did not depend on sweated labor, nor were working conditions bad. There were no latifundia in the province. There were large *bodegas* (winepresses) and small ones, but most were small, of family size, and primitive in method. Mendoza is an Andean province, and very beautiful. It depends in great measure on irrigation, unlike the littoral. During the thirties the national government set up the Junta Reguladora de Vinos to control production, and as a result, 15,000 hectares (out of a total of 100,000) of vineyards were pulled up and destroyed.[33] There are also vineyards in San Juan, but Mendoza is the grape province par excellence.* The Junta was severely criticized for its plow-under policies, and for fomenting an artificial scarcity of wine to keep the price up. Wine is one of the necessities of life in Argentina, for all classes drink it as a table beverage. Its price has risen constantly since the creation of the Junta, and brands that were selling for 90 centavos the liter in 1935 were selling for 2.20 pesos in 1943. Part of the rise, of course, was a reflection of better business conditions; but part was the action of the Junta. Another criticism levelled against this agency was that it secured profits to the big bodegas, but had no interest in the problems of the vineyards that furnished them their grapes. Thus, in 1942, when a question arose between the bodegas and vineyards as to the price of the current crop, the Junta gave the bodegas permission to sell the wine they had stored for aging. This meant that they did not have to buy the current crop in order to fulfill their market obligations, and broke the strike of the growers. The Junta Reguladora de Vinos was abolished in 1943 as one of the first acts of the Ramírez government when it came to power by revolution. But in its place was put another agency which is probably the same thing under a different name.

Sugar, wine, and yerba could not exist in Argentina without tariff protection, and here lies the conflict of interests with the agricultural littoral. As they had always done, the estancieros and farmers argued that these industries were artificial and harmful: that, without protection of any kind, Argentina could sell wheat

* In 1937, of a total of 140,000 hectares planted to grapes, 100,000 were in Mendoza.

corn, beef, and mutton in the world market at a profit, and that the more tariffs the country raised against European and British products, the more it hurt itself. The protected industries, on the other hand, argued that Argentina needed a balanced economy if it were not to be at the mercy of world markets. Where would Argentina be today, they asked, if it did not have its own sugar, wine, tobacco, cotton, and petroleum? The war had shut off access to Europe, to the East Indies, and even in large measure to the United States. Yet Argentina was hardly feeling the war. It was smoking cigarettes made with national tobacco, eating sugar grown in Tucumán, wearing linens made from Argentine flax, woollens made from Argentine wool, and cottons made from Argentine cotton. The streets were full of cars powered by gasoline from Comodoro Rivadavia. And everyone agreed that the infant industries had been the salvation of the country. Where would Argentina have been if its factories had not made dishes, electric-light bulbs, pots and pans, stoves, furniture, shoes, hats, and textiles? Where would the State Railways have been without the new coaches made in the workshops of Tafí Viejo in Tucumán? If the livestock interests had had their own way, Argentina in the face of world war would have been without resources of any kind.

This, in brief, was the argument. The group that was the most potent force against nineteenth century liberal economics was the new and rising industrial class, which had grown up in little more than a decade. Two conditions favored it: the world depression which caused a depreciation of the peso and forced Argentina to make many things which it could no longer afford to buy; and the world war, which had virtually isolated the country. Industry was without a voice in the government; the industrial class was a social cipher; but control of the nation's wealth, and with it, of the nation's economy, was gravitating into its hands.

BIG BUSINESS

In six years, Argentine industry grew amazingly. Here are the figures: Number of establishments in 1935, 40,000; in 1941, 60,000. Number of employees in industry in 1935, 462,000; in 1941, 829,-000. Salaries and wages in 1935, 737,000,000 pesos; in 1941, 1,284,-000,000. Value of products elaborated in 1935, 3,500,000,000 pesos; in 1941, 6,300,000,000.[34]

There were several facts of importance in this general industrial picture. The first was the concentration around Buenos Aires and its suburbs. The Industrial Census of 1939 showed that 60 per cent of the establishments, 70 per cent of the workers, and 74 per cent of the salaries were concentrated in the city and province of Buenos Aires.[35] This fact was serious, for Buenos Aires already had a monopoly of the agricultural wealth, and of the money spent by the national government in salaries. Of all the taxable incomes in Argentina in 1941, *74 per cent by value were in the Federal Capital.*[36] The unbalance in Argentine economy, not to mention political power, was more serious than it had ever been; and those sanguine porteños who believed that the provinces complained because it was their tradition to complain, and who refused to see the seriousness of this national problem—they were in the majority—were doing nothing to better the situation. Nature in the first place gave Buenos Aires a strategic location on the Río de la Plata which made it the port of the United Provinces. To this was added the advantage of the climate and soil of the province. Its location first made it great. But what nature began, man finished. The railroads in the nineteenth century were built out like the spokes of a wheel, so that all traffic radiated from Buenos Aires. When highways were constructed, they, too, began and ended in the Federal Capital. When the Republic was constituted, the government was located in Buenos Aires—a most serious mistake. In short, economically and politically the gravitation toward the Capital augmented in geometric progression. With each passing year, the city grew in wealth and population, while the provinces remained poor and backward. The sugar millionaires from Tucumán, the rich estancieros from Patagonia, the owners of the wine industry, went to Buenos Aires to live, and took their money—which came from the provinces—with them. Nine provinces had less than 1 per cent each of the taxable incomes in Argentina in 1941.[37] They were Entre Ríos, Corrientes, Salta, San Juan, Santiago del Estero, Jujuy, Catamarca, San Luis, and La Rioja. The more beautiful and populous Buenos Aires became, the more industries settled there, the stronger was the attraction of population from the provinces. Rich and poor alike gravitated to Buenos Aires—the poor to make money, and the rich to spend it.

Another interesting aspect of the industrial picture was that even now, more than half of the owners of commercial and industrial establishments in Argentina were foreigners.[38] The proportion had descended since the nineteenth century. But in view of the fact that foreigners in the total population came to only about 20 per cent, the predominance of immigrants in industry was significant. Among foreign owners, the most important were Italians and Spaniards in that order. There were also Russians, Poles, Germans, and French, but they were not numerous.

The largest single industry in Argentina in 1939, in value of production, was the frigoríficos, with an output of 526,000,000 pesos. The second was the building industry, with a production valued at 300,000,000 pesos. And then in succession came the electric companies, petroleum refineries, flour mills, and textile mills.[39] Take out the frigoríficos, power companies, and refineries—the first two because they were foreign corporations, and the third because they were either Argentine government monopolies or foreign corporations—and the building industry, flour milling, and the manufacture of textiles were left as the most important private industries in Argentina.

The building industry had been booming for several years, especially in Buenos Aires, where since the middle of the last decade there had gone up numberless apartment houses in the style made popular in Europe by Le Corbusier: slender, white, and functional, with marble and glass entranceways and curved balconies. In the United States they would be called "streamlined" or "modernistic," though the terms are misleading. They were expressions of the architectural philosophy that a house is a machine for living. There had been a fever of building in the Capital and its suburbs, like Vicente López and San Isidro; and especially in the fashionable Atlantic beach resort where well-to-do porteños spend their summers—Mar del Plata. Construction was not too well supervised, and, especially after the war brought a steel shortage, buildings collapsed with frequency and numerous workmen were killed, without eliciting any investigation by the authorities. The apartment buildings of Buenos Aires were of brick and concrete with almost no reinforcement; and most of the bricks were hollow. This no doubt accounted for the collapses. The building industry was apparently not too remunerative to the contractors, because large numbers annually went into bankruptcy. According to estimates of the Unión Argentina de Asociaciones de Ingenieros, 70 per cent of the money invested in construction in 1940 was in Buenos Aires and its suburbs. In per capita investment, however, Mar del Plata topped the list with 232 pesos; and after Mar del Plata came Vicente López (181), San Isidro (166), Buenos Aires (56) and Santa Fe (44).[40] Except for Santa Fe, all these represented the spending power of Buenos Aires, for they were either suburbs or resorts of the Federal Capital. The construction industry, unlike many others, was not a monopoly.

Flour milling, however, and the related cereal exporting, which was the fourth largest industry in the country, was 85 per cent controlled by four firms. They were Bunge y Born, De Ridder, La Plata Cereal, and Dreyfus. Bunge y Born exported 30 per cent of all the cereals of Argentina, and was the middleman for half the nation's cereals. The Bunge y Born group controlled more than fifty companies with a capital of 170,000,000 pesos. The company's founders, E. A. Bunge and J. Born, were Belgian Jewish financiers of world-wide connections. So great was their power in the Belgian Congo, for instance, that one of their officers, who was an Argentine, was named governor of the Congo, and thus lost his Argentine citizenship. One of the firm in Belgium was Count Henri Carton de Wiart, who was Minister of Justice from 1911 to 1920, and Premier in 1920-1921.

In 1943 this firm was not run by either Bunge or Born, but by Alfredo Hirsch and Jorge Oster. Both were Germans, the former Jewish, the latter Catholic. There were Bunges in the group, however. Members of both the Bunge and Hirsch families had intermarried with the Argentine landed aristocracy, Mario Hirsch with a Blaquier Unzué and Eduardo Bunge with an Urquiza Anchorena. Bunge y Born operated in Brazil and Paraguay as well as in Argentina, and by means of interlocking directorates controlled flour mills, estancias, quebracho concessions, chemical companies, and loan associations.[42] The great importance of the cereal milling and exporting monopoly derived from the fact that these cereal brokers had most of the foreign exchange available to Argentina, and it was from them that the national government bought its pounds and dollars.

The textile industry was not a monopoly, but it was the industry in which the largest individual fortunes were now being made. Among the hundred largest incomes in 1941, there were seventeen textile manufacturers, and three manufacturers of stockings. War had been a boon to this business, but what peace would do to it remained to be seen. At the end of hostilities England would have to unfreeze millions of pounds of blocked exchange which it owed Argentina; and, since one of England's chief exports was textiles, Argentina might be, like the United States in 1918, unwilling to have the debt repaid in merchandise. One thing seemed certain, and that was that the Argentine textile manufacturers were going to be strong exponents of high tariff protection. If they saw themselves faced with ruin, they were going to exert all the political pressure they could. But in 1943 it was still an estanciero's government. The largest family fortune in Argentina, estimated by many to be well over a billion dollars, was the industrial-financial empire of the Bembergs, headed in the third Argentine generation by Otto and Federico Bemberg. The Bembergs controlled a vast brewing fortune that produced most of the beer in Argentina, including Quilmes and Palermo, with a monopoly on sales in the Federal Capital.* They held malt companies, industrial credits, factories, land, colonies, yerbatales (there was a Puerto Bemberg on the Paraná), cotton companies, winter resorts, and mortgages.[43] All the privately held shares in the Corporación de Transportes were theirs, and these alone were valued at 70,000,000 pesos.[44] They owned stock in the Unión Telefónica (national telephone company—a subsidiary of International Telephone and Telegraph). They had a chain of estancias producing the Argentine cheeses which were becoming famous in the American market, especially now that war had shut off normal supplies of Roquefort and Gorgonzola. In short, the Bembergs had one of the largest family fortunes in the world. Yet when Otto Sebastián Bemberg, father of Otto and Federico, had died in Paris in 1934, the Bembergs had declared—and paid inheritance taxes on—a fortune of 600,000 pesos. Argentines could not forget that, nor swallow the indifference of a Conservative government that from motives of—was it venality?—allowed this vast fortune to pass virtually tax-free to the hands of Otto and Federico.

The Bembergs had a heritage of public ill will possible only to the very rich. They were hated for their business astuteness, for buying bankrupt estancias from impoverished aristocrats at something like their real value, for lending on mortgages and foreclosing on them. They were known for their political loans: perhaps as insurance, they lent money to hard-pressed politicians, and if these loans were poor risks in dollars and cents, they were not from the political point of view. Popular mythology viewed the Bembergs as the vultures that benefited from the misfortunes of others. Yet their *consorcio*, with that of Bunge y Born, was almost the only source of industrial loans in a country where people lent only on land; and if their estancias made money where others went bankrupt, it was because they did not buy at inflated values. Many of those who criticized them most severely were families whose holdings dated from the 50-centavo-a-hectare sales of Rosas.

* The Bembergs also controlled Rheingold beer in the United States.

Were they less guilty of bargain buying than the hardheaded Bembergs?

Unfortunate it was that the Bembergs and Hirsches and Dreyfuses could be signalled out as Jews by the anti-Semites. They had married criolla aristocracy for two generations, and were usually Catholics; but the Jewish surnames remained and were the focus for the anti-Semitism of the nationalists. In much the same way, the frigorífico, railroad, and public utility monopolies were the occasion for a hate-the-foreigner campaign. The question that the nationalists did not ask, however, was: Since the criollos had been in Argentina before there were any immigrants, before the hated Jews and foreigners came, how had economic control passed to their hands? And if the nationalists did not know the answer they knew what they would do if they should ever come to power. They would drive the hated money-changers, the Jews and the foreigners, from Argentina forever. They had a motto: *Sovereignty or Death.*

MYOPIA

> *The phenomenon of regression that has taken place in Argentina is strange. It is the phenomenon of an inspiration cut short. In the beginning—our whole history proves it—Argentines to a man seemed inspired by active zeal. . . . Then suddenly, when the century was well advanced, the original motive force, the spirit of the march, broke down. . . . It is as if we were to imagine an enormous factory in which, at a given moment, all the workers were suddenly to operate mechanically, producing objects without object, deprived of conscious will power, not knowing how long or for whom, or why, or to what end they were laboring.* —EDUARDO MALLEA, *The Bay of Silence.*

Buenos Aires was not Argentina.

One was deceived by statistics. The foreigner coming to Argentina to trade, to represent his country diplomatically, or to be a tourist settled in the city and thought that he knew the country.

Here were the wealth, the population, the trade, and the government. This was the city that ruled. To understand how it overshadowed everything else in Argentina, one must imagine New York in the same situation. New York, let us suppose, with a population of 30,000,000, has all the nation's industry, and is the Federal Capital. In that case, New York would be to the United States what Buenos Aires is to Argentina.

But Buenos Aires was not Argentina; and when I say this I mean in spirit and in personality. The porteño's was still a mentality apart, just as surely in 1943 as it had been a century earlier. In some ways the indifference toward the rest of Argentina was more characteristic than it had ever been, because in Rosas' time the protest of the provinces was felt in civil war, and now it was too weak to be felt. The average porteño did not know what the rest of Argentina was like. His mental picture of his country was something like this: There is a rich, vast farming land filled with wheat and corn and fat cattle; in the Andes is Nahuel Huapí National Park, more beautiful than Switzerland; in the northeast is Iguazú Falls, larger and more beautiful than Niagara; somewhere in the mountainous provinces are undiscovered deposits of iron, coal, and copper which will some day make Argentina as rich as Brazil; the people of Argentina are white. Since the porteño left Buenos Aires only to visit the hillside resorts of Córdoba, or the seaside resort of Mar del Plata, he carried this vision, uncorrected, to the grave with him.

He was quite deceived. Argentina was not like this. What was spiritually indigenous to the country could be seen in San Juan, or Santiago del Estero, or Catamarca, where the population was not a European white, but a criollo brown that showed the blending of two races; where the people did not eat well, and lived in adobe or twig huts with earth floors; where the poor bred but did not marry. This was the Argentina of the caudillos, the gauchos, and Sarmiento's despised chiripá. If Sarmiento had visited the mountain villages of his native San Juan, or San Luis, in 1943, he would have found them little changed, and he would still have seen plenty of evidences of the "barbarism" that was his bête noire.

There would still have been children without shoes, houses without floors, and people who could not read or write. And probably the table manners of the poor would have struck him as terrible.

In the country as a whole he would have found innumerable primary schools as a monument to his labors. But if he had gone to a country school in the desert of Santiago del Estero, he would have seen that the children were hungry and, what was worse, thirsty. In some places he would have seen the schoolteacher with a jar of water on her desk. To the children who behaved she would give a drink, and those who did not, would get no water. And the only meal of those children in twenty-four hours would have been the doughy paste fed them at noon in the schoolhouse. If he had gone to Tucumán he would have seen children whose eyes were rimmed with trachoma, and who shivered with malaria. In Jujuy they would be sleeping in the schools at night on sheepskins because their homes were so far away. This was also Argentina.

In Buenos Aires the middle class got its bath a day, and probably wasted water. But there were a thousand towns that had never known what it was to have running water. And even on the outskirts of the provincial capitals whole sections had no water. Santa Fe, for instance, was a beautiful city of many parks. But on the outskirts were people who lived by picking up rags and bottles from the city dump. Their huts were of tin, or branches, or adobe, and when they needed drinking water they carried their cans to a faucet by the side of the road; there, in summer, they stood in line in the sun, while millions of flies from the dump buzzed around them. In Jujuy, across the river bed from the city, the poor people lived in huts, too, and drank and washed in the stream because there were no pipes where they lived. Here milk was still ladled from cans slung over a horse's back, as it had been in Buenos Aires a century before. Vegetables were carried into town on horseback by Indian women, and sold from baskets. The porteños read about it in books, but this was the daily living of the north.

The porteños who read about the gauchos' huts of a century

ago did not know that these were still the habitations of the *majority* of provincianos. Sometimes they were of straw, sometimes of mud, sometimes of branches. Even in rich Santa Fe the country people lived in ranchos that were no different from the rancho of the gaucho, except perhaps that now there were cane chairs where before there had been horses' skulls. The floor was still of trampled earth. Water still came from a well. And the asado was cooked on a stake driven into the ground, not because this was a picnic, but because there was no stove.

All this the porteño did not know. Occasionally he would visit the provinces. Once Eduardo Mallea, one of the best known modern Argentine novelists, went overnight by train to Santa Fe. It was only a ten hours' trip, but it shocked him into writing about it in a book. One of the most interesting chapters of this book, which is called *Historia de una Pasión Argentina*, describes the sleepy little town of San José del Rincón, just fifteen miles from Santa Fe. To Mallea Rincón was horrible, a symbol of decay and death. It is, as a matter of fact, an enchanted village over which a spell seems to have been laid a hundred years ago. It is a jungle of orange groves and old, old adobe houses beside the Paraná. There is no intruding electric light or telephone. If you visit it in a summer's twilight, there is perfect silence, as if the people had been sleeping for several lifetimes. The air is heavy with orange blossoms and the scent of flowers. But there is no movement. When night falls, kerosene lamps shine from the homes and the pulpería. It is interesting that Mallea should have thought San José horrible because it seemed to be living in a dream from another century. What would he have thought, I wonder, of Santiago del Estero, where people were not only from another century, but hungry and thirsty as well?

It was possible for the porteño even to live in the provinces without seeing anything around him. The porteño in the provinces was the porteño in exile, which meant that in his mind's eye he was back in Buenos Aires, or Corrientes, going into his favorite confitería for his evening vermouth. Perhaps that was why he could not see what was in front of him. One evening, in Tucumán, an

Irish lady made the comment that, since she had been living in the city, not one but many poor women had come to her back door with babies in their arms, offering to sell them for servants. The others of the company were porteños. One, who had been living in Tucumán for more than two years, was shocked at her remark, and protested:

"But that is perfectly preposterous. Everyone knows that, if anything, the Argentines have too *strong* a sense of the family. There is no country in the world where family relations are more sacred."

"My dear sir," said the Irish lady, "do you know that in this province half of the births are illegitimate?"

The porteño, in answer, merely continued to protest about the sacredness of the family in Argentina, and the Catholic feeling for home and children.

"But we are talking about two different social classes," she said. "You are talking about the middle class and about Buenos Aires. I am talking about the lower classes, and about Tucumán."

What the Irish lady said, of course, was perfectly true. Poor women who had unwanted children did sell them, or even gave them away to be raised as servants in a family. But the curious thing was that a porteño who had been living in Tucumán for two years, in one of the provinces with the saddest social problems of the Republic, had seen nothing of what was under his nose, and was still living in the imaginary Argentina of the Avenida Alvear and the Calle Florida.

Most porteños would have been surprised to know what the provincianos thought of them. Outside Buenos Aires, city and province, there was only the greatest bitterness toward the Federal Capital. It was a symbol of political and economic tyranny. From Buenos Aires came the interventions that deposed elected governments and managed elections to the taste of the party that ruled the capital. Popular movements began and ended in Buenos Aires. Three military schools and a couple of regiments marching from the city's outskirts to the Plaza de Mayo for Argentina were enough to bring about a change of government. Each year the concentration of wealth and industry around the federal district grew more preponderant. Once the government sent a committee to Iguazú Falls to consider the feasibility of harnessing their tremendous hydroelectric power. But when the committee reported that it was cheaper to bring coal from Wales than to bring electricity *to Buenos Aires* from Iguazú, the matter was dropped. There was a possibility of hydroelectric development in the Andes; but dams were not built because *the Andes were so far from Buenos Aires.* In short, it apparently never occurred to the government that any other city than Buenos Aires needed power, or that any other city than Buenos Aires could or should be a center of industry. But the porteños did not know what the interior thought of them. One explained to me once that the rivalry between Buenos Aires and the provinces was good-natured and joking, "like the Harvard-Yale football game, you know." This was what he, and most porteños, thought. But I had seen tears of anger in the eyes of provincianos when they spoke of Buenos Aires.

The early development of Buenos Aires was favored by nature, for it had access to Europe by sea, and to the heart of the grazing country by land. The colonial regime also favored it by making it the only port of the Río de la Plata, and giving it the customs monopoly. When the railroads were built, they added another advantage by converging on the capital city. Finally, the concentration of population made it the logical site for industry. Perhaps airplane transportation will do for the interior what not even the civil wars could accomplish. It used to be that every stranger that came to the Plata entered, and left, by Buenos Aires. Now he might fly over the Andes from Santiago, Chile, in which case his first glimpse of Argentina would be Mendoza; or he might fly down from La Paz, and see first the snow-rimmed valley of Salta. The age of flight could make some interior city—Salta, Mendoza, Córdoba—a crossroads of air transportation.

There was power in the Andes, and if it were ever developed, there would be growth and change in the mountain cities. Cheap electricity could overcome the handicap of long train hauls. To the grazing interests of the littoral which still dominated Argentina in

1943 the development of hydroelectric power was a menace to the trade with England. One of the largest items in Anglo-Argentine trade was Welsh coal, and if it should disappear, England would sell and buy less in Argentina. That is why an estanciero's government did not see fit to harness Iguazú, the Paraná, and the cascades and lakes of the Cordillera. The littoral argued that it possessed by nature all the nation's wealth, and that to create artificial wealth in the provinces was unjustified. The argument was specious. Salta, in the north, not only had oil and iron, but could raise fruit and even cattle. What had kept it poor was the transportation problem. The rivers of the Andes, properly dammed, would provide water for electricity and for irrigation. There was probably no potentially richer section than the territory of the Río Negro, but the fruits it sent to market arrived either green or rotten, so slow and bad was the freight service. In Patagonia flowers and fruit grow to giant size. In Buenos Aires in 1941 there was on exhibit a Patagonian squash weighing *two hundred pounds*. But who would go to live in Patagonia, where there were no railroads and no cities? The real potentialities of Argentina had never been scratched and never would be so long as the ruling mentality was bounded on all sides by the city limits of Buenos Aires.

The crisis that began with Uriburu is a puzzle, unless one understands that the economic bases of the old Argentina were in dissolution. From 1930 to 1943 Argentina was governed by the Conservative party; but there was a deep difference between its conservatism and the conservatism of the same class in the nineteenth century. There was something cheap, false, and artificial about the conservatism of Uriburu-Justo-Castillo. The estanciero class in the late nineteenth century was dynamic and strong, and its politicians, men like Roca and Pellegrini and Sáenz Peña, whatever their faults, had personal dignity and intelligence. Conservative governments gave Argentina presidents like Sarmiento and Mitre. They brought in the foreign capital that developed the country, and gave it its railroads and packing plants. It was true that this was a class rule, and that many, if not most, of the Conservative presidents were men with a profound mistrust of the mob. It did not matter. They truly represented the Argentina of the nineteenth century.

The phenomenon of the early twentieth century was the rise of Radicalism. The Radical party spoke for the urban middle class, and it gradually and peaceably superseded the rule of the Conservative oligarchy. The party had outstanding figures. The Noventa had attracted the best and most progressive elements in the younger generation. Radicalism, too, was an element of progress, and was dynamic. Criticize Yrigoyen as one likes—his faults were evident enough—one cannot deny that he stood for an ever widening basis of democracy.

But what, on the other hand, had been happening since 1930? First, the September Revolution itself. Among its leaders, we look in vain for a young man, or a man of ideas. The men who made the September Revolution were the worst element in the country. Not a single one of them had a new idea. They were military men, men of the most limited education. They were not aristocrats, but were middle class, with social pretensions. They gave orders, but they were not strong; and they finally played into the hands of the most reactionary and discredited people in the country. The Conservative governments of the thirties were corrupt, fraudulent, unimaginative. They were in moral, spiritual, and intellectual bankruptcy. Whom did they truly represent? They were trying to turn the clock back to the nineteenth century, when the aristocracy had much land and few mortgages, and stood for something both politically and economically. But the world depression was wiping out these fortunes. There were still the same names on the same estancias, and there were the same parties at the Alvear Palace and Plaza hotels, reading like the roll call of Rosas' land grants. But the estancias were mortgaged to the hilt, and values were no longer rising, wiping out the debts by their increment. It has been untrue for the last decade to speak of the "landed aristocracy." The economic structure of the estanciero class was eaten away at the base.

The 1930 revolution and what went after represented regression. The aristocrats in government office were there because their estancias were bankrupt and they had to make a living and give jobs to their relatives. The government bureaucracy was filled with bankrupt gentlemen. Everything the government did showed an unintelligent clinging to outworn ideas. And yet changes came, in spite of everything, and the very Conservative government laid the basis for its fall. It was in the thirties, for instance, that the depreciation of the peso, agricultural unemployment, and the breakdown in trade created the new Argentine industry. The same decade brought government regulation to most phases of Argentine economy. Argentina, like all the other states of the world, became a directed economy.

It is easier to understand the bankruptcy of Conservatism than the bankruptcy of Radicalism. After all, Argentina was outgrowing its cow-country phase and maturing. But why the complete failure of the Radical party? Why did it attract no young men to its ranks? The Radical party of the thirties was on most scores worse than the Conservative party: it lacked morale, it lacked leadership, there was no fight in it.

The crisis of Radicalism was double. First, in the purely Argentine aspect, the Radical party was the reverse of the same coin which had Conservatism on its face. In short, the commercial classes that had created the Radical party were living from one end of the Argentine-British bilateral trade. They were in origin importers of French, British, and Italian merchandise. At the same time, the estanciero class were the exporters of what the land produced. Thus the immigrant commercial class of Buenos Aires, which made the Revolution of 1890, were a part of the old Argentina, the colonial Argentina. They were *not* the same as the new industrial class. The change in Argentine economy meant a change for them, too, although they had nothing to lose from industrialization if they could continue as middlemen.

But the real crisis of Radicalism was a reflection of the world crisis of the petty bourgeoisie. What happened in Argentina happened in France, in Germany of the Weimar Republic, in Austria, and throughout Europe. The middle-class governments, instead of accepting spiritual leadership, were as afraid of change as anyone; and so change, when it came, simply mowed them down. Radicalism did not offer Argentina anything, any more than Radical-Socialism offered anything to a disunited and demoralized France. Radicalism had introduced the principle of universal suffrage. It had admitted the middle classes to university education. Beyond that, it had nothing to offer.

This was the Argentina of June, 1943: disunited, deeply cynical, without purpose or direction. Its spiritual bankruptcy was as patent as its physical prosperity in the war boom, and at the helm of government was a class that no longer had the power to change its direction, or to prevent outside influences from bringing a change of direction. A nation, a society with all its values, was adrift on a wide ocean, with no one to set the course and no one even to point a destination. Argentina had reached the end of an era.

THE NATIONALIST REVOLUTION

JUNE 4, 1943

We of the Argentine army are playing a daring game, the most daring there is, and we are disposed to give our lives for our country. We will not tolerate impositions of an international order, and much less of an internal order.—COLONEL JUAN D. PERON to *El Mercurio* of Chile, November 11, 1943.

In the early dawn of June 4, 1943, the garrison of the Campo de Mayo in Buenos Aires marched from its barracks, and the army took over the government of Argentina. When time has lent perspective, this event will be seen for what it was: economically, politically, socially the most important event in Argentine history since the Noventa. For this blow, struck swiftly and without warning, marked the end of a society, an economy and a way of life. With it were buried the Argentina that lived from beef alone, the Argentina of the Enlightened Oligarchy, liberal Argentina, the free trader, and the hopes, the power, and the predominance of the landed aristocracy.

The June Revolution had much in it that was accident and improvisation. The ground for dissatisfaction among nationalist army officers was prepared when President Castillo picked Robustiano Patrón Costas to succeed him in office. Patrón Costas was detested by everyone except the British in Argentina. He was hated by the left because of his unsavory record as a feudal landholder in the north. The Naziphiles and nationalists hated him worse because he was known to be strongly pro-British, and his foreign policy as President could not but lean toward the Allies. But the Patrón Costas candidacy was the underlying, rather than the immediate, cause of revolt in the army.

The coup against Castillo was precipitated by a rumor that the Radical party was going to invite War Minister Pedro P. Ramírez to be its candidate in the September elections. The President, reading the rumor in the papers, called General Ramírez in to explain. Ramírez denied the story, and on June 1 his denial appeared in all the papers. But it was assumed the War Minister would resign, to be replaced by either Diego I. Mason or Juan Carlos Bassi. Castillo waited from Tuesday June 1 to Thursday June 3, for Ramírez's resignation, and it did not come.

In those two days, hurried consultations among leaders of the armed forces culminated in a meeting the morning of June 3 at the Campo de Mayo in which the army chiefs decided on revolution.[1] Ramírez favored the blow to save himself; but there is little doubt that the motives were as mixed as the plotters. The faction led by General Arturo Rawson wanted to repair Argentine prestige and acquire arms by adopting an out-and-out policy of collaboration with the Allies. The Radical generals wanted to end Conservative rule and bring their own party to power. And the faction of fanatic nationalists known as the G.O.U. (Group of United Officers) wanted to end the pretense of democracy once for all and build a totalitarian state. The G.O.U. was the military wing of Argentine nationalism, and perhaps the only army faction that knew exactly what it wanted, and was prepared to get it. Its chief was Colonel Juan Domingo Perón, who had been in Italy and had observed totalitarian government at first hand. How divergent were the intentions of the men who made the June Revolution did not appear until later. But they met on the common ground that Castillo must go.

Thursday night June 3, the President realized for the first time that something big was afoot. At two o'clock in the morning he called a cabinet meeting. At the presidential estate in Olivos there was a stormy interview between the President and the Minister of War. Ramírez, when he left, went directly to the barracks of the Campo de Mayo. Castillo and the rest of the cabinet now knew what to expect: it was revolution. They ordered the Minister of War placed under arrest, and at dawn drove to Buenos Aires, to the Casa Rosada. The revolution was already under way. There had been troop movements all night, and at four in the morning the soldiers started from the Campo de Mayo toward the center of the city. The revolutionary troops included the 4th Infantry, the school of arms, the cavalry school, the school for noncommissioned officers, the 10th Cavalry, the 1st Artillery, the 1st Anti-Aircraft Artillery, and the communications school [2]—total, about 10,000 men.

The soldiers converged on Buenos Aires in several columns with General Arturo Rawson, the cavalry commander, at their head. Ramírez drove to the Casa Rosada to present his ultimatum to President Castillo. The demand was that Castillo's ministers resign—all of them—to be replaced by four generals and four admirals. The President refused, and Ramírez was placed under arrest. Rawson, in the meantime, at the head of one of the revolutionary columns, had reached the Naval Mechanics' School, and there the only encounter of the revolution took place. The director of the school ordered the sailors to fire on Rawson's men, and at the first volley about a hundred fell dead or wounded. The revolutionists had not expected this opposition, and in their confusion fired on each other, killing more men. Then the Mechanics' School was surrounded and blasted with artillery fire. The encounter was brief and bloody, and the true number of casualties was never released to the public.

In the gray dawn, Buenos Aires slept, unaware of the events that were taking place. The morning papers carried no hint of revolution, but the reporters were already out in the streets, trying to find out what was happening. The first trams and colectivos came into the center of town, carrying their passengers to work. Between nine and ten o'clock the first shoppers reached the central district, to find business houses shuttered, and banks admitting customers by small side doors. When they asked what was the matter the clerks could only give the rumor that there was a revolution. Who was making it? Nobody knew. No extras had reached the street, the government had control of the radio. The city was blanketed with silence. Police went about armed, but did not know whom they were defending, or against what. The revolution had been a perfect surprise.

When President Castillo realized the size of the movement against him, he and his ministers drove to the port and took refuge on the minesweeper *Drummond*. The state radio was still broadcasting reassurances that all was well, that the movement was under control. By now the first extras were on the street, and were selling for as much as three pesos each. Curious crowds were converging on the Plaza de Mayo, sure that whatever was happening, it would all finish there. When Rawson and his troops finally reached the Plaza, it was packed with people shouting for liberty, democracy, and *la patria*, and waving little blue and white flags. Nobody knew who was in, but everybody knew who was out. Castillo was on his way to Uruguay. Good riddance! By midafternoon the first acts of violence took place, and they were, characteristically, directed against the Corporación de Transportes. Porteños, in doubt as to how to express themselves when public order breaks down, burn the nearest streetcars. In 1919 it had been the Lacroze. Now it was the Corporacíon de Transportes. The crowds turned on the busses and colectivos of the hated monopoly, smashed their windows, turned them over, and set them on fire. By three o'clock the scene in the Plaza de Mayo was Dantesque with the smoke of burning vehicles.

This was the revolution of June 4. Castillo was out. Very well. Who was in? That was a question harder to answer. On Saturday it was announced that General Arturo Rawson was the provisional President of the Republic. The cabinet showed every evidence of haste and improvisation. For instance, the Minister of Foreign Relations was a former chief of police of Buenos Aires. The Minister of Finance was José María Rosa, chief stockholder of *El Pampero*, who was on both British and American blacklists. The Minister of Justice, Dr. Horacio Calderón, was on the American blacklist. Ramírez was Minister of War. In as Minister of Agriculture was General Mason, whom Castillo had been considering just three days before as a successor to Ramírez. The government issued various proclamations. It was, it said, against fraud and venality. It was for collaboration with the other American countries. It was against "usurious capital." [3]

That was Saturday. On Sunday there was a new President, and an entirely new cabinet. The President was not General

Rawson, but General Ramírez. The Minister of Finance was Jorge Santamarina, president of the Banco de la Nación, who represented the historic interests of the estancieros. Rosa and Calderón were out. The first cabinet had all been a bad mistake. It had been evident that a government which wanted recognition from the United States could not include in its cabinet men who were blacklisted as fascists. There was a rumor that Rawson was out because he had announced his intention of shooting Culaciati, Castillo's Minister of the Interior, and Daniel Amadeo y Videla, the ex-Minister of Agriculture, in the Plaza de Mayo (Ramírez, on the other hand, thought that jailing them was enough). Culaciati had managed Castillo's interventions and fraud, and Amadeo y Videla was accused of having stolen a fortune in the Ministry of Agriculture.

On Monday the Supreme Court gave the Ramírez government *de facto* recognition. On Wednesday Bolivia, Brazil, Chile, and Paraguay recognized the new government. On Thursday, Italy and Germany recognized it. On Friday, the United States and Great Britain recognized it.

All sectors of public opinion were delighted. The democratic press had nothing but kind words for the army. The fascist press printed eulogies. All the political parties except the Conservatives presented their adhesion to the June 4th revolution. Only the Communists declared at once that the government was fascist, and they were immediately arrested, and their papers suspended. On the whole, the body of democratic opinion did not know what to make of the new government. It showed no evidences of a long-range policy, and behaved in the most contradictory ways. The new Minister of Foreign Relations, Admiral Segundo R. Storni, made public declarations of friendship toward Great Britain and the United States; but at the same time the Minister of the Interior banned the Junta de la Victoria, Acción Argentina, and the Confederación General del Trabajo. The government seemed to be at loggerheads with itself, a fact fortunate for its own survival: it was precisely because its policies were not clear, because of the ambiguities, that so many political groups were betrayed into supporting it. Because its own inner conflicts were not resolved, it did not appear either dangerous or resolute. One faction, led by Rawson, still hoped for rapprochement with the United States, which to their minds meant Lend-Lease war supplies that would put the Argentine army on a par with its neighbors. Another, led by Colonel Perón, stood for uncompromising nationalism. At the top, maintaining a precarious equilibrium between both extremes, was Ramírez himself. His objective was reform, which to his rather simple military mind meant Turn the Rascals Out. Away with politicians, away with grafters. Argentina needed a thorough housecleaning. And so the June Revolution entered its first, or disinfectant, stage.

HOUSECLEANING

> *Our task is to see to it that some day Argentines may again breathe freely, may have work, bread, and an honest home, with sons that are pure in body and soul, that respect their parents, venerate their heroes, and pray to God for our country. When we have attained this objective, we shall have solved every social, political, and institutional problem, and shall have set our country firmly and finally on the path to the fulfillment of its destiny.*—President Pedro P. Ramírez at the Army-Navy banquet, July 6, 1943.

In the first months of military rule, Argentina was left breathless with a succession of decrees designed to repair errors of speech, public morals, finance, agriculture, and political opinion. No reform was too small to receive full and solemn attention from the army officers who now took over all public offices, and were under the impression that one runs the body politic as one does an army corps.

The first act of the Ramírez government was to intervene in the provinces. That attended to, it turned to the ills of the nation. Seeing that the cost of living was high, the government cut the Gordian knot of inflation and scarcity by asking food merchants to lower the price of potatoes and butter, and by ordering landlords to reduce rents 5 to 20 per cent.[4] It was as simple as that. Salaries of public employees were raised to meet the cost of living, again by a stroke of the pen. The government ordered the Corporación de Transportes to stop the confiscation of colectivos, in this way solving the transportation question. As for turning the rascals out, this was done by the wholesale discharge of the government bureaucracy, product of thirteen years of the Conservative spoils system. Public employees, the government announced, would henceforth be appointed strictly on merit. Investigating the fraud of the Castillo government, the military arrested both Culaciati and Amadeo y Videla. It also arrested Communists, and sent them to Patagonia. For the new government there was only praise. On the anniversary of Argentine independence, the 9th of July, crowds such as had not turned out in years filled the streets to cheer General Ramírez as he passed, and to throw flowers from the balconies.

At first the haze of good intentions and bad politics was evident. There was improvisation. The military mind saw many evils in Argentine society, and set out to correct them. It was decided to purify the language by eliminating slang from the radio, and a censorship was set up to listen to announcers and make sure that their idiom was elegant. Public employees were used to arriving at work late and leaving early: new orders told them to be at their desks ten minutes before the hour, and said that they were not to put on their overcoats before closing time. Names of popular but slangy tangos were changed into Academy Spanish, and lyrics reformed. Business houses were told at what hour to close. Taxis were told on which side of the street to pick up passengers. Women were arrested for wearing skirts too short.

In high places the feeling was evident that the public needed military discipline. Stern and Spartan virtues were to be injected into public life. Shortly after the revolution, the new Vice-President, Admiral Sabá H. Sueyro died. Few people had ever heard of him before June 4, and he had done nothing since. Nevertheless, President Ramírez ordered national mourning for two days, one of them, alas, Sunday. Every race track, theater, movie, and confitería in Buenos Aires was shut. Pleasure-loving porteños wandered disconsolately from shuttered theater to shuttered confitería, unable to get a cup of tea or glass of vermouth. They were angry at Sueyro for dying and spoiling their week end, and angry at the President for the exaggerated national mourning.

As more and more government employees were discharged, admiration for reform changed to personal injury, because every family had an uncle or brother who had been *comisario* of police, or postal clerk, and had lost his job. As the government sent interventors to take over the Corporación de Transportes, the labor unions, the universities, American power companies, replacing governors, university presidents, and corporation directors with colonels and captains, criollo wits could not refrain from celebrating the reforms with jokes of the most various kinds. When the police ordered a popular Andalusian singer back to Spain because his morals were so publicly bad, the wits said that the government would name a colonel to take his place. Minister of Finance Jorge Santamarina, one of two civilians in the cabinet, was nicknamed "La Fille du Régiment."

However, in the welter of decrees, several points began to be clear. The new government had no conception of democratic processes. It dissolved Congress and called off the September elections. It did not believe in freedom of speech, freedom of the press, or freedom of assembly. Plain-clothes men circulated in bars and public places, listening for public expressions of disagreement with the regime. For the first time since the rule of Juan Manuel de Rosas, people looked over their shoulders before expressing a political opinion. The waiter might be a spy. What was worse, increasing the sensation of fear, was that the police were arresting people suddenly and shipping them without trial to concentration camps in Patagonia. There was no *habeas corpus*, and private citizens no longer had the certainty—which was taken for granted until it was lost—that the law protected them from the arbitrary whim of a government of force. There were stories of tapped telephone wires, admitting the government to the private conversations of persons it suspected. People were not even sure of the mails any longer. They ceased to discuss politics with strangers and withdrew unto themselves, afraid of those who had come as friends and had now taken over the house. Fear of the government was a new feeling to the Argentine. It was strange that so few had foreseen, and so few had protested. Almost alone was Enrique F. Mihura, governor of Entre Ríos, who was not deceived when the military intervened in his province. "It is with sorrow I discover that the Provisional Government has decided to end the autonomy of Entre Ríos," he wrote to Ramírez. "You, the Chief of State who came to power in a movement that was based on the need for reestablishing democracy and administrative decency, have fallen into the paradox of destroying all that was constructive in this revolution which, as is now apparent, this country will some day bitterly regret." [5]

Ramírez was not a strong man or a demagogue. His position at the head of the government was almost accidental; and, within the government, division was apparent. Arturo Rawson insisted that Argentina must break with the Axis and get United Nations support. But more insistent and progressively more audible was the extreme nationalism voiced by the still obscure army colonel, Juan Domingo Perón. Perón was intelligent, as most of his colleagues were not. He was ambitious. His program was a strong, nationalistic Argentina, jealous of its sovereignty, well armed, socially disciplined, industrialized, cut free from Britain. He had no sympathy for the landed aristocracy that had directed the nation and had, he believed, sold it to foreign capital. Perón had a strong weapon against his fellow officers: in his files were the signed resignations of 3,300 out of the total of 3,600 officers in active service.[6] But, if Perón looked strong, the government looked weak. There were rumors of dissension among the military, and the government had no political support, no party behind it. The nationalistic fractions had always been splintered, and numerically they were not strong. Manuel Fresco, whose newspaper *Cabildo* gave strong support to the government, was known to be the enemy of General Juan Bautista Molina, leader of the Alianza de la Juventud Nacionalista, which also supported the government. Government jobs were going to officers rather than to civilian nationalists. The government stood by strength of arms alone, without backing of either the people at large or a determined and organized party.

Events played more and more into the hands of army nationalists. The policy of rapprochement with the United States, never very explicit, was discredited once for all by the Hull-Storni exchange of September. Foreign Minister Segundo R. Storni sent an incautious note to United States Secretary of State Cordell Hull that was intended as a gesture of good will. Clumsily attempting to explain why Argentina had not broken with the Axis, it said that, although Argentine public opinion was predominantly pro-Ally, it would be incompatible with Argentina's sense of fair play to hit the Axis nations when they were down. At the same time the note complained that the United States was not sending necessary supplies to Argentina, and that it would not furnish arms to "preserve the military equilibrium" in South America.

Secretary of State Cordell Hull sent a chilling reply. Argentina, he said, had freely entered into the undertaking to break relations with the Axis and had not fulfilled it. The government had supplied newsprint to totalitarian newspapers in Buenos Aires. As for the fact that supplies were not being sent to Argentina, Argentina would of course understand that the necessities of war came first. Argentina had done nothing to help her neighbors, who were without oil at a time that Argentina was producing more oil than it ever had done. As for the "military equilibrium" of which Admiral Storni spoke, Secretary Hull wished to emphasize that "questions of military and naval equilibrium between the American republics are certainly inconsistent with the inter-American doctrine of the pacific solution of international controversies," and "the furnishing of arms and munitions for the ends mentioned by Your Excellency would seem to this government to be an action clearly inconsistent with the juridical and moral bases" of inter-American understanding.[7]

Apparently the government believed that this exchange put its diplomacy in a good light, because the papers were asked to print the full texts of the two notes, and were told that the censorship would be lifted for one day to give them complete liberty of editorial comment. *Noticias Gráficas* took the government at its word, and used the note as the occasion for speaking of those who were trying to give the new government a totalitarian bent, and of those "Axis sympathizers who disguise themselves in a Catholicism they neither feel nor practice." [8] The paper was hastily confiscated from the streets where it was on sale. Early trains for the provinces carried *Noticias Gráficas,* and were intercepted at provincial railroad stations by the police. The editor was put in jail charged with spreading "false rumors" about the revolutionary government.

Public reaction to the Hull-Storni exchange was immediate and unanimous. All sides agreed Storni had been undiplomatic in the extreme. The fascist sympathizers did not like what the note said about a majority of the Argentines being sympathetic to the democracies, and the democratic sympathizers did not like the remarks about not hitting the Axis when it was down, and the foolish slip about "military equilibrium." So universal was the condemnation of the government for its diplomatic blunder that Storni resigned, taking all the blame for what was said. As a matter of fact, probably neither the ideas expressed nor the form of the note was his, and he let himself be made the scapegoat. In any case the American slap had one effect on the government, and that was to discredit those who, like Rawson, favored a rapproachement with the Allies. The nationalists could, and did, show that the policy of placating the United States led to humiliation. Argentina, they said, must assert its sovereign will once for all. And so the government turned more and more from the moderates toward a fanatic nationalism, and each turn brought it closer to the policies of the G.O.U., whose chief was Juan Domingo Perón.

THE OPPOSITION

> *Much remains to be done, and in order to do it we must put an end to this state of alarm in which agitators of all kinds would have us live; we must create a union of all Argentines, as well as a cordial understanding with foreigners; we must Christianize the country, in harmony with its history and constitution; we must encourage births rather than immigration; we must assure the wages of labor and a decent roof over each home; we must root out doctrines of hatred and atheism.* —GUSTAVO MARTÍNEZ ZUVIRÍA, November 2, 1943.

By October sentiment about the government had crystallized. The trend of its policies was clear. Internally they led to a growing authoritarianism without respect for civil liberties or processes of law. Externally they were nationalistic, anti-American, and passively, if not actively, sympathetic to European fascism. Much that the government was doing had needed to be done—a fact which nobody could deny, and which redounded to the everlasting discredit of the democratic parties. But it was ultimate ends that gave Argentines the feeling of uneasiness. If this government imposed itself, what would Argentina be in five—ten years? Another Italy?

In mid-October a large group of Argentina's most distinguished citizens signed a petition to the government, asking for a return to democratic processes and for a foreign policy of honest cooperation with the other American nations. The signatures were a roll call of the nation's most distinguished figures: university professors, elder statesmen, politicians, writers, scientists, they cut across party lines, and Radicals, Socialists, and Conservatives were mixed indiscriminately. The petition was of Socialist origin, but was in no sense a political document. Many of those who signed held government posts from the Castillo regime, the professors in particular. But the reaction of the Ramírez government was immediate and angry. All within reach of its anger paid for their exercise of free speech by losing their posts. It did not matter that one was the nation's most distinguished physiologist, a man of international reputation; that another was a university president; that all were household names to the Argentine people. While the nation watched numbly, those who had dared to ask for democracy were struck down by the revolution which crowds had welcomed only four months before with "Viva la democracia!"

The opposition went underground, and as it did so a surprising fact became clear: that only two major parties were effectively opposed to the regime, the *Socialists and the Conservatives.* Here was a juxtaposition that could only be astonishing to persons acquainted with the history of the last thirteen years, but that was immensely revealing as to the character and origin of the present government. Truth was that the Radical party would not be identified with the opposition, that it resisted all efforts to get it into an anti-government coalition, and that its leaders believed that sooner or later they would inherit the Ramírez revolution. They persisted in this belief even though no Radical held a government post, and even though there was no evidence national elections were to be called.

It will be remembered that the June coup was precipitated by the rumor that the Radical party was going to offer the presidential candidacy to General Ramírez. The Minister of War did not choose to wait for the outcome of a doubtful election, and took power by force. But the Radical party position had origins more complex than the accident that Ramírez might have been its candidate. The fact was that the revolution was a middle-class seizure of power from the landed oligarchy: denied entrance by the front door, the middle class had entered by the rear. Thirteen years of fraud and systematic frustration had left the democratic majority among Argentina's middle millions disorganized and without real hope of power. The thirties had also convinced a minority of the middle class that democracy was a cheat. In the army hierarchy, which was a stronghold of the Argentine bourgeoisie, middle-class resentment, nationalism, and a belief in direct action fused. The army dictatorship was middle-class because the dictators were middle-class, because their outlook was bourgeois: they did not love the landed oligarchy nor the economic regime this stood for; they feared the working class and were determined to make only such concessions as were necessary in order to keep it satisfied without altering in any way its fundamental position of subservience; they feared leftist revolutionary ideologies which could in any way rob *them*—the middle class—of their comforts and prerogatives; they feared the postwar for what it could bring of social unrest and alien doctrines; they took power because they did not want another *Semana Trágica* that might grow to revolutionary proportions, and because they knew the Castillo regime was too weak and stupid to save Argentina from the cataclysm to come.

That was why Socialists, Communists, and Conservatives reacted together in a common gesture of self-defense, and why the Radicals were too confused to act. The nationalist government did not have the majority of the middle class behind it. But the quandary of the Radicals was real, for this government was their own child: a bastard perhaps—not publicly acknowledged certainly—but their own. The Radicals could not like the partners the Ramírez government had drawn into the coalition. There was too much of the *niño bien* element from impoverished landed families, there were too many fanatical Catholics and Hispanists, and there were the ruffians of the Alianza de la Juventud Nacionalista. The common denominator in the whole nationalist hodgepodge was a shared frustration. They were politically frustrated. They found their roads to power blocked by the old, the cynical, and the tired in all parties. They shared an envy of the small minority that owned all the land. Here there was a perfect coincidence of views between the middle class who had never owned land, and the impoverished sons of bankrupt estancieros, who no longer owned land. The partnership between British capitalists and Argentine estancieros to exploit the public was galling because they had no share in the benefits. And finally, the nationalists had gone right rather than left because they did not identify themselves with the working class, for whom they had only contempt. There was little real difference between the economic programs of right and left—both were against foreign capital, against the political stranglehold of the landholding classes, and for the public ownership of utilities; but they differed fundamentally in that the Communists wanted a thorough revision of social relationships, while the nationalists wanted to create for themselves a system of social privilege. There was nothing they feared more than a working-class revolution.

The whole device of intervention by which succeeding Argentine executives had more and more centralized power was employed full force against any institution or province that might provide a focus of resistance to the nationalist revolution. In the view of the intellectuals of the new regime, control of education was fundamental to its success. On October 15 the anti-Semitic Dr. Gustavo Martínez Zuviría, who had been head of the National Library under Castillo, and who wrote books under the name "Hugo Wast," was made Minister of Justice and Public Instruction and began the active spiritual renovation of Argentine universities. Almost within the week of taking office he had a student strike on his hands. Students of the Littoral University (located in Rosario and Santa Fe) objected to their fascist interventor, Dr. Jordán Bruno Genta, signed a democratic manifesto, and were expelled. Although all the university interventions antedated Martínez Zuviría's assumption of office, he was by far the most nationalist and fascist-minded man to hold the portfolio of education; and he was determined to break the opposition in the universities.

The student strike spread quickly. After 190 chemistry students were expelled by Genta from the Littoral University, the Federación Universitaria of Córdoba staged a twenty-four-hour sympathy strike. The national Federación Universitaria Argentina (F.U.A.) issued a manifesto. "We saw our ideals betrayed on June 4th," it said, "—our country sold out and isolated from its sister republics." Four months after coming to power the government "threatens to plunge the nation into the darkness of tyranny, to divide Argentines, to annul all liberties and destroy the democratic basis of our nationality. . . . What we students want is the unity of the nation and freedom of its inhabitants, without distinctions of race, creed, or religion." Sovereignty? Yes, but with "that sense of American unity whose first lesson was taught us by José de San Martín." [9]

The national government had a weapon against rebellious students, a weapon so strong that in the history of the Argentine universities no individual, and no group, had been able to stand out against it. The weapon was that monopoly on higher education by the state which deprived every expelled student of the possibility of an education. To enter the profession of engineering, teaching, law, or medicine, one needed a university degree; to obtain the degree one had to graduate from a national university; and to graduate one had to receive the political stamp of approval of the government in power. Against this rock the Reform had broken time and again. In the struggle with the nationalist government the Reform was represented by the Federación Universitaria, which was its creation. The new government intended not only to break the F.U.A., but to end the Reform. On October 28 Martínez Zuviría ordered the universities closed. It was only a month before examinations, and the only protest possible to the F.U.A. was to stay away from the November finals. The Minister of Education knew this would hurt the strikers more than the government; and he ordered that those who stayed away from examinations should be suspended on the ground that their lack of interest showed they had mistaken their calling. Nevertheless, when November came, the majority of students at La Plata, Santa Fe, and Córdoba refused to attend examinations, and those who did were so badly treated by their fellows that they had to be protected by the government. Only at the University of Buenos Aires, whose Law School had gradually come to be the intellectual seat of Argentine nationalism, did the majority of the students take their finals. Across the Andes, the liberal Republic of Chile offered the hospitality of its universities to all the suspended students.

In October, unrest became strong in the ranks of labor. One of the first acts of the Ramírez government on taking power had been to intervene in all unions, put them under army control, and confiscate their funds. Leaders suspected of leftist tendencies were sent to prison in Neuquén or Río Gallegos, in Patagonia. Argentine labor had never been strongly militant, but suddenly trouble broke out which mere repression could not solve. Ten thousand packing-house workers went on strike in La Plata, and the trouble spread to Avellaneda and Buenos Aires, until nearly twenty-five thousand workers were out. The government made arrests by the hundreds. Finally, on November 5, it solved the problem by the kind of direct action which would occur to the military mind: the police at gun point rounded up all men in worker's clothes that they found in the streets and herded them into the Armour and Swift frigoríficos. The stratagem worked, and the strike was broken.[10]

Simultaneously a strike broke out among construction workers in the beach resort of Mar del Plata. The issue seems to have been bicycle license fees, but the strike threatened to tie up the resort precisely at the opening of the season—which would have greatly incommoded the middle and upper classes of Buenos Aires, who migrate *en masse* to Mar del Plata during the hot summer months. The government took a serious view of the question, and again solved it by mass arrests.[11]

Thus far the nationalist government had no answer to the labor problem beyond the crudest repression. But if the majority of the *militares* were so shortsighted, the shrewd Juan Domingo Perón was not. So far his position in the government had been extra-official: as leader of the G.O.U. he was a power behind the scenes. But on October 28 the government created a National Department of Labor directly responsible to the President, and Perón was put at its head. He was known best by the rumors about him. Among the known facts were his activities in the Uriburu revolution, his job as teacher of military history, his service in Chile as Argentine military attaché, his two years of study in Germany and Italy, 1937–1939. Among the rumors was the story that he had been declared *persona non grata* by the Chilean government for espionage, and had left under a cloud. But the point on which most rumors agreed was that it was he who really ran the government. Curious to know the truth, Abel Valdés, editor of *El Mercurio* of Santiago, Chile, called on Colonel Perón and had a long interview.

Was it true, he asked, that Colonel Perón really ran the country?

"Don't pay any attention to those stories," the Colonel replied, "because they are nothing but rumors, like most of what you will hear in Buenos Aires."

Perón expressed his opinions freely. "I personally believe in corporate unions,* and as such I am anti-Communist, but I believe that labor should be organized under the government so that the workers and not the leaders and agitators may have the greatest benefit from their efforts. That is why I consider the National Labor Department so important that I have taken it under my own direction; and I believe it should be organized as a ministry, which will be done as soon as it is possible. . . . I am determined," he went on heatedly, "that the riches of our country shall remain among us, so that each Argentine may benefit more and more from his labor. That is why I shall not allow elements of dissolution and agitation, which in the majority of cases are not even Argentine, but foreign and without respect for the nationality of my country."

Valdés led the conversation to the subject of big business. He had noted, he told Perón, a certain coldness toward the present government in various "spheres of great economic power . . . that would not be at all displeased if the present Argentine government should fall." Perón laughed at first, then became angry. "We are interested in the progress of our country," he replied, "and in this labor we shall not permit capitalist interference. In the previous cabinet there was a minister who genuinely represented the great economic interests, many of which are foreign.† Personally, I be-

* What Perón said was *soy sindicalista;* but the rest of the sentence makes it clear that he had in mind government-controlled unions like those in Italy.

† Perón was referring to Jorge Santamarina, who had recently resigned as Minister of Finance. Santamarina was the first, the last, and the only member of the Ramírez government left over from the Conservative oligarchy. A member of one of the outstanding landed families, Santamarina had been president of the Banco de la Nación during the Castillo government.

lieve that that gentleman was above reproach; but he should have attended to the Ministry of Finance and not have tried to meddle in our foreign policy. It is natural this should have occurred, because the powerful foreign interests, which in Argentina have been used to dominating on the level of a real economic dictatorship, took advantage of that gentleman's presence to increase their intolerable pressure. So that when American or other foreign capital tried to change our foreign policy, we had to tell the Minister of Finance: 'No, sir: You are in the Ministry of Finance—but don't think you are going to run Argentine foreign relations.' He resigned, and the foreign policy of my country, which will not be altered to suit any capital, is that which Minister General Gilbert has fixed. . . . Now," he concluded, "if the gentlemen of money think we are going to fall, they are mistaken. *We shall see who is going to fall.*"

Valdés left the interview thoughtful. "My impression," he wrote, "is that if things continue as they are going, and if there are no international complications, Colonel Juan Perón may very shortly be the greatest caudillo in the Argentine Republic—and who knows for how long?"[12]

FOREIGN AFFAIRS

In October the cabinet ceased to represent anything but nationalism. In that month the last three moderates were ousted,* and Brigadier General Alberto Gilbert was called to fill Storni's place in the Ministry of Foreign Relations.

National policy was now a choice between extremes of nationalism. Within the army camarilla, a behind-the-scenes struggle for power was going on. On the one hand was Perón, a fanatic nationalist, and on the other Minister of the Interior Luis César

* Minister of Finance Jorge Santamarina, Minister of Justice and Public Instruction Elbio Anaya, and Minister of Public Works Ismael Galíndez.

Perlinger, also a fanatic nationalist. Of the two fanatics, Perlinger was considered to be the more extreme because he advocated outright confiscation of foreign companies; but the real struggle was not a political one, but one for power. Perón wanted to rule. So did Perlinger.

Where foreign policy was concerned, the nationalists were in perfect agreement. Their efforts centered on building a politico-economic bloc of states in the southern part of the continent, strong enough to defy the United States and to "defend" itself against Brazil. In its essentials the idea was the old one of the "reincorporation" of the Viceroyalty of the Río de la Plata: of Uruguay across the river, and Paraguay and Bolivia to the north. Slightly more elaborated, it was the dream of the nationalist economist Alejandro Bunge of uniting Argentina, Uruguay, Paraguay, Bolivia, and Chile in a customs union. Bunge believed that this wedding of agricultural and mineral economies would give the union virtual self-sufficiency: that the small nations united would outweigh the ever menacing and fabulously wealthy neighbor, Brazil. Brazil was the *bête noire* of Argentine imperialists. Among army men, it was an obsession. So long as Brazil remained a menace, Argentina could never be sure of her continental leadership. And Brazil, larger in area than the United States, three times as populous as Argentina, rich in minerals as Argentina was poor, and with a growing and prosperous industry, was an obstacle too large to be avoided.

Bunge's dream became a distinct possibility when the Ramírez government signed treaties first with Chile and then with Paraguay providing for eventual customs union. Chilean Foreign Minister Joaquín Fernández y Fernández visited Buenos Aires in September, and Paraguayan President Higinio Morínigo in November. Each was fêted and accorded all honors. Morínigo would have been quite willing to agree to a customs union on the spot, for his little country, long a vassal of Argentina, had suffered from Argentine tariffs on yerba mate. Both treaties merely specified future negotiations on the question of a zollverein. But they represented forward steps.

Relations with Uruguay were another and a very different problem. Uruguay was a buffer state between Brazil and Argentina, created to serve as a buffer, and with the psychology of a buffer. It was England which had created Uruguay to guarantee international navigation of the Río de la Plata. Had Uruguay joined the Argentine Republic, the Plata would have been an interior river, hence closed to foreign shipping. The tiny republic, smaller than the one Argentine province of Buenos Aires, had survived only by keeping on good relations with her two big neighbors, and because they had kept the peace. Uruguay is indistinguishable from Argentina in speech, ethnology, topography, or economy. It is a continuation of the pampa, it bred the same gauchos, raises the same cattle, is white like Argentina, has had the same Italian immigration, shares the same customs. Buenos Aires is the mecca of the *orientales,** who think it the finest city in South America. Nevertheless, the tiny republic is very jealous of its independence, and has preserved it by letting itself be entangled with neither Argentina nor Brazil, and by assiduously cultivating the friendship of the most powerful nation in the hemisphere, which is the United States.

The coming to power of a nationalistic and militaristic dictatorship in Argentina caused the greatest alarm in Montevideo. Uruguay knew the dangers of a war with Brazil: that such a war would necessarily be fought on her soil. And she knew that the men now in power in Buenos Aires had for years advocated the restoration of the Viceroyalty of the Río de la Plata. Uruguay was constructing air and naval bases throughout her territory as a measure of national and hemisphere defense. Two of the airdromes—one at Carrasco and one at Melilla—were being built by American engineers; and at Laguna del Sauce, near Montevideo, United States specialists and machinery were building one of the largest air and naval bases on the continent.[13] The small republic was well aware that, should the Argentine government choose to consider such activity as unfriendly, a serious crisis would result.

* Uruguayans: from the name of the country, *República Oriental del Uruguay* (Eastern Republic of the Uruguay).

Under the Pan American conventions, bases throughout the hemisphere were open to all the American republics, and Argentina knew as well as Uruguay that American ships and planes used the Montevideo base. But could Uruguay afford to forgo American protection in order to appease her neighbor? That was the dilemma.

Within Uruguay there was a large and militant fifth column that stood ready to help Argentina take over the country. They were followers of Luis Alberto Herrera, who owned the Montevideo daily *El Debate*, and their Senate leader was Eduardo Víctor Haedo. The Herreristas were numerically few: out of thirty Senate seats they controlled seven, and in the Chamber of Deputies they held twenty-three seats out of ninety-nine. But they were extremely vocal, and were in such close contact with the Argentine military that they constituted a real threat to the nation.

Thus, at the southern tip of the continent, Argentina was turning her foreign policy to the creation of a strong system of states under her leadership. But in the north lay the greatest stumbling-block to her ambitions. What of the United States?

Argentina, not only under the Ramírez government but under the Conservative government that preceded it, had an almost unbroken record of bad relations with the United States. But they were rapidly nearing the point of breakdown. The nationalists who were now in power had no more use for the United States than they had for England. Yet Argentine shipments of meat, grains, dairy products to both countries were booming. The entire meat production was going to Britain to feed the Allied armies, and the United States was paying the bill under Lend-Lease. The nationalist government knew that they had a trump card here: in a hungry world, nobody could afford to boycott so essential an exporter of foodstuffs. If the Argentine beef market were shut, the United States would have to supply the meat herself, a measure that would cut internal consumption of meat in the United States by 25 per cent.

On the other hand, the nationalists were uneasy at talk in the United States of freezing Argentine funds. Argentina had a gold balance of nearly a billion pesos in New York.[14] Afraid that economic action by the United States might mean loss of this money, the government in October began repatriation of the gold from the Federal Reserve Bank of New York to the Central Bank in Buenos Aires.

For months Argentina had been under virtual blockade by the United States. Argentina was the only country in the hemisphere that had not broken with the Axis, the only one where Axis agents were free to operate, where blacklisted firms were patronized by the government. With each passing month less and less in the way of necessary supplies reached Buenos Aires. Motors were breaking down for lack of replacements, cars were going off the streets for lack of tires, industrial expansion had reached its limit for lack of machinery. Although the United States was taking everything it could get in the way of needed food supplies, it was shipping back only gold bars: the gold that had so fascinated the Castillo government, gold that the country could not wear as clothes, burn as fuel, nor drive as transportation. How long could the nationalists withstand the pressure? Their last hope was to drive a wedge between Britain and the United States. They knew from experience that the two nations had always worked at cross purposes in the Río de la Plata, and that it had been the tacit policy of the British to keep Argentina out of the Pan American fold. Would Britain follow the United States blockade, or would she take advantage of the bad feeling to consolidate her own postwar position in the Argentine market? It was not Britain which had objected to the Argentine policy of neutrality, as the Argentines very well knew.

But in January, 1944, the Ramírez government suddenly capitulated. Fearful that the United States was going to order the freezing of all Argentine funds, and discouraged by the virtual economic blockade, President Ramírez on January 26 announced to the world that Argentina had severed diplomatic relations with the Axis. For Ramírez and his Foreign Minister, Alberto Gilbert, it was too late. They had long since alienated the democratic elements in the country by their nationalist program, and no belated gesture was likely to win them popular support. And on the other hand, by capitulating to American pressure they cut themselves off from the die-hard nationalists in their own government. In the city of Tucumán Dr. Federico Ibarguren, the nationalist interventor, ordered all flags flown at half-mast in mourning for the "humiliation" of his country. At the University of Tucumán the interventor, Dr. Santiago de Estrada, ordered all university offices closed, and sent in his resignation to the Minister of Education. Only General Rawson from Brazil sent his congratulations to the President, and he was so instantly and crushingly rebuked by Ramírez himself that he was forced to resign his ambassadorship.

In Buenos Aires the first reaction of such die-hards as Martínez Zuviría and Perlinger was to resign; but within a month the G.O.U. had taken over the government. On February 16 the rightists seized power in a bloodless coup, and Ramírez was out. In his place was his "constitutional" successor, Vice-President Edelmiro Farrell, a convenient front man for the G.O.U., and the nationalists were more securely in the saddle than they had ever been. But now there could be no question as to this government's foreign policy. Britain, the United States, and most of the American embassies ceased to have any relations with the Casa Rosada, and Argentine foreign relations entered a twilight period when foreign ambassadors, continuing to reside in the country, pretended the government did not exist.

TOWARD THE CORPORATE STATE

> *The internal organization of the army is conceived with an authentic organic-social feeling and is an exemplary seat of discipline, camaraderie, patriotism, hierarchy, and respect. There there exist neither unjustifiable postponements nor undeserved promotions. The scale is followed without exceptions or privileges, with a strict sense of selection and justice which neither is nor can be—nor do we wish it to be—the exclusive benefit of the armed forces, but is rather a social conquest for all Argentines.*
>
> —Juan Domingo Perón, May 1, 1944.

On the building of the new National Labor Department, once the seat of the Buenos Aires City Council, the government engraved this motto: "We seek to suppress the class struggle, supplanting it by a just agreement between workers and employers, in the light of the justice emanating from the state." [15]

That justice which was to emanate from the state was now the concern of Juan Domingo Perón. It was clear from his statements that he had no patience with autonomous unions, which to his mind were political weapons for anarchists and Communists; but it was to become clear from his actions that if he demanded state control of all labor organizations, he also believed in the concrete betterment of wages, working conditions, and standards of living. The condition which Perón faced when the National Labor Department was created was one of widespread rebellion by labor. Unions had suffered interventions, their funds had been confiscated, their leaders were in prison or in exile. The government had absolutely forbidden them to act in politics. Taking over from this point, Perón set out to give them substantial pottage in exchange for their birthright. Argentine labor had heard much about freedom, justice, and the class struggle from its leaders, but had received remarkably little in the way of bread. Perón decided to give it bread.

The new chief of the Labor Department worked around the

clock studying conditions of farm labor, of labor on the railroads, of the Cajas de Jubilación (pension funds), which were in a state of virtual bankruptcy. The government had already increased the wages of municipal and national employees, adopting the policy of the family wage, which meant that a man with children got more pay than one with no family. This was in accord with the best Catholic doctrine, and with the new government policy of encouraging "births rather than immigration." The nationalists wanted a big population without risking the importation by foreigners of exotic doctrines to the Río de la Plata.

Within a few months of taking office, Perón had set minimum wage and work standards for agricultural labor, which had long been the most neglected part of the working class. He ordered the British-owned railroads to grant wage increases to their employees, a measure that to the nationalists meant killing two birds with one stone: they pleased Argentine railroad workers, and got in a blow at the hated British capital. Government and railroad pension funds were taken over by the government,[16] thus giving hope at last to thousands of retired workers that they would get the pensions that they had been paying for during their working years, and that had been denied to them on retirement because the funds were virtually in a state of bankruptcy. For the first time, Argentina was given a civil service: the government established job tenure, retirement pay, and disability insurance among public employees.[17]

All these social measures were long overdue. Perón had taken away the autonomy of the unions; but he was gambling on the concrete social gains to win labor's support. The working class had seen its rents lowered by 20 per cent, its wages raised, its children provided for, food prices pegged, and tenure and pensions guaranteed. It did not matter that the measures were at best palliatives, or that the destruction of labor's right to social protest might mean far less possibility of gain in the future. It did not matter that the government's ultimate objective was total control of the working class under a system of discipline and hierarchy. It did not matter that, in the end, this was Mussolini's corporate state. The point was, Juan Argentino had more food under his belt and more money in his pay envelope, and under "democracy"—if that was what you could call all that had gone before—he had had nothing at all.

"We have proclaimed the right to better conditions of life," Perón told Córdoba workers, "and nothing shall stop us in the task of making them possible. Nearly a million workers in city and country, men who work with their brains, men who work with their muscles, already enjoy the benefits to which I refer. . . . While enterprises flourish, the men who gave their best energies to make them great decline through lack of foresighted and humane legislation. . . . We legislate for all Argentines, for the present and for the future, so that the inevitable convulsions of the postwar period shall not shake our country through its failing to realize those precepts of social justice whose absence we could never justify to our consciences and to history." [18] Perón began to call himself "the first worker of Argentina." On July 8, 1944, when he took over the office of Vice-President, delegates from forty unions (in all of which the government had intervened) stood outside the Casa Rosada to cheer him.* At noon, as he was taking the oath of office, railroad workers stopped all trains for half an hour to demonstrate their solidarity.

But the subjugation of labor was only one aspect of a total effort at the control of all segments of political, social, and economic life. On January 1, the papers published a decree dissolving all political parties, and a few days later the nationalist groups were ordered to close down. The move was a prelude to the creation of a single party, and the inclusion of the nationalists in the political ban was never intended as a reflection on them, as the President's secretary, Enrique P. González, made quite clear a few days later: "Perhaps because of a certain ambiguity of expression in the press

* Among the unions: Railroad Workers' Union, Federation of Catholic Professors and Teachers, Municipal Employees and Workers, Federation of Brewery Workers, Tramway Workers' Union, Bakers' Federation, Garment Workers, Taxi Drivers' Union, Argentine Telegraph Operators' Association, personnel of the Molinos del Río de la Plata (Bunge y Born company), Argentine Dentists' Federation, Port Workers of the Capital, Argentine Teachers' Union, Autonomous Butchers' Union, Swineherds' Union, moving picture extras, Federation of Workers' Associations, Glassworkers' Union, Posts and Telegraph Workers, Union of Government Workers and Employees.

communiqué it was possible to infer that the nationalist groups were being put in the same category as political parties," he said. But this was not so. "The terms 'venality' and 'fraud' and 'political corruption' do not refer to them. The nationalist groups are made up of young men, full of spirit, of self-esteem, of great patriotism, and they felt hurt by the lack of clarity in the communiqué . . . but I must say that the nationalist groups were by no means dissolved because they were considered as a perturbing element or one lacking in moral values." [19] Let the nationalists then take heart. *They* were not the "perturbing element": the "perturbing element" was democracy.

While the nationalist government was silencing political opposition from the democratic parties, it attacked the hegemony of the landed class on all fronts. With the end of the Conservative party went the end of the instrument through which the landed oligarchy had ruled Argentina. But the nationalist government went further than mere political attack: it lent effective aid to the one economic segment that was becoming strong enough to challenge the cattle barons, which was industry. In April it issued a decree setting up an Industrial Credit Bank to make loans available for long-term development.[20] The Bank, with a capital of 50,000,000 pesos, was to have a directorate representing the Ministry of Finance, the Ministry of Agriculture, the Ministry of War, the Ministry of the Navy, the Banco de la Nación, the Banco Central, and the Unión Industrial Argentina.[21] Behind the action was the obsession of "national defense": as Perón said at the dedication of the chair of National Defense at the University of La Plata, "National defense demands a powerful industry, and not just any kind, but heavy industry." [22] But indirectly the whole impulse of the nationalists toward industrialization was aimed at cutting the umbilical tie with England, at putting an end to the cycle of sending raw materials to Europe and getting them back processed. That was the cycle by which the landed oligarchy had existed and grown fat.

For all their talk of criollo virtues, of *Argentinidad,* for all their glorification of gaucho virtues, and their desire to return to the

Golden Age of Juan Manual de Rosas, the nationalists had little use for the landed oligarchy. In their minds the landholding aristocracy stood not for the pristine gaucho virtues, but for the despised liberalism of the Unitarios, and for the ninety years of Anglo-Argentine bilateralism. The rule of the Enlightened Oligarchy had meant free trade, foreign capital, political and economic liberalism, and a turning away from the stern Catholic and Spanish tradition of the Sword and the Cross. "What is called the Enlightened Oligarchy," *El Federal* * sneered, ". . . has been the most disastrous group of men the nation has ever had, worse even than the Unitarian oligarchy, which could not survive against the popular and traditionalist caudillos. . . .

"What was enlightened about that oligarchy? Mitre, Sarmiento, Avellaneda: let them pass, they were personalities of undisputed stature. But the rest? What is the intellectual standing of the Quintanas, the Figueroa Alcortas, the Sáenz Peñas, the Uriburus, the Pellegrinis, the Rocas? They are people who have not bequeathed anything either to Argentine or to classic culture. . . . The famous Enlightened Oligarchy was nothing but a group of clubmen, Voltairians, supposedly of progressive and liberal ideas, imitators of French and English salons, and many of them without the slightest roots in the Argentine patriciate. . . . Their only function in the state was by means of decrees and laws to turn over (at times without even realizing it) all our communications, our agriculture, our mineral wealth, our cultural formation—our schools, and even our public opinion, newspapers—to the all-embracing rule of British capital." [23]

The government showed little concern for the traditional privileges of the landlords of Argentina. Not only did one of its first decrees lower urban rents, but in December, 1943, land rents on the farms and estancias of Buenos Aires, Santa Fe, Córdoba, Entre Ríos, San Luis, and Santiago del Estero were lowered 20 per cent.[24] The government said land was overvalued, which was true;

* In January, 1944, *El Pampero* was suppressed by the Ramírez government as a gesture of appeasement to the Allies; but it reappeared within a few days under the new name *El Federal*.

but this measure was a direct blow at the pocketbooks of the gentry who for generations had lived on the incomes derived from renting their land to tenants. Few of the landholding aristocracy worked their own estancias. The tenant farmers were a prosperous rural middle class, and the land decree benefited them directly.

The pattern of government action was clear. It aimed at the totalitarian state, and not just any kind of totalitarian state (for all the hue and cry in the American press, the nationalists cared nothing for Nazi Germany): it was to be a Catholic, corporate state, founded on Hispanic tradition, and based on the social precepts of the Church. In the United States, accustomed to thinking of a landed aristocracy as the bulwark of Catholic reaction, the Argentine pattern was confusing, and there were many who mistakenly believed (and wrote) that the nationalist revolution was a grab for power by the landholders. Nothing was further from the truth. In Argentina the landed oligarchy stood for liberalism in its purest nineteen century concepts: for noninterference by the Church in the State; for republican government based on limited suffrage; for free speech; above all, for free trade and economic laissez faire. The rise of nationalism meant the end of government by and for the estancieros.

From the first the new state sought support from the Church. Traditionally, the Argentine clergy did not mix in politics except extraofficially; and this sudden embrace from the secular power did not meet with immediate and enthusiastic response from the Church hierarchy. Ramírez showed his Catholicism by taking a priest, Father James Wilkinson, to the Casa Rosada with him; but Father Wilkinson soon left. Far more significantly, the government decreed what had been forbidden by law in Argentina: compulsory religious education in all the public schools. A papal nuncio had once been expelled for asking religious instruction. Now, for the first time in the history of the Argentine Republic, it was not only to exist but to be compulsory. In what is surely one of the most remarkable decrees of the nationalist regime, the measure was based on Article 76 of the Constitution (which specifies that the President must be a Catholic), saying that "the official school without religion is anti-democratic and unconstitutional, that it does not prepare the child for the supreme honor to which every Argentine may aspire, that is, to be President of the nation." [25]

The decree fell like a bombshell on the country. It was a dramatic and complete reversal of the whole trend of a century. Since 1884 it had been unlawful to give any religious instruction during school hours; since 1904 it had been a punishable offense to give it to children whose parents had not previously requested it.[26] Argentina had maintained as complete a divorce between Church and State as a Catholic country can: secular education, secular cemeteries, civil marriage. Ex-President Castillo, who was living in retirement in the country, gave an interview to the New York *Herald Tribune* in which he not only attacked the decree on compulsory religious instruction, but added: "I hope I am mistaken, but I fear I am right when I say civil war appears likely very soon." [27]

The clergy was very much divided on the national government's efforts to associate itself with Catholicism. Although Cardinal Luis Copello congratulated the President on the decree, there was a widespread uneasiness among the Catholic hierarchy, which remembered the Spanish Civil War too vividly to enjoy being associated in the popular mind with an unpopular government. "The independence of the Church is above all else," Monseñor Alfonso Buteler, Bishop of Mendoza, warned *Acción Católica*. "Let us take care not to create by our attitudes certain ties and understandings in the eyes of society, by which the Church never gains and almost always loses." [28] Democrats like Monseñor Miguel de Andrea gave thinly veiled speeches on human liberty. But there were no veils on the policies of the men in power. They were going to make Argentina over in the image of the Catholic, Hispanist corporate state: a state where each class had its hierarchy and accepted it, and where Marx's class struggle was relegated to the past tense, not for lack of anything to struggle for, but for lack of the instruments or the right to make protest felt. The government motto was simple and austere: *Honesty, Justice, Duty*. It was engraved on postage stamps for all to read.

THE NATION IN ARMS

> *The words "national defense" may make some of you think this is a problem whose presentation and solution are of interest only to the nation's armed forces. The truth is very different: into its solution go all the inhabitants, all their energies, all their wealth, all their industries and production, all their means of transport and communication, the armed forces being merely . . . the fighting instrument of that great whole which is "the nation in arms."*—PERÓN, dedicating the chair of National Defense at the University of La Plata, June 10, 1944.

The economic program of the nationalists had five clear objectives. First, and essential to the rest, was to cut the tie with England once for all by ending the exchange of Argentine raw products for British manufactures. Second was to take over all public utilities which were in foreign or in Jewish hands: this meant smashing the street railways, the railroads, and the big grain middlemen. Third was to "develop" the "vast" mineral deposits in the Andes, the coal and iron which wishful thinking had put there, and the potential hydroelectric power which was there. Without these it would be impossible for Argentina ever to match her rival, Brazil, as a power on the continent. Fourth—and the others were directed to this—was to create a powerful industry, and above all, a *heavy* industry in the nation. This would put an end to the colonial economy which, for more than a century, had benefited only one class, and brought poverty to other classes and weakness to the nation as a whole. And finally, the nationalists proclaimed the intention of developing a real balance between the impoverished interior and the rich and proud capital city, where all the wealth and power of the country had been gathered into a few hands. This was the program, and it was not an end in itself. Colonel Mariano Abarca, Director General of Industries in the reorganized Ministry of Agriculture, explained the end clearly to the Unión Industrial (Argentina's National Association of Manufacturers). "Modern warfare," he said, ". . . requires a sound and strong economy and industry. An efficient army and navy are not enough to keep a nation free and sovereign, because they would be like a coat of mail on a body unable to carry it. We must develop an athlete in armor to insure our country's freedom; in other words, *the country must be made strong economically*." [29]

If Argentina was to be free of Britain at war's end, it was imperative to cut the tie of mutual indebtedness that held the nations together. Britain had her vast investment in government bonds and public utilities, and so long as Argentina had to carry the burden of interest and profit payments—in 1942 the service on the foreign debt alone came to a billion pesos [30]—it was imperative to have sterling exchange, which meant selling to England. This was the reason why the estancieros had never seriously tried to nationalize the railroads when they were in the government: their meat trade depended on keeping Argentina in debt to Britain. But it was not *selling* to Britain that the nationalists objected to. It was the price of keeping that market, which meant the bilateralism of the Roca-Runciman Pact. Now, during the war, Argentina was piling up so many hundreds of millions of pesos of blocked sterling exchange in London after four years of selling without buying in return, that the nationalist government had the solution. It could retire its British debt with the blocked sterling exchange. Unless it did, when the war was over Argentina would have to buy almost everything she imported in Britain to liquidate it.

Between December, 1943, and April, 1944, the Argentine government embarked on the repatriation of 500,000,000 pesos of her British debt. What had been an external debt became an internal one, the Central Bank issuing 4 per cent bonds to cover the operation.[31] This was merely the largest and latest of a series of moves to take advantage of war prosperity to end foreign indebtedness. But, even before this operation, the rise in the value of the peso and the retirement of foreign debts had reduced the external service spectacularly: from 1,063,000,000 pesos in 1942, it had dropped to 797,000,000 in 1943.[32]

The public debt was only one item in the sterling exchange

problem. Far bigger, not only financially, but socially, was the problem of the semi-bankrupt British utilities: the railroads, with their obsolete rolling stock, the tram lines, the gas and light companies. For years they had been draining money from the country and giving the worst possible service in return. They had been the particular *bête noire* of both the left and the right. The nationalists decided to expropriate.

In Buenos Aires the national government took over the British gas company, the Compañía Primitiva de Gas, offering less than a tenth of what the company claimed it was worth,* and put an end to the autonomy of the virtually bankrupt Corporación de Transportes for failure to meet bond payments.[33] The capital of the Corporación was written down from 326,875,000 pesos to 169,927,000 pesos.[34] So far as the railroads were concerned, the handwriting was on the wall. They were ordered to pay all the back wages they had been allowed to retain from their employees since 1934, a sum that now totalled 64,000,000 pesos.[35] This was a double blow by the nationalists: financially, it was almost enough to sink the railroads, and was an excellent weapon to bring them to terms on expropriation; and on the other hand, the measure increased the government's popularity with the powerful railroad workers' union.

American capital did not escape. In the province of Tucumán the nationalist interventor, Alberto Baldrich, ordered expropriation of two subsidiaries of the American and Foreign Power Company, the Compañía Tranvías Eléctricos de Tucumán, and the Compañía Hidroeléctrica de Tucumán. Both companies had long been under fire for their wretched service and high rates, but the seizure was motivated by the xenophobia of the nationalists. Baldrich in his

* The company claimed a value of 43,064,051 pesos (*La Nación*, May 4, 1944). The government allowed a value of 19,201,579, but deducted from that 15,442,839 for the cost of removing the installations from the streets (not that the government was going to remove them). This left 3,758,740 for the company (*La Nación*, Apr. 18, 1944). Although there is little doubt that the government was taking advantage of the company, there is little reason to believe the company had not long ago amortized its original investment, which amounted to only 256,266 gold pesos (*Noticias Gráficas*, May 2, 1944).

decree of expropriation of the Hidroeléctrica explained the act on the ground that "almost all the shares . . . are in the hands of a company incorporated outside the country," [36] which for him was reason enough. In Entre Ríos the nationalist interventor expropriated another American and Foreign Power subsidiary, the Compañía de Electricidad del Este Argentina.[37] The expropriation was accompanied by nationalist demonstrations in the city of Paraná, where crowds stoned the offices of the liberal dailies *El Diario* and *La Acción*.[38] In Buenos Aires the national government ordered the Post Office Department to study plans for the nationalization of the Unión Telefónica, a subsidiary of International Telephone and Telegraph.[39]

But not only was the government out to break foreign capital: it was equally determined to break the national capital that was the other side of the coin, the men who had a monopoly on cereals, the gigantic conservative fortunes of the Bembergs, the Hirsches, the Dreyfuses. On April 20 the Buenos Aires and La Plata grain elevators of Bunge y Born, De Ridder, Dreyfus, La Plata Cereal, were declared public utilities and expropriated.[40] Two months later, on Otto Bemberg's fifty-seventh birthday, police entered the office of the Crédito Industrial y Comercial Argentino, heart of the Bemberg empire, forced him to open his safes, and took all that they could find: piles of stocks and bonds that reached from the floor to the ceiling, including government securities, shares in the Unión Telefónica, all the privately held stock of the Corporación de Transportes, and bars of solid gold.[41] The government intended to find out at last just what the Bembergs were worth, and get to the bottom of the extraordinary inheritance of Otto Sebastián, whose heirs had claimed the decade before that their father had left them only 600,000 pesos. If fraud could be proved, the Bemberg family might owe the national treasury nearly 200,000,000 pesos. The blow at the cereal middlemen and at the Bembergs was another example of killing two birds with one stone. Having grain elevators as publicly owned utilities could only benefit the country, just as getting inheritance tax from the Bembergs would fill the treasury; but here, too, was an excellent chance for the anti-Semites in the government to get in a blow at Jewish capital.

The third and fifth points of the nationalist program—development of mineral and power resources, and of the interior provinces —went together: "We want to locate factories near raw materials," Juan D. Pistarini, Minister of Public Works, told the people of Córdoba; "and that can be done by giving industry abundant power at low cost." He spoke at the dedication of a dam on the Río Segundo which would be one of the largest in the western hemisphere when it was completed. "The work has another importance from the national point of view: we want to reduce the congestion of industries in the littoral and locate them in the interior, bringing about a better general economic equilibrium for the country." [42]

The search for minerals in the Andes was redoubled. In the government's mind was the tantalizing vision of national self-sufficiency—the same chimera of autarchy which Mussolini's Italy had pursued to its ruin. "We must be self-sufficient: that is our motto!" Lieutenant Colonel Alejandro G. Unsain, vice-president of the Argentine Chamber of Mines, told the Unión Industrial. ". . . A country cannot become industrialized unless mineral production is previously assured. The example of Japan admits of no reply. That far eastern country developed a heavy industry which depended largely on the acquisition of scrap iron in the United States. This industrial error led Japan inevitably to war." [43] Or, what was more to the point, defeat. With military men in all branches of government, and as interventors in private institutions, thought on all subjects came eventually to the same point: the nation's fitness and preparation for war.

The keystone to the preparedness program was the creation of a strong industry. Argentine industry, which had grown up in depression and burgeoned in war, thanks to the now total breakdown in world trade, would be in peril when peace returned. It was in no position to compete with cheaper and better products from abroad. An estanciero's government would have let it wither as it grew—and good riddance. To the cattlemen the trade with

England was more important than local manufacture. But the nationalists were determined not to let their infant industries go by default, and on June 7, 1944, made public a decree on industrial development and defense. The measure provided for additional tariffs, import quotas, and production subsidies to industries of "national interest." These were defined as those using Argentine raw materials exclusively, and those necessary to national defense.[44] "World economy is tending toward a more uniformly distributed industrialization," Abarca told the Unión Industrial. "General industrialization does not mean a decrease in foreign trade; on the contrary, trade will be more active, although the movements from one market to another will consist preferentially of finished goods and not raw materials. For example, Argentina will give preference to the exportation of linseed oil and not linseed, of shoes and not hides, and so forth. . . . In the twentieth century all countries are trying to process their own raw materials; they know that they can obtain very low prices by direct sale; they know on the other hand that when they are industrialized they will not only manufacture their own products but utilize by-products which will give employment to their labor; and furthermore, they know that self-determination is possible only when a country has all that is necessary for existence. Everybody now knows that a country has either the economy of a colony or that of a world power. . . . Peoples, like individuals, have to win their political and economic freedom. The first may be won by arms, and the second by work; one requires a revolution, and the other an evolution, but in some cases also a revolution."[45]

The Argentine nationalists, to judge from what they said, had a mercantilist concept of the state. They sought a stronger economy, more wealth, a healthier, better paid citizenry to serve the ends of the powerful national state. In short, the national economy was not an end in itself, but the means to "national defense." Not only did they insist on the theme of a strong industry as an aspect of "the nation in arms," but they set out to create an arms industry. An American article on Argentina used a phrase that stuck in the military craw: "Fortunately for Argentina's neighbors," it said, "its army is a lion without teeth." [46] A few weeks later Perón was in Córdoba to dedicate an airplane made by Fritz Mandl's Impa Corporation. The former Austrian munitions king was now making arms for the new government. Asked by a bystander what "DL" on the plane's wing stood for, Perón replied that it might mean "Dele, dele!" (Give it to him!), or it might—here, perhaps, a malicious twinkle—stand for *dientes del león* (lion's teeth).[47]

On all sides there were evidences of Argentine rearmament. Backbone of the program was Mandl's Impa Corporation, formed with joint private and government capital, and including Impa Aeronáutica, Impa Central, and Impa San Martín.[48] Eighty establishments were put to work turning out thirty-five-ton "Nahuel" tanks (from the Indian word for tiger).[49] The government expropriated all materials necessary for "national defense": at will the army could take private automobiles, tires, spare parts, binoculars, theodolites, even wagons and leather and canvas products.[50] The university students' freedom from more than three months of military service was ended by decree.[51] Now officer candidates would take their year's training like anyone else. In a year the army was doubled in size, and it became a crime to publish reports in the press of army promotions, the organization of commands, military contracts, military works, garrison movements, or arms.[52] Military roads were built to the Paraguayan frontier, to the frontier with Brazil.

Chile grew worried at the string of garrisons being set up in the Andes, stretching from San Juan and Mendoza to southernmost Patagonia. In Mendoza and San Juan the 16th and 22nd Infantry Regiments were sent to Uspallata and Barrial. To Junín de los Andes, in Neuquén, went the 26th Infantry. To Bariloche and Esquel, territory of Río Negro went the 21st. And in Chubut and Santa Cruz, in the southern end of Patagonia, the 25th Infantry was set up in Puerto Deseado, the 8th in Comodoro Rivadavia, and the 24th in Río Gallegos. To the archipelago of Tierra del Fuego went a unit from the 24th. In Corrientes and Misiones, facing Paraguay and Uruguay, a new division, the 7th, was created.[53] Now the government could say that every territory and province of the Republic except La Pampa had a garrison of troops. But La Pampa did not touch any foreign border.

When July 9, 1944, gave the new government a chance to stage the traditional military parade in honor of Argentine independence, Argentines and foreigners were astonished at the display. There were tanks, planes (five of them Argentine-made), artillery and motor repair shops, parachutists, air-borne troops, white-clad mountain units. Ten Nahuel tanks were on display: weighing thirty-five tons, they had a speed of forty kilometers an hour, and carried a 75-millimeter cannon, a 13-millimeter machine gun, three 8-millimeter machine guns, and a crew of five men. Six of the planes that flew over Buenos Aires towed three gliders apiece.[54] On the reviewing stand, beside the President and ministers, stood Senator Eduardo Victor Haedo of Uruguay, guest of honor.

If Argentine and foreign observers were impressed, so were Argentina's neighbors. In Uruguay, Haedo's militant fifth column attacked Yankee bases on the Río de la Plata and spoke out for union with Argentina. In Paraguay there were rumors of Morínigo's imminent fall, to make room for a more manageable Argentine puppet. In Chile, the Senate went into secret session with the Foreign Minister, Joaquín Fernández y Fernández, over Argentine military preparations and the new mountain garrisons. What did they mean? Was it merely, as Perón insisted, that a disarmed Argentina was bringing her military establishment up to parity with her neighbors'? [55] Or did warlike preparations add up to war? In the southern end of the continent tension mounted. What was going on under the military hats in Buenos Aires could only be surmised, but outsiders occasionally got a glimpse, as when the incautious Juan Domingo Perón, dedicating a chair of National Defense at La Plata, told his audience:

"Many believe in the possibility of world peace, but it has never been achieved. . . . Peoples which have neglected their defense preparations have always paid for their error by disappearing from history, or falling into the most abject servitude. . . .

"I have tried, during the course of my talk, to put over these ideas: (1) That war is an inevitable social phenomenon. (2) That the so-called pacifist nations, as ours is, if they want peace had best prepare for war. (3) That national defense is a problem involving all activities; that it cannot be improvised in the moment of war, but is the work of long and conscientious years of preparation; that it cannot be accomplished unilaterally, by the armed forces alone, but must be done through the combined efforts of government, of private institutions and all the Argentine people; that its problems are so diverse and require such technical skills that no capacity or intellect can be dispensed with; and finally, that its demands will only contribute to the increased greatness of the nation and to the happiness of its sons." [56]

From the skies over Buenos Aires, on the first anniversary of the revolution that put the army into power, war planes dropped leaflets: "The Americans say that Argentina is a tiger [*sic*] without teeth. But we shall have teeth, and well clenched." [57]

Convinced that it was useless to hope for a return to reason in Buenos Aires, the United States recalled Ambassador Norman Armour, and he was followed out of Argentina by virtually every representative of the American republics and the United Nations. Argentina faced the future alone.

THE SCARLET AND THE BLUE

> *June 4 is the return to Rosas without Don Juan Manuel. It is the absolute negation of our historic past. . . . It is the counter revolution, the anti-Argentine counter revolution. . . .*
>
> —*El Himno Nacional*, May, 1944.

The Argentine Republic, the liberal, free-trading nation that had built on blooded beef and land, that had been thirteen years dying, came to an end on June 4, 1943. Whether the nationalists ruled or fell, whether they gambled their country's future on a crazy military adventure, whether, even, they led it to a bloody and tragic civil war, the revolution of June 4 had written *Finis* to the Republic of 1853.

For nearly a century Argentina had been the special preserve of the men who owned her land. Legislation served their needs, reflected their philosophy, and assured the economic order on which their wealth was based. Until 1930 there was no more generous land on earth for immigrant and foreigner alike. There, that liberalism which had been the glory of the best nineteenth century thought assured them the freedom to worship as they wished, to build their fortunes and to speak their minds, so long as they did not seriously challenge the economic and political order on which the state was built. That order was assured by the tie to Britain that kept open the beef market, and by the limitations on suffrage that assured political rule by the Enlightened Oligarchy.

But the world changed, and Argentine Conservatism did not. The tides of European immigration brought thousands of new people to the Plata for whom there could be no place without a fundamental change in the landholding system. World depression and the breakdown in trade put an end to that freedom of interchange on which the whole Argentine-British relationship had been built. New industries and new industrial fortunes meant a fundamental shift in economic power. The day the landowners lost control of the nation's purse, it was certain that their hold on politics must follow. But for thirteen years the Conservatives had hung on by sheer audacity, unwilling to face the change that had to come.

Both the Right and the Left saw it. But where the Socialists and Communists wanted a fundamental change in all the social and political and economic relationships—the break-up of the latifundia, universal suffrage, creation of a new and balanced economy between Buenos Aires and the interior, between agriculture and industry—the nationalists were in their hearts as fearful of real revolution as the Conservatives. The nationalist revolution was the full turn of the wheel back to Rosas. It was the scarlet, blind nationalism, xenophobia, dictatorship, clericalism, authoritarianism, denying all that had come to Argentina with its immigrants. As

Education Minister Alberto Baldrich told the students of Cuyo University, "It would not be out of place if the program of the new generation permitted us to return to the traditional cultural sources of Argentine strength—the old Spanish-creole trunk, born in Spain, the only medium for making youth understand the high mission of this country among the nations, and the Christian and heroic conception of living." [58] Yet the very men who proclaimed the criollo virtues bore names that proclaimed their immigrant origins: Peluffo, Pistarini, Farrell, Teisaire, Mason, Ameghino, Perlinger. It was not that they loved the aristocracy the more, but that they loved the rabble less.

In 1853 the blue banner of the liberals had driven the red from Buenos Aires. The red was back, presiding at the grim funeral of Argentine Conservatism. But where could it lead, and what future did it offer? What had Argentina been under the scarlet flag of Rosas? Isolated from the society of nations, backward, feudal, stricken with terror, suspicious of foreigners, without railroads, telegraphs, gas, or running water, it represented the purest criollo virtues of the nationalist mythology. Now the twentieth century Rosistas had had a chance to observe streamlined dictatorships, and they were talking of industrialization, rearmament, and power politics. Power politics? War? With a nation of *thirteen million people?* Yet the men of government had vowed to put an end to immigration. On the first anniversary of the revolution schoolteachers throughout the Republic had to chalk this motto on the blackboard: "Argentina for the Argentines, because only they created it, defended it, and are worthy of it." [59] Megalomania could lead a nation to war, but megalomania could not conjure up the iron and coal of a heavy industry, the technics of warfare, the soldiers for foreign conquest, or the wealth to make victory possible. If what the nationalists were aiming at was military domination, they would lead their nation to certain and irrevocable ruin.

But they were not the voice of the people. In the last days while expression was still free, they had not been able to muster a tenth, not a twentieth of the Argentines. Now the democratic parties had gone underground, and for the first time since Echeverría's little band had met secretly in the Buenos Aires of Juan Manuel de Rosas, there was an Asociación de Mayo, publishing its clandestine paper, *La Voz de Mayo*. Arrayed against the nationalists were all the forces in the country except their own: the landed Conservatives, the democratic majority of the middle class, the Socialists, and the Communists. Perón had taken over the Confederación General del Trabajo and robbed the unions of their autonomy, but they, too, had gone underground. The liberals, the intellectuals, the social reformers were in prison or in exile, and now from Montevideo, as they had a century before, the progressive forces of Argentina fought the reaction in their country. They knew that their country had a great and peaceful destiny if she would be true to it, but it was not that of the narrow horizons of Juan Manuel de Rosas. There were many who had seen it, and some had broken their hearts over it. Their names were Bernardino Rivadavia, Domingo Sarmiento, Leandro Alem, Juan B. Justo, Lisandro de la Torre.

The democratic forces knew that they had betrayed themselves, and that it was they who had let the nationalists take power by default. The great question for Argentina was whether they had learned their lesson, and whether it was not too late to avert civil war. Would a nation as comfortable, as remote, and as prosperous as this wartime Argentina have the courage of its real faith, or would it be betrayed again, as it had been for so long, by the vast apathy of the well fed? Eduardo Mallea had put it very well:

> *For a country to achieve a great destiny it must have suffered intensely. Only tenors are trained while listening complacently to their own singing. . . .*

ACKNOWLEDGMENT

I wish to thank Radcliffe College for the money that made possible my two years in Argentina. I wish to express my gratitude in addition to the many persons and institutions whose kindness and help were invaluable: to Sr. Carcavallo of the Seminario de Ciencias Jurídicas y Sociales of the Buenos Aires Law School for his suggestions on the finding of materials; to the librarians of the Ministry of Foreign Relations, the Banco Tornquist, the Banco Central, and *La Prensa* for their help with bibliography; to the United Press for its permission to use the files of its mailer service; to *La Nación* for the use of its archives; to the Buenos Aires National History Museum, and the Colonial and Historical Museum of Luján for permission to photograph their engravings.

I wish also to thank Mr. William Bristol of the University of Pennsylvania for making available his studies of Hispanism; Mr. Robert A. Rennie of Harvard University for his invaluable help on the economic aspects of Argentine history, especially the period of the Noventa; Dr. Nicolás Repetto for his many personal kindnesses and attentions; and the unnumbered friends in Buenos Aires and in the provinces whose honesty and intelligent criticisms made it possible for me to see and understand much that I should never have known about without them.

FOOTNOTES

The Setting

1. Domingo F. Sarmiento, *Facundo*, in *Obras de D. F. Sarmiento* (Santiago de Chile, 1889), VII, 19.
2. William McCann, *Two Thousand Miles' Ride Through the Argentine Provinces* (London, 1853), I, 157.
3. Sarmiento, *op. cit.*, 19.
4. Wilfrid Latham, *The States of the River Plate* (London, 1866), 13–14.
5. J. A. B. Beaumont, *Travels in Buenos Ayres* (London, 1829), 21.
6. Pedro Inchauspe, *Voces y Costumbres del Campo Argentino* (Buenos Aires, 1942), 81.
7. W. H. Hudson, *The Naturalist in La Plata* (London, 1892), 207.
8. *Ibid.*, 264.
9. *Censo Agropecuario, 1908* (B.A., 1909), 11.
10. Beaumont, *op. cit.*, 64.
11. *Ibid.*, 42.
12. *Ibid.*, 63.
13. McCann, *op. cit.*, 157.
14. *Ibid.*, 155.
15. Sarmiento, *op. cit.*, 46.
16. T. J. Hutchinson, *Buenos Aires and Argentine Gleanings* (London, 1865), 48.
17. Beaumont, *op. cit.*, 65.
18. McCann, *op. cit.*, 102–103.
19. Inchauspe, *op. cit.*, 106–107.
20. Alfredo Ebelot, *La Pampa* (B.A., 1890), 53.
21. McCann, *op. cit.*, 161.
22. Beaumont, *op. cit.*, 35.
23. Figures of the League of Nations, 1936, in Emilio Llorens, *El Subconsumo de Alimentos en América del Sur* (B.A., 1941), 38–40.
24. Hutchinson, *op. cit.*, 51.
25. *Ibid.*, 123.
26. E. Vera y González, *Historia de la República Argentina* (B.A., 1926), XI, 128–129.
27. Ebelot, *op. cit.*, 15–20.
28. Lucio V. Mansilla, *Una Excursión a los Indios Ranqueles* (B.A., 1939), I, 30.
29. Woodbine Parish, *Buenos Ayres and the Provinces of the Rio de la Plata* (London, 1852), 101–106.
30. *Ibid.*, 103.
31. Francis Bond Head, in *Buenos Aires Visto por Viajeros Ingleses, 1800–1825* (B.A., 1941), 66.
32. Samuel Haigh, in *Buenos Aires Visto*, etc., 73, 76.

33. *Ibid.*, 79.
34. J. P. Robertson, in *Buenos Aires Visto*, etc., 59.
35. *Ibid.*, 58–59.
36. Samuel Haigh, in *Buenos Aires Visto*, etc., 59.
37. Parish, *op. cit.*, 362–368.
38. Alexander Gillespie, in *Buenos Aires Visto*, etc., 21, 39.
39. Rodolfo Puiggrós, *La Herencia que Rosas Dejó al País* (B.A., 1940), 7, 18.
40. Beaumont, *op. cit.*, 133–136.
41. Puiggrós, *op. cit.*, 9–10.
42. U. S. Tariff Commission, *The Foreign Trade of Latin America* (Washington, 1940), Part II, Section I, 1–3.
43. McCann, *op. cit.*, 207–209.
44. Parish, *op. cit.*, 276–277.
45. Thomas Mannequin, *Les Provinces Argentines et Buenos-Ayres* (Paris, 1856), 19.
46. *Segundo Censo de la República Argentina, Mayo 10 de 1895* (B.A., 1898), 624–625.
47. Domingo F. Sarmiento, *Recuerdos de Provincia*, in *Obras*, III, 129.
48. Joseph Andrews, *Las Provincias del Norte en 1825* (B.A., 1915), 17–84.
49. Sarmiento, *Obras*, VII, 62.
50. *Ibid.*, 60–61.

Bloody Rosas

1. J. A. B. Beaumont, *Travels in Buenos Ayres* (London, 1828), 158-159.
2. Letter written from Mendoza Jan. 10, 1830, in *Gaceta Mercantil*, Feb. 17, 1830.
3. *Loc. cit.*
4. Beaumont, *op. cit.*, 101.
5. *Ibid.*, 127.
6. *Ibid.*, 130.
7. *El Diario*, special financial supplement, 1928. See also financial history of Argentina by José A. Terry in special supplement of *La Nación*, May 25, 1910. For law authorizing loan see *Registro Nacional*, II (1822-52), No. 1620.
8. William McCann, *Two Thousand Miles' Ride Through the Argentine Provinces* (London, 1853), I, 220.
9. Jacinto Oddone, *La Burguesía Terrateniente Argentina* (B.A., 1930), 47-64.
10. Adolfo Saldías, *Historia de la Confederación Argentina* (B.A., 1914), I, 15.
11. D. F. Sarmiento, *Obras* (Santiago, Chile, 1889), VII, 73.
12. E. Vera y González, *Historia de la República Argentina* (B.A., 1926), XI, 146.
13. Sarmiento, *op, cit.*, 72.
14. José M. Paz, *Memorias* (B.A., 1917), II, 135.
15. *Ibid.*, I, 166.
16. Rodolfo Puiggrós, *La Herencia que Rosas Dejó al País* (B.A., 1940), 17.
17. *Ibid.*
18. Letter to Doña Josefa Gómez, March 2, 1869. From the private archives of Adolfo Saldías. In Saldías, *op. cit.*, I, 15.
19. Vera y González, *op. cit.*, XI, 39.

20. Beaumont, *op. cit.*, 59, 73.
21. McCann, *op. cit.*, I, 220.
22. Woodbine Parish, *Buenos Ayres and the Provinces of the Rio de la Plata* (London, 1852), 114.
23. Vera y González, *op. cit.*, XI, 133.
24. Parish, *op. cit.*, 116.
25. Puiggrós, *op. cit.*, 151.
26. Vera y González, *op. cit.*, XI, 231.
27. *Gaceta Mercantil*, Dec. 31, 1830. Italics my own.
28. Jacinto Oddone, *El Factor Económico en Nuestras Luchas Civiles* (B.A., 1937), 190-191.
29. Vera y González, *op. cit.*, XI, 151-152.
30. *Censo Agropecuario 1908* (B.A., 1909), III, 69.
31. Vera y González, *op. cit.*, XI, 242.
32. *Ibid.*, 277.
33. José Ingenieros, *La Evolución de las Ideas Argentinas* (B.A., 1920), II, 34.
34. Verse 4. *Gaceta Mercantil*, Aug. 2, 1843.
35. Ingenieros, *op. cit.*, 528.
36. *Ibid.*, 533.
37. Oddone, *op. cit.*, 236.
38. *Ibid.*, 238-239.
39. Parish, *op. cit.*, 358.
40. Paz, *op. cit.*, II, 386.
41. Vera y González, *op. cit.*, XII, 26.
42. Esteban Echeverría, *Dogma Socialista* (B.A., 1915), 183.
43. *Ibid.*, 102-103.
44. J. M. Gutiérrez, "Vida de Echeverría," in *ibid.*, 50.
45. Ingenieros, *op. cit.*, II, 89.
46. Echeverría, *op. cit.*, 89.
47. Vera y González, *op. cit.*, XII, 294.
48. Paz, *op. cit.*, II, 454–456.
49. Vera y González, *op. cit.*, XI, 416.
50. Letter to Urquiza, Yungay, Oct. 13, 1852. In D. F. Sarmiento, *Las Ciento y Una—Polémica con Alberdi* (B.A., 1939), 58.
51. *Ibid.*, 37.
52. Lucio V. Mansilla, *Una Excursión a los Indios Ranqueles* (B.A., 1939), I, 178.
53. *Ibid.*, 185–186.

The Land—I

1. J. A. B. Beaumont, *Travels in Buenos Ayres* (London, 1828), 34.
2. Wilfrid Latham, *The States of the River Plate* (London, 1865), 33.
3. William McCann, *Two Thousand Miles' Ride Through the Argentine Provinces* (London, 1853), I, 161.
4. Rodolfo Puiggrós, *La Herencia que Rosas Dejó al País* (B.A., 1940), 19–22.
5. *Ibid.*
6. Adolfo Saldías, *Historia de la Confederación Argentina* (B.A., 1911), I, 10. I, 10.

7. T. J. Hutchinson, *Buenos Ayres and Argentine Gleanings* (London, 1865), 29–32.
8. Latham, *op. cit.*, 114.
9. Jacinto Oddone, *La Burguesía Terrateniente Argentina* (B.A., 1930), 74–83.
10. *Ibid.*, 84.
11. Miguel Angel Cárcano, *Evolución Histórica del Régimen de la Tierra Pública 1810-1916* (B.A., 1925), 113.
12. Antonio Zinny, *Historia de los Gobernadores de las Provincias Argentinas* (B.A., 1879), I, 186-190.
13. Oddone, *op. cit.*, 93–118.
14. *Ibid.*, 145.
15. *Twentieth Century Impressions of Argentina* (London, 1911), 275.
16. *Informe de las Condiciones Financieras, Comerciales, etc., de la República Argentina, Recopilado en 1866 por el Sr. D. Francisco Clarc Ford*, 8–9.
17. Woodbine Parish, *Buenos Ayres and the Provinces of the Rio de la Plata* (London, 1852), 357.
18. Emilio Lahitte, *Informes y Estudios de la Dirección de Economía Rural y Estadística* (B.A., 1918), II, 4.
19. McCann, *op. cit.*, I, 67–68.
20. Heriberto Gibson, "La Evolución Ganadera," in *Censo Agropecuario 1908*, III, 70.
21. Godofredo Daireaux, "La Estancia Argentina," in *ibid.*, III, 8.
22. Gibson, *loc. cit.*, 78.
23. Latham, *op. cit.*, 34.

Urquiza and the Liberals

1. D. F. Sarmiento, *Recuerdos de Provincia*, in *Obras* (Santiago, 1885), III, 130.
2. *Ibid.*, 131.
3. Aníbal Ponce, *Sarmiento* (B.A., 1938), 32.
4. *Ibid.*, 180.
5. *Ibid.*, 95.
6. D. F. Sarmiento, letter to Urquiza, Oct. 13, 1852, in *Las Ciento y Una* (B.A., 1939), 39.
7. E. Vera y González, *Historia de la República Argentina* (B.A., 1926), XII, 164.
8. "Acusación del General Urquiza contra el Dr. d. Evaristo Carriego. Defensa en l[a] instancia hecha por el defensor del acusado, Dr. d. Manuel G. Argerich. Buenos Aires, Oct. 9, 1866." In *Antecedentes para el Proceso del Tirano de Entre Ríos, J. J. de Urquiza* (B.A., 1867), 103.
9. Vera y González, *op. cit.*, 158.
10. J. B. Alberdi, *Bases y Puntos de Partida para la Organización Política de la República Argentina*, in *Obras Completas* (B.A., 1886), III, 427.
11. *Ibid.*, 430.
12. *Ibid.*, 432, 434.
13. Vera y González, *op. cit.*, 342.
14. Sarmiento, *Las Ciento y Una*, 55.

15. Agustín Rivero Astengo, *Hombres de la Organización Nacional* (B.A., 1937), 81.
16. *Ibid.*, 252-254.
17. Raúl Scalabrini Ortiz, *Historia de los Ferrocarriles Argentinos* (B.A., 1940), 85.
18. *Primer Censo de la República Argentina . . . de 1869* (B.A., 1872), xviii, xx.
19. Ministerio de Hacienda, *La Población y el Movimiento Demográfico* (B.A., 1940), 146.
20. *Ibid.*, 12.
21. Alberdi, *op. cit.*, 527.
22. Vera y González, *op. cit.*, 358.
23. *Sesiones del Congreso Legislativo sobre la . . . Ley Estableciendo Derechos Diferenciales* (Paraná, 1856), 9, 11.
24. V. Martin de Moussy, *Description Géographique et Statistique de la Confédération Argentine* (Paris, 1860), II, 514.
25. *Ibid.*, II., 549, 563, 569–570.
26. J. A. Alsina, *La Inmigración Europea en la República Argentina* (B.A., 1898), 50–52.
27. Moussy, *op. cit.*, II, 325.
28. *Ibid.*, II, 287, 329–330.
29. *Ibid.*, 175–198.
30. *Ibid.*, I, 552–553.
31. *Ibid.*, III, 703–704.
32. Scalabrini Ortiz, *op. cit.*, 23.
33. *Twentieth Century Impressions of Argentina* (London, 1911), 273.
34. *Ibid.*, 275.
35. Alberdi, *op. cit.*, 434.
36. J. B. Alberdi, *Autobiografía* (B.A., 1927), 262–264.
37. *Censo General de la Provincia de Buenos Aires . . . de 1881* (B.A., 1883), xxxii–xxxiii.

Civilization and Barbarism

1. Sarmiento-Mitre *Correspondencia, 1846–1868* (B.A., 1911), 182, 179.
2. D. F. Sarmiento, *Aldao y El Chacho* (B.A., 1938), 64–65.
3. Lucio V. Mansilla, *Retratos y Recuerdos* (B.A., 1927), 24.
4. Sarmiento, *op. cit.*, 69.
5. Sarmiento-Mitre *Correspondencia*, 251.
6. E. Vera y González, *Historia de la República Argentina* (B.A., 1926), XIII, 209.
7. Aníbal Ponce, *Sarmiento* (B.A., 1938), 172.
8. *Primer Censo de la República Argentina . . . de 1869* (B.A., 1872), xviii.
9. Ministerio de Hacienda *La Población y el Movimiento Demográfico* (B.A., 1940), 12.
10. *Primer Censo . . . de 1869*, xxxvi, xlix–l.
11. Mansilla, *op. cit.*, 25.
12. Paul Groussac, *Los que Pasaban* (B.A., 1939), 150.
13. M. G. and E. T. Mulhall, *Handbook of the River Plate Republics* (London, 1875), 22.

14. Luis H. Sommariva, *Historia de las Intervenciones Federales en las Provincias* (B.A., 1929), I, 409.
15. *Obras de D. F. Sarmiento* (Santiago, 1889), L, 330.
16. Sommariva, *op. cit.*, 410.
17. *Ibid.*, 427.
18. Ponce, *op. cit.*, 197.
19. Groussac, *op. cit.*, 165.
20. A. de Nevers, *Atentado a la Constitución Nacional Argentina y su Consecuencia, la Revolución de Setiembre de 1874* (B.A., 1876), 31.
21. Eduardo E. Ramayon, *Adolfo Alsina, Ministro de Guerra en Campaña, 1876* (B.A., 1939), 20.
22. Letter of Alsina to Roca, Oct. 6, 1875, in Manuel J. Olascoaga, *La Conquista del Desierto: Estudio Topográfico de la Pampa y Río Negro* (B.A., 1940), I, 19–21.
23. Lucio V. Mansilla, *Una Excursión a los Indios Ranqueles* (B.A., 1939), II, 18–19.
24. Roca to Alsina, Oct. 19, 1875, in Olascoaga, *op. cit.*, I, 24, 25, 27.
25. Leopoldo Lugones, *Roca* (B.A., 1938), 181.
26. Olascoaga, *op. cit.*, I, 210.
27. *Ibid.*, 201.
28. Eduardo Racedo, *La Conquista del Desierto: Memoria Militar y Descriptiva de la 3ª División Expedicionaria* (B.A., 1940), 21.
29. Olascoaga, *op. cit.*, 202–203.
30. Elvira Aldao de Díaz, *Reminiscencias sobre Aristóbulo del Valle* (B.A., 1928), 103–104.
31. Sarmiento in *El Nacional*, July 18, 1879, quoted in Lugones, *op. cit.*, 204–205.

THE LAND—II

1. Alejo Peyret, *Una Visita a las Colonias de la República Argentina* (B.A., 1889), 209–210.
2. *Ibid.*, 214–216.
3. *Ibid.*, 219–220.
4. *Ibid.*, 6–12.
5. J. A. Alsina, *La Inmigración Europea en la República Argentina* (B.A., 1898), 192–197.
6. José Mendelson, "Génesis de la Colonia Judía de la Argentina (1889–1892)," in *Cincuenta Años de Colonización Judía en la Argentina* (B.A., 1939), 112.
7. *Ibid.*, 113–118.
8. Antonio Gómez Langenheim, *Colonización en la República Argentina* (B.A., 1906), 160–165.
9. *Ibid.*, 166.
10. D. G. de la Fuente, *Tierras, Colonias y Agricultura: Recopilación de Leyes, etc.* (B. A., 1894), 52–54.
11. Jorge M. Bullrich, *La Evolución de los Valores de los Campos en la República Argentina* (B.A., 1935), 3.
12. *Ibid.*, 3.

13. Jacinto Oddone, *La Burguesía Terrateniente Argentina* (B.A., 1930), 195–196.
14. De la Fuente, *op. cit.*, 98–99.
15. *Ibid.*, 117–118.
16. *Ibid.*, 263, 296, 299.
17. Oddone, *op. cit.*, 197–198.
18. De la Fuente, *op. cit.*, 164.
19. Gómez Langenheim, *op. cit.*, 178–180.
20. Miguel Angel Cárcano, *Evolución Histórica del Régimen de la Tierra Pública 1810–1916*, (B.A., 1925), 411.
21. "La Industria Azucarera en Tucumán," in *La Argentina* (Tucumán), July 9, 1925.
22. *Memoria Histórica y Descriptiva de la Provincia de Tucumán* (B.A., 1882), 398–400.
23. *Ibid.*, 516–525.
24. Emilio Frers, *Cuestiones Agrarias* (B.A., 1918), II, 153.
25. Heriberto Gibson, "La Evolución Ganadera," in *Censo Agropecuario 1908*, III, 78.
26. *Ibid.*, 79.
27. Antonio M. Poy Costa, *Los Frigoríficos* (B.A., 1918), 8–10.
28. *Ibid.*, 12.
29. Juan E. Richelet, *La Ganadería Argentina y su Comercio de Carnes* (B.A., 1928), 34, 83.
30. José Hernández, *Instrucción del Estanciero: Tratado Completo para la Plantación y Manejo de un Establecimiento de Campo* (B.A., 1882), 50.
31. *La Prensa*, June 5 and 8, 1887.
32. Report of Dr. Carlos Remy, in Ramón Bidart, *La Fiebre Aftosa* (B.A., 1928), 8–9.
33. *La Agricultura y la Ganadería Argentinas* (B.A., n.d.), 64.
34. Richelet, *op. cit.*, 83.

Boom: 1860–1889

1. *Nuestra Industria Rural* (B.A., 1866), 43–44.
2. V. Martin de Moussy, "La Cordillera de los Andes," *Revista de Buenos Aires* (B.A., 1863), I, 39–44.
3. Raúl Scalabrini Ortiz, *Historia de los Ferrocarriles Argentinos* (B.A., 1940), 92–93.
4. *Ibid.*, 104, 113, 115.
5. *La Agricultura y la Ganadería Argentinas* (B.A., n.d.), 497–498.
6. William Rögind, *Historia del Ferrocarril Sud* (1937), 20–26.
7. Scalabrini Ortiz, *op. cit.*, 115–119.
8. *La Agricultura y la Ganadería Argentinas*, 491.
9. Scalabrini Ortiz, *op. cit.*, 129–133.
10. *Ibid.*, 136.
11. Cámara de Diputados, *Diario de Sesiones*, Sept. 3, 1909, II, 124.
12. *Ibid.*, 48–56.
13. Scalabrini Ortiz, *op. cit.*, 148, 154.

14. *Ibid.*, 48–56.
15. Cámara de Diputados, *op. cit.*, 115.
16. V. Martin de Moussy, *Description Géographique et Statistique de la Confédération Argentine* (Paris, 1860), I, 564.
17. *Buenos Aires Visto por Viajeros Ingleses, 1800–1825* (B.A., 1941), 79.
18. Woodbine Parish, *Buenos Ayres and the Provinces of the Rio de la Plata* (London, 1852), 116.
19. D. F. Sarmiento, *Life in the Argentine Republic* (N.Y., 1868), 11. This is Mrs. Horace Mann's translation of *Facundo.*
20. J. A. Alsina, *La Immigración Europea en la República Argentina* (B.A., 1898), 45.
21. Alfredo Ebelot, *La Pampa* (B.A., 1890), 173–174.
22. M. G. and E. T. Mulhall, *Handbook of the River Plate Republics* (London, 1875), 103 f.
23. Alsina, *op. cit.*, 39–43.
24. Damián M. Torino, *El Problema del Inmigrante y el Problema Agrario en la Argentina* (B.A., 1912), 47.
25. Benito Marianetti, *Los Trabajadores de la Industria Vitivinícola* (Mendoza, 1939), 42.
26. Ministerio de Hacienda, *La Población y el Movimiento Demográfico* (B.A., 1940), 146.
27. *Anuario del Departamento Nacional de Estadística Correspondiente a 1893* (B.A., 1894), 476.
28. Michael G. Mulhall, *The English in South America* (B.A., n.d.), 599–600.
29. *Segundo Censo de la R.A., 1895* (B.A., 1898), II, clxxvii; III, cxlii, cxliv.
30. José A. Wilde, *Buenos Aires desde 70 Años Atrás* (B.A., 1908), 22–25.
31. Manuel Bilbao, *Buenos Aires desde su Fundación hasta Nuestros Días* (B.A., 1902), 150.
32. *Ibid.*, 535.
33. T. J. Hutchinson, *Buenos Aires and Argentine Gleanings* (London, 1865), 57.
34. Bilbao, *op. cit.*, 210–224.
35. *Ibid.*, 533, 289, 496.
36. *Ibid.*, 188–193, 496.
37. Mulhall, *Handbook*, etc., 73–74, 80.
38. H. Armaignac, *Voyages dans les Pampas* (Tours, 1883), 74.
39. E. Vera y González, *Historia de la República Argentina* (B.A., 1926), XIII, 274–290.
40. Rögind, *op. cit.*, 74–76.
41. *La Prensa*, Jan. 1 and 2, 1890.
42. Santiago Alcorta, *La República Argentina en la Exposición Universal de París de 1889* (Paris, 1890), I, 12–15; II, 376.
43. *La Prensa*, Jan. 1, 1890.
44. Messages of Juárez Celman to Congress, 1887, 1888, 1889, in H. Mabragaña, *Los Mensajes, 1881–1890* (B.A., n.d.), IV, 188–189, 194, 223–228, 266, 300, 318.

The Noventa

1. John H. Williams, *El Comercio Internacional Argentino en un Régimen de Papel Moneda Inconvertible, 1880–1900* (B.A., 1922), 18–19.
2. *Anuario del Departamento Nacional de Estadística Correspondiente a 1893* (B.A., 1894), 473.
3. *Ibid.*, 365.
4. Williams, *op. cit.*, 44.
5. *La Prensa*, Mar. 4, 1890.
6. *Ibid.*, Jan. 1, 1891.
7. Juan Balestra, *El Noventa* (B.A., 1934), 70.
8. *Ibid.*, 63.
9. *La Prensa*, Jan. 1, 1890.
10. *Anuario . . . de Estadística*, 365.
11. *Estadística del Comercio y de la Navegación de la República Argentina Correspondiente al Año 1890* (B.A., 1891), 338–339.
12. Balestra, *op. cit.*, 70.
13. Cámara de Senadores, *Diario de Sesiones* (B.A., 1891), May 29, 1890, 38–39.
14. Francisco A. Barroetaveña, "La Unión Cívica," in Jorge W. Landenberger and Francisco M. Conte. eds., *Origen, Organización y Tendencias de la Unión Cívica* (B.A., 1890), xvi.
15. Manuel Gálvez, *Vida de Hipólito Yrigoyen* (B.A., 1939), 26.
16. Balestra, *op. cit.*, 57–58.
17. *La Prensa*, Jan. 1, 1891.
18. Letter of Lisandro de la Torre, May 17, 1937, in Elvira Aldao de Díaz, ed., *Cartas Intimas de Lisandro de la Torre* (B.A., 1941), 74–75.
19. Ismael Bucich Escobar, *Historia de los Presidentes Argentinos* (B.A., 1923), II, 290.
20. *La Prensa*, Jan. 1, 1891.

Hipólito Yrigoyen: The Rise and Fall of the Radical Party

1. Manuel Gálvez, *Vida de Hipólito Yrigoyen* (B.A., 1939), 32.
2. Lisandro de la Torre, "Página de Historia," *La Nación*, June 24, 1919.
3. *Ibid.*
4. *Anuario del Departamento de Estadística Correspondiente a 1893* (B.A., 1894), 473.
5. *Ibid.*, 365.
6. B. González Arrili, *Vida de Lisandro de la Torre* (B.A., 1940), 49.
7. De la Torre, *loc. cit.*
8. *Ibid.*
9. Elvira Aldao de Díaz, *Reminiscencias sobre Aristóbulo del Valle* (B.A., 1928), 102.
10. Emilio Frers, *Cuestiones Agrarias* (B.A., 1918), II, 120–121.
11. De la Torre, letter to Mariano Demaría, Rosario, Jan. 21, 1921, in De la Torre, *Las Dos Campañas Presidenciales (1916–1931)* (B.A., 1939), 148.

12. González Arrili, *op. cit.*, 76.
13. De la Torre, speech at Teatro Coliseo (Buenos Aires), Sept. 13, 1931, in *Las Dos Campañas*, 156.
14. Juan B. Justo, *El Socialismo Argentino* (B.A., 1915), 25.
15. Emilio Lahitte, *Informes y Estudios de la Dirección de Economía Rural y Estadística* (B.A., 1918), II, 4.
16. Cámara de Diputados, *Diario de Sesiones*, May 21, 1906, I, 98–100.
17. *South American Journal*, Oct. 24, 1942, p. 195.
18. *Tercer Censo Nacional . . . 1914* (B.A., 1916), V, 3.
19. Paul Groussac, *Los que Pasaban* (B.A., 1939), 426–427.
20. *Leyes Nacionales, 1911:* Laws 8129 and 8130.
21. De la Torre, letter to Demaría, in *Las Dos Campañas*, 145.
22. *Ibid.*, 122–123.
23. *La Prensa*, Oct. 13, 1916.
24. *Album Presidencial de la Reorganización Nacional, 1916–1922* (B.A., n.d.).
25. Jorge M. Bullrich, *La Evolución de los Valores de los Campos en la República Argentina* (B.A., 1935), 13–14.
26. Departamento Nacional del Trabajo, *Investigaciones Sociales, 1940* (B.A., 1941), 2.
27. U.S. Dept. of Commerce, Bureau of Foreign and Domestic Commerce, *The Economic Position of Argentina During the War* (Washington, 1920), 12.
28. F. A. Kirkpatrick, *South America and the War* (Cambridge, England, 1918), 38.
29. Luis M. Drago, "La Cuestión Internacional," *Anales de la Facultad de Derecho*, Vol. III, Ser. 3, 5–7.
30. *Album Presidencial.*
31. Virgil Salera, *Exchange Control and the Argentine Market* (N.Y., 1941), 28.
32. *Tercer Censo Nacional . . . 1914* (B.A., 1917), VIII, 207.
33. Julio V. González, *La Emancipación de la Universidad* (B.A., 1929), 246.
34. Julio V. González, *Principios y Fundamentos de la Reforma Universitaria* (1930), 19.
35. Austin F. Macdonald, *Government of the Argentine Republic* (N.Y., 1942), 170.
36. E. Vera y González, *Historia de la República Argentina* (B.A., 1926), XIII, 419.
37. Letter of Aug. 2, 1938, in Aldao de Díaz, *Cartas Intimas de Lisandro de la Torre* (B.A., 1941), 120.
38. This, and the subsequent chronicle of the Semana Trágica, are taken from *La Nación*, Jan. 4 to 15, 1919.
39. *La Nación*, Jan. 11, 1919.
40. *Ibid.*, Jan. 13, 1919.
41. *Ibid.*, Jan. 15, 1919.
42. Dr. Enrique Siewers, "Les Possibilités de Colonisation en Argentine," *Revue Internationale du Travail*, Oct., 1934, p. 13; Feb.–Mar., 1937, p. 41. Also, *Censo Agropecuario, 1937* (B.A., 1940), lviii–lxii.
43. *Crítica*, Sept. 13, 1930.
44. Salera, *op. cit.*, 40.

45. V. Gutiérrez de Miguel, *La Revolución Argentina: Relato de un Testigo Presencial* (B.A., 1930), 98–103.
46. De la Torre, letter of Feb. 16, 1934, in Aldao de Díaz, *op. cit.*, 43.
47. *Ibid.*, 43–44.
48. Gutiérrez de Miguel, *op. cit.*, 134.
49. De la Torre, *Las Dos Campañas*, 181–182.
50. De la Torre, speech in Córdoba, Oct. 13, 1931, in *ibid.*, 208–209.
51. De la Torre, *Otra Página de Historia* (1932), 12.
52. J. Beresford Crawkes, *533 Días de Historia Argentina* (B.A., 1932), 399.
53. De la Torre, *op. cit.*, 15.
54. *Pregón*, Jan. 5, 1939, quoted in Aldao de Díaz, *op. cit.*, 228.
55. De la Torre, *La Cuestión Social y un Cura* (B.A., 1943), 152.

The Struggle for Economic Sovereignty

1. *South American Journal*, quoted in *The Standard*, Apr. 8, 1941.
2. Ministerio de Agricultura, *Informe del Comité Mixto Investigador del Comercio de Carnes Anglo-Argentina*, 1938 (London, 1938), 8.
3. *La Ley de Coordinación de los Transportes Urbanos* (1936), 14.
4. Virgil Salera, *Exchange Control and the Argentine Market* (N.Y., 1941), 46.
5. *La Nación*, Nov. 25, 1932.
6. *Crisol*, Nov. 26, 1932
7. *La Vida de los Ferrocarriles y la Competencia en los Transportes: Memorial Presentado al Gobierno de la Nación Argentina por las Compañías de Ferrocarriles* (B.A., 1931), 7–8, 11.
8. *The Standard*, Apr. 8, 1941.
9. *Informe del Comité Mixto*, 8.
10. Telegrams of Jan. 7 and Feb. 10, 1932, published in the Senate *Diario de Sesiones*, Sept. 29–30, 1936, p. 1295.
11. Salera, *op. cit.*, 75.
12. Ministerio de Relaciones Exteriores, *Memoria Presentada al Honorable Congreso Nacional Correspondiente al Período 1933–34* (B.A., 1934), 464.
13. *Anuario del Comercio Exterior* (1940), lxv–lxxvii.
14. Salera, *op. cit.*, 81, 129.
15. Ministerio de Relaciones Exteriores, *op cit.*, 471–473, 486–487, 491–492.
16. *Daily Express*, May 1, 1933. *Daily Mail*, Apr. 28, 1933.
17. *Memoria de la Dirección General de Vialidad* (B.A., 1940), 76.
18. Rafael García Mata and Emilio Llorens, *Argentina Económica* (B.A., 1940), 175.
19. Cámara de Senadores, *Diario de Sesiones*, Sept. 28, 1936, p. 1278.
20. *Ibid.*, Sept. 29–30, 1936, p. 1306.
21. *Ley de Coordinación*, 5, 10, 49.
22. University of Buenos Aires, Facultad de Ciencias Económicas, Instituto de Economía de los Transportes, *Los Ferrocarriles Argentinos de Capital Privado en los Ultimos Once Años*, 1928–39 (B.A., 1940), 30.
23. Salera, *op. cit.*, 133.
24. Great Britain, Department of Overseas Trade, *Report* (Apr. 1938), 21–22.

25. *Crisol,* Nov. 26, 1932.
26. Quoted in *Noticias Gráficas,* Nov. 28, 1932.
27. Cámara de Diputados, *Diario de Sesiones,* Sept. 25–26, 1935, p. 349.
28. *Commercial Pan America: Annual Economic Survey of Latin America, 1940,* Vol. X, nos. 4, 5, 6 (Washington, 1941), 107–109. U.S. Tariff Commission, *The Foreign Trade of Latin America* (Washington, 1940), Part I, Section I, 62–63.
29. Pact of 1936, Art. 9.
30. For these figures I am indebted to the study made by Robert A. Rennie, of Harvard University.
31. Salera, *op. cit.,* 175.
32. *Ibid.,* 204.
33. *Memoria de la Dirección Nacional de Vialidad* (B.A., 1940), 77–79.
34. Salera, *op. cit.,* 205.
35. *Ibid.,* 216–217.
36. Hugo R. Iannini, *Comercio de Carnes Importadas en Inglaterra: Mercados de Smithfield* (B.A., 1936), 5.
37. Ministerio de Agricultura, *Informe del Comité Mixto Investigador del Comercio de Carnes Anglo-Argentino,* 1938 (London, 1938), 12–19.
38. *Ibid.,* 30–32.
39. *Ibid.,* 34–39.
40. *Ibid.,* 66, 127.
41. Cámara de Senadores, *Diario de Sesiones,* June 18, 1935, p. 191.
42. *Ibid.,* 197–198.
43. *Ibid.,* 220.
44. Lisandro de la Torre, *Investigación del Comercio de Carnes* (B.A., 1935), 212.
45. *Ibid.,* 20, 66, 68, 212.
46. Cámara de Senadores, *op. cit.,* July 23, 1935, xi–xii, Sept. 10, *et seq.*
47. De la Torre, *op. cit.,* 195.
48. Ernesto Tornquist y Cía, *Report on Business Conditions in Argentina,* No. 209 (Jan., 1936), 1.
49. Cámara de Diputados *Diario de Sesiones,* Aug. 28, 1942, pp. 2925–2926.
50. *South American Journal,* Oct. 24, 1942, p. 195.
51. Manuel A. Fresco, *El Negociado del Puerto de Rosario* (Oct., 1942), 10.
52. *La Vanguardia,* Sept. 28, 1939.
53. Testimony of Mario Bravo before the Constitutional Committee of the Chamber of Deputies, quoted in Benjamín Villafañe, *La Tragedia Argentina* (B.A., 1943), 220.
54. Elvira Aldao de Díaz, ed., *Cartas Intimas de Lisandro de la Torre* (B.A., 1941), 57.
55. *La Razón, Anuario 1938,* 15–16.
56. Aldao de Díaz, *op. cit.,* 61–62, 86.
57. *Ibid.,* 67–68.
58. *Ibid.,* 92.
59. B. González Arrili, *Vida de Lisandro de la Torre* (B.A., 1940), 298.

War

1. Cámara de Diputados, Comisión Investigadora, *Informe No. 2 (Sept. 5, 1941)*, 10.
2. *Ibid.*, 10, 11, 34, 36.
3. Cámara de Diputados, Comisión Investigadora, *Informe No.* 3 (Sept. 17, 1941), 41.
4. *Ibid.*, 12–13, 19–20.
5. *Ibid.*, 45–48. For much of my information about the nationalist press I am much indebted to Mr. William Bristol of the University of Pennsylvania, who has made a special study of Hispanism in Latin America.
6. *Informe No.* 2, 23. *Informe No.* 3, 37.
7. *La Razón, Anuario 1941*, 129.
8. *Crítica*, Dec. 7, 1941.
9. *Ibid.*, Dec. 16, 17, 1941.
10. *La Prensa*, Dec. 10, 1941.
11. Adolfo Lanús, *Campo Minado* (B.A., 1942), 117.
12. *La Nación*, Jan. 14, 1942.
13. *La Prensa*, Jan. 18, 1942.
14. *Crítica*, Jan. 18, 1942.
15. *Noticias Gráficas*, Jan. 24, 1942.
16. *Nueva Política*, No. 19 (Feb., 1942), p. 16.
17. *La Nación*, May 27, 1942.
18. *La Nación*, Sept. 10, 1942.
19. Report of the Comisión de Control de la Corporación de Transportes, quoted in *La Nación*, Aug. 27, 1943.

1943: Argentina on the Eve

1. Ministerio del Interior, Departamento Nacional del Trabajo, *Investigaciones Sociales* (B.A., 1940), 10–13, 28.
2. *Estadística Industrial de* 1939 (B.A., 1942), 29.
3. *Investigaciones Sociales 1940* (B.A., 1941), 58.
4. League of Nations Statistics, 1936, quoted in Emilio Llorens, *El Subconsumo de Alimentos en América del Sur* (B.A., 1941), 38–40.
5. Alejandro E. Bunge, *Una Nueva Argentina* (B.A., 1940), 167.
6. Emilio A. Coni, "Plan de Estudio Técnico sobre la Duración del Trabajo en la Agricultura," *Boletín Oficial de la Bolsa de Comercio del Rosario*, Feb. 28, 1935, pp. 7–13.
7. Juan A. Solari, *Trabajadores del Norte Argentino* (B.A., 1937), 55.
8. Alfredo L. Palacios, *El Dolor Argentino* (B.A., 1938), 87–93.
9. F. Rojas, "La Distribución de la Propiedad Territorial y el Desarrollo de la Industria Azucarera en Tucumán," *Argumentos*, Nov., 1938, p. 10.
10. Bunge, *op. cit.*, 167.
11. Nicolás González Iramain, *Tres Meses en Jujuy: La Intervención Nacional de 1942* (B.A., 1942), 170.
12. Solari, *op. cit.*, 80.

13. González Iramain, *op. cit.*, 41.
14. Palacios, *op. cit.*, 144, 115.
15. Solari, *op. cit.*, 14–15.
16. *Ibid.*, 21, 23, 32.
17. Cámara de Diputados, *Diario de Sesiones*, Sept. 14, 1942, pp. 3861–3862.
18. Figures of the Departamento de Estadística in *La Nación*, Sept. 3, 1943.
19. *Censo Nacional Agropecuario, 1937, Economía Rural* (B.A., 1940), lviii–lxii.
20. *Ibid.*, 5.
21. *Por los Trabajadores del Campo en Buenos Aires: Los Problemas del Agro en la Provincia* (La Plata, 1942), 18–20.
22. Jacinto Oddone, *La Burguesía Terrateniente Argentina* (B.A., 1930), 206.
23. Institut International d'Agriculture, *Annuaire International de Statistique Agricole 1938–1939* (Rome, 1939), 265–267, 281–285, 291.
24. Comisión Nacional del Azúcar, *Informe* (B.A., 1931), 19.
25. Solano Peña Guzmán, *Problemas Económicos de Tucumán* (1941), 118.
26. *Ibid.*, 64.
27. Emilio Frers, *Cuestiones Agrarios* (B.A., 1919), III, 304, 308–309.
28. José R. Rosenvald, *El Privilegio Azucarero y sus Deberes* (B.A., 1936), 12.
29. Cámara de Diputados, *Informe de la Comisión Investigadora de los Trusts* (B.A., 1919), 105.
30. Carlos D. Girola, *La Yerba Mate* (B.A., 1931), 3.
31. Ernesto Dumas, *El Problema de la Yerba Mate* (B.A., 1930), 7.
32. Veritas, Apr., 1942, pp. 395–436.
33. Benito Marianetti, *Los Trabajadores de la Industria Vitivinícola* (Mendoza, 1939), 7.
34. Ministerio de Hacienda, *Censo Industrial* de 1935 (B.A., 1938), 43. And *La Nación*, Sept. 3, 1943.
35. Ministerio de Hacienda, *Estadística Industrial* de 1939 (B.A., 1942), 43.
36. Ministerio de Hacienda, *Dirección General del Impuesto a los Réditos, Memoria*, 1941, 33.
37. *Ibid.*, 33.
38. *Censo Industrial* de 1935, p. 34.
39. *Estadística Industrial* de 1939, p. 40.
40. Unión Argentina de Asociaciones de Ingenieros, *El Momento Actual de la Construcción* (B.A., 1941), 27, 32–33.
41. Roque Paz, "El Grupo Bunge y Born en la Economía Nacional," *Argumentos*, Feb., 1939, pp. 304–313.
42. Ibid., 312–313.
43. Cámara de Diputados, *Diario de Sesiones*, Sept. 22–23, 1942, p. 4242 (speech of Américo Ghioldi).
44. New York *Herald Tribune*, June 30, 1944.

The Nationalist Revolution

1. Declarations of General Rawson, *La Prensa*, Dec. 7, 1943.
2. *La Nación*, June 5, 1943.
3. *Ibid.*

4. *Crítica*, July 2, 1943.
5. *Urquiza, Despierta!* No. 5, Feb., 1944.
6. Perón's statement in his interview to *El Mercurio* of Chile, quoted in *La Nación*, Nov. 12, 1943.
7. *La Nación*, Sept. 8, 1943.
8. *Noticias Gráficas*, Sept. 8, 1943.
9. United Press, Oct. 28, 1943.
10. Associated Press, Oct. 4. United Press, Oct. 5, 1943.
11. Associated Press, Dec. 12, 1943.
12. *El Mercurio* interview, quoted in *La Nación*, Nov. 12, 1943.
13. Statement of the Uruguayan Ministry of Defense, June 1, 1944, quoted in *La Nación*, June 2, 1944.
14. Central Bank *Memoria*, for 1943, quoted in N.Y. *Journal of Commerce*, July 19, 1944.
15. Perón speech, quoted in *La Nación*, May 2, 1944.
16. Decree of Apr. 28, 1944, quoted in *El Cronista Comercial*, Apr. 29, 1944.
17. Decree No. 16,672 of Dec. 16, 1943.
18. *La Nación*, May 31, 1944.
19. *Ibid.*, Jan. 15, 1944.
20. *El Cronista Comercial*, Apr. 5, 1944.
21. *El Federal*, May 18, 1944.
22. *Ibid.*, June 11, 1944.
23. *Ibid.*, May 18, 1944.
24. *La Nación*, Dec. 15, 16, 1943.
25. *La Prensa*, Jan. 1, 1944.
26. J. L. Mecham, *Church and State in Latin America* (Chapel Hill, N.C., 1934), 301–302.
27. N.Y. *Herald Tribune*, March 22, 1944.
28. *Tiempo* (Mexico City), June 30, 1944.
29. *El Cronista Comercial*, June 1, 1944.
30. Central Bank *Memoria* for 1943, quoted in N.Y. *Journal of Commerce*, July 19, 1944.
31. *La Prensa*, Dec. 30, 1943.
32. *Journal of Commerce*, July 19, 1944.
33. *La Nación*, June 15, 1944.
34. *Ibid.*, Feb. 1, 1944.
35. N.Y. *Times*, July 25, 1944.
36. *La Razón*, May 2, 1944.
37. N.Y. *Times*, May 13, 1944.
38. Associated Press, May 14, 1944.
39. Associated Press, Dec. 18, 1943.
40. Associated Press, May 15, 1944.
41. N.Y. *Herald Tribune*, June 30, 1944. *El Federal*, June 24 *et seq.*
42. *La Nación*, July 5, 1944.
43. *El Cronista Comercial*, June 17, 1944.
44. *La Nación*, June 7, 1944.
45. *El Cronista Comercial*, June 1, 1944.

46. Ysabel Fisk and Robert A. Rennie, "Argentina in Transition," *Foreign Policy Report*, May 1, 1944.
47. N.Y. *Herald Tribune*, June 3, 1944.
48. *Ibid.*, July 12, 1944.
49. *La Nación*, June 4, 1944.
50. *El Cronista Comercial*, Jan. 20, 1944.
51. *La Nación*, May 18, 1944.
52. Decree 7323 of 1944.
53. *La Nación*, Apr. 13, 1944.
54. London *Times*, July 11, 1944. N.Y. *Herald Tribune*, July 12, 1944.
55. N.Y. *Times*, Aug. 6, 1944.
56. *El Federal*, June 11, 1944.
57. *Tiempo* (Mexico City), June 30, 1944.
58. *Christian Science Monitor*, Aug. 7, 1944.
59. *El Mundo*, June 1, 1944.

NOTE ON SOURCES

Although I have made every effort to be scrupulous in the use of sources and of statistics, the reader must be warned not to accept them too uncritically.

Travellers' accounts, on which I have drawn heavily for the early chapters of my book, are frequently misleading. Most of the present-day books by Americans are quite inaccurate, and there is little reason to believe that nineteenth century Englishmen were any better in this respect. The commonest failing of the casual observer is to infer from his own particular experiences that what he has seen is generally true. This is not always the case.

Such books as Sarmiento's *Facundo* and Paz's *Memoirs,* splendid as they are, were nevertheless works of propaganda against Rosas and the caudillos, and must be recognized as such. All the books of the Unitario exiles were motivated by passionate convictions of injustice and outrage, and must be discounted with this fact in mind.

Such works of Argentine history as those of Saldías and Vera y González, from which I have filled in pieces of my narrative, nowhere cite their sources. Although this in itself does not mean the books are untrustworthy, it does mean that I personally cannot vouch for what they say. The works appear to be complete, and carefully done. Beyond this I cannot vouch for them.

Statistics must be accepted with utmost reservations, especially those from private sources. Economists like Bunge, whose figures I have avoided as much as possible, are frequently astonishingly inaccurate. Official government statistics, especially those of recent years, are much better. Present-day Argentine statisticians are excellently trained, and except where they are purposely trying to obscure an issue * their figures may be accepted without reservation. The older censuses, however, were often incomplete. Comparisons between censuses are usually misleading, and in this regard I should like to warn the reader against the industrial censuses. Between the first industrial census of 1935 and succeeding ones, the government discovered all kinds of industries which had been there all the time, but which it had not counted in the first census. Thus, even though I compare figures from the 1935 *Censo Industrial* and 1941 *Estadística Industrial,* the real growth is somewhat less than the absolute figures would lead one to believe.

* *E.g.,* the import figures which have been used to minimize the value of United States purchases in Argentina; and the categories of the 1937 agricultural census, so arranged as to disguise the huge concentrations of land in a few hands.

From what I have said above, I do not wish the reader to infer that this book, its sources and its statistics, are entirely worthless. I wish only to indicate that they should not be accepted uncritically. On the other side it must be said that however inaccurate they may be in detail, I believe that the general trends which they show do exist. In the long run, this is the important thing. In future years, monographic studies which today are almost entirely lacking in this field, will make the necessary additions and corrections; when that day comes, each chapter of *The Argentine Republic* will be subject to detailed criticism and revision. But in the meantime I hope it will have served its purpose, which was to point the way to future investigators, and throw much-needed light on a country about which the average American knows almost nothing.

SELECTIVE BIBLIOGRAPHY

(Books of unusual interest or value are starred *)

OFFICIAL PUBLICATIONS

CENSUSES

Censo Agropecuario Nacional: La Ganadería y la Agricultura en 1908. B.A., 1909.

Censo General de la Provincia de Buenos Aires, Demográfico, Agrícola, Industrial, Comercial, etc., Verificado el 9 de Octubre de 1881. B.A., 1883.

Censo Nacional Agropecuario, 1937. B.A., 1940.

Ministerio de Hacienda, *Censo Industrial de 1935.* B.A., 1938.

———, *Estadística Industrial de 1939.* B.A., 1942.

———, Dirección General de Estadística, *La Población y el Movimiento Demográfico de la República Argentina en los Años 1939 y 1938, y Síntesis de Años Anteriores.* B.A., 1940.

Primer Censo de la República Argentina, Verificado en los Días 15, 16, y 17 de Septiembre de 1869. B.A., 1872.

Segundo Censo de la República Argentina, 1895. 3 vols., B.A., 1898.

Tercer Censo Nacional Levantado el 1° de Junio de 1914. 10 vols., B.A., 1916.

COMMERCE

Anuario del Departamento Nacional de Estadística Correspondiente a 1893. B.A., 1894.

Estadística del Comercio y de la Navegación de la República Argentina Correspondiente al Año 1890. B.A., 1891.

Ministerio de Hacienda, Dirección General de Estadística, *Anuario del Comercio Exterior de la República Argentina Correspondiente a 1940, y Noticia Sumaria del Período 1910–1940*. B.A., 1941.

CONGRESSIONAL COMMITTEES

Cámara de Diputados, *Comisión Especial Investigadora de Servicios Eléctricos de la Capital: Informes y Conclusiones*. 2 vols., B.A., 1941.

———, Comisión Investigadora de Actividades Antiargentinas, *Informe No. 1* (Aug. 29, 1941), *Informe No. 2* (Sept. 5, 1941), *Informe No. 3* (Sept. 17, 1941), *Informe No. 4* (Sept. 30, 1941), *Informe No. 5* (Nov. 28, 1941). B.A., 1941.

———, *Informe de la Comisión Investigadora de los Trusts*. B.A., 1919.

CONGRESSIONAL DEBATES

Congreso General Constituyente de la Confederación Argentina, *Sesión de 1852–1854*. B.A., 1871.

Congreso Nacional, *Diario de Sesiones de la Cámara de Diputados*.

———, *Diario de Sesiones de la Cámara de Senadores*.

Sesiones del Congreso Legislativo sobre la Importante Discusión de la Ley Estableciendo Derechos Diferenciales. Paraná, 1856.

FOREIGN RELATIONS

Eighth International Conference of American States, *Final Act*, December, 1938. Lima.

Final Act of the Inter-American Conference for the Maintenance of Peace. B.A., 1936.

Inter-American Conference for the Maintenance of Peace, *Proceedings (Stenographic Reports), Buenos Aires, December, 1936*. B.A., 1937.

Ministerio de Relaciones Exteriores, *Decretos sobre la Neutralidad de la República Argentina en el Estado de Guerra en Europa, de 4 de Septiembre de 1939, 11 de Junio de 1940, Abril 16 y 17 de 1941, y Mayo 13 de 1941*. B.A., 1939–1941.

———, *La República Argentina en la Conferencia de Panamá (1939)*. B.A., 1940.

———, *La República Argentina en la Octava Conferencia Internacional Americana Reunida en Lima del 9 al 27 de Diciembre de 1938*. B.A., 1939.

———, *Memoria Presentada al Honorable Congreso Nacional Correspondiente al Período 1933–1934*. B.A., 1934.

———, *Tercera Reunión de Consulta de Ministros de Relaciones*

Exteriores de las Repúblicas Americanas, Río de Janeiro, 15 al 29 de Enero 1942: Participación Argentina. B.A., 1942.

Octava Conferencia Internacional Americana, *Diario de Sesiones (Versiones Taquigráficas), Lima, Diciembre de 1938.* Lima, 1938.

SPECIAL STUDIES AND REPORTS

Comisión Nacional del Azúcar, *Informe sobre el Estado de la Industria Azucarera y Medidas Aconsejadas al Gobierno Provisional de la Nación.* B.A., 1931.

Memoria de la Dirección Nacional de Vialidad. 1933–1940.

Ministerio de Agricultura, *Análisis del Problema Vitivinícola.* B.A., 1934.

*———, *Informe del Comité Mixto Investigador del Comercio de Carnes Anglo-Argentina, 1938.* London, 1938.

———, Junta Reguladora de Vinos, *Comunicado sobre la Evolución de la Industria Vitivinícola a Través de Cuatro Años de Regulación.* B.A., 1939.

Ministerio de Hacienda, Dirección General del Impuesto a los Réditos, *Memoria, Año 1941.* B.A.

Ministerio del Interior, Departamento Nacional del Trabajo, *Condiciones de Vida de la Familia Obrera.* B.A., 1937.

———, *Investigaciones Sociales,* 1936, 1937, 1939, 1940.

———, *La Desocupación en la Argentina, 1940.*

———, *Organización Sindical: Asociaciones Obreras y Patronales (1941).*

Oficina Central de Tierras y Colonias, *Informe del Director Don Nicasio Oroño sobre Colonización de Tierras Nacionales.* B.A., 1890.

PRIVATE COLLECTIONS OF DOCUMENTS

Colección de Leyes y Decretos Vigentes sobre Tierras Públicas Promulgadas desde 1830 hasta Julio de 1862. B.A., 1862.

de la Fuente, D. G., *Tierras, Colonias y Agricultura: Recopilación de Leyes, Decretos y Otras Disposiciones Nacionales.* B.A., 1894.

Mabragaña, H., *Los Mensajes: Historia del Desenvolvimiento de la Nación Argentina Redactada Cronológicamente por sus Gobernantes,* Vols. III and IV. B.A., n.d.

LETTERS

Aldao de Díaz, Elvira, ed., *Cartas Intimas de Lisandro de la Torre.* B.A., 1941.

Correspondencia Literaria, Histórica y Política del General Bartolomé Mitre. 3 vols., B.A., 1912.

Sarmiento-Mitre Correspondencia, 1846–1868. B.A., 1911.

JOURNALS, MEMOIRS, AND TRAVELS

Alberdi, Juan Bautista, *Autobiografía.* B.A., 1927.

Aldao de Díaz, Elvira, *Reminiscencias sobre Aristóbulo del Valle.* B.A., 1928.

Andrews, Joseph, *Las Provincias del Norte en 1825.* B.A., 1915.

Armaignac, H., *Voyages dans les Pampas de la République Argentine.* Tours, France, 1883.

*Beaumont, J. A. B., *Travels in Buenos Ayres and the Adjacent Provinces of the Rio de la Plata, with Observations Intended for the Use of Persons Who Contemplate Emigrating to That Country, or Embarking Capital in Its Affairs.* London, 1828.

**Buenos Aires Visto por Viajeros Ingleses, 1800–1925.* B.A., 1941.

Ebelot, Alfredo, *La Pampa: Costumbres Argentinas.* B.A., 1890.

Espinosa, Antonio, *La Conquista del Desierto: Diario del Capellán de la Expedición de 1879, Monseñor Antonio Espinosa, Más Tarde Arzobispo de Buenos Aires.* B.A., 1939.

Giménez, Juan, *Paraná, Capital de la Confederación Argentina: Recuerdos Históricos.* Paraná, 1906.

González Iramain, Nicolás, *Tres Meses en Jujuy: La Intervención Nacional de 1942.* B.A., 1942.

Groussac, Paul, *Los que Pasaban: José Manuel Estrada, Pedro Goyena, Nicolás Avellaneda, Carlos Pellegrini, Roque Sáenz Peña.* B.A., 1919.

*Head, Francis B., *Rough Notes Taken During Some Rapid Journeys across the Pampas and among the Andes.* London, 1861.

Hutchinson, Thomas J., *Buenos Aires and Argentine Gleanings, with Extracts from a Diary of Salado Exploration in 1862–1863.* London, 1865.

*McCann, William, *Two Thousand Miles' Ride Through the Argentine Provinces: Being an Account of the Natural Products of the Country, and Habits of the People; with a Historical Retrospect of the Rio de la Plata, Monte Video, and Corrientes.* 2 vols., London, 1853.

Mansilla, Lucio V., *Retratos y Recuerdos.* B.A., 1927.

**———, *Una Excursión a los Indios Ranqueles,* 2 vols. B.A., 1939.

Olascoaga, Manuel J., *La Conquista del Desierto: Estudio Topográfico de La Pampa y Río Negro.* 2 vols., B.A., 1940.

*Parish, Sir Woodbine, *Buenos Ayres and the Provinces of the Rio* *de la Plata from Their Discovery and Conquest by the Spaniards to the Establishment of Their Political Independence.* London, 1852.

*Paz, José María, *Memorias Póstumas.* 2 vols., B.A., 1917.

*Peyret, Alejo, *Una Visita a las Colonias de la República Argentina.* 2 vols., B.A., 1889.

Racedo, Eduardo, *La Conquista del Desierto: Memoria Militar y Descriptiva de la 3ª División Expedicionaria.* B.A., 1940.

**Sarmiento, Domingo F., *Estados Unidos.* B.A., 1942.

GOVERNMENT REPORTS ON ARGENTINA

Argentina (American Nations Series, No. 1). Washington, 1938.

Great Britain, Department of Overseas Trade, *Report of the British Economic Mission to Argentina, Brazil and Uruguay.* London, 1930.

———, *Reports on Economic, Commercial, Industrial and Financial Situation of Argentina,* 1921–1925, 1927–1931, 1933, 1935–1939. London.

Halsey, Frederic M., *Investments in Latin America,* Vol. I, *Argentina.* Washington, 1925.

Informe de las Condiciones Financieras, Comerciales, etc., de la República Argentina Recopilado en 1866 por el Señor D. Francisco Clarc Ford, Secretario de Legación de su Magestad Británica, Presentado entre Otros a Ambas Legislaturas del Parlamento Inglés en Marzo del Presente Año 1867.

*Latham, Wilfrid, *The States of the River Plate: Their Industries and Commerce, Sheep-Farming, Sheep Breeding, Cattle-Feeding and Meat-Preserving; Employment of Capital; Land and Stock and Their Values; Labour and Its Remuneration.* London, 1866.

**Moussy, V. Martin de, *Description Géographique et Statistique de la Confédération Argentine.* 3 vols., Paris, 1860–1864.

**The Reports on the Present State of the United Provinces of South America, Drawn Up by Messrs. Rodney and Graham, Commissioners Sent to Buenos Aires by the Government of North America and Laid Before the Congress of the United States.* London, 1819.

U.S. Department of Commerce, Bureau of Foreign and Domestic Commerce, *The Economic Position of Argentina During the War.* Washington, 1920.

U.S. Department of Labor, Bureau of Labor Statistics, *Bulletin No. 510: Foreign Labor Laws—Argentina.*

U.S. Tariff Commission, *The Foreign Trade of Latin America:* (1) *Trade of Latin America with the World and with the United*

States; (2) *Commercial Policies and Trade Relations of Individual Latin American Countries*; (3) *Selected Latin American Export Commodities*. 5 vols., Washington, 1940.

HANDBOOKS AND YEARBOOKS

Baedeker de la République Argentine.

Comité Nacional de Geografía, *Anuario Geográfico Argentino*. B.A., 1941.

Figaro (*Le*), *Album de la République Argentine: Ses origines, Sa Vie, Sa Culture, Son Commerce, Ses Industries, Ses Richesses, Ses Progrès*. Paris, 1929.

García Mata, Rafael, and Llorens, Emilio, *Argentina Económica*, B.A., 1940.

Institut International d'Agriculture, *Annuaire International de Statistique Agricole 1938–1939*. Rome, 1939.

League of Nations, *Statistical Year Book*. Geneva, 1927–1941.

———, *World Economic Survey 1939/41*. Geneva, 1941.

Mulhall, M. G. and E. T., *Handbook of the River Plate Republics*. London, 1875.

Razón (*La*), *Anuario*, 1938, 1939, 1940, 1941. B.A.

SECONDARY WORKS

Academia Nacional de la Historia, *Historia de la Nación Argentina*. Vols. IX and X, B.A., 1941, 1942.

Acuña, Angel, *Mitre Parlamentario*. B.A., 1940.

(*La*) *Agricultura y la Ganadería Argentinas: Su Origen, Su Desarollo, Sus Progresos, las Industrias Derivadas*. B.A., n.d.

Aikman, Duncan, *The All-American Front*. N.Y., 1941.

Alazraqui, José, *La Viticultura Nacional frente a la Política Libre-Cambista*. B.A., 1913.

Albarracín, José M., *Sarmiento*. B.A., 1940.

Alberdi, Juan Bautista, *De la Anarquía y Sus Dos Causas Principales, del Gobierno y Sus Dos Elementos Necesarios en la República Argentina, con Motivo de Su Reorganización por Buenos Aires*. Besançon, France, 1862.

———, *Estudios Económicos*. B.A., 1916.

———, *Obras Completas*, Vol. III, *Bases y Puntos de Partida para la Organización de la República Argentina*.

Album Presidencial de la Reorganización Nacional, 1916–1922. B.A.

Alcorta, Santiago, *La República Argentina en la Exposición Universal de Paris de 1889*. 2 vols., Paris, 1890.

Aldao, Carlos A., *Los Caudillos: Cuestiones Históricas.* B.A., 1925.
Alsina, Juan A., *El Obrero en la República Argentina.* 2 vols., B.A., 1905.
———, *La Inmigración en el Primer Siglo de la Independencia.* B.A., 1910.
———, *La Inmigración Europea en la República Argentina.* B.A., 1898.
———, *Población, Tierras y Producción.* B.A., 1903.
Amadeo, Octavio R., *Vidas Argentinas: Rivadavia, Mitre, Sarmiento, Avellaneda, Rosas, Irigoyen, Roca, Pellegrini, Alem, Sáenz Peña.* B.A., 1934.
Amadeo, Rómulo, *La Acción Social Católica.* B.A., 1930.
Antecedentes para el Proceso del Tirano de Entre Ríos, Justo José de Urquiza: Colección de Artículos Publicados en el "Pueblo." B.A., 1867.
Aramburu, Julio, *Historia Argentina.* B.A., 1939.
Argentina, *La Obra de la Revolución: Reseña Sintética de la Labor Desarrollada. 1930—6 de Septiembre—1931.*
Arrendamientos Rurales. B.A., 1935.
Artuso, Francisco S., *La Industria Molinera Argentina: Producción, Consumo y Exportación del Trigo.* B.A., 1917.
*Astesano, Eduardo, *Contenido Social de la Revolución de Mayo—La Sociedad Virreinal.* B.A., 1941.
Auzón, Eugenio, *Historia de la Revolución de Julio de 1890 en Bueno Aires, con Planos de las Operaciones Militares y Navales y Piezas Justificativas.* B.A., 1890.
Avellaneda, N., *Estudios sobre las Leyes de Tierras Públicas.* B.A., 1865.
Ayarragaray, Lucas, *La Anarquía Argentina y el Caudillismo: Estudio Psicológico de los Orígenes Argentinos.* B.A., 1925.
———, *Socialismo Argentino y Legislación Obrera.* B.A., 1912.
Balestra, Juan, *El Noventa: Una Evolución Política Argentina.* B.A., 1934.
Baque, Santiago, *Influencia de Alberdi en la Organización Política del Estado Argentino* (Thesis, Facultad de Derecho of the University of Buenos Aires). B.A., 1914.
Barros, Alvaro, *La Memoria Especial del Ministro de la Guerra.* B.A., 1877.
Beals, Carleton, *The Coming Struggle for Latin America.* London, 1939.
Beresford Crawkes, J., *533 Días de Historia Argentina, 6 de Septiembre de 1930—20 de Febrero de 1932.* B.A., 1932.

Bidabehere, Fernando A., *Acción de la Economía Dirigida en la República Argentina*. B.A., 1937.

Bidart, Ramón, *La Fiebre Aftosa*. B.A., 1928.

Bilbao, Manuel, *Buenos Aires desde su Fundación hasta Nuestros Días*. B.A., 1902.

Blanco, Eusebio, *Las Viñas y los Vinos en Mendoza*. B.A., 1884.

Bucich Escobar, Ismael. *Historia de los Presidentes Argentinos*. 2 vols. B.A., 1923.

Bullrich, Jorge M., *La Evolución de los Valores de los Campos en la República Argentina: Sus Causas y sus Indices*. B.A., 1935.

Bunge, Alejandro E. *La Economía Argentina*. 4 vols., B.A., 1928–1930.

———, *La Independencia Económica Argentina*. B.A., 1932.

———, *Las Industrias del Norte*. B.A., 1922.

———, *Una Nueva Argentina*. B.A., 1940.

*Cady, J. F. *Foreign Interventions in the Rio de la Plata, 1835–1850*. Philadelphia, 1929.

Calvet, A. *L'Immigration Européenne, le Commerce et l'Agriculture à la Plata, 1886–1888*. Paris.

*Cárcano, Miguel Angel, *Evolución Histórica del Régimen de la Tierra Pública, 1810–1916*. B.A., 1925.

Carrasco, Gabriel, *La Producción y el Consumo del Azúcar en la República Argentina*. B.A., 1894.

Cassagne Serres, Alberto, *Establecimientos Ganaderos. Formación— Explotación — Administración — Contabilidad — Rendición de Cuentas*. B.A., 1925.

Cattle and Beef Survey: A Summary of Production and Trade in the British Empire and Foreign Countries, Prepared by the Intelligence Branch of the Imperial Economic Committee. London, 1934.

Centro de Estudios de Derecho Internacional Público, *La Política Exterior de la República Argentina*. B.A., 1931.

Cincuenta Años de Colonización Judía en la Argentina. B.A., 1939.

Compañía Swift de la Plata, S.A. *Breve Reseña sobre la Industria Frigorífica en la Argentina*. B.A., 1934.

(*Las*) *Cuatro Jornadas de Julio: La Revolución de la Unión Cívica*. B.A., 1890.

**Darwin, Charles, *Journal of Researches into the Natural History and Geology of the Countries Visited during the Voyage of H.M.S. Beagle Round the World*, 2 vols. N.Y., 1846.

de la Torre, Lisandro, *Cuestiones Monetarias y Financieras*. B.A., 1941.

———, *El Convenio de Londres*. B.A., 1933.

———, *El Gobierno contra los Elevadores de Granos Cooperativos.* B.A., 1933.

———, *Intermedio Filosófico. La Cuestión Social y los Cristianos Sociales. La Cuestión Social y un Cura. Grandeza y Decadencia del Fascismo.*

*———, *Investigación del Comercio de Carnes.* B.A., 1935.

———, *La Situación Financiera. Otra Página de Historia.* 1932.

———, *Las Dos Campañas Presidenciales* (1916–1931). B.A., 1939.

de la Vega Díaz, Dardo, *Mitre y el Chacho; La Rioja en la Reorganización del País.* La Rioja, 1939.

del Mazo, Gabriel, *La Reforma Universitaria como Conciencia de Emancipación en Desarrollo* (1918–1938). B.A., 1938.

Dumas, Ernesto, *El Problema de la Yerba Mate.* B.A., 1930.

Echeverría, Esteban, *Dogma Socialista: Precedido de una Ojeada Retrospectiva sobre el Movimiento Intelectual en el Plata desde el Año 1837.* B.A., 1915.

(Las) Empresas de Ferrocarriles de Jurisdicción Nacional: *La Futura Ley de Coordinación Nacional de los Transportes Explicada al Público.* B.A., 1936.

Estudios de la Unión Industrial Argentina.

Feuerlein, Willy, and Hannan, Elizabeth, *Dollars in Latin America: An Old Problem in a New Setting.* N.Y., 1940.

Foreign Bondholders' Protective Council, Inc., *Annual Report, 1940.*

Frers, Emilio, *Cuestiones Agrarias.* 3 vols., B.A., 1918.

Fresco, Manuel A., *Como se Habla y se Gobierna en la Primera Provincia Argentina: Nuevo Nacionalismo, Campaña Anti-Comunista, Política Obrera, Legislación del Trabajo. Mensajes y Discursos Políticos del Gobernador Dr. Manuel A. Fresco.* La Plata, 1937.

Fundación de Escuelas Públicas en la Provincia de Buenos Aires durante el Gobierno Escolar de Sarmiento, 1856–1861, 1875–1881. La Plata, 1939.

Gallo, Vicente C., *Avellaneda.* B.A., 1928.

Gálvez, Manuel, *Vida de Hipólito Yrigoyen, el Hombre del Misterio.* B.A., 1939.

Gandulfo de la Serna, Adolfo, *La Oposición Doctrinaria entre Sarmiento y Alberdi.* B.A., 1917.

*García, Juan Agustín, *La Ciudad Indiana.* B.A., 1909.

García, Tubal C., *La Industria Azucarera Argentina y las Consecuencias de su Protección.* B.A., 1920.

Gil, Enrique, *Pan Americanism and the International Policy of Argentina.* N.Y., 1916.

Girola, Carlos B., *La Yerba Mate*. B.A., 1931.
González Arrili, B., *Vida de Lisandro de la Torre*. B.A., 1940.
González Calderón, Juan, *Derecho Constitucional Argentino: Historia, Teoría y Jurisprudencia de la Constitución con un Prólogo del Dr. Joaquín V. González*. 3 vols. 3rd ed., B.A., 1931.
———, *El General Urquiza y la Organización Nacional*. B.A., 1940.
———, *Función Constitucional de los Ministros*. B.A., 1911.
González, Julio V., *La Emancipación de la Universidad: Contribución al Estudio de un Nuevo Régimen de Enseñanza Pública Superior en la Argentina*. B.A., 1929.
———, *Principios y Fundamentos de la Reforma Universitaria*. 1930.
———, *I. Realización Integral de la Reforma. II. El Partido Nacional Reformista*. B.A., 1927.
Graty, Alfred M. du, *La Confédération Argentine*. Paris, 1858.
Gutiérrez de Miguel, V., *La Revolución Argentina: Relato de un Testigo Presencial*. B.A., 1930.
Hanson, S. G., *Argentine Meat and the British Market*. Stanford University, 1938.
Hernández, José, *Instrucción del Estanciero: Tratado Completo para la Plantación y Manejo de un Establecimiento de Campo*. B.A., 1882.
*———, *Martín Fierro*, ed. Eleuterio F. Tiscornia. B.A., 1941.
Hudson, W. H., *Birds of La Plata*. London, 1920.
———, *The Naturalist in La Plata*. London, 1892.
Hundimiento de Barcos durante la Guerra Europea. B.A., 1929.
Iannini, Hugo R., *Comercio de Carnes Importadas en Inglaterra, Mercado de Smithfield*. B.A., 1936.
Ibarguren, Carlos, *Juan Manuel de Rosas, Su Vida, Su Tiempo, Su Drama*. B.A., 1930.
(*El*) *Imperialismo Yanqui y la "Buena Vecindad."* B.A., 1938.
Inchauspe, Pedro, *Voces y Costumbres del Campo Argentino*. B.A., 1942.
*Ingenieros, José, *La Evolución de las Ideas Argentinas*. 2 vols., B.A., 1920.
Jefferson, Mark, *Peopling the Argentine Pampa*. N.Y., 1926.
Jurado, Mario, ed., *Antecedentes Parlamentarios de la Legislación Argentina: I, Comercio de Carnes* (1862–1941). B.A., 1941.
Justo, Juan B., *El Socialismo Argentino*. B.A., 1915.
———, *Estudios sobre la Moneda*. B.A., 1921.
Kirkpatrick, F. A., *A History of the Argentine Republic*. Cambridge, England, 1931.
———, *Latin America and the War*. Cambridge, England, 1918.

Kurtz, Roberto, *La Argentina ante Estados Unidos*. B.A., 1928.

*Landenberger, Jorge W., and Conte, Francisco M., eds., *Origen, Organización y Tendencias de la Unión Cívica: 1889—1 de Septiembre—1890. Obra Oficila*. B.A., 1890.

Langenheim, A. G., *Colonización en la República Argentina*. B.A., 1906.

Lanús, Adolfo, *Campo Minado*. B.A., 1942.

Lascano, Victor, *Argentine Foreign Policy in Latin America*. Miami, 1940.

(*La*) *Ley de Coordinación de los Transportes Urbanos*. B.A., 1936.

Llorens, Emilio, *El Subconsumo de Alimentos en América del Sur*. B.A., 1941.

López Idoyaga, Pedro, *Corporación de Transportes de la Ciudad de Buenos Aires*. B.A., 1940.

Lugones, Leopoldo, *Roca*. B.A., 1938.

Luzuriaga, Lorenzo, *La Enseñanza Primaria y Secundaria Argentina Comparada con la de Otros Países*. Tucumán, 1942.

Macdonald, Austin F., *Government of the Argentine Republic*. N.Y., 1942.

Marianetti, Benito, *Los Trabajadores de la Industria Vitivinícola*. Mendoza, 1939.

Martínez, A. B., and Lewandowski, M., *The Argentine in the 20th Century*. London, 1911.

Mecham, J. Lloyd, *Church and State in Latin America*. Chapel Hill, 1934.

Memoria Histórica y Descriptiva de la Provincia de Tucumán. B.A., 1882.

Micele, Antonio, *La Industria Azucarera en la República Argentina*. B.A., 1936.

Moreno Quintana, Lucio M., *La Diplomacia de Yrigoyen*. La Plata, 1928.

Mulhall, Michael G., *The English in South America*. B.A., n.d.

Nevers, A. de, *Atentado a la Constitución Nacional Argentina y Su Consecuencia, la Revolución de Septiembre de 1874*. B.A., 1876.

Nuestra Industria Rural o Rápida Ojeada sobre el Estado de Nuestra Ganadería y los Efectos de Nuestra Legislación Agraria. B.A., 1866.

Oddone, Jacinto, *El Factor Económico en Nuestras Luchas Civiles*. B.A., 1937.

———, *Historia del Socialismo Argentino*. B.A., 1934.

———, *La Burguesía Terrateniente Argentina*. B.A., 1930.

Padilla, Miguel M., *La Cuestión Azucarera en el Congreso, 1917*. B.A., 1917.

Palacios, Alfredo L., *El Dolor Argentino: Plan Sanitario y Educativo de Protección á los Niños.* B.A., 1938.
Partido Demócrata Nacional, *Carta Orgánica.* La Plata, 1933.
Partido Socialista, *Estatutos, Carta Orgánica, Reglamentos, Declaraciones, Programas, Resoluciones.* B.A., 1939.
Pascale, Silvio, *El Factor Arrendamiento en el Problema Agrícola.* B.A., 1931.
Pellegrini, Carlos, *Discursos y Escritos, con un Prólogo de Enrique de Vedia, recopilados por Domingo de Muro, 1881–1906.* B.A., 1910.
Peña Guzmán, Solano, *Problemas Económicos de Tucumán.* Tucumán, 1941.
Phelps, Vernon Lovell, *The International Economic Position of Argentina.* Philadelphia, 1938.
Ponce, Aníbal, *La Vejez de Sarmiento.* B.A., 1939.
———, *Sarmiento, Constructor de la Nueva Argentina.* B.A., 1938.
Por los Trabajadores del Campo de Buenos Aires: Los Problemas del Agro en la Provincia. La Plata, 1942.
Poy Costa, Antonio M., *Los Frigoríficos: Datos Históricos, Descriptivos, Constructivos y Económicos. Aplicación del Frío en las Industrias Agrícolas.* B.A., 1918.
*Puiggrós, Rodolfo, *La Herencia que Rosas Dejó al País.* B.A., 1940.
Quesada, Julio A., *Orígenes de la Revolución del 6 de Septiembre de 1930. La Campaña Presidencial de 1928. La Agitación Popular de 1930.* B.A., n.d.
Ramayon, Eduardo E., *Adolfo Alsina, Ministro de Guerra en Campaña, 1876.* B.A., 1939.
Ramos Mejía, José María, *Rosas y Su Tiempo.* 3 vols., B.A., 1907.
Ramos Mexía, Ezequiel, *La Colonización Oficial y la Distribución de las Tierras Públicas.* B.A., 1921.
Repetto, Nicolás, *Política Internacional.* B.A., 1943.
Richelet, Juan E., *La Ganadería Argentina y Su Comercio de Carnes.* B.A., 1928.
Rivera Indarte, José, *La Intervención en la Guerra Actual del Río de la Plata.* Rio de Janeiro, 1845.
Rivero Astengo, Agustín, *Hombres de la Organización Nacional: Retratos Literarios.* 2 vols., B.A., 1936, 1937.
Rögind, William, *Historia del Ferrocarril del Sud.* 1937.
Rosenvald, José Ricardo, *El Privilegio Azucarero y Sus Deberes.* B.A., 1936.
Rossi, Vicente, *El Gaucho, Su Origen y Evolución.* La Plata, 1921.

Rotary Club de Rosario, *El Municipio de Rosario y la Acción de los Poderes Públicos*. Rosario, 1939.

Rotger, Pedro F., *Historia de la Revolución Radical Año 1893, Precedida por los Discursos Pronunciados por los Ministros Doctores del Valle, López, Demaría, Benavente y Otros*. B.A., 1913.

Royal Institute of International Affairs, *The Republics of South America: A Political, Economic and Cultural Survey*. London, 1937.

Ryan, Ricardo, *La Política Internacional y la Presidencia Yrigoyen*. B.A., 1921.

Sáenz Peña, Roque, *Escritos y Discursos*. B.A., 1935.

Saldías, Adolfo, *Historia de la Confederación Argentina. I—Rozas y Su Epoca*. B.A., 1911.

*Salera, Virgil, *Exchange Control and the Argentine Market*. N.Y., 1941.

*Sarmiento, Domingo F., *Aldao y El Chacho*. B.A., 1938.

——, *Las Ciento y Una: Polémica con Alberdi*. B.A., 1939.

**——, *Life in the Argentine Republic in the Days of the Tyrants; or, Civilization and Barbarism*. N.Y., 1868.

——, *Obras*. 52 vols., Santiago, Chile, 1887.

Scalabrini Ortiz, Raúl, *Historia de los Ferrocarriles Argentinos*. B.A., 1940.

——, *Política Británica en el Río de la Plata*. B.A., 1940.

Soares, Ernesto A., *Ferrocarriles Argentinos, Sus Orígenes, Antecedentes Legales, Leyes Que los Rigen y Reseñas Estadísticas*. B.A., 1937.

Sociedad Rural Argentina, *El Pool de los Frigoríficos: Necesidad de la Intervención del Estado*. B.A., 1927.

Solari, Juan A., *Trabajadores del Norte Argentino*. B.A., 1937.

*Sommariva, Luis H., *Historia de las Intervenciones Federales en las Provincias*. B.A., 1929.

Terry, José A., *Finanzas*. B.A., 1927.

——, *La Crisis (1885–1892): Teoría de la Crisis—Inconversión de 1885—Desarrollo de la Crisis—Sistema Bancario*. B.A., 1893.

Tornquist (Ernesto) y Cía, *Business Conditions in Argentina: Quarterly Report*.

(La) *Vida de los Ferrocarriles y la Competencia en los Transportes: Memorial Presentado al Gobierno de la Nación Argentina por las Compañías de Ferrocarriles*. B.A., 1931.

NEWSPAPERS

Crisol

Crítica

El Cronista Comercial
El Diario
El Pampero
El Federal
Gaceta Mercantil (1826–1850)
La Argentina (Tucumán)
La Nación
La Prensa
La Razón
La Vanguardia
Noticias Gráficas
The Christian Science Monitor (Boston)
The Daily Express (London)
The Daily Mail (London)
The Daily Telegraph (London)
The Herald Tribune (New York)
The Journal of Commerce (New York)
The Standard
The Times (London)
The Times (New York)

PERIODICALS

Anales de la Facultad de Derecho y Ciencias Sociales
Argumentos
Foreign Commerce Weekly
La Argentina Económica
La Revista de Buenos Aires: Historia Americana, Literatura y Derecho (1863–1867)
Nueva Política
Revista Argentina de Ciencias Políticas (1910–1928)
Revista de Derecho, Historia y Letras (1917–1919)
Revista de Economía Argentina
Revista Económica del Banco de la Nación Argentina
Revue Internationale du Travail
The South American Journal
Veritas

CLANDESTINE PRESS

El Garrote
La Voz de Mayo
Urquiza, Despierta!

INDEX

Double surnames are listed in the Spanish style, under the *first* (not last) surname. Example: León Ortiz de Rozas will be found under Ortiz, not Rozas.

S

T

Avenida Alvear. Buenos Aires

QUICHUA WOMAN. Santiago del Estero

Old Woman, Santa Fe

Peon and Horse. Lago Situación, Chubut (Patagonia)

ANDEAN LAKE PORT. Puerto Blest, Lake Nahuel Huapí, Río Negro (Patagonia)

(Courtesy of Luján Museum.)

GAUCHOS, LATE NINETEENTH CENTURY. Province of Buenos Aires

Naval Mechanics on Parade. Buenos Aires

STREET SCENE. Buenos Aires

Country Pulpería. Santiago del Estero

Cooking the Supper. Santiago del Estero

Town Square and Cathedral, Tucumán

Sugar Cane. Tucumán

PAISANO. Termas de Río Hondo, Santiago del Estero

(Courtesy of Ferrocarriles del Estado.)

FISHERMEN. Laguna de Giancanello, Mendoza

Dawn Over Salta

House on the Pampa, Santa Fe